1st
Race

Notes of a Pianist

NEW EDITIONS

of Classic Commentaries on America's Past

◇◇◇◇◇◇◇◇◇◇

William Bradford—OF PLYMOUTH PLANTATION
with an introduction and notes by Samuel Eliot Morison

Richard Burton—THE CITY OF THE SAINTS
with an introduction and notes by Fawn M. Brodie

Dan De Quille (William Wright)—THE BIG BONANZA
with an introduction by Oscar Lewis

Louis Moreau Gottschalk—NOTES OF A PIANIST
with a prelude, a postlude, and explanatory notes by Jeanne Behrend

Horace Greeley—AN OVERLAND JOURNEY
with an introduction and notes by Charles T. Duncan

Frances A. Kemble—JOURNAL OF A RESIDENCE ON A GEORGIAN
PLANTATION IN 1838–1839
with an introduction and notes by John A. Scott

Frederick Marryat—A DIARY IN AMERICA
with an introduction and notes by S. W. Jackman

Frederick Law Olmsted—THE COTTON KINGDOM
with an introduction by Arthur M. Schlesinger

"Dame Shirley" (Louise A. K. S. Clappe)—THE SHIRLEY LETTERS
with an introduction and notes by Carl I. Wheat

Alexis de Tocqueville—DEMOCRACY IN AMERICA
with an introduction, notes, and bibliographies by Phillips Bradley

Anthony Trollope—NORTH AMERICA
with an introduction and notes by Donald Smalley and
Bradford Allen Booth

Mrs. Frances Trollope—DOMESTIC MANNERS OF THE AMERICANS
with an introduction and notes by Donald Smalley

These are BORZOI BOOKS, *published in New York by* ALFRED A. KNOPF

Frontispiece of the first edition
of Notes of a Pianist, Philadelphia, 1881

NOTES
of a Pianist

Louis Moreau Gottschalk

EDITED, WITH A PRELUDE, A POSTLUDE,
AND EXPLANATORY NOTES, BY

Jeanne Behrend

New York : Alfred · A · Knopf
1 9 6 4

Acknowledgments

❦

A TRANSCRIPT of *Notes of a Pianist* was made in the 1870's by the author's sister Clara and translated into English by his brother-in-law, Dr. Robert E. Peterson. Since, to date, Clara Gottschalk's transcript of the journal's scattered pages has not been discovered and is therefore presumed lost, the original edition (1881) of necessity formed the basis for this one. It posed many problems, foremost among them Dr. Peterson's translation. One could often only surmise what Gottschalk actually had written or meant to say. "You others" obviously must have been *"vous autres,"* or, correctly translated in this particular case, "you people." Havana obviously does not lie at the *bottom* of a bay. Kamehameha could not have *predicted* European civilization, he *preached* it—the former word obviously a faulty translation of the verb *prédiquer.* Many such instances can be cited. An effort has been made, however, to preserve in essence the prose of one who expressed himself most readily in French. It has unfortunately been impossible to differentiate among dollars, francs, and *reales* where the translator (and perhaps the author as well) did not.

There were problems inherited from Clara's own difficulties with her brother's handwriting. Many personal names and place names were misspelled. Most perplexing of all was the jumbled sequence of entry, particularly in the West Indian account and that of Peru. As for entries made in the United States, whole sections dated 1863 actually had been written in 1862. The journal's continuity is now in order, to the best of my knowledge. Connecting links inserted in brackets fill in the gaps occasioned by the author's long silences and serve to clarify the narrative.

I wish to express my appreciation to the many who assisted me in this task—first, to Miss Adele Freedman of RCA Victor, for her part in persuading me to accept it.

Through the kind offices of Dr. Carleton Sprague Smith and

Alfred A. Knopf, Inc., I was given access to the vast compilation of Gottschalk material made by Dr. David James.

In matters of translation, Miss Blanche A. Price, Mrs. Samuel Lifschey, Mr. John de Lancie, Mr. Max de Schauensee, Hon. and Mrs. Ramón Fina, Hon. Renato Bayma Denys, Mr. Eusebio Gonzalez Afonso, and Mr. Walter Burle Marx generously gave assistance.

Mrs. John Duke, Mr. John G. Doyle, and Mr. John Hottensen facilitated the preparation of the Bibliography.

The editorial acumen of Mr. Herbert Weinstock and Mr. Henry Robbins was of great benefit, and correspondence with Mr. Ernst C. Krohn, Mr. H. Earle Johnson, and Mr. Joel A. Rogers proved enlightening. Thanks are due also to Sra. Isabel Aretz de Ramón y Rivera, Mr. Calvert Bean, Jr., Dr. Moses Behrend, Mr. and Mrs. John Edmunds, Miss Sophie Elfont, Mr. Warren R. Howell, Dr. David James, Mr. Hershy Kay, Dr. Bertram W. Korn, Mr. George S. MacManus, Mr. John F. Marion, Mr. Anthony Milner, Sra. Mercedes Reis Pequeno, Mr. Ray Riling, Mr. Cyrus C. Rogers, Miss Ann Ronell, and Mr. Maxwell Whiteman.

The staffs of the following historical societies were invaluable in helping to trace Gottschalk's itinerary in the United States: the Chicago Historical Society; the Erie County Historical Society; the Geneva Historical Society; the Illinois State Historical Library; the State Historical Society of Missouri; the Niagara County Department of History; the Historical and Philosophical Society of Ohio; Department of History, State University College, Oswego, N. Y.; the Historical Society of Pennsylvania; the Toledo Public Library.

And finally, I thank the staffs of the Library of Congress, the New York Public Library, the New Orleans Public Library, the Free Library of Philadelphia, the Library Company of Philadelphia, the libraries of the Curtis Institute, University of Pennsylvania, and College of Physicians of Philadelphia, the National Library of Rio de Janeiro, and the Carnegie Library of Pittsburgh, for their co-operation.

J. B.

October 1963

Contents

❋

PRELUDE   xi

NOTES OF A PIANIST
   Notes of the Author   3
   The West Indies, 1857–62   5
   The United States, Panama, Mexico, 1862–65   39
   Mexico, Panama, South America, 1865–68   321

POSTLUDE   399

A NOTE ON GOTTSCHALK'S COMPOSITIONS   411

BIBLIOGRAPHY   415

INDEX   *follows page*   420

List of Illustrations

❦

FRONTISPIECE from the first edition of *Notes of a Pianist*

FOLLOWING PAGE 56

PLATE

I   *Gottschalk as a very young man*
(COURTESY OF DR. DAVID JAMES)
Gottschalk after his return from Europe
(COLLECTION OF JEANNE BEHREND)

II   *Photograph of Gottschalk, 1867*
(COURTESY OF DR. DAVID JAMES)

III   *The first Gottschalk monster concert, 1869*

IV   *Caricature of Gottschalk's hands, 1869*
(COURTESY OF DR. DAVID JAMES)
Gottschalk the virtuoso

V   *Caricature of Gottschalk, 1869*

VI   *The great Gottschalk Festival, 1869*

VII   *Gottschalk's funeral cortege*
Gottschalk's body embalmed

VIII   *Bust of Gottschalk*
(COURTESY OF DR. DAVID JAMES)

Unless otherwise attributed, the illustrations are by courtesy of Mercedes Reis Pequeno, Chief, Music Section, National Library, Rio de Janeiro.

Prelude

O N FEBRUARY 8, 1870, Amy Fay, a young American student in Berlin, wrote home to her family:

> I was dreadfully sorry to hear of poor Gottschalk's death. He had a golden touch, and equal to any in the world, I think. But what a romantic way to die!—to fall senseless at his instrument, while he was playing *La Morte*. It was very strange. If anything more is in the papers about him you must send it to me, for the infatuation that I and 999,999 other American girls once felt for him, still lingers in my breast![1]

The death of Louis Moreau Gottschalk in December 1869 was indeed an occasion of widespread mourning. One of the great pianists of his time, he had, as a youth still in his teens, excited the admiration of Chopin and Berlioz and charmed much of Europe with Creole melodies of his native Louisiana; he had

---

[1] Amy Fay: *Music-Study in Germany* (New York: The Macmillan Company; 1897), p. 42. Miss Fay's impression concerning Gottschalk's death was not entirely accurate.

successfully toured France, Switzerland, and Spain, the United States and Canada, the West Indies, and South America—scandalizing with his amours, endearing himself through charities and his own compositions geared to the popular taste. And now, at Rio de Janeiro, aged forty, he was dead.

Twelve years later, in 1881, his journal, *Notes of a Pianist*, was published by J. B. Lippincott & Company. Parts of it had appeared during his lifetime, principally in *La France musicale*, *L' Art musical*, and the *Atlantic Monthly*. Entangled in bureaucratic red tape for four years at Rio de Janeiro, the journal was finally obtained by Gottschalk's sisters in London. It was in a chaotic state. The editor, Clara Gottschalk, needed two more years to decipher and transcribe her brother's legacy, a nearly illegible mass of loose, torn, faded scraps of paper. It was then translated (rather ineptly) from the original French by Clara's brother-in-law, later her husband, Dr. Robert E. Peterson of Philadelphia.

Despite these vicissitudes the journal emerges as an important personal document of the nineteenth century. Out of print for some fifty years, the lucky owners of a few remaining copies have resembled a kind of unofficial Gottschalk Society, quoting favorite passages to each other and exchanging conjectures. *Notes of a Pianist* covers five years in the West Indies (1857–62), three years in the United States (1862–65), and three in South America (1865–68). Its author, although born in the Western Hemisphere, was educated mostly in Europe: he could determine to what extent the New World was new, and could extract the very essence of its atmosphere. People of various cultures, races, and environments came under his notice; we see them through his eyes. The vignette, the anecdote, the opinion enliven his account. Although neither unprejudiced nor consistent,[2] it often sparkles with Gallic wit, evidence of his own personal charm. Clearly, the author of this journal was a well-educated person of many interests, superior sensibilities and intelligence—not, to quote his own modest preface, just "a musician, and only a pianist!"

Gottschalk, an American, confided to his journal in French and spoke English with an accent. This was no anomaly. He was born in New Orleans on May 8, 1829, only twenty-six years after

---

[2] *Notes of a Pianist* begins with an inaccuracy, after a preface declaring the journal's only merit to be its veracity.

NOTES OF A PIANIST.

BY

LOUIS MOREAU GOTTSCHALK,

PIANIST AND COMPOSER,

CHEVALIER OF THE ORDERS OF ISABELLA THE CATHOLIC, CHARLES III., AND
LION OF HOLSTEIN-LIMBOURG; MEMBER OF THE PHILHARMONIC
SOCIETIES OF BORDEAUX, NEW YORK, HAVANA,
RIO DE JANEIRO, ETC. ETC.

DURING HIS PROFESSIONAL TOURS IN THE UNITED STATES,
CANADA, THE ANTILLES, AND SOUTH AMERICA.

PRECEDED BY A

SHORT BIOGRAPHICAL SKETCH WITH CONTEMPORANEOUS CRITICISMS.

EDITED BY HIS SISTER,

CLARA GOTTSCHALK.

TRANSLATED FROM THE FRENCH BY

ROBERT E. PETERSON, M.D.

"We see that nothing is wanting in the works of Gottschalk, neither variety in the
subjects treated of, nor originality of style. He merits then, as composer and as artist,
a separate place alongside of the great masters of modern art."—A. MARMONTEL.

PHILADELPHIA:
J. B. LIPPINCOTT & CO.;
LONDON: 16 SOUTHAMPTON STREET, COVENT GARDEN.
1881.

Title page of the first edition of Notes of a Pianist, Philadelphia, 1881 the Louisiana Purchase. Vestiges of French and Spanish rule made Gottschalk's birthplace a world apart, a checkerboard of streets and houses (Le Vieux Carré) bordering a curve on the Mississippi River. Predominantly French in culture, it is still known as the French Quarter of New Orleans.

Negroes, from ebony to pale sepia, from slaves to slaveowners, gave Le Vieux Carré a lively aspect. Slaves danced the bamboula, vendors sang their wares, pretty quadroons walked in rhythmic grace. Within this colorful ambiance—except for a sojourn at Pass Christian, Mississippi—Gottschalk passed his first thirteen years. Here were formed the native stamp of much of his music and the attitudes that were to shape his life.

Gottschalk's father, Edward Gottschalk (1795–1853), was a native of London, educated in Germany, a gentleman of wide cultural background. New Orleans became his home through his establishment there in business and his marriage to young Aimée de Bruslé, daughter of upper-class refugees from the slave rebellion in Santo Domingo. Their first child, Louis Moreau—or Moreau, as he was called by his family—was named after his great-uncle Count Moreau de l'Islet, a prominent New Orleans jurist. He was the eldest of seven children. The responsibilities of primogeniture were taken for granted in this close-knit family, whose sense of blood loyalty stemmed as much from his father's Jewish heritage[3] as from his mother's titled French one.[4] It was always understood that the role of paterfamilias would eventually be assumed by Moreau.

The symptoms of musical precocity are easily recognized. Moreau abounded in them. When he was three years old, he began to play the piano. When he was seven, on short notice he substituted at the organ at High Mass for his teacher, François Letellier, organist and choirmaster at the St. Louis Cathedral.

---

[3] Throughout the mass of biographical material on Gottschalk written by Upton, Kellogg, Howard, Lange, Loggins, and others, the assumption that he was partly of Jewish origin persists. The only dissenter is Fannie L. Gwinner Cole: Dictionary of American Biography (Vol. VII, 1931), pp. 441-42. However, recent investigations made by Dr. Bertram W. Korn (*American Jewish Archives*, November 1963) and Mr. Ronald J. D'Arcy Hart, M. A., London genealogist, strongly suggest that Moreau's paternal grandparents were Jewish.

[4] The titles are given in *Notes of a Pianist*. However, in the annals of law in Louisiana, the name of Moreau's great-uncle becomes L. Moreau Lislet, Esq.

By the time Moreau was eleven, Letellier was declaring that the boy must be sent to Paris to complete his musical education. On April 23, 1841, he gave a farewell concert assisted by several adult performers.[5] The following year, after continuing to participate in various *soirées musicales*, he sailed for France on May 17, a well-prepared student, having also studied violin with Félix Miolan, concertmaster of the Théâtre d'Orléans, brother of the well-known French singer Mme. Miolan-Carvalho.[6] The musical elite of New Orleans included as well the Parisian émigré Jean-Baptiste Guiraud, whose son Ernest, born in New Orleans, like Moreau went to Paris as a youth. At this point, however, their paths took different courses. Ernest Guiraud remained in Paris, winning, like his father, a Prix de Rome, becoming closely associated with Berlioz and, especially, Bizet. He set the originally spoken recitatives of *Carmen* to music after Bizet's death and became Debussy's first professor at the Conservatoire.

Moreau's Paris educated him on three levels. He studied piano with Charles Hallé[7] and Camille Stamaty,[8] composition with Pierre Maleden.[9] He acquired an aristocrat's graces—fencing, riding, Latin, Greek, and the modern classics—all of assistance in his conquest of the Parisian *haut monde*. And he absorbed Paris in the glowing extravagance of "the Romantic Century." Within his orbit came, among others, Victor Hugo, Théophile Gautier, Alexandre Dumas *père*, Alphonse de Lamartine, Rachel, Count d'Orsay, Frédéric Chopin, Hector Berlioz, Jacques Offenbach,

---

[5] "Master Gottschalk was greeted by a brilliant and crowded assemblage on Friday night, and the beautiful St. Louis ballroom glittered with Creole beauty and fashion. The receipts must have been some five or six hundred dollars." *The Daily Picayune*, April 25, 1841.

[6] There seems to be a conflict of testimony between Gottschalk's sisters as to the name of his violin teacher. Clara says that he was Mr. Miolan; Célestine identifies him as a Mr. Ely.

[7] Charles Hallé (1819–95), né Karl Halle, later Sir Charles Hallé, was a native of Westphalia, Germany. Fleeing the Paris Revolution of 1848, he went to Manchester, England, where in 1857 he founded the Hallé Orchestra.

[8] Camille-Marie Stamaty (1811–70), of Greek-French parentage, was born in Rome. He studied with Kalkbrenner and Mendelssohn and became a well-known pedagogue, numbering among his students Camille Saint-Saëns.

[9] Pierre Maleden (1806–?), native of Limoges, studied in Germany with Gottfried Weber. He became established in Paris as a teacher in 1831. "The greatest benefit I got from my studies with Stamaty was my acquaintance with Maleden," Saint-Saëns said.

Georges Bizet, and Camille Saint-Saëns. A French critic, Oscar Comettant, declared in 1857 that Gottschalk was American only by birth: *"Il est Français d'esprit, de coeur, de goût et d'habitudes."*

The transition from student to artist was effected brilliantly. In France, Switzerland, and Spain, from 1845 to 1852, his appearances in salon, court, and concert hall were a series of unqualified triumphs. Eager to equal them at home and to rival Jenny Lind's American success, he arrived in New York in January 1853. The first four years of his repatriation (1853-57) are dealt with retrospectively in the journal itself. They included his New York debut, P. T. Barnum's offer, the happy return to New Orleans, the unlucky tour of New England, the financial difficulties after his father's death, the first visit to Cuba (February 1854-February 1855), and the success of his most popular composition, *The Last Hope*, sales of which helped to pay off his father's debts and contribute to the support of his mother, brothers, and sisters. *The Last Hope* became the fond property of every young lady with a piano in the parlor and dampened many a handkerchief with tears.

Early in February 1857, Gottschalk arrived in Havana to begin a concert tour with Adelina Patti, then only fourteen and accompanied by her father. At this stage in his career, we first come face to face, as it were, with Gottschalk. For shortly after disembarkation, perhaps even before, he began to write his journal. It covers a span of eleven years, the last entry having been made at Montevideo on December 15, 1868, almost exactly twelve months before his death. These were years mostly of travel. Although certain localities held him for lengthy sojourns, at no time could he claim any of them as his home. And, although he complained piteously of his lot, he did nothing to change it. The journal—perhaps more than his profession, of necessity often imperfectly served—became an anodyne for his woes, almost a means of preserving his sanity.

What provides the incentive to start a diary? Is it a need to come to terms with self, to maintain identity, to emerge from the enslavement of circumstance through the discipline of language? What provided an incentive for this one? A crisis, perhaps. He had had to make many adjustments. The impact of his native land had been shattering to a young man who was, in his own

words, still "poorly prepared for the realities of American life."
He had seen, probably for the first time, hostile reviews of his
programs. His friend Ada Clare[1] had publicized in the New
York *Atlas* his recent rejection of her, darkly hinting that she
was pregnant by him. His mother had recently died in Paris.[2] To
sum up, Gottschalk reached Cuba emotionally spent. In the diary
he found a trustworthy confidant, and in the tropics, a refuge—
"l'isle joyeuse" of his maternal ancestors. His five-year stay there
more than answered an atavistic urge: it was a kind of necessary
reversion to the conditions of his childhood. Perhaps it is no
coincidence that he had gone to Cuba after his father's death
years before.

Soon after arriving there on this first visit in 1854, he met the
Cuban composer and pianist Nicolás Ruiz Espadero, an eccentric recluse who became one of his closest friends. One day in
January 1862, Espadero accompanied him to the American Consulate, where he swore allegiance to the union of American states,
then in danger of disintegration. On January 18 he sailed from
Havana, never—it was presaged in the *Gaceta de la Habana*—to
return to the beloved isle. He had spent half of the West Indian
sojourn there.

Now Gottschalk matched his country's fratricidal conflict with
his own unrest. The tours were arduous: up into Canada, down
to Virginia, westward to Wisconsin, from San Francisco eastward
to mining towns in Nevada. "The devil take the poets who sing
the joys of an artist's life," he cried. A review by no means
entirely favorable to Gottschalk as a musician noted nevertheless
that "a knight out of a fairy-book in search of adventure could
hardly have done and suffered more."[3]

On September 18, 1865, Gottschalk sailed from San Fran-

---

[1] Ada Clare was the pseudonym of Jane McElhinney (1836–74), a
member of an eminent South Carolina family; actress, journalist, novelist,
New York's "Queen of Bohemia," and friend of many writers including Walt
Whitman. Toward the conclusion of her novel, *Only a Woman's Heart*
(1866), she delineated Gottschalk ("Victor Doria") with surprising effective-
ness as a Don Juan. Their son died when still a boy.

[2] It is characteristic of the journal that several persons with whom its
writer was most involved are not mentioned by name—among them his
mother, his brother Edward, and Ada Clare. Their exclusion can be attributed
either to his sister's revision or simply to his own reticence.

[3] Charles S. Holt: "Gottschalk's Diary," *The Dial*, November 1881, pp.
141–43.

cisco for South America. It was a sudden departure. A trumped-up charge against him had been aired in some local newspapers. He was forced to flee on board in the dead of night. The incident became known, and for a time soiled his name across the northern continent.

A sense of failure now engulfed him. Repeated successes in Lima and Santiago could not entirely dispel it. Entries in the journal become less frequent and are marked by the macabre, the bizarre, the grotesque. Revolution in Lima,[4] corruption almost everywhere—he was becoming more and more disillusioned with countries that were republics only in name.

Public education, he realized, was needed in South American countries. "Of all forms of government," he said, "the republic is that which exacts from the people the greatest degree of enlightenment: under it each citizen ought to participate actively in its destinies, as he constitutes, so to speak, a fraction of the government itself." He continued:

> Those favored by fortune can educate themselves in all countries, and it is for that reason that the American thinkers did not dedicate their cares to the aristocratic element of society, but rather to the lowest ranks of the great mass of people, whom they have struggled to enlighten, comprehending that education ought not to be a privilege, but something which belongs to all as much as the air we breathe, and that every citizen has as imprescriptible a right to the light of the Spirit as he has to the light of the sun which illuminates him.

He was expressing ideas that, though still not accepted in his country without reservations, remain its basic aspirations. Although he could now have returned to the United States with impunity, his friends there were still unaware of the heights to which he was rising as a fellow citizen. He goes on:

> The popular system of education in the United States, in that austere elaboration, which, of a child, makes successively a man and later a citizen, has, for its principal object, to prepare him for the use of liberty—that cuirass of

---

[4] Gottschalk's report on the agony of Lima suggests Goya's *Desastres de la guerra*.

the strong, but which frequently, for the weak, is transformed into the shirt of Nessus.

In my country, it is not its eminent individuals, but the superiority of the intellectual level of the people, which attracts the attention of the observer; for, however great Prescott, Longfellow, Everett, Bancroft, and many others may be, these noble characters are lost to view in the presence of the enlightenment of the collective entity—the "people." It is of great interest indeed to our political existence and to our prosperity, that the most obscure of the farmers of the "Far West" can lay aside the plow to ascend the tribune and thence spread abroad the most patriotic and progressive ideas.[5]

Gottschalk was offering a benefit concert for the Society of the Friends of Education, founded in Montevideo by José Pedro Varela, friend and disciple of Sarmiento. The pianist was one of the cofounders of this organization; his concert earned it more than a thousand pesos.

Soon after his arrival in Montevideo in 1867, he made the acquaintance of another future biographer, Luis Ricardo Fors, an exiled Spanish republican. They became inseparable companions, dividing their time for two years between Montevideo and Buenos Aires, working in behalf of social reform. By the close of 1868, Gottschalk had resumed composing. His success with the public of the Río de la Plata had awakened in him long-dormant plans: he would return to the United States; he would return to Europe; he would have his operas performed; he would, in deference to his mother's oft-expressed wish, visit the Holy Land. . . .

The end came twelve months later.

A compendium of contemporaneous views on Gottschalk's playing serves to give an idea of what it was like.

It was superlative.

Evidently it was a lapidary's art. The "cascades of pearls," the "golden touch" and "glittering star dust" all excited mention, en-

---

[5] Octavia Hensel: *Life and Letters of Louis Moreau Gottschalk* (Boston: Oliver Ditson and Company; 1870), pp. 165–67. Octavia Hensel was the pseudonym of Mrs. Mary Alice Ives Seymour, one of Gottschalk's pupils. After her book was published, it was believed by some that she had had a liaison with Gottschalk.

hanced as they were by grace and brilliance and dazzling effects of shading encompassing the entire tonal gamut of the instrument. "The piano does not sound like a piano when he plays it," was, in essence, a frequent comment.

Over and above all these purely sensuous aspects of his pianism, however, was the presence of a genuinely musical soul. This was what most commanded the admiration of his friend and mentor Hector Berlioz: his musicianship, his taste, and his fine sense of proportion. Often irritated by undeserved ovations, Berlioz took pleasure in Gottschalk's success, happy to see an artist receive his just due. "Mr. Gottschalk," he said, "is one of the very small number of those who possess all the different elements of the sovereign power of the pianist, all the attributes that environ him with an irresistible prestige."[6]

The standards of comparison then were Chopin, Liszt, and Thalberg. In varying degrees they had freed piano playing, restoring to it and extending dimensions realized by Beethoven but undreamed of by such pianists as Herz and Kalkbrenner. And it was to the innovators that Gottschalk was most often compared, sometimes even to their disadvantage.

Victor Hugo characterized Gottschalk as "a poet, a man of gay imagination, an eloquent orator who can move his audience."

The most conclusive American comments on at least one aspect of Gottschalk's playing are those of his colleague and friend William Mason:[7]

I knew Gottschalk well, and was fascinated by his playing, which was full of brilliancy and bravura. His strong, rhythmic accent, his vigor and dash, were exciting and always aroused enthusiasm. He was the perfection of his school, and his effects had the sparkle and effervescence of champagne. He was as far as possible from being an inter-

---

[6] Louis Moreau Gottschalk: *Notes of a Pianist* (Philadelphia: J. B. Lippincott and Company; 1881), pp. 50, 51.

[7] William Mason (1829–1908), pianist and composer, was a son of the hymn writer and music educator Lowell Mason, brother of Henry Mason, founder of the Mason and Hamlin Piano Company, manufacturers; he was an uncle of the composer Daniel Gregory Mason. A pupil of Liszt, he became acquainted with Wagner, Brahms, Schumann, Meyerbeer, Anton Rubinstein, von Bülow, and Grieg. His revolutionary ideas on piano touch antedated those of later pedagogues.

preter of chamber or classical music, but, notwithstanding
this, some of the best musicians of the strict style were frequently to be seen among his audience, among others Carl
Bergmann, who told me that he always heard Gottschalk
with intense enjoyment. He first made his mark through
his arrangement of creole melodies. They were well-defined
rhythmically, and he played them with absolute rhythmical
accuracy. This clear definition in his interpretation contributed more than anything else to the fascination which he
always exerted over his audience.[8]

This superbly endowed pianist was born just after the dawn
of Romantic music: Weber had died in 1826, Beethoven in 1827,
Schubert in 1828. And in March 1829 the first public performance of Bach's *St. Matthew Passion* since Bach's death took
place in Berlin under the direction of Mendelssohn, ushering in
an important phase of the so-called Romantic era, that of discovery. A spirit of restless inquiry now animated the art of music
in Europe, resulting in a discovery of past epochs and alien cultures, in new forms and practices. Composers set their stamp on
the epoch, not alone with their music, but also with their prose.
Mendelssohn, Schumann, Berlioz, and Wagner demanded in
articles and essays an end to the domination of facile Italian and
French operas, declared war on philistinism, and pleaded for
attention to the values of Gluck, Bach, Beethoven, and Schubert.

Gottschalk's path through this period of change and upheaval
resembles the course of a motley, vagrant filament, original in
texture and direction, through a rich tapestry. It begins in New
Orleans, proceeds to Europe, and returns to the Western Hemisphere, where it snaps off prematurely.

Arriving in Paris in 1842, Gottschalk straightway was initiated
into the wonders of Bach and Beethoven by his teacher, Hallé.
This was strong fare for a boy reared in a city of operatic traditions.[9] His next teacher, Stamaty, prepared him for his private
debut in April 1845, when he played Chopin's Concerto in E

---

[8] William Mason: *Memories of a Musical Life* (New York: The Century
Company; 1901), pp. 205, 206.
[9] Only one year after the première, in 1831, of Meyerbeer's *Robert le
Diable* in Paris, Moreau, upon hearing his mother sing an aria from it, essayed
it on the piano—his first keyboard venture. He was three years old. The influence of this opera was to remain with him.

Minor, Thalberg's transcription of excerpts from Rossini's *Semiramide* and Liszt's Fantasy on Meyerbeer's *Robert le Diable*. Assisting artists included the cellist August Franchomme and Jean Géraldy, baritone. Chopin was present, among other notables. According to Clara Gottschalk, he said to her brother: "Give me your hand, my child; I predict that you will become the king of pianists."[1]

At his public debut in Paris, on April 17, 1849,[2] Gottschalk established himself as a figure not only *in* the Romantic epoch but also *of* it. He introduced the New World via his own compositions, which already had been received enthusiastically in influential circles and were being published by Escudier.[3] These nostalgic evocations of New Orleans were electrifying, putting him in a class by himself. *"Pianiste compositeur louisianais,"* he was the first to bring to Europe the Afro-Caribbean rhythms of that amalgam of cultures, American folk music. The critics responded with Chateaubriand-like effusions:

> If Mr. Gottschalk has been able, although still young, to acquire this individuality that escapes so many others, it is perhaps owing to the fact that, after having formed his talent by solid studies, he has left it to wander carelessly in the fragrant savannas of his country, from which he has brought back to us its colors and perfumes.[4]

> Mr. Gottschalk was born in America, whence he has brought a host of curious chants from the Creoles and the Negroes; he has made from them the themes of his most delicious compositions. Everybody in Europe now knows *Bamboula, Le Bananier, Le Mancenillier, La Savane,* and twenty other ingenious fantasies in which the nonchalant graces of tropical melody assuage so agreeably our restless and insatiable passion for novelty.[5]

---

[1] Gottschalk: *op. cit.,* p. 33.

[2] He had already appeared publicly in the provinces.

[3] Léon Escudier (1821–81) and his brother Marie (1819–80) were busy Parisian musical entrepreneurs, publishing *La France musicale, L'Art musical,* and books on music. They brought out many of Verdi's works and were the first to publish Gottschalk, whom they advertised as *"Gottschalk de la Louisiane."*

[4] Théophile Gautier: *Feuilleton de la Presse,* Paris, March 31, 1851.

[5] Hector Berlioz: "Mr. Gottschalk's Concert," *Feuilleton, Journal des Débats,* Paris, April 13, 1851.

A youth not yet twenty had become a pioneer in musical folklore. Glinka had recently published his Russian melodies; Chopin his mazurkas and polonaises; Liszt was soon to follow with "Hungarian" rhapsodies. Gottschalk's contribution was part of this wave of nationalism.

He stirred the imagination. Pale, dark, and slender, he came from afar, from the land of "the noble savage." He was aware of the value of such attributes, for by 1847 he was beginning to realize that as a musician he would have to support himself and several dependents. The profession of concert pianist, always precarious, was subject to certain special conditions a century ago. We are afforded, in Gottschalk's diary, a glimpse of their nature, which varied slightly in different localities.

The solo recital was only very gradually being adopted.[6] ("Gave a concert alone at Worcester, Massachusetts," Gottschalk says by way of reporting something unusual, and there are other instances of this kind.) A concert was just what the word implies: a concerted effort on the part of various individuals or groups to entertain the audience. It could sometimes include such diverse elements as an act from an opera or various operatic selections, a movement from a symphony or a concerto, a play, a juggler, a few piano solos. The visiting artist's program often was rounded out by selections offered by local talent. If a certain piece pleased the audience, the performer was expected to repeat it—several times, in fact, if the enthusiasm warranted it. Thus an encore was exactly what the word means: *again*. A benefit could be one for the artist, all the proceeds of the evening going to him. On such occasions he might be crowned onstage with a laurel wreath or a jeweled wreath of gold or silver.

Another characteristic of concert life was the multiple-piano vogue.[7] Any number of pianos on-stage, from two to forty, with one or two players to a keyboard, attracted the public. This

---

[6] The first effort in this direction was made by Ignaz Moscheles (1794–1870) in London in 1837. Fearing monotony on this occasion, he used some vocal assistance. Two years later in Rome, Liszt gave recitals that he called "musical soliloquies." Judging from one of his programs, they bore little resemblance to the format now generally accepted. After he gave one in London in 1840, the term "piano recital" came into use.

[7] See Arthur Loesser: *Men, Women and Pianos* (New York: Simon & Schuster; 1954), pp. 363–65, 487.

practice gave amateurs a chance to perform with professionals, local and foreign, and promoted the sale of pianos. Gottschalk resorted to this practice, literally, one might say, to drum up trade for piano music.

Patronage, as always, was a help: in Paris the salon; in Spain and even republican Switzerland the court. At Geneva, in 1851, he became the favorite of the Grand Duchess Anna of Russia, her consort, who was the Baron de Vauthier, and their entourage, largely through his performance of Weber's *Concertstück*—the baron had been a friend and admirer of Weber. In Madrid, Gottschalk gathered from Queen Cristina's remarks that he could win the Spanish people best with "acrobatics." An appeal to their patriotism, Gottschalk discovered, was infallible. Already he had flattered the Swiss with his arrangement of excerpts from Rossini's *Guillaume Tell*. He was to drive the Spanish populace wild with his *El Sitio de Zaragoza* (*The Siege of Saragossa*), a "symphony" for ten pianos based on Spanish tunes and national airs. It had all the effects dear to the battle pieces that had raged in parlors and concert halls since Franz Kotzwara's *Battle of Prague* (1789)—trumpet calls, military marches, drum rolls, cannon fire, etc.—effects later used stunningly by Tchaikovsky in his *1812 Overture*.

Gottschalk continued to beguile the masses in this way. After returning to the United States, he is supposed to have taken parts of *El Sitio de Zaragoza*, substituted American anthems for the Spanish ones and entitled the result *Grand National Symphony for Ten Pianos: Bunker Hill*. Probably as a solo piece he renamed it *American Reminiscences* or *National Glory*, adding to it Foster's "Oh! Susanna" and "Old Folks at Home." During the Civil War he gladdened Northern hearts with *The Union*. In Chile, he accomplished his purpose with *Solemne Marcha Triunfal a Chile*; in Uruguay, with *Marche Solennelle* and *Montevideo*; in Brazil, with *Grande fantaisie triomphale sur l'hymne national brésilien* and *Marcha solemne brasileira*.

It is quite possible that Gottschalk learned from Berlioz how to rally an entire community by means of a festival. Berlioz who, himself could whip up a patriotic tune on occasion, as witness the *Rákóczy March*, conceived the idea in the summer of 1844 of commemorating the Paris World's Fair of Industrial Products with a music festival[8] using 500 choristers and 480 instrumentalists. Possibly Gottschalk assisted him in this enterprise, which involved rehearsing various groups separately and then en masse.[9] The performance on August 1, 1844, was effected with the aid of seven deputy conductors. Following this ordeal, Berlioz went to Nice for a month to recuperate. The conglomerate program, the numerous performers, the method of rehearsal and performance, the conductor's labors, the growing anxiety, and the ensuing state of utter exhaustion are familiar elements of Gottschalk's career in Latin America.

Such was the concert world in which Gottschalk moved, subject to its conditions but giving to it the impress of his own individuality. In Europe his fame and influence became considerable. Rossini, in 1866, recommended Teresa Carreño to a friend in London as "a charming pianist, pupil of the celebrated Gottschalk."[1] Bizet as a boy played his works; *Le Bananier, Le Mancenillier* and *La Moissonneuse* were in his library.[2] Offenbach, long before the commencement of his career in the musical theater, played on the cello his own arrangement of *Le Bananier*. When Verdi's *Aïda* received its La Scala première in 1872, a critic fancied that he found Gottschalk's influence in it.[3] As for Debussy's *Golliwog's Cakewalk*, might it not be a collateral descendant of *The Banjo?*

On February 11, 1853, Gottschalk made his New York debut. The format of his program was more or less an example of current custom; it remained basically the same for his grand return to New York from the West Indies exactly nine years later.

---

[8] By the 1870's, in the United States at least, a festival had come to mean a series of performances spread out over several days. With the advent of the twentieth century, festivals, sometimes lasting for weeks and even months, became dominated by particular themes, such as Bach, the Renaissance, contemporary music, music of the Western Hemisphere.

[9] In 1846-7, Gottschalk gave a series of concerts with Berlioz at the Théâtre des Italiens.

[1] Marta Milinowski: *Teresa Carreño* (New Haven: Yale University Press; 1940), p. 74.

[2] Mina Curtiss: *Bizet and His World* (New York: Alfred A. Knopf; 1958), p. 472.

[3] Carlo Gatti: *Verdi, The Man and His Music* (New York: G. P. Putnam's Sons; 1955), p. 246.

L. M. Gottschalk

respectfully announces to the musical public of New York
that he will give a grand concert on
FRIDAY EVENING, FEBRUARY 11,
at Niblo's Salon.

MR. GOTTSCHALK will be assisted by

MME. ROSE DE VRIES   MR. KYLE
MR. HOFFMAN   MR. FRASER

PROGRAMME — PART I

DUET—Grand Concertante for Flute and Piano Forte
    Messrs. A. Kyle and G. F. Bristow

FANTASIA—The Chase of Young Henry[4]   Gottschalk
    by THE AUTHOR

SONG—I Will Love Thee to the Last   Montgomery
    by Mr. Frazier

FANTASIA—"Jerusalem",[5] Grand Triumphal   Gottschalk
    (Fantasia for two Pianos)
    by Mr. RICHARD HOFFMAN and the Author

GRAND ARIA—"I due Foscari"   Verdi
    Sung by Mme. ROSE DE VRIES

SEPTUOR, from Lucia di Lammermoor[6]   Liszt
    GOTTSCHALK

PART II

DESCRIPTIVE BALLAD—"The Young Soldier", composed
    expressly for him by Balfe   by Mr. Frazier

POETIC CAPRICES "The Moissoneuse" Mazurka
    "The Ossianic Dance"   Gottschalk
    "The Bananier, Negro Dance"
    by THE AUTHOR

ARIA—Ah, mon fils—"Prophet"   Meyerbeer
    by Mme. ROSE DE VRIES

Waltz di Bravura (for two pianos)   Gottschalk
    by Mr. R. HOFFMAN and THE AUTHOR

Carnival of Venice,[7] composed and executed by   Gottschalk

Tickets One and Two Dollars, according to location.
Doors open at 6½ o'clock, Concert to commence at 7½

---

[4] The overture to Méhul's opera Le jeune Henri.
[5] From the French version of Verdi's I Lombardi.
[6] The opera by Donizetti.
[7] After Paganini?

The notice that appeared on the amusements page of the New York *Times* the day of the concert is shown on the facing page.

Although the press was not unanimous in his favor—the *Herald* ecstatic, the *Times* somewhat condescending—this proved an auspicious debut, albeit financially unsuccessful. At his second concert he filled Niblo's Theater.

Other pianists from abroad had preceded him, but they had not been presented with quite the same éclat. And he was a special case: an American who had made good in Europe. In New York and elsewhere he was well received, especially, of course, in New Orleans. Then, in October of that year, in Boston, the "Athens of America," he met with a stinging professional defeat. It was administered by the recalcitrant John Sullivan Dwight (1813–93), a former Unitarian minister and transcendentalist of Brook Farm. Although *Dwight's Journal of Music* (1852–81) had a small circulation, it was the arbiter of taste in musical circles. The acclaim accorded Gottschalk in Europe mattered not a whit to Dwight. Right after the New York debut he had begun sniping at the young pianist via his New York correspondent. His objection, on the face of it, was a legitimate one echoed to this day—Gottschalk did not play the piano classics.

Dwight[8] was a member of a scattered group of heroic souls attempting the impossible—this in itself a tenet of Romanticism. They were seeking to form the musical taste of a heterogeneous mass of people in a state of flux. Results of their efforts were already perceptible: all of Beethoven's symphonies save the first were performed in Boston during the season of 1852–53, the ninth twice. An open letter to Dwight in Leipzig's *Neue Zeitschrift für Musik* of June 17, 1853, marveled at this and other such Boston wonders. Written by the German magazine's editor, it saluted Dwight and his *Journal*, and concluded: "WESTWARD MOVES THE HISTORY OF ART."

Boston, of course, might have been expected to lead at the time. But throughout the nation, there were evidences of a growing dissatisfaction with the limitations of Gottschalk's repertoire.

---

[8] His gods were Bach, Mozart, Beethoven, Mendelssohn, and Chopin. Listing him as John Sebastian Dwight was an apposite mistake, perhaps an intentional one. Thomas Ryan: *Recollections of an Old Musician* (New York: E. P. Dutton & Company; 1899), p. 118.

Theodore Thomas (1835–1905), German-born, was to have much to do with this change of cultural climate. In 1862, he resolutely faced a twofold, self-imposed task: to develop the American public's taste for symphonic music and to establish a permanent, privately subsidized symphony orchestra such as did not yet exist in Europe. By dint of some thirty years of Herculean labors, he achieved what he set out to do.[9]

Gottschalk, whose musical formation had taken place in the Paris of the 1840's after childhood in a French milieu, now found himself in an increasingly German-dominated country. Although mainly successful he encountered more difficulties in pleasing the public in the United States than anywhere else. He had to walk a tightrope over a terrain of widely divergent tastes. His own salon pieces and opera transcriptions, too trivial for listeners demanding Beethoven and Mendelssohn, were too advanced for some of the simple folk in outlying communities, who were asking for a tune they could follow.

However, Gottschalk responded more than is generally realized to the challenge posed by the *cognoscenti*, sometimes thereby incurring a penalty.[1] In New York and other large cities, he played such works as Chopin's "Funeral March," Grand Scherzo (opus 31), impromptus, waltzes, Etude in F Minor, and Prelude in D-flat Major; of Schumann, the Andante and Variations for Two Pianos. Of Beethoven, he played the Andante from the Sonate "Pathétique" and participated in performing the last two movements of the "Kreutzer" Violin Sonata and other chamber works; of Mozart, a violin sonata in A Major; of Weber, quite often the *Concertstück, Perpetual Motion,* and Liszt's arrangement of the *Invitation to the Waltz;* chamber works by the French-English composer George Onslow (1784–1853); of Berlioz, Liszt's ar-

---

[9] Truth to tell, these worthy pioneers ignored or discredited the very musical lifeblood of a young nation: old tune books, minstrel shows, Gottschalk's works based on American folk tunes, Stephen Foster, spirituals—the entire wealth of music in the vernacular that was to culminate in jazz and the musical comedy.

[1] "He also gave a couple of Chopin's pieces, but their effect was lost in the large theatre. His own arrangement from *Norma* seemed to be much better understood and more enjoyed by most of the audience. He was most warmly applauded." From the *Evening Bulletin,* Philadelphia, May 27, 1862. The Chopin works were an étude in F minor and a waltz in A-flat major, opus numbers not given.

rangement of the Sermon and Benediction from *Benvenuto Cellini*. The last named cannot be called a piano classic, but Gottschalk's performances of it in 1856 must have been among the very first in the Western Hemisphere of music by Berlioz.

He sought as well to enlighten the public, announcing a series of "*Matinées d'Instruction*" at Irving Hall, New York, to illustrate "the method by which modern effects are produced on the piano." Apparently only one was given, "in the round," on March 18, 1862, just before his first tour of the West.

The North American years of the journal (1862–65) were catalysts to its most frequent entries. Impression crowded upon impression. The pace became breathless as he recorded the growth of cities, technological advances, and the development of advertising and journalism.

An intimate observer of the Civil War, Gottschalk noted particularly the suffering it brought. (His description of panic at Harrisburg is a masterpiece of reporting.) There was no question as to where his sympathies lay: although "a son of the South," he favored the Union cause. But the extreme partisanship of American women, North and South, rather dismayed him. Evidently it was part of the active role they played in society. He marveled at the freedom enjoyed by unmarried women here, and generally approved of it, despite his dislike of "strong-minded women." To the reader, *Notes of a Pianist* provides a panorama of nineteenth-century American womanhood—adventuresses like Adah Isaacs Menken, an occasional prostitute, reformers like Amelia Bloomer, the new waitresses, and the countless "faces to make one play wrong notes"—the Daisy Millers and Amy Fays exchanging books at the library and playing *The Last Hope*.

As an American citizen, Gottschalk vacillated constantly between pride and irritation. He recognized achievements and potentialities in the United States, but regretted the lack of traditions. (And there were times when democracy seemed a little too democratic.) He was that timeless figure, the unaware American: unaware because, while wanting to take pride, he does not know what values to seek in order to justify it. An expatriate in his own country, he is ignorant of its heritage.

Nowhere is this more apparent than in an entry for March 14, 1864. On a train bound for Norwich, Connecticut, a fellow

musician had introduced himself to Gottschalk, who explains for
our benefit:

> He is a traveling music master, whose species is known
> only in the United States. They go from village to village
> and organize classes, which they teach collectively—religious
> hymns, national songs, etc. There are collections of little
> airs published for this purpose.

Gottschalk, sighing for traditions, had stumbled on a vital
choral tradition of eighteenth-century New England, rooted partly
in the English Reformation and Restoration: the singing school.
It is still alive in the rural South. It had not yet completely disappeared from New England, as this chance meeting proves. He
was as far removed from its early composers as he was from the
school of late-nineteenth-century American composers which followed him. Edward MacDowell remains the best-known member
of that school. John Knowles Paine (1839–1906), its forerunner,
resembled a neat version of the bespectacled, bearded German
professor so despised by Gottschalk.

In MacDowell's smaller pieces and various works by George
W. Chadwick and Arthur Foote, Gottschalk might have found
much to admire. Conversely, the approval of a musician of Gottschalk's ilk would have mattered little to the senior members of
this august galaxy. Although his music in the native vein was exactly what Dvořák was demanding from American composers
during his visit to the United States (1892–95), only the national-
istic Arthur Farwell (1872–1952) could have realized it. With the
exception of Horatio Parker,[2] members of the Old Guard, as Farwell called them, were as remote from Gottschalk as they were
from Charles Ives (1874–1954), herald of the twentieth century.

Gottschalk was a pivotal figure. His forty years spanned a
period of transition, John Sullivan Dwight being one of its chief
oracles. In the West Indies and most of South America, however,
no such thorn in the side existed for Gottschalk. There he was
adored almost without reservations. He entered intimately the
cultural life of communities large and small, whether exhorting
hundreds of musicians to their best or quietly improvising at the
piano among friends. Of his final sixteen years in the Western

---

[2] Horatio Parker (1863–1919) taught Ives at Yale University.

Hemisphere, only six were spent in the United States. Creole by tradition and temperament, he felt an affinity with Latin American tempos and was keenly perceptive of their nuances.

By way of explaining the excesses of partisanship aroused by two rival prima donnas, he wrote: "The Havanese public is essentially Hispano-American, that is to say, *ardent et primitif.*"[3] He himself had experienced the warmth of such adulation in Cuba and elsewhere. At Santa Clara he had been induced to enter the town riding a white Andalusian steed. After his concert at Trinidad (Cuba), we are told, a hidalgo brushed aside the coachman to conduct Gottschalk's carriage on foot through the adoring crowd. At Puerto-Príncipe (Cuba), on his leaving the concert hall a procession was formed: first, the orchestra playing the *Royal March*, then the artists and assorted talent of the town, then Gottschalk with the governor and his municipal council and aides-de-camp, then a "court" of distinguished ladies—all proceeding through a ranged battalion of soldiers carrying torches, while the townspeople sang: "Glory to Moreau!"[4]

In those warm, beautiful isles, where time seemed to stand still, Italian opera bloomed like a tropical flower. Gottschalk himself was engaged to conduct operas at Matanzas and Havana in 1860. And heaven help a maestro who tried to get by with a truncated, sleazy performance in a small town! He was sharply taken to task by the local newspaper critic and advised either to mend his ways or not to return.

Opera, yes, and the luxuriant profusion of native songs and dances meant music in the West Indies. Gottschalk dispensed them both with incomparable pianism, the former through transcriptions and fantasies, the latter through his own arrangements and compositions ensnared in local color, compositions that no doubt provided an impetus to the exquisite piano works of Ignacio Cervantes (1847–1905) of Cuba and Juan Morel Campos (1857–1896) of Puerto Rico.

In Latin America, Gottschalk pushed the festival idea to extreme limits. Every musical element in the community, professional and amateur, was pressed into service, including military

---

[3] *La France musicale*, October 28, 1860, pp. 425, 426.
[4] *L'Abeille*, New Orleans, June 29, 1857, quoting the *Courrier des États-Unis*.

bands and visiting opera companies. For weeks the newspapers, always generous in Latin America to cultural items, reacted as if caught by a contagion. Gottschalk, normally indolent and, he assures us, fond of reverie, suddenly became a dynamo of energy, rehearsing, composing, copying, giving out interviews, busying himself with the thousand and one details necessary to the undertaking.

Latin Americans were treated to sonorities unknown to them. The festivals became *their* festivals, in which *they* participated. The familiar—operas and native music—became exalted; the unfamiliar became familiar. Apparently he was the first professional pianist to use this form of mass music education. The accusation made against him in the United States, that he lagged behind enlightened musical taste, could not be made in Latin America.

In the year of Gottschalk's birth, there was born in Russia a pianist who was to outlive him by twenty-five years: Anton Rubinstein (1829–94). He arrived in the United States in 1872, seven years after Gottschalk's departure, three years after his death, and he consolidated in this country a changing approach to the piano and its literature.

More than choice of repertoire was involved in the advent of Rubinstein, however. Here was something new. A leonine presence on-stage already foretold the sounds that would emanate from the piano—a Steinway, of deeper resonance than Gottschalk's choice, the Chickering. Crystalline clarity and brilliance no longer sufficed. Not that Gottschalk could not produce volume —he must have made the cannons roar when he played *The Union*, and when he conducted his multiple-piano groups in the March from *Tannhäuser*, the sound must have been overpowering at times. But Rubinstein's playing had an emotional intensity that thrilled his audiences. He stormed and raged, and if notes were missed along the way, they mattered but little in the grand design.[5] Musicians schooled in the German tradition—and there were many—rejoiced at hearing the classical repertoire. They might have heard it played also by Otto Dresel and others, but Rubinstein, first in the invasion of Slavic pianists, possibly

---

[5] See, however, Amy Fay: *op. cit.*, p. 47, for comment on both pianists' reliance on "tricks" and "*effect*."

interpreted it with more abandon than those who had paved the way for him.

In 1875, Hans von Bülow gave the first North American performance of Tchaikovsky's new Piano Concerto in B-flat Minor, in Boston. The pattern was set. Nobody who was anybody could be content any longer solely with salon trifles, patriotic ditties, and fantasies on operatic airs.

And yet, when eleven-year-old Josef Hofmann arrived in 1887 to astound the public, he included Gottschalk's *Le Bananier* on his programs. A Philadelphia historian wrote toward the close of the century:

> Even today, forty years afterwards, in quiet villages, like lonely cavities where rain-pools linger, it is Gottschalk's music, with his portrait on the cover, that still reigns supreme among "fashionable pieces."[6]

The old tradition died hard—if it died at all. Not so long ago, Horowitz was playing his *Variations on Themes from Bizet's Carmen* and his arrangement of Sousa's *Stars and Stripes Forever.* Among recent recruits to this form of anachronism are pianist Jorge Bolet (*Liszt's Paraphrase on Rigoletto*) and violinist Aaron Rosand (Sarasate's *Carmen Fantasy*).

Although the publication of *Notes of a Pianist* produced a flurry of reviews in *The Dial, Lippincott's Magazine,* and *The Nation,* and although the October 1908 issue of *The Musician,* "The Gottschalk Number," contained five different articles on the pianist, his reputation slowly declined. Luis Fors noted this in Europe as early as the 1870's. Interest in him flared up briefly here because of Homer Bartlett's article in *Musical America,* January 30, 1915: "First American Composer Received Abroad." Thereafter, for over a decade, Gottschalk's reputation reached its lowest point. *The Last Hope* still went its saccharine way, both as a church hymn named "Mercy" and as an indispensable aid to the silent movies. But the young twentieth century was all too willing to sack relics of the past, whether fine old houses or Gottschalk's name.

---

[6] Louis C. Madeira, compiler; Philip H. Goepp, editor: *Annals of Music in Philadelphia and History of the Musical Fund Society* (Philadelphia: J. B. Lippincott & Company; 1896), p. 161.

The revival began early in the 1930's. For the next thirty years, a succession of magazine articles, recordings, and reissues of his music brought to light a forgotten figure. He has been a tempting subject for biographers, but thus far only one biography has reached publication, the first to be brought out in the twentieth century, well written but fictionalized and sparsely documented.[7]

A graph representing one hundred seventeen years, cascading from wild acclaim to the nadir of neglect and now rising again, would provide an abstract of this drama. Its main protagonist, however, has not yet been heard from in this study. It is time to ask: What did Gottschalk think of himself?

He said that he was the first American pianist, "not by my artistic worth, but in chronological order." His friend William Mason, being his senior by some fourteen weeks, could dispute this claim and did in fact point out that, although Gottschalk had been concertizing before his own return in 1854 from Europe, he always was assisted by other performers. Mason, on the other hand, helped to initiate piano recitals per se. But Mason stopped touring after one year, appalled at the monotony of playing the same pieces, town after town. He settled in the New York area to teach and to introduce new chamber music[8] Gottschalk, although also a successful teacher, toured almost constantly, as though possessed by a demon. His claim to being the first American pianist could be substantiated by the clarification: first American *concert* pianist to win international acclaim.

Far from accepting the charge of having lowered standards, he took pride in having raised them. "The American taste is becoming purer," he said, because for years young ladies had been playing such of his works as *The Last Hope, Berceuse,* and *Murmures éoliens* and attending his performances of them.

All things are relative. It depends on whether we are looking down on a plateau from a mountain or up at it from a valley. If we wish to flatter ourselves that we are looking down on *The*

---

[7] Vernon Loggins: *Where the Word Ends, The Life of Louis Moreau Gottschalk* (Baton Rouge: Louisiana State University Press; 1958).

[8] Together with Theodore Thomas and Carl Bergmann he gave Brahms's Trio, Opus 8, its world première in New York on November 27, 1855. Brahms, then only twenty-two, scarcely had been performed in public.

Last Hope from a great height, then indeed, its pious posturing in
a frame of fancy arabesques seems pretty poor stuff. If, however,
we view it from the valley of a library's dusty archives (that re-
pository of household castoffs), we may realize that this soaring
arc of melody deserved to outlive tons of Victorian trash, as it
has.[9] Gottschalk's best sentimental pieces are immeasurably superior to others of their genre and time. His claim to have raised
standards, therefore, can be given the same consideration as
Foster's wish to show the "opera mongers" that good popular
songs could be written.

But this unaware American did not realize his place in history.
Neither did his public. Posterity plays its tricks. Today it is not
the sentimental pieces that we most cherish (even though
Ricordati and *Berceuse* possess an undeniable charm), but rather
The Banjo, Souvenir de Porto Rico (*Marche des Gibaros*), *La
Gallina, Pasquinade, Bamboula, Le Bananier, La Savane, Le
Mancenillier*—the last four written when he was still in France.
They are exhilarating, fresh, vigorous, in the best tradition of
American popular music and straight from the hemisphere's very
loins.[1] Even *The Union*, a Civil War montage based on "The
Star-Spangled Banner," "Hail, Columbia," and "Yankee Doodle"
can be appropriate on the Fourth of July.

Gottschalk considered catholicity of taste to be the mark of a
cultivated musician. He liked a certain Beethoven quartet especially because it reminded him of an Italianate aria by Mozart.
But he presented Wagner when that composer was still a contro-
versial figure. A long letter to his Cuban friend the poet Don
Rafael Mendive,[2] published in *El Siglo* on August 29, 1863, reveals an individual of very decided tastes and predilections,
possessing a more truly musical orientation than that of many of
his detractors.[3]

Privately, for his friends, Gottschalk often played Bach and

---

[9] *The Last Hope* was in print until 1953. It is still available in a recently
published collection of Gottschalk's works and, simplified, in many hymnals.

[1] The relationship between Gottschalk's music and jazz often has been
pointed out—in the rhythms, phrase forms, and heritage of New Orleans
which they have in common.

[2] Longfellow translated one of Mendive's poems in 1849.

[3] Luis Ricardo Fors: Gottschalk (Havana: Propaganda Literaria, 1880),
pp. 124–34.

Beethoven. One can take with a certain skepticism his oft-quoted
remarks derogatory to Schumann, reported by Mason.[4] A spirit of
raillery lies behind them; one imagines the Creole, relaxed,
wreathed in cigar smoke, eying with amusement his earnest Anglo-
Saxon friend.[5]

He defended well, by way of his little homily on Thackeray
versus Shakespeare, his role as *composer*-pianist. He was, after all,
of a school not far removed from an earlier epoch, when the ability
to compose and improvise had been a criterion by which a performer was judged. Others were better qualified to play the
classics, he said candidly and with reason, but nobody could play
his own works as well as he could. Besides, he added, the public
liked them, and what difference would it make a thousand years
hence, anyway?[6]

Dashed hopes can be read in this cynicism. Although in-
escapably an American, he never relinquished the dream of returning to Europe for further study and maturation, of returning
wealthy. Yet his whole mode of life made this improbable. If
only, when acquiring his education in music, in languages, and
the classics and all the trappings of a gentleman—if only he had
also learned that two and two can make only four, no more. The
money that would have made possible the opulent return to the
scene of his youthful triumphs was lavished on charities, public
and private, and on festival speculations. Little did he keep of the
earnings that might have contributed to his own stability. To the
very end he supported his sisters in London, a substitute father
forever trapped by, but for the most part separated from, his
family. Professional researchers of the soul will recognize the con-
flicts in this one. Friends noted the melancholy face, the bitten
fingernails. His own words betray him: the sense of isolation,
the recurring burden of New Year's Day, the mirage of marriage,
"ennui—ennui—ennui."

During the last four years of exile (playing "Home, Sweet
Home" on some programs), Gottschalk must have thought en-

---

[4] William Mason: *op. cit.*, p. 207.
[5] According to Fors, Gottschalk admired Schumann under certain aspects,
in general considering him "a real genius" (*op. cit.*, p. 406).
[6] George P. Upton: *Musical Memories* (Chicago: A. C. McClurg & Company; 1908), p. 77.

viously of the young musicians he had known in Paris—Bizet, Saint-Saëns, Offenbach—and of his compatriot Guiraud, who were making their marks there. From a vantage point a century later, many see Gottschalk as a minor actor on the scene of a changing musical taste. In Europe the major ones included Louis Spohr, to some extent, and Mendelssohn, Berlioz, Liszt, Moscheles, Wagner, Robert and Clara Schumann, Hallé, Von Bülow, Rubinstein; in the United States, besides Mason, Thomas, and Bergmann, there were, among many others, Henry Christian Timm, William Scharfenberg, Otto Dresel, Theodor Eisfeld, Gustave Satter, and Carl Wolfsohn. These were the propagandists for Great Music,[7] the standard-bearers of a worthy cause, the disseminators of old and new classics too long neglected, works that remain basic to the repertoire. And some of these artists had their lapses.[8] In 1841, at a concert devoted to works by Beethoven—moreover, a concert largely instigated by Liszt for the purpose of raising funds for a Beethoven statue at Bonn—Liszt felt obliged to accede to the audience's demand for his own fantasia on themes from Meyerbeer's *Robert le Diable*. William Mason, on tour in 1855, was not above finishing his recitals with improvisations combining "Yankee Doodle" with the psalm tune "Old 100," and there were other such shotgun weddings not mentioned in his *Memories*. Rubinstein, too, and later Paderewski—he really liked the tune—attempted a *Yankee Doodle* bit.[9] Even Theodore Thomas had to proceed cautiously in his programming, easing auditory nerves with light music (of quality, be it said) while he gradually introduced symphonic and operatic music, old and new, of the highest caliber.

Gottschalk as musician was basically no reformer. He gave the

---

[7] "The great dead! How many little crimes are committed in their name!" —Gottschalk.

[8] Opinions, too, were expressed that seem incomprehensible today. Schumann, among the very first to recognize Chopin's genius, nevertheless characterized his B-flat Minor Sonata as "dissonances through dissonances into dissonances." While acknowledging its qualities, he said that an adagio, perhaps in D flat, would have been more effective than a gloomy, repellent funeral march, and as for the "unmelodious" last movement: "this is not music."

[9] Both arrangements were dedicated to Mason. By this time, however, educated concert-goers no longer cared for this music. Mason apparently dissuaded Paderewski from playing his arrangement in public.

public what it wanted, and it wanted what he was best able to give. Circumstances allowed him no alternative in his own mind. He was a public entertainer and as such gave pleasure to many. But he was no mere matinee idol. On the contrary, he was an important composer and folklorist arriving between two developments in music of the United States, valuable also as a link in the chain of changing taste. An artist buffeted by circumstance, he was obliged to succeed as an American concert pianist during years of his country's most unsettled period. That he succeeded is testimony to his own resourcefulness. In an entertainment field dominated by opera, minstrel shows, singing families, lectures, and the incipient splendor of the American symphony orchestra, he helped to create an audience for piano recitals, even in places where a grand piano never before had been seen.

Chronicler of his epoch, cultural ambassador, pioneer in music therapy, he was dedicated to the rights of man and the aid of the needy. His magnanimity and sense of social responsibility were proverbial.

These attributes distinguished him from most of the concert pianists who visited America during his time, pianists now largely forgotten. Together with the many native-born ones who began to flourish after Gottschalk's death, their faces look out from old volumes—unfamiliar faces and names—a sobering thought for present-day performers in pursuit of careers.

Gottschalk remains.

He has survived, not only because of his music, but also because of himself. He has survived because of his qualities as a sentient, articulate human being. Into this journal he poured thoughts and images; it is a kaleidoscope of his extraordinary existence. Personages figure in it, countless lesser people appear briefly and vividly. The fields, mountains, and cities, rivers, lakes, and seas of three continents, in view or remembered, are its scene. Winter's freezing cold and summer's burning heat rend it; war and pestilence, the homelessness of a wanderer wrack it. Transcending all in the perpetual gold of spring and autumn is Gottschalk's own nature—urbane, mercurial, adventurous, impassioned, and compassionate.

Here now is his story as he tells it.

J. B.

Notes of a Pianist

NOTE

Connective passages supplied by the present editor are enclosed in brackets and set in this type.

[1] Numbered footnotes have been supplied by the present editor.

* Footnotes designated by asterisks are from the original edition (1881) of this work.

Notes of the Author

Which May Serve as Preface[1]

W̲RITTEN WITHOUT ORDER and without connection, with hasty pen upon the leaves of my pocket-book, these Notes, which someday I propose to publish, were at first destined to be read only by myself. I have taken, during the long years that I have traveled, the habit of fixing daily my impressions of my journey. They possess no literary merit, but they speak absolutely the truth: is that a sufficient compensation for the numerous deficiencies of style which the critic can find in them? The recollections of my travels have often supported me in the ennui and fatigue of my wandering life. In writing about the present I often forgot the bitterness of the past, and when, on the contrary, the present became wearisome, I plunged into happy memories of the times that are no more, and I reawakened its charming emotions. These poor leaves

---

[1] A lengthier version of this preface formed the beginning of Gottschalk's article for the *Atlantic Monthly*, March 1865, the second in a series of three entitled *Notes of a Pianist*. Traces of it appear also in *L 'Art musical*, August 13, 1863.

have received my joy, my griefs, and my pains for the long time that I have whirled in that monotonous and agitated circle that is called concert life. May the reader lend to them a little charm when it is wanting, and when he shall find too flagrant proofs of awkwardness in my pen, let him remember that I was but a musician, and only a pianist!

The West Indies
1857–62

[*February 12, 1857*]

MY FIRST VISIT to Cuba was in 1853.[1] It was on my return from Europe. I had just spent eighteen months in Spain, five of them at the Court of Madrid. I spoke Spanish; the Queen had conferred upon me the Cross of Isabella the Catholic; and El Chiclanero,[2] after having heard the performance of my symphony *The Siege of Saragossa, had* presented me with the sword of Montes, the famous bullfighter. I was therefore in the best condition to be well received in the "Pearl of the Antilles," without relying upon the hundred letters of recommendation, which it was not necessary for me to present in order to receive the most generous and friendly hospitality.

---

[1] Gottschalk's first visit to Cuba actually took place in 1854, after a year of concertizing in the United States.

[2] José Redondo y Domínguez, called El Chiclanero because he came from Chiclana, Spain. He was a bullfighter and a protégé of Francisco Montes, also a native of Chiclana.

So much has been written about Havana that I shall not essay to speak of what is so well known: that Havana is situated on a bay (may not this be the origin of its name, which up to this time remains doubtful, notwithstanding the researches of the etymologists—Havre, Haven, Havana?), the very narrow entrance of which is defended by the famous Morro [Castle] on the left, whose cannons gape in a frightfully suggestive manner, within reach of your hand; on the right by the no less formidable Fort Cabaña, built in the rock and bristling like its opposite neighbor with a triple row of open jaws. Hardly have you passed these two threatening sentinels when the sight reposes on red, white, yellow, pink, and green houses, with square, flattened roofs like those of an Arab's. We come to anchor. The never-ending torture of customhouse officials, doctor of the port, captain of the port, clerks of the port, and porters of the port commences. After a great deal of noise and little work (it is rather the manner of doing things by all Spanish employees) we take a canoe painted blue and rose and disembark. They then pen us in a square hall in sight of the civil guards, and establish our identity by means of our passports, given previously to the captain of the steamer. The passports will not be returned to us until we quit the island; in the meantime they give us a permit to land.

During the voyage from New Orleans to Havana [in 1854] I had noticed among the passengers on the steamer two Italians whose modest traveling clothes had exposed them to the rudeness of some rich tradesmen, a species of individuals found on all the steamers of the world and always recognized by their cravats of every shade and color, their insolence and bad taste. The two strangers, who appeared to be but slightly affected by their ostracism, stood apart. Desirous to make up for the rudeness of my fellow countrymen, I sought an opportunity to introduce myself to them. One evening, when, according to their custom, they were conversing at the stern of the boat, I heard them pronounce the name of Count Mamiani, an exiled Catholic poet and philosopher whom I had known in Paris. I seized the occasion and introduced myself. At the end of half an hour we were the best friends in the world. I learned that the large old man with the red beard was the Count de Cassato, and that his friend was the Count de

Malaperta, both traveling for their pleasure, and in possession of a fortune of many millions. O wealthy shopkeepers, if you had but known it!

There was something touching in their friendship, which had been contracted under very singular circumstances. Both of these old bachelors, philosophers, and travelers, fifty-six years of age, had made up their minds, the one in Tuscany, the other in Turin, to visit the five parts of the globe. They had laid their plans methodically by fixing the probable time of their death at the age of sixty-five, and they had commenced their travels. One evening the Count de Cassato had sought refuge for the night in an inn in the north of Spain, and had monopolized for his supper the scanty provisions that from time immemorial are found (when found at all) in the larder of a Spanish inn—that is to say, a cup of chocolate, some hard-cooked eggs, and olives. When another hungry traveler presented himself, the landlord, pressed by the reiterated demands of the newcomer, exposed his situation to the first. The Count de Cassato, with much earnestness and good humor, offered half of his supper and his bed to the newcomer, who was none other than the Count de Malaperta. The singularity of this meeting, the similarity of their positions, tastes, and projects bound them to each other, and they have never separated since that day. When I became acquainted with them, they had already visited Asia, Africa, all of Europe, and South America, and they were now going to Havana en route to Mexico, whence they expected to leave for Australia, and whence, the time they had fixed for their death being very near, *Deo volente*, they would return to Turin. They both wrote their impressions of their travels daily. The Count de Malaperta, a learned philosopher whom a light shade of misanthropy perhaps rendered less agreeable than Count de Cassato, was to undertake the task of condensing and combining the two journals at the end of the voyage.

As they were Italians and enthusiasts, two hours had not elapsed after landing before they had found a music shop and a piano, and my first evening in Havana was spent in playing for these two charming and venerable men the whole repertory of their dear Italian music.

This manner of traveling hardly resembled that of the two Englishmen I met some years ago at El Toboso. They had their courier, who spoke Spanish (of which they did not understand a word); they carried their tea with them, wore green veils on their hats, and had their eternal field glass suspended in its case by a band around the shoulder. They read every number of *The Times* that had been issued since they had left home, and which had been sent to them from England. I found them eight months afterward, at Cádiz, at the Hotel d'Angleterre, with their tea, green veils, gray hats, field glasses, and courier. The only change that had taken place in them was that they had *Uncle Tom's Cabin* (then all in vogue), which their ambassador had given them at Madrid. They did not understand one word of Spanish, had never seen the country, only the *hôtels anglais* of Cádiz, of Seville, and of Madrid. The result of their studies might have been reduced to this: that the beefsteak of the Hotel Péninsulaire of Madrid was tenderer than that of the Hotel d'Angleterre of Cádiz.

This is not to travel. To know a country—that is to say, to observe its customs, and the manners of its inhabitants—one must lay aside all preconceived opinions, forget one's own habitudes, and, above all, speak the language of the people one wishes to study; to do otherwise is to travel like a trunk or a carpetbag. But I strongly suspect that the English in general are an illustration of this aphorism by Alphonse Karr:[3] "Nobody travels for the purpose of traveling, but for the purpose of having traveled." Is it not much more commodious in such cases and much less expensive to purchase a traveler's guidebook and study it? How many do not act otherwise!

At Saratoga I knew a young man from the Southern states whom everyone called a millionaire. He had never been in Europe, but he had effrontery and had made a reputation with many mammas and young marriageable girls as a traveler by recounting to them his impressions of Italy. Who does not know the Colosseum, the Bridge of Sighs, the Arno, St. Mark's Square, the cathedral at Milan, the Leaning Tower of Pisa, and the Bay of Naples? He knew his guidebook for Italy by heart, and his descriptions were truthful to weariness. I have a horror of beauties consecrated by millions of classical descriptions and the admiration of hundreds of centuries. What I like in traveling is the unexpected,

---

[3] Jean-Baptiste-Alphonse Karr (1808-90), French novelist, journalist, and satirist. In 1839 he became editor of *Le Figaro*.

the personal observations that I make; to penetrate into the minds of the people; to know them, not as they feel when they are aware that they are observed (in these circumstances men are almost all alike), but in their deshabille; and to probe their consciences. What is it to me if you tell me that the English are stiff, arrogant, and exclusive; that the French are good soldiers and make puns; that the Spaniards are suspicious, play castanets, and are smugglers; that the Turks have a tendency to obesity and polygamy; that the Germans are beer barrels in the morning and barrels of beer in the evening; that the Italians are given to assassination and to making macaroni, etc. All this I know, or rather it has been told to us too often for me not to know it.

Some travelers, out of imbecility or bad faith in speaking of the plantations in Cuba, deny the assertions of the enemies of slavery by assuring us that the slaves on the plantations visited by them have a happy air, and that during their stay they had not heard a single blow of the whip. Happy tourists! Suppose that, instead of looking upon those joyous faces that smile in the presence of their master, you had had the curiosity to take off the clothes of these unfortunates and to examine their shoulders. You would have learned more in a few seconds by the sight of certain scars badly healed, and perhaps of wounds still bleeding, scarcely healed, than all your observations, founded upon your own suppositions, had taught you.

~~~~~~~~~

[After playing for the captain general at his palace on February 16, 1857, Gottschalk made his first public appearance in Havana on February 20, at the immense Grand Tacón Theater (Gran Teatro de Tacón). He was assisted by Adelina Patti singing a cavatina by Bellini, "O luce di quest' anima" from Donizetti's Linda di Chamounix, the polacca from I Puritani, and the final rondo from La Sonnambula; by Juan and Francisco Van der Guth, prize-winning professors from the Brussels Conservatory, the former playing on the cello a Beethoven fantasy "on El Deseo," the latter a violin fantasy on Linda di Chamounix; by his friend Espadero, who played with him, as Thalberg recently had, in New York, his "Gran Duo" on Il Trovatore. Gottschalk's solos were his transcription from Jérusalem (Verdi), and original pieces: El Cocoyé, Marche de nuit, and The Banjo.

Flowers rained, poetry flourished, and after two more appearances and a visit to Matanzas, Gottschalk and Patti went on tour: in March he gave several concerts each at Cárdenas and Cienfuegos, as well as concerts at Villa Clara, Trinidad, and Santa Clara; in April, three at Puerto Príncipe; in May, three at Santiago. By this time he was struggling to regain his health after a serious illness. One gathers, from a perusal of newspapers over a number of years, that Havana was not a satisfactory "concert town." Gottschalk was not to return to it until late in 1859.]

◇◇◇◇◇◇◇◇◇◇

[*June 1857*]

I embarked at Havana on June 3 for St. Thomas. On the sixth we were in sight of the coast of Haiti. The night began to fall. All the passengers went below. I remained alone. Leaning against the rigging, I contemplated the desolate country that opened out before me: high mountains whose angular peaks seemed as if they wished to pierce the clouds; solitary palm trees hanging sadly over the desert shore; a horizon whose lines were lost on a stormy sky. Everything, and more especially the name of Santo Domingo, seemed to speak to my imagination by recalling to me the bloody episodes of the insurrection,[4] so closely associated with my childhood memories. When very young, I never tired of hearing my grandmother relate the terrible strife that our family, like all the rest of the colonists, had to sustain at this epoch; the narrative of the massacre at the cape, and the combat fought in the *mornes*[5] by my great-grandfather against the Negroes of Gonaïves.

My recollections, drawn toward them by a mysterious affinity, rose one by one in a striking and lucid manner from the long-forgotten past. I again found myself before the large fireplace of our dwelling on the Rue des Remparts at New Orleans, where, squatting on the matting in the evening, the Negroes, myself, and the children of the house formed a circle around my grandmother. We would listen, by the trembling fire on the hearth, under the

---

[4] The slave rebellion of the late 1790's, which began in the western part of Santo Domingo, the portion that is now Haiti.

[5] Hills, bluffs; possibly Gottschalk is referring to Gros Morne, a hotly fought point in the struggle.

coals of which Sally, the old Negress, baked her sweet potatoes, to the recital of this terrible Negro insurrection. She was the same old Sally who, while listening all the time, spoke in a low voice to a portrait of Napoleon hung above the fireplace, which she obstinately believed was bewitched because it seemed to look at her in every corner of the room, wherever she might be. I was without any doubt Sally's favorite, to judge by the stories with which she filled my head. I was not tired of listening for the hundredth time to the marvelous adventures of Compé Bouqui (the clown of the Negroes) and the knavery of Compé Lapin, whose type represents the Punchinello of Europe. We listened to Sally so well that we knew all of her stories by heart—with an interest that has lasted till today and still makes me find an inexpressible charm in all these naïve legends of our old Negroes. I should like to relate, in their picturesque language and their exquisite originality, some of those Creole ballads whose simple and touching melody goes right to the heart and makes you dream of unknown worlds.

To return to my grandmother's stories: one of my favorites was that of John Bras Coupé, captain of the runaway Negroes of Bayou Sarah, who filled all Louisiana with reports of his sanguinary exploits. He resisted alone, this hero of our savannas, all the expeditions sent in pursuit of him. Strange rumors were in circulation on this subject. Sometimes it was a detachment of troops that had ventured to the haunt of this brigand, who disappeared without anyone's being able to discover any trace of him. Sometimes it was the hunter whose bullet was flattened against the breast of Bras Coupé, his skin rendered invulnerable by certain herbs with which he rubbed it. The Negroes asserted that his glance cast a spell and that he fed on human flesh. He was finally captured and condemned to be hanged in the square opposite the Spanish Cathedral. He had been attacked by a terrible scurvy, and the infecting odors exhaled by his corpse two hours after his execution made it necessary to bury him, contrary to the law that condemned him to remain suspended from the gallows for two days. Sometimes Sally interrupted my grandmother's narrative to exorcise a "*zombi*,"[6] of which, she said, she felt the impure breath on her

---

[6] The biographical sketch in the original edition of *Notes of a Pianist* relates that when Gottschalk, as a small child, started to play the piano the awestruck Negroes whispered, "*Zombi!*"

face. Shivering with fright, we narrowed our circle around my grandmother, who, after crossing herself and scolding Sally, took up her story where she had left off.

I will not repeat the long series of misfortunes and bloody episodes to which my family succumbed at the time of the terrible insurrection of Santo Domingo. It would be too long, and besides it is only the history of all the colonists of Santo Domingo toward the close of the last century. My great-grandfather, the Comte de Bruslé, governed at that time the quarter of Petite Rivière. His family was naturally one of the first with whom the bands of Biassou[7] were infuriated. My great-uncles were all massacred. Their daughters and wives, fallen into the power of their former slaves, were put to death after having been subjected to the most horrible outrages. My great-grandfather escaped in the dress of his nurse, an old mulatto *"woudou"* (witch), and ran, notwithstanding his seventy years, to place himself at the head of the colonial troops, where he died heroically. My grandmother saved herself, half naked and dying of hunger, by wandering many days in the woods, finally being found by the captain of an English vessel that made sail for Jamaica.

Can anyone be astonished that the mere name of Santo Domingo awakens somber memories in me, or that I could not help feeling an indescribable sentiment of melancholy while for the first time beholding this fatal land, with which so many grievous recollections are associated? Our dwellings burned, our properties devastated, our fortunes annihilated—such were the first effects of that war between two races who had in common only that implacable hatred which each nourished for the other.

Can anyone, however, be astonished at the retaliation exercised by the Negroes on their old masters? What cause, moreover, more legitimate than that of this people, rising in their agony in one grand effort to reconquer their unacknowledged rights and their rank in humanity? In contemplating the events of that memorable epoch, at the distance of time that today separates us from them, we see the work of regeneration purged from the stains imprinted on it by human passions. It disengages itself from the shadows that obscured it; the blood has disappeared; the stains are

---

[7] An early leader of the insurrection, a rival of Toussaint l'Ouverture.

wiped out; and, from the bosom of this world which crumbles away, rises, somber and imposing, the grand form of Toussaint l'Ouverture, the enthusiastic liberator of a race that nineteen centuries of Christianity had not yet been able to free from the yoke of its miseries. The greater part of the colonists immigrated to New Orleans (my grandmother, then very young, was of this group); a great number also to Santiago de Cuba, which is why even now French Creole is spoken in preference to Spanish in many parts of the island of Cuba.[8]

◈◈◈◈◈◈◈◈◈

St. Thomas, July 1857

I have been here for fifteen days, but ought notwithstanding to go immediately to Venezuela, where I have been expected for six months, but as soon as the news of my arrival reached the governor-general he wrote to me inviting me to dine with him. I was recommended to him by former President General Ech[enique] of the Republic of Peru. At the dessert His Excellency proposed a toast in my honor and expressed the desire that I might be heard at least once before leaving the island. A subscription list was opened at the table, and next day a deputation of amateurs of the city came to offer me fifteen hundred dollars for three concerts. The last took place day before yesterday; the *Marche de nuit*, *Valse poétique*, and *The Banjo* were encored. The event of the evening was a gigantic bouquet of roses and of Cape jasmin which two Negroes, bending under the burden, came to present to me upon the stage in the name of the Chevalier de L——, a Genoese gentleman, a dilettante singer who also possesses very uncommon musical erudition. The bouquet was not less than four feet in circumference.

The Chevalier de L—— has lived on this island for many years and has built a mansion at the foot of the tower of Frederick

---

[8] A longer version of this entire entry, dated December 20, 1857, appeared in *La France musicale*, Paris, January 24, 1858. It ends:
"*Une singulière particularité des contes nègres, c'est qui'ils sont généralement précédés de certaines formules bizarres de paroles sacramentelles dont le sens mystérieux nous échappe, mais dont l'origine est évidemment africaine. Avant de commencer, le conteur prononce à haute voix le mot:* 'Tim-tim', *l'un des assistants répond gravement:* 'Bois sec.'—'Bois cassé, tchou macaque!' *ajoute un troisième, et seulement alors le conte commence . . .*"

Barbaroussa on the summit of a hill overlooking the harbor. It
was the haunt of the buccaneers and filibusters. Frederick Barbaroussa, their chief at St. Thomas, made it into a veritable fortress,
as its position rendered it impregnable. I found the cannons still
there in the embrasures, and some piles of balls. Nothing is more
melancholy or speaks more to the imagination than these ruins and
some old harquebuses on the wall, and I acknowledge that I could
not help feeling a certain uneasiness on descending into the subterranean vaults, dug out of the living rock, in which they shut up
their prisoners of war. The porter of the villa showed us several
instruments of torture and many skeletons of men and women in
chains found at a shallow depth beneath the soil. They recalled
to the imagination the most somber pictures of the bloody dramas
that according to tradition have taken place here. I listened, shivering, to the story told me by an old Negro officer. He spoke in a
low voice as if he feared that Federico el Verdugo[9] still might
hear him. He knew the tradition through his father, who had it
from another old Negro, whose father had known Barbaroussa.
Everytime he pronounced the name of Frederick Barbaroussa he
lowered his voice and gave me a mysterious look by which, no
doubt, he wished to make me understand that the spirit of El
Verdugo still inhabited the tower.

The island of St. Thomas is hardly twenty-five miles in circumference. The Danish Government, understanding at a glance the
advantage it might draw from the geographical position of this little
island, has made it a free port, owing to which it has today acquired a commerical importance that none of the large islands of
the Antilles can now dispute. Today St. Thomas is the exchange
center of the two continents, the market in which the products
of the two worlds are bartered. Santo Domingo sends her mahogany; Havana tobacco; Cuba and Puerto Rico sugar; Jamaica rum;
Santiago cocoa; Antioquia[1] emeralds and gold; Venezuela hides.
All these are stored in vast warehouses, true chaoses, where all
the products of Europe are found, from the muslins of Manchester
and the silks of Lyon to the bottles of Dr. Girandeau of St.-Ger-
vais. It is a kind of fair to which all the peddlers of the two con-

---

[9] Frederick the Hangman.
[1] A province of Colombia.

tinents of Spanish America come twice a year. Specialized trade is doubtless unknown here, for everybody sells everything. The perfumer keeps plowshares and sells English needles.

Europe furnishes her the more or less reliable products of her commerce: Nantes the wines of Spain and the hams of Westphalia; Hamburg Erard's pianos; Cádiz the oils of Aix; Birmingham hardware; Paris crepes de Chine; Sheffield, Toledo blades, etc, etc. St. Thomas is a naval station of the greatest importance. Her port, surrounded by high mountains, affords a safe asylum to vessels of all kinds during the hurricanes so terrible in the Antilles. It is also the junction point of all the English and American steamers, a network of which extends from Southampton and New York to the Isthmus of Panama and covers all the coasts of the Atlantic and Pacific as far as Cape Horn.

Unfortunately yellow fever rages cruelly at St. Thomas. According to the official statistics, it carries off more than one-third of the sailors who remain in port during the months of July and August.

On my arrival the epidemic was raging in all its violence. The authorities had taken the severest measures to prevent boats from landing. The steamer was forced to anchor one mile out at sea. The marine hospital had been transported to the other side of the bay and surrounded by a sanitary cordon to prevent all communication between the town and the harbor. Despite all these precautions, two days after our arrival our steamer had already lost seven men belonging to it; three servants on board who were attacked with the same plague succumbed in a few hours. Another steamer, leaving St. Thomas for Southampton during the same period, lost twenty-eight sailors and fourteen passengers during the voyage.

My intention on arriving was to take immediately the schooner *Isabel,* which leaves for Venezuela twice a month. I remembered that Herz[2] was not willing to venture a concert at St. Thomas, and I knew too well the great experience that my illustrious predecessor had acquired in the art of giving concerts, not to follow his

[2] Henri Herz, né Heinrich Herz at Vienna in 1803, died at Paris in 1888. Fashionable pianist, professor of piano at the Paris Conservatoire for twenty-six years, he was an industrious fabricator both of pianos and of flashy sets of variations for piano. (Gottschalk's farewell New Orleans concert in 1841 included Herz's *Variations on Themes from Meyerbeer's Il Crociato.*) He concertized during 1845-51 in the United States, Mexico, and the West Indies. His *Mes Voyages en Amerique* was published in Paris in 1866.

example and "burn" St. Thomas. The consignee's office of the
Isabel was open, and I hastened there and bought my passage.
"The schooner will leave in two days," the captain said to me.
How spend two days unless by visiting the environs on horseback?
It is what I undertook to do.

There is nothing so picturesque as St. Thomas. Imagine one
of those painted wooden boxes of toys from Nürnberg, with
their polished white little houses with red roofs and their trees of
symmetrical foliage. Place the houses one behind the other on
three little hills, throw here and there clusters of palms and coco-
nut trees, add a background of mountains like sugar loaves, a fore-
ground of neat, pretty dwellings coquettishly stuck here and there,
a sky like that of Switzerland, a pretty little whitewashed fort
pierced for six guns, enabling the fluted breeches of six pretty little
green bronze cannon to emerge—do not forget the big German
sentinel sleeping or smoking his pipe in his sentry box—and you
will understand the charm that detained me before this agreeable
and peaceful scene. I stayed there until the beginning of evening.
The night came on, I retraced the road to town, and I did not
leave in two days.

Everything at St. Thomas wears an air of gentility and good
nature which soothes the eye and the mind, especially after leaving Cuba, where everything seems in a state of decay. The Negroes
are free at St. Thomas. The female mulattoes seemed to me remarkably pretty—they have preserved the *tignon* (a sort of turban)
of bright colors.

◇◇◇◇◇◇◇◇◇

[*Late summer, 1857*]

My health is good. I have for some months invariably commenced
all my letters with the same phrase for the purpose of falsifying
the absurd stories that have circulated, and still circulate, about
me since my illness at Santiago—stories that the newspapers
of the United States and of Cuba hasten to publish with a great
many commentaries. I wish to speak of my death. This sad event
took place at Santiago three months ago. I was carried off in three
days by a frightful attack of black vomit; it is the newspaper *Savana
la Grande* that tells it; but the *Revue de Villa Clara*, without doubt

better informed, makes me succumb to an aneurism of the heart, which I much prefer, the aneurism being much more poetical than the vomit.

I have written to these gentlemen assuring them that I am still alive and requesting them to publish my letter when it reaches them. The newspaper *Savana la Grande* already has gone to the expense of a lithograph of the *"deceased"* and *"ever to be regretted Gottschalk,"* which it furnishes gratis to its subscribers. By what means, in such a case, can they make me return to life? As to the *Revue de Villa Clara,* it already had announced to its *numerous* subscribers a superb colored engraving, and a *romance* composed by an amateur of the town—the whole entitled *Funeral Homage to the Bard of the Tropics.* I understood what I owed to those who so much regretted me, and I consented to remain dead for some days. I will not say anything of the funeral *romance* by the amateur of Villa Clara, but the colored engraving merits, by its originality of design and of color, a very particular notice. The subject of it is allegorical. *The genius of music sheds tears over a broken lyre and casts a black veil over a bust,* which the *Revue de Villa Clara* says is mine. The genius of music is muffled in a troubadour's robe and a pale rose tunic, with a most amusing effect, which recalls that of the Christ of the Cathedral of Burgos, which Christ, the sacristan assured me when I visited the church in 1852, *was human flesh, and had been found swimming in the river.* They took it and carried it in *triumph* to the convent of the Franciscans; *but* it *escaped from there,* and came to *place itself in the little chapel* of the cathedral, to the right on entering, where you can still see it by the help of the trifling sum of two *reales,* which the sacristan demands to show you the miraculous effigy of the Saviour and to tell you its very truthful history.

To return to the engraving in the *Revue*: the genius of music has his mouth open and seems prepared to swallow a long serpent, which, on closer examination, I recognized to be a black ribbon on which are these words, which the genius of music lets fall in the depth of his affliction: *"¡Cruel Apolo, lo mirabas con envidia y nos lo has arrebatado!"* [Cruel Apollo, thou didst covet him and take him away from us!] I intend to keep the *romance* and the engraving. Some newspapers in the United States have persisted, in spite of a letter addressed by me to the *Courrier des États-Unis,* in believing me still very ill. Notwithstanding what they say, I was never in better health.

~~~~~~~~~

[A letter from Gottschalk, dated May 29, 1857, printed in the Courrier des États-Unis and quoted in the New Orleans L'Abeille on June 15, at once reassuring and jocular, foretells the journal's mood at this time:

> ... A peine la nouvelle de ma maladie se fut-elle répandue, que tous les médecins, pharmaciens, apothicaires, vétérinaires de la ville s'emparèrent de moi comme d'une proie longtemps convoitée—j'en comptai jusqu'à sept à la fois autour de mon lit, et je ne doute pas que ce soit à cette circonstance qu'il faille attribuer la nouvelle anticipée de ma mort si légèrement accueillie par les journaux de l'île. En effet, un homme seul contre sept médecins cubanais?—"que vouliez-vous qu'il fît?" comme dit le vieux Corneille "—Qu'il mourut!" sans doute. Pas du tout. J'ai protesté, et je m'en suis tiré un peu avarié, il est vrai; mais après tout, on n'affronte pas impunément de pareilles épreuves—je suis donc à peu près bien, quoiqu'un peu faible.

It is somewhat more difficult to fix the following short paragraph into the calendar. Evidently Gottschalk visited Haiti, where fellow Masons honored him. He arrived in Puerto Rico around the beginning of September 1857.]

~~~~~~~~~

I have succeeded at Port-au-Prince and on the islands of St. Thomas and Puerto Rico. I explored these last two on horseback, and have gone over them in every sense. I have made some notes on what has appeared to me interesting.

~~~~~~~~~

[La France musicale called the Gottschalk-Patti concerts in Puerto Rico "les triomphes les plus éclatants." They performed at Plazuela, Mayagüez, Cabo Rojo, and four times at Ponce—on November 11, 18, and 25 and December 1.]

◇◇◇◇◇◇◇◇◇◇

[December 1857]

At Ponce I have encountered the most flattering and most hospitable reception. Four concerts given at the theater before a brilliant
audience, whose enthusiastic demonstrations testified to their
great taste for music, have more than justified, in my eyes, the
reputation that Ponce enjoys. The ladies are charming and dress
with the most refined taste. If I were still at that happy period of
seventeen to twenty years of age, when the brilliant illusions of
our youth carry us with rapid flight on their variegated wings,
when only one glance from the loved one, only one grasp of her
hand, would have filled me with ecstasies, I do not doubt that I
should have fallen in love with many of the charming creatures
who graced the ranges of boxes in the theater at each of my concerts. But alas! It is a long time—thanks to cares and to affairs
that time has thrown in my path—since my heart has become
deadened and feels no more these tender emotions; so I am content with admiring, without desiring more.[3]

◇◇◇◇◇◇◇◇◇◇

Ponce [approximately close of December 1857]

I have spent four weeks on the plantation of Mr. K. There I
found that cordial and assiduous hospitality which has become
proverbial when we speak of Plazucla. But what cannot be imagined is the grace, the distinction, and the cordiality with which
Monsieur and Madame K. do the honors of their comfortable
mansion. What charming souvenirs these four weeks, so rapidly
elapsed, have left me!—the happiness this peaceful country life
gives me! Solitude, for me, is repose—is the absence of the thousand distractions of this unquiet, giddy existence to which my career of nomad artist condemns me. In solitude, in reveries, and in

---

[3] Gottschalk saluted the "charming creatures" of Ponce by composing at
this time a piece called *Las Ponceñas*. See Emilio J. Pasarell: *"El Centenario
de los conciertos de Adelina Patti y Luis Moreau Gottschalk en Puerto Rico,"
Revista del Instituto de Cultura Puertorriqueña*, Vol. II, No. 2 (January–
March 1959), pp. 52–55.

contemplation I find fertile sources of inspiration. Then I turn my thoughts inward; all my faculties are strengthened, recover their original vigor, which the incessant contact with society and the constrained actions of men had occasioned them to lose. Only then am I myself. I collect my scattered thoughts in the silence; in the face of the majestic and imposing serenity of a beautiful sunset I listen to the inner voices that tell me marvelous things, which art seeks to translate into its language, but of which its most beautiful *chefs-d'oeuvre* are, alas, only the pale and distant reflections. For myself, who, because of a sickly and nervous nature, always have had a propensity to melancholy, the stirring and noisy existence that the career of nomad virtuoso imposes on me is that to which I have the greatest antipathy.

Thus, above all, I have enjoyed at Plazuela what I have been deprived of for so many years, the first of all joys: "not having to give a concert"—that is to say, not being obliged, at a fixed hour, to bestow a certain quantity of inspiration for the price of a few dollars, but to find one's self in the home life of the family; that is to say, to have the heart warmed by the contact of good and amiable people and to forget the thousand and one jealousies and miseries to which the talented artist is exposed.

At Plazuela I again met a distinguished and clever man, old Dr. B., whom I already had encountered in my travels and whom I loved at first sight for his youthful enthusiasm for poetry and his enlightened taste for the arts. Frequently some visitors came from Manatí, Arecibo, or some of the neighboring plantations. The doctor then recited to us some fragments of Racine. I played or improvised according to the caprice of my imagination; Adelina and Madam K. sang a duet.

[A "farewell concert" on January 7, 1858, took the form of a gran festival in which Patti assisted, playing both solo and then second piano. After touring other localities of the island, such as Guayama, the two artists gave their first concert at the capitial, San Juan, in May, and another on June 23. The Courrier de la Louisiane referred to Gottschalk's "monster concerts" in Puerto Rico as "very successful."

In July 1858, Gottschalk was about to leave Puerto Rico for Venezuela. The rest of that year may well have been the time of

his travels "on the Spanish Main . . . the Guianas and the shores
of Pará," and is so designated by Loggins. A correspondent of La
France musicale of February 20, 1859, discloses the presence of
Gottschalk at Martinique, accompanied by the flutist Allard.]

◇◇◇◇◇◇◇◇◇◇

St. *Pierre* [*Martinique*]

The latest political events at Barcelona[4] (La Côte ferme) are of a
nature to cure radically all artists who have the insane idea of
making a tour there. There has arrived here within these last few
days a family of Italian singers named Busati, escaped by miracle
from the horrors of famine, thanks to the intrepidity of a captain
whose small-decked vessel was able in the night to slip between the
armed vessels that now close the mouth of the Barcelona River—
the only and last entrance through which the unfortunate besieged
can hope to receive succor. The details we have gathered are
nauseating: they are dying of hunger in the town, and infants and
women are being killed in the streets as a pastime by drunken
soldiers. The American consul, barricaded in his house, sustained
himself and his family for a month on boiled dry peas, without
bread or salt. The French consul, being so imprudent as to open
his window, received a ball in his shoulder. Ten or twelve pretenders are tearing to pieces, in the midst of every excess of bloody
anarchy, the fragments of that unhappy country. What a fate
awaits all the foreign artists who insist on going to try their luck
in the Spanish republics!

The Busati family has found here a reception worthy of the
sentiments of confraternity, which, although I say it myself, exists
in the hearts of all artists. The Creoles are, of all people, the most
hospitable and the most prompt to feel. The Busatis' first concert
took place at the theater. Madame Busati, a soprano *sfogato*[5]
passed to the state of soprano *sfiatato*,[6] sang nevertheless in good
style the cavatinas from [Verdi's] *Attila* and from [Rossini's]
Semiramide. It is too much to demand more of a singer who has
been the best Adalgisa to Pasta in the best period of that incom-

---

[4] Barcelona, Venezuela.
[5] A very high, light, virtuosic soprano.
[6] Breathless.

parable Norma. Mademoiselle Busati sang with all the inexperience of her sixteen or seventeen years the cavatina from [Doni-
zetti's] *Betly* and the *alla polacca* from *I Lombardi* by Verdi.[7]
She lacks warmth and technique; I was almost about to say—voice.
What, then, remains to her? There remain very fine black eyes
filled with fire, which are not a slight compensation for all she still
lacks as an artist. Mr. Busati, a baritone, an old *caricato*[8] of the
Italian Opera at Astor Place and impresario at Caracas, has caused
amusement in the duet of the Turk from *Attila*.

An opera troupe is very much wanted—the island demands it
with might and main. The theater at St. Pierre is very handsome.
The subsidy granted by the town is fifteen hundred francs per
month. It would, then, be possible for a director who understands
his business to make not a bad speculation by coming to Martinique and Guadeloupe with some passable singers.

I am urgently requested to procure a professor of the piano, a
conscientious musician who knows, on pressing occasions, how to
tune pianos. They will assure him twenty-five hundred francs per
annum for two years, and, according to all probabilities, he should
be able to make from eight to ten thousand francs by his lessons.
As a matter of fact, this figure could not be attained without very
great regularity and assiduous activity. The expenses in this country in leading a regular life could not go beyond three thousand to
thirty-five hundred francs per annum. If with this information
some Parisian journal could disembarrass me from the importuni-
ties of a crowd of music-mad fathers and save from the miseries of
the professorship at Paris one of those innumerable estimable artists
whom the crushing prestige of great stars condemns to obscurity
in a great theater, but who takes his rank again in a more humble
sphere, it would confer a great favor on them. The professorship
at St. Pierre is represented by Mr. Maurice Z——, the able leader
of the orchestra, formerly at Amiens and Strasbourg; Sikler, a violinist, whom the handbills of his first concerts, on his arrival at
Martinique, presented to us as first violin of the King of Naples;
and Parnain, a distinguished violoncellist, formerly second-prize

---

[7] *I Lombardi* was first given at Milan, February 11, 1843. A revised
version, *Jérusalem*, produced at Paris, November 26, 1847, was the basis of
Gottschalk's fantasy by that name.
[8] Or *buffo*, a male singer of comic roles.

winner at the Conservatoire, now organist and professor of piano. Every one makes me feel how much it was to be regretted that so many brilliant talents should be lost for want of a good director. Seriously, I have found among many young Creole girls an ability such as more than one *artiste* might wish for.

You who know the *ban et l'arrière-ban* of the pianists, come to my aid. Save me from these respectable fathers adorned with charming daughters who, in defiance of common sense, drum the keyboard from morning to night and make me curse the day when I brought into the world the *Bananier, The Banjo,* and all the other exotic products that my concerts have brought into vogue in America.

[Gottschalk arrived at the island of Guadeloupe approximately in the early spring of 1859. An anticipated vacation proved to be an impossibility, for the people clamored to hear him. To this end, a wealthy merchant at Le Moule had all the partitions of his house torn down in order to provide a concert hall for the virtuoso. By the middle of July he had played eight times at Basse-Terre. He began to teach, charging forty francs an hour.

In August he was at Matouba, near an extinct volcano, the highest in the Antilles. There he wrote a work at the request of the Venezuelan general and politician José Antonio Páez (1790–1873), "thrice liberator of the Spanish Americas and my friend" (La France musicale, September 4, 1859.) Called La Bataille de Carabovo, it was intended as a triumphal march for Páez.

Around September, Gottschalk was back in Martinique, at St. Pierre.]

◊◊◊◊◊◊◊◊◊

[*Martinique, November 1859*]

The fêtes at Fort-de-France, on the inauguration of the statue of the Empress Josephine, have been very brilliant. For three days the town was literally overrun by innumerable strangers attracted from all the neighboring islands to witness the brilliant solemnity. The hotels were not large enough; some slept *à la belle étoile* (that is, in the open air). I supped with five English officers who had hired for the night, from a retailer of liquors, the place beneath his counter. It was doubtless impossible for anybody to sleep—thanks to a crowd of invading colonists with whom it was necessary to dispute the ground inch by inch.⁹

Tired of the war from the first night, I had abandoned the field of battle to them, and had gone to walk, by the light of the moon, on the *place* of the town—an immense square bordered with gigantic tamarind trees, in the middle of which rises the statue of Josephine. This statue is cut out of one block of beautiful white marble. The attitude is simple and noble. The empress, standing erect, holds a medallion of the emperor in one hand, and with the other seems to indicate a point on the horizon, which her eyes seek to pierce. That point is Trois Islets, the birthplace of the illustrious Creole.

The vessels of the government, the *Fulton, Lucifer,* and *Ardent,* sent to all the Lesser Antilles to bring their governors, who had been invited, returned with the deputations of the consul general and the governor of Guadeloupe, the consuls general of Dominica, of Barbados, Grenada, Santa Cruz, etc., etc. A chamberlain of the king of Denmark represented all the Danish Antilles. The first day was devoted to a banquet for two hundred persons, given by the island to its guests. The next day there was a government ball. Fifteen hundred invitations had been given—that is to say that for four hours people crushed each other with a desperation the more inexplicable because the weather had become insupportably hot. At supper the enthusiasm reached its highest point, particularly after a very felicitous speech in French made by the English governor of St. Lucia. The seminary students were in the upper gallery, and at a signal from the governor of Martinique they sang the national air "God Save the Queen," which the French officers had the politeness to make them repeat in the midst of prolonged applause. Apropos of the seminary students, I ought in passing to congratulate them on the manner in which they executed the "*Miserere*" from *Il Trovatore,* arranged for military band with solo for the saxophone, by their able Professor Don José Ruiz, a dis-

---

⁹ Sleep for him was impossible for another reason: the Negroes descended on the town with their "deafening orchestra of bamboulas [drums], razas, and tam-tams," singing and dancing incessantly through the streets for three days. So Gottschalk reported in a letter to *La France musicale* published on December 11, 1859, p. 488.

tinguished guitarist, who, after traveling and giving concerts through all America, has come to establish himself in St. Pierre. The program announced for the last day a grand concert to be given by Gottschalk. The consul general had called on me to contribute by my talent to the success of the fete, which so far had been brilliant.

I had accepted a subsidy of twelve hundred dollars, which had been voted to me by the colony for the expenses of a concert, and had asked the services of Madame Budan, a distinguished singer, an old pupil of the Conservatoire, who is better known in the profession, especially at Bordeaux, where about twelve years ago she had great success under the name of Madame Koska. All the governors with their staffs were present at the concert. In the middle of my piece *The Siege of Saragossa,* under a full fire of chromatic grapeshot and deadly octaves, I thought of looking into the hall, where I saw the fine large head of an English major, red and snoring (the major, not the head) like a German humming top. You may imagine the blow given to my *amour propre.* At the moment when the first cannon gives the first signal for the assault on Saragossa, I boldly commenced "God Save the Queen," which I combined admirably with "*Partant pour la Syrie*". My big major started out of his sleep at the noise of the plaudits. The hearer, enchanted with the *entente cordiale* of these two themes in spite of their opposing rhythms, recognized his national air, and, delighted at hearing it, applauded wildly and so warmly that I forgave him, and I even believe that since that time we have been good friends.

Madame Budan sang the air from [Halévy's] *Charles VI* and the *polacca* from *Jérusalem* in a remarkable manner, which brought her warm and prolonged applause.

◇◇◇◇◇◇◇◇◇

[Cuba, approximately early spring 1860]
I left Martinique with great regret. There also I have made devoted friendships too warm not to cost me a great deal in leaving this good little island, so charming in its poverty, its hospitality almost having given me back all the joys that I had not experienced since I left my family.

A few days ago I was present at a soirée given by Mr. de L[ar-rinaga], one of the most opulent Creoles. There was music, and I played upon a marvelously fine piano manufactured by my illustrious confrere Henri Herz. This piano, which cost fifteen thousand francs, is a piece of furniture—a veritable chef-d'oeuvre of Parisian industry; it is all of ebony, with moldings of gilt bronze, chiseled like a bijou by Froment-Meurice.[1] But its exterior, beautiful as it was, struck me less than its qualities of sound, its crystalline limpidity, and the equality of its round tone, like the human voice in all its registers. I compliment the illustrious pianist and manufacturer on his work.

On my arrival at Havana I forgot the distance that I just had traveled, and kept on my linen clothes.[2] The winter was truly one of the most rigorous that ever had been experienced in Havana. So on the day after my arrival I was taken ill and was confined to my bed for three weeks by a threatened inflammation of the lungs. I was scarcely well when the captain general, Marshal Serrano, invited me to the palace, and two days later I gave a very successful concert, but the fatigue I experienced after my long illness caused a great irritation of the bowels, which again rendered it necessary for me to stay in my room and adhere to a diet.

Two months later (on the offer made to me by the general-in-chief to place at my disposal all the military bands) I had, as I say, the idea of giving a grand festival, and I made an arrangement with the director of the Italian company, then in possession of the Grand Tacón Theater. He contracted with me to furnish his chief performers, all the choruses, and his whole orchestra on condition of having an interest in the result. I set to work and composed, on some Spanish verses written for me by a Havanese poet, an opera in one act, entitled *Fête champêtre cubaine*. Then I composed a *Triumphal Hymn* and a *Grand March*. My orchestra consisted of six hundred and fifty performers, eighty-seven choristers, fifteen solo singers, fifty drums, and eighty trumpets—that is to say, nearly nine hundred persons bellowing and blowing to see who

---

[1] Jacques-Charles-François-Marie Froment-Meurice, French sculptor of the nineteenth century.

[2] Gottschalk had arrived at Havana from Martinique late in November 1859.

could scream the loudest. The violins alone were seventy in number, contrabasses eleven, violoncellos eleven!

You can imagine the effect. No one can have any idea of the labor it cost me. The copying of the orchestral parts alone amounted to five thousand francs. There were two thousand pages of the single act of the opera; for the *Fête cubaine* more than four thousand pages, and nearly two thousand pages for the *Hymn*. I was obliged to write out the original score for all. Besides, I had to devise page by page the whole eight or ten thousand pages. During the last week I had such an amount of labor that I remained at work seventy-two hours, sleeping only two hours out of every twenty-four. I was to pay a very heavy fine in case I was not ready at the time fixed in the contract made with the impresario of the theater.

"Notice to artists: To give a concert at the Tacón is equal to laying a plan for a campaign, to putting an opera of Meyerbeer on the stage, or to publishing *Le Père Goriot*, by Balzac; finally it is an immense effort, requiring a great deal of money, time, diplomacy, and muscles of steel in the service of an iron will."

For a very long time my health has been precarious, and it is very far from being altogether re-established. Excessive labor and change of climate have tried it greatly. I must not, according to the advice of my physician, encounter the cold of the north, which, during the past winter, has been excessive. In eight days, I probably shall be at New Orleans, and I will remain there only one or two weeks.

The heat here already is insupportable, and in spite of the efforts made by the opera and two or three American circuses, nearly everybody has left for the country.

[The festival took place on February 17, 1860. As early as January 7, the Gaceta de la Habana was announcing certain plans: Berlioz's manner of performing Rossini's Moïse at his first festival in Paris would be followed, i.e., the principal phrase sung successively by soprano, tenor, and baritone would be sung by all the sopranos, all the tenors, and all the baritones of the Maretzek Company, with members of chorus and orchestra joining in to make a thrilling crescendo. Although Moïse was not performed, this effect probably was used in some other work. A month later, the paper reported that in order to foil the speculators Gottschalk would sell tickets from his residence. The festival was definitely a success. In April and May, Gottschalk participated in various concerts. As for another large, successful concert at the Salon of the Louvre, the Gaceta declared that only Gottschalk could perform such a miracle at this time, adding that in his Escenas campestres he had conserved the character and poetry of the country that had inspired him.]

◇◇◇◇◇◇◇◇◇

[*Havana, September 1860*]

We expect from day to day the zarzuela[3] company that Don Carlos Raya, the present impresario of the Tacón, has gone to Spain to engage. It is to alternate during the whole theatrical season with a numerous and brilliant Italian troupe that the same impresario promises at the beginning of December. Up to now I do not know anything definite about the personnel of this latter company. So many different artists are spoken of that it is impossible to foresee who will be chosen. Basseggio, Lotti, Medori, Tedesco all have been announced successively. The latest number of the *Diario de la Marina*, of Havana, asserts that all four will come. This assertion is so much the more singular because, besides these four "*prime donne di cartello*,"[4] Kennett, a contralto, already is engaged, as well as Fanny Natale, a *soprano sfogato*, and Agnes Natali, a contralto. Total: seven "*prime donne di primo cartello*." The tenors are Pancarri, Volpini (whose wife is engaged as second prima donna for the operas of *mezzo carattere*[5])!! and Testa, a charming *tenorino*[6] whose exquisite style makes up for the deficiency of an agreeable but feeble voice. The baritone and bass are equally good. The choruses are to be augmented by four men and four women engaged in Paris by Mr. Raya. The orchestra too will be engaged there. The artists engaged for the Spanish opera are—prima donnas: La Natarre, La Nastariz, and La Santa María; tenor: Gonzales; baritones: Folgueras and Fuentes. The leaders of the

---

[3] A traditional form of Spanish opera, dating from the seventeenth century and still popular.
[4] That is, prima donnas whose names bring sold-out houses.
[5] Between lyric and dramatic in quality.
[6] A very small, light tenor voice.

orchestra for the two companies are six in number—a number that seems exaggerated but nevertheless hardly sufficient for an audience that constantly wishes something new and deserts the theater on a second performance. *La Traviata* is the only opera that has triumphed over the apathy of the Havana public. Max Maretzek[7] gave it twelve or fifteen times before crowded houses last winter, nineteen times the preceding season.

It is a fact sufficiently interesting to be noticed that the ladies literally took possession of the theater every time the posters announced *Traviata.* On the part of the ladies were sobs, transports, ejaculations at each of the different catastrophes of the drama by Alexandre Dumas *fils,* the sight of which was very amusing, and more than once excited unbecoming laughter in the pit. Two years ago, Gazzaniga,[8] whose gestures and acting are somewhat violent and often exaggerated and adapted to a southern audience, had become the idol of the feminine public of Havana. The enthusiasm she excited bordered on madness. The gentlemen threw their hats to her, the ladies their embroidered handkerchiefs and bracelets. Two factions were formed whose disputes, begun in the theater, were kept up in the streets, and often threatened to become riots. One of these factions took the part of Frezzolini;[9] it was the enlightened and conservative party. The other, for Gazzaniga, was composed of the ladies and the Havanese. The young girls were *gazzaniquistas* or *frezzolinistas,* and at the aristocratic balls of one or the other faction the unfortunate dancers who belonged to the opposite party were snubbed mercilessly. The dressmakers, the tailors, the confectioners, the cafés were partisan. The sign of one bore "*à la Traviata,*" and all the *gazzaniquistas* supplied themselves at his shop; another, "*à la Sonnambula,*" and all the *frezzolinistas* ran there. It seems incredible that human passions should be ex-

---

[7] Max Maretzek (1821–97), "Maretzek the Magnificent," a native of Moravia, arrived in America in 1848. An enterprising manager of opera companies, he toured the United States, Cuba, and Mexico, wrote two operas, and was the author of several diverting little books among them *Crotchets and Quavers:* or, *Revelations of an Opera Manager in America* (New York: S. French; 1855).

[8] Marietta Gazzaniga sang extensively in Europe and America.

[9] Erminia Frezzolini (1818–84) was past her vocal prime when she arrived here in 1853. One of Verdi's favorite singers, she sang in the first performance of *I Lombardi* at La Scala and in the first performances of *Giovanna d'Arco* and of *Rigoletto* in Paris.

cited so violently by such ridiculous puerilities. It is certain that speculation took advantage of the general effervescence and that great and rapid fortunes were made in a few months. At her benefit, Gazzaniga received from the public a lyre and a cup of massive gold in commemoration of the double triumph she had obtained in Pacini's *Saffo* and the *brindisi* from *La Traviata*. The receipts were over twenty-five thousand francs, besides the jewels that were thrown to her on the stage, which were without exaggeration valued at from thirty to forty thousand francs.

La Cortesi, *soprano sfogato*, had a fine success last year in *Trovatore*, and particularly in *Traviata*. The exuberance of her gestures and certain ultramontane exaggerations recalled Gazzaniga. Besides, she had the immense advantage of appearing beautiful on the stage. Nothing more was wanting to awaken the hatred of the partisans. The *gazzaniquistas* adopted her. La Gassier, her happy rival, was sustained by the people of taste, and the strife recommenced. The authorities had to interfere, and the encoring of pieces was prohibited. The benefits of both prima donnas produced magnificent and fruitful ovations. Each of them received wreaths of massive gold. The receipts at each performance were estimated at fifty thousand francs.[1]

◇◇◇◇◇◇◇◇◇

[*September 1860*]

I have been to Cárdenas to give a concert, the subscription for which had been secured to me in advance by the Philharmonic Society of that charming city, which is not more than thirty years old and already is reckoned among the most flourishing of the Antilles. Nearly one-half of the sugar of the island of Cuba (nearly seven hundred thousand cases of sugar and one hundred thousand hogsheads of molasses) is exported every year from Cárdenas. Its jurisdiction contains five hundred thousand souls and six hundred sugar houses. With such elements it must be one of the richest of the island. Its business is almost exclusively with the United States. Visited principally by the Yankees, whose activity, enter-

[1] A more detailed version of this entry appeared in *La France musicale* on October 28, 1860, pp. 425, 426, entitled "*La Musique à la Havane*," in which Cortesi is designated as "*soprano de force*" rather than "*soprano sfogato*."

prising spirit, and industry agree marvelously with the necessities and character of its inhabitants, it is at the head of every enterprise and all the progress that for some years past have transformed ancient Cuba, and made of her today one of the richest, most civilized, and most beautiful countries of the world.

Perhaps the preceding statistics will be found useless and tiresome, but it seems to me, now that regenerated Spain has revealed all her resources to Europe and again takes the rank that formerly belonged to her among the great nations, it will not be without interest to many persons in the community to know the importance of one of the new ports of its principal colony. The theater at Cárdenas is only a provisional one and but little worthy of notice. They are constructing a new one, which is only about one-third up, already has cost one hundred ninety thousand francs, and promises to be like the Tacón Theater at Havana. The church is of the Gothic style and has so much the more charm, as I am accustomed to the massive, heavy architecture that the talent of Herrera[2] has made the fashion to such a great degree for the last two centuries. It is elegant and boldly supports two aerial clock towers that, at a distance, give a picturesque effect by detaching it from the dark verdure of the cocoa trees and palms.

A church and a theater are the two prime necessities of a Spanish-American city. In the United States, when they found a new city, they commence building a hotel, afterward a church, and finally the newspaper office. Given the hotel, church, and political discussions, you have the existence of the Yankee. Immediately after the newspaper office comes the lecture or concert hall. The lectures, of which French people can have but an imperfect idea, are essentially an American invention, and have become an imperative necessity for a people constantly occupied with popular elections, political or religious discussions, and public discourses on every possible subject. The profession of lecturer is one of the most lucrative that I know of. Everybody speaks with facility and with a certain eloquence that demands no special study.

---

[2] Juan de Herrera (1530–97), Spanish architect who was employed on the Escorial after 1567 and built the royal pleasurehouse of Aranjuez. He had a strong influence on the church architecture of Latin America in the sixteenth and seventeenth centuries.

My concert at Cárdenas was a complete success, and I was enchanted with the enthusiastic reception they gave me.

Decidedly my trip to Cárdenas has taken fabulous proportions and becomes an Odyssey. Alexandre Dumas would have made two large volumes of impressions out of it. What still adds to its interest is that I am ignorant as to how it may end. I am writing in a railway carriage that is carrying me I know not where, and its jerks make my pencil describe curves, angles, and spirals charming to look at; they are very pretty, and afford the eye the same interest as the clouds in whose fantastic forms everyone can see what he likes. The page I have just finished almost resembles an Egyptian obelisk. Perhaps I may be told that jerks are not indispensable to the making of hieroglyphics. But the train stops:

"Where are we?"

At Marajas.

"Where are we going?"

We are going back!

These questions and answers give me a little knowledge as to my position, of which I have been ignorant for the three days, or nearly so, during which I have made my residence in a train, on the road from Cárdenas to Havana, for it should be known (I should have begun with it) that for three days I have been trying to return to Havana. Invited by the Philharmonic Society of Cárdenas, who wished to hear me, I accepted with all the ardor that the desire to see again my numerous friends and a charming town—whose remembrance is connected with the happiest memories of my first voyage to Cuba—could give me.

The locomotive scarcely makes six miles an hour and advances with the worst possible will, now and then uttering lamentable groans. Our conductor insists on explaining the bad conduct of the locomotive as resulting from the want of coal and the abundance of green wood. I myself, enlightened by three days of vicissitudes and tribulations, begin to comprehend what tears my ears and penetrates my heart. This groan seems to say to me: "Hast thou then no pity on my sweat and my fatigues? How far wilt thou thus travel on the iron road? Dost thou forget that I have panted and have been tormented for the last three days because I have indulged the fallacious hope of going to Havana?"

"Alas," I replied, "poor sister in misfortune, our misery is equal. I also am the victim of my sanguine credulity. I reasoned that since the proverb says that every road leads to Rome, there was the stronger reason for thinking that the railroad from Cárdenas to Havana must conduct me to Havana.

"An error, an illusion of my excited imagination. If not, what signifies the business I have been engaged in for the last three days? Tossed from station to station, from inn to inn, and finding myself farther off than ever from the end of our journey! Do not complain, for if thy conductor gives thee only green wood, I endure the horrors of hunger, only partially appeased by the lean breast of a venerable fowl which has been served up to us on the road."

After this dialogue between the locomotive and myself, I placed myself in a comfortable position for a nap, from which I was not awakened until my arrival at Havana, broken down, but happy for having escaped the dangers of a long and fatiguing journey.

~~~~~~~~

[On March 21, 1861, the Gaceta de la Habana announced a forthcoming "gran proyecto," a festival including forty pianists, all the musicians of the military garrison, and all the amateur vocalists of Havana—a "festival gigantesca" compared with which the preceding one, in 1860, had been "just child's play." It took place on April 17, and was notable more for what it attempted than for what it achieved. Gottschalk used six "harmoni-flautas . . . to give an idea of the calm and serenity of a night in the equinoctial regions." He also imported from the eastern tip of the island, at Santiago, the king of the Association of French Negroes, with a whole arsenal of drums—an innovation presaging Amedeo Roldán's Overture on Cuban Themes (1925).[3]

It was a fiasco. "Quantity rather than quality," said the Gaceta, citing problems of ensemble and lack of rehearsal. It lasted five and a half hours, toward the last playing mostly to empty seats. The presence of Ada Clare at this time must have been disturbing to Gottschalk.

In May, Gottschalk played several times at Pinar del Río, in October at Guanabacoa, Marianao, and Havana, in November at

---

[3] Alejo Carpentier: *La Música en Cuba* (Mexico: Fondo de Cultura Económica; 1946), p. 158.

Havana and Matanzas. Over the years the press had been an-
nouncing his imminent departure for Europe, for the United
States, or for South America, even naming the steamer. But now
the West Indian chapter actually was coming to its close.]

The islands of the Antilles impart a voluptuous languor that
is contagious; it is a poison that slowly infiltrates all the senses and
benumbs the soul with a kind of ecstatic torpor.

I shall never forget the two months I passed at Caimito, in
the interior of Cuba.[4] I had just recovered from a serious illness;
some newspapers, indeed, had mourned for me in very fine necro-
logical articles. My two physicians, fearing a malignant fever, had
prescribed absolute rest for me, and I was to pass my convalescence
in the district of Guanajay, near the Sierra de Anafe. It was a vast
plain, in the center of which rose a large, square, modern building, having only a ground floor, like most of the Cuban houses. A
friend of mine, who had intended to establish a sugar plantation
on this land, placed at my disposal *la casa del amo* (the master's
house), the only one yet built. A sugar plantation invariably consists of the following buildings, which, for hygienic reasons, and
for convenience, are identical: *casa del amo*, which occupies the
center and is isolated from the rest of the *finca*; *casa del mayoral*,
the commandant's, or manager's, dwelling; *casa de la molienda*,
the building containing the steam engine for grinding the canes
and communicating with the *casa de las calderas* (boilers). Afterward come *el hospital, el corral*, in which the domestic animals are
kept; and finally, at some distance, *las casuchas de la negrada*,
the cabins of the Negroes. Every evening the *mayoral* shuts them
up under lock and key, after having called the roll and made them
repeat the Pater Noster and the Ave Maria.

Nothing of all this yet existed at my friend's. There was one
house only, which we reached through an immense avenue of
palms. A kind of wooden ascent of twelve steps led to an exterior gallery, a sort of Indian veranda, which is to a Cuban dwelling what a porter's lodge is to the French. From the gallery you

[4] This was during the summer of 1860. Most of the account here given,
up to the close of the moonlit scene, appeared in a letter to Escudier from
Gottschalk, dated June 25, 1862 (New York), published in *L'Art musical*,
July 31 of that year.

look out upon the country: it is an observatory. Visitors can be seen coming, and in the distance Negroes can be watched at their work. There, life is passed in the hammock or the *butaca*,[5] in smoking, in sleeping, in drinking coffee, and, above all, in breathing the air of the savanna.

To serve in the *casa del amo* or to belong to the plantation sums up the whole life of the Negro. To serve *el amo* is the marshal's baton of the model slaves. By way of punishment the Negroes of the town who have committed any peccadilloes are sent by their master to the fields, which serve, in a way, as galleys. The beasts of burden of the *finca* are infinitely better treated, and their existence is less compromised than that of the poor slaves, who are obliged, during the grinding season, to work from eighteen to twenty hours a day, to brave the heat of the devouring sun, and to endure the deluging rains with no other clothes than calico drawers. The *mayorales*, or overseers, treat the sick Negroes in their own way. I do not know that they understand anything at all, but these gentlemen have a passion for systems, the consequences of which are disastrous. Leroi (a patent medicine) is generally the universal panacea most commonly employed. I knew at Santiago de Cuba a Basque (almost all the overseers of Cuba are Asturians or French Basques) who could hardly read and who treated all the sick with cold water. A large cistern in the middle of the coffee plantation was the only remedy in the house. During a visit I made there, I was present at the cure of a hysterical young Negress, whom they threw into the basin twice a day. She struggled horribly in the water, not knowing how to swim, and by a miracle was not drowned. It is true that she died five days afterward.

The house I lived in was at an hour's distance from the first cabins of Caimito. Throughout the vast plains and the fields of cane not a vestige of a habitation, a true wilderness for a league around, with the mountains of Anafe on the horizon. Méry[6] and Théophile Gautier would have gone mad in contemplating this paradise, in which only an Eve was wanting. Unfortunately, the

---

[5] Armchair.

[6] Joseph Méry (1798–1865) French littérateur, author of numerous poems, novels, and dramas. With Camille du Locle, he wrote the libretto of Verdi's *Don Carlos.*

only company in my Eden was a very ugly Negress, who, every evening after having roasted the coffee, crushed her maize in a hollow piece of wood, recited the Ave Maria before an old colored image of the Virgin, came and squatted down at my feet on the veranda, and there, in the darkness, sang to me in a piercing, wild voice full of strange charm, the *canciones* of the country. I would light my cigar, extend myself in a *butaca*, and, surrounded by this silent, primitive nature, plunge into a contemplative revery, which those in the midst of the everyday world can never understand. The moon rose over the Sierra de Anafe. The crickets chirped in the fields; the long avenue of palms, which extended from the *casa* to the entrance of the plantation, was separated into two black bands on the uniform ground of the fields. The phosphorescent arabesques of the fireflies flashed suddenly through the thick darkness that surrounded us. The distant noises of the savanna, borne softly by the breeze, struck my ears in drawn-out murmurs. The cadenced chant of some Negroes belated in the fields added one more attraction to all this poesy, which no one can ever imagine.

My thoughts flew away with the fumes of my cigar; my ideas were effaced, and I finished by feeling my brain benumbed by that delicious beatitude which is the extreme limit between sleep and life. I would have remained thus until the morning had it not been for the voice of the *sereno* (night watchman), who came to tell me that it was eleven o'clock—that is to say, the hour for retiring. Once more I threw a last look at all this marvelous nature and withdrew into my chamber.

Sometimes I read before going to sleep. Now and then a bat, dazzled, struck my lamp and extinguished it. The number of these little animals in the Cuban country houses is immense. The apartments having no ceilings but the roof itself, and as they are separated from each other only by partitions rising about six or seven feet, the bats establish themselves there in perfect security. Every hole, every chink, every obscure corner conceals a nest. The enormous beams, particularly those which cross the structure of the roof and which the equivocal taste of the natives covers with indentations by a cutting punch, seem to be their preferred quarters. As soon as night comes on, the noise that all this hairy,

winged colony makes becomes deafening. I liked to follow with
my eyes their wild flight, whose circles, always narrowing, had
my lamp for their center. I liked, also, their sharp little cry, which
peopled the immense depths of my chamber.

Now and then I read. Unfortunately the library included but
four books, the invariable foundation of all the rustic libraries in
Cuba, to wit: *El Buen cristiano* (The Good Christian), *El Manual
del Hacendado* (*The Farmer's Manual*), and Raspail's *Médecine,*
translated into Spanish. I must not forget *El Oficio de la santa
misa* (*Office of the Holy Mass*). There was little of variety and
of relative interest, as may easily be understood.

Thus it was a precious discovery I made of a large folio, printed
in the eighteenth century, with tailpieces, blue and red letters,
impossible engravings, and a preface by the Reverend Father Don
Antonio de los Heros, Canon of Toledo, of the Holy Inquisition,
of the Chamber and Private Council of His Majesty Charles III,
deputed by the archbishop to examine this work, in which he de-
clares that he has found nothing contrary to the commandments
of our Mother the Holy Church. This book contained the poetical
works of the valiant and very illustrious (thus ran the title of the
work) captain of infantry, Señor Don Heraclio Augusto José de
los Ángeles de Lobo e Ximenes. This brave man of war informs us
in an epistle to the reader, that "Mars had adopted him for his
well-beloved son"; that "Apollo, in gratitude for the worship he had
vowed to the Muses, treated him as a spoiled child." Well, at last
here is a sincere preface. One feels at ease with good Captain Lobo
who, in spite of the bullying airs he takes on, is fundamentally the
most amiable of creatures. His casque has all the appearance of
Mambrino's helmet.[7] His sonnets, when he does not turn them
against the enemies of the proud Castilian, are the bouquets of
Chloris. In the midst of all this silly rubbish I found some charming things, some truly striking *manières picaresques,* and some very
minute details. A poem on the taking of Gibraltar, for instance,
where, swimming in the midst of Homeric denunciations and furious imprecations against the English, I discovered some very interesting facts of an undoubted historical character. I found in it

---

[7] This is an allusion to an incident in Cervantes' *Don Quixote de la
Mancha* in which the "proud Castilian" dons an ordinary shaving bowl,
believing it to be the golden helmet of a Saracen hero, Mambrino.

the whole gallery of Gil Blas's characters. Whether Lesage[8] has stolen or borrowed his work, he is certainly the only one who has made old Spain known to France.

Apropos of Lesage, what most irritates the national susceptibility of the Spaniards? Gibraltar, it may be replied; or rather the witty but slightly veritable gasconades of Alexandre Dumas apropos of Madrid. No! What has rendered, and still renders the Spaniards unhappy is the glory usurped by the author of *Gil Blas*. I recollect a work I read in Spain, entitled "*Gil Blas*, stolen and translated into French by a M. Lesage, and restored here to Spanish by a Spaniard, jealous of his honor, and who does not permit anyone to ridicule his nation."

Must not this Spaniard be slightly related to the illustrious Knight of la Mancha? Whether or not this be the case, it is almost certain that Lesage only compiled different works already published at Madrid, which fact, however, does not prevent *Gil Blas* from being an exact mirror of the Spain of the eighteenth century and sometimes, also, of the nineteenth.

---

[8] Alain-René Lesage (1668–1747) was a French novelist and dramatist who wrote several works more or less borrowed from Spanish originals, including the novel *Gil Blas* (1715–35).

The United States, Panama, Mexico

1862–65

New York, February 1862

HERE I AM AGAIN, after an absence of six years,[1] once more in New York! Six years foolishly spent, thrown to the wind, as if life were infinite, and youth eternal; six years, during which I have roamed at random under the blue skies of the tropics, indolently permitting myself to be carried away by chance, giving a concert wherever I found a piano, sleeping wherever the night overtook me—on the grass of the savanna, or under the palm-leaf roof of a *veguero* [a tobacco-grower] with whom I partook of a tortilla, coffee, and banana, which I paid for on leaving in the morning,

---

[1] Gottschalk had left New York for the West Indies in February 1857; he returned to it in February 1862, five years later, not six. In his backward glances he generally lengthens his sojourns in Europe and Latin America, shortens those in the United States.

with *"Dios se lo pague"* (God repay you); to which he responded with a *"Vaya usted con Dios"* (God go with you)—these two formularies constituting in this savage country, the operation so ingeniously perfected among civilized peoples, that is called "settling the hotel bill."

When I became tired of the same horizon, I crossed an arm of the sea and landed on a neighboring island or on the Spanish Main. In this manner I have successively visited the Spanish, English, French, Dutch, Swedish, and Danish Antilles, the Guianas, and the shores of Pará. Sometimes the idol of an ignorant *"pueblo,"* to whom I have played some of their simple ballads, I have stopped for five, six, or eight months among them, putting off my departure from day to day, and have at last resolved seriously to go no farther; or, detained in a village where the piano was still unknown, by the ties of an affection with which my fingers had nothing to do (O rare and blessed affections!), I forgot the world, and lived only for two large black eyes, which veiled themselves with tears whenever I spoke of beginning my vagabond course again, again living as the bird sings, as the flower opens, as the brook flows, forgetful of the past, careless of the future. I sowed my heart and my purse with the ardor of a sower who hopes to harvest a hundred ears for every seed, but the fields in which spent doubloons are harvested and the loves of springtime blossom again were not yet ready for the husbandman, and my heart and purse, exhausted by this double prodigality, one fine day were discovered to be dry. Then, seized with a profound disgust of the world and of myself, tired, discouraged, suspecting men (and women), I hastened to hide in the wilds on the extinguished volcano of N——, where I lived for many months like a cenobite, with no companion other than a poor fool I had met on a small island and who attached himself to me, followed me everywhere, and loved me with that absurd and touching constancy which one meets with only in dogs and madmen. My friend, whose folly was quiet and inoffensive, believed himself to be the *greatest genius in the world*. He suffered, he said, from a gigantic and monstrous tooth (and it was only by this that I recognized that he was insane, the other symptoms being found among too many individuals to be considered as an abnormal trait of the human mind)—a monstrous tooth that periodically increased and threatened to encroach upon the whole jaw. Tormented with the desire to regenerate humanity, he divided his time between the study of dentistry, which he learned for the purpose of combating constantly the fantastic progress of his molar, and a voluminous correspondence that he carried on with the Pope, *his brother*, and the Emperor of the French, *his cousin*, in which he pleaded the interests of humanity, and called himself the Prince of Thought, and raised me to the dignity of his illustrious friend and benefactor. In the midst of this intellectual ruin only one thing survived—his love for music. He played the violin, and—a singular thing—although insane, he understood nothing of the music of the future![2]

Perched upon the edge of the crater, on the very top of the mountain, my cabin overlooked the whole country. The rock on which it was built hung over a precipice whose depths were concealed by cacti, convolvuluses, and bamboos. The one who had preceded me had surrounded this lower ground with a parapet and had made it a terrace level with the bedroom. He had requested to be buried there, and at night from my bed I could see the white tombstone a few steps from my window in the moonlight. Every evening I moved my piano out upon the terrace, and there, in view of the most beautiful scenery in the world, which was bathed by the serene and limpid atmosphere of the tropics, I played, *for myself alone*, everything that the scene opened before me inspired — and what a scene! Imagine a gigantic amphitheater, such as an army of Titans might have carved out in the mountains; to the right and left virgin forests filled with wild and distant harmonies that are like the voice of silence; before me sixty miles of country whose magic perspective is rendered more marvelous by the transparency of the atmosphere; over my head the azure of the sky; below the declivities, surmounted by the mountain, descending gradually toward the plain; farther on, the green savannas, then, lower, a gray point—it is the town; and farther on again the immensity of the ocean, whose line of deep blue forms the horizon.

Behind me was a rock on which broke a torrent of melted snow that turned from its course, leaped with a desperate bound, and

---

[2] This is a sly dig at the kind of music that then seemed to be what we now know as "modern music." In Gottschalk's time it was called the "music of the future." Its chief protagonists were considered to be Berlioz, Liszt, and Wagner.

engulfed itself in the depths of the precipice that gaped under my window.

It was there that I composed *Réponds-moi, La Marche des Gibaros, Polonia, Columbia, Pastorella e cavaliere, Jeunesse,* and other unpublished works. I let my fingers run over the keyboard, wrapped up in the contemplation of these marvels, while my poor friend, to whom I did not listen, divulged to me with childish loquacity the high destiny to which he proposed to elevate humanity. Do you comprehend the contrast between this ruin of intelligence that, like a clock out of order, strikes all its ideas at random, and the majestic serenity of that nature which surrounded me? I felt it instinctively, and my misanthropy softened, became indulgent toward others and myself; I was cured of my wounds, my despair vanished, and soon the sun of the tropics, which gilds all things—dreams as well as fruit—gave me back my vagabond life, strong and confident.

I again began to live according to the customs of these primitive countries, which, if they are not strictly virtuous, are nonetheless terribly attractive. I saw again those beautiful *trigueñas,* with red lips and brown bosoms, ignorant of evil, sinning with frankness, without fearing the bitterness of remorse. All this is frightfully immoral, I know, but life in the savannas of the tropics, in the midst of a half-civilized and voluptuous race, cannot be that of a London cockney, a Parisian idler, or an American Presbyterian.

In the depths of my conscience I sometimes heard a voice that recalled me to what I was, to what I ought to be, and imperiously commanded me to return to a healthy and active life. But I had permitted myself to become so morally benumbed by languor— the *far niente*—that the idea of again appearing before a polished audience seemed to me, very honestly, absurd. For what good? I said to myself. And besides it is too late, and I continued to live, to sleep, to awaken, to gallop over the savannas on horseback, to listen to the female parrots coquet in the guava trees at sunrise, to the crickets chirp in the fields of sugar cane at nightfall, to smoke my cigar, to drink my coffee, to cradle myself in my hammock— finally, to enjoy all the pleasures beyond which the *guajiro*[3] sees

---

[3]Cuban peasant.

only death or, what is still worse, the feverish agitation of northern society. Here is the secret of the atrophy of the new Spanish colonies. Go then and talk of stocks, of loan banks, of exchange, to that sybarite, king of the savanna, who can live the whole year on exquisite bananas, on savory cocoa that he has not had the trouble to plant, who smokes the best tobacco in the world, who replaces the horse of yesterday with a better chosen in the first *caballada* that he meets with, who, clothed in his linen drawers, sees the seasons succeed each other in perpetual summer; and who, in the evening, under the palmtrees, finds beautiful, dreamlike girls impatient to bestow their love on him—who will know how to murmur in his ears these three words, eternally beautiful, "Yo *te quiero*" (I love thee).

The moralists, I well know, condemn all this; and they are right. But poetry is often in antagonism with virtue; and now that I am shivering under the icy wind and gray sky of the north, now that I hear discussions on Erie, Prairie du Chien, Harlem, and Cumberland, now that I read in the newspapers the lists of dead and wounded, the devastation of incendiaries, the abductions and assassinations that are committed on both sides under the name of retaliation, I find myself excusing the demisavages of the savannas who prefer their poetic barbarism to our barbarous progress.

Recalled suddenly to real life by a great grief, I wished to break all the ties that bound me to those six lost years.

It was at this period that Strakosch[4] wrote, offering me an engagement for a round of concerts in the United States. I hesitated an instant, cast a last glance at the past, gave a sigh, and signed. The dream was finished—I was saved, but who shall say if, in this salvage, youth and poesy had not been wrecked? Poesy and youth are by nature vagabonds; they are butterflies. Shut them up in the cage of reason, and their transparent wings are broken against the prison bars. Regulate their flight and you take from them their scope and boldness—two qualities that often are found in inexperience and whose loss is not always compensated by maturity of talent.

---

[4] Max Strakosch (1834–92) was Gottschalk's manager for most of his tours in the United States. His brother was Maurice Strakosch (1825–87) pianist-composer, brother-in-law and manager of Adelina Patti. The brothers, natives of Moravia, sometimes were partners in managerial ventures.

◇◇◇◇◇◇◇◇◇

New York, February 15, 1862

My first concert in New York, after six years of absence, took place on the eleventh.⁵ I played badly. I felt too much emotion for my fingers and my mind not to be affected by it. I recognized among the audience all the well-disposed physiognomies of unknown friends, who, during my long series of concerts at Dodsworth's Hall in 1855,⁶ constantly had encouraged and sustained me and had been the first to contribute to the success of *Marche de nuit* and *Last Hope*, which I had just composed. Richard Hoffman,⁷ one of the rare brotherhood of the piano, who has always given me proofs of good-fellowship, had lent me his co-operation to play my *Guillaume Tell* and my *Ojos criollos*.

Of all the pianists who have visited the United States, there is not one whose talent merits more esteem than that of Richard Hoffman. A conscientious artist, a perfect musician, a distinguished and modest man, he has arrived legitimately and without effort at the high position that he occupies. His taste and the moderation of his judgment have preserved him from coteries. He is neither the chief nor the instrument of any clique. He admires and understands the great dead (I mean the classics), but he does not conclude from this that he must kill the living who possess talent. He does not believe that in admiring Schumann he is compelled to believe that Rossini is a fool. He comprehends Bach but does not shrug his shoulders on hearing the name of Bellini. In conclusion, he is an artist and a *gentleman*.

My impresarios, Strakosch and Grau,⁸ having discovered that

---

⁵ On February 8, 1862, Gottschalk played privately for some of his colleagues and the elite of New York's journalists. It was apparent to them that his art had matured in the intervening years.

⁶ The series began on December 20, 1855, and concluded on June 7, 1856. The concert on January 31 consisted of his Spanish and Cuban compositions.

⁷ Richard Hoffman (1831–1909), English-born pianist and composer, pupil of Moscheles, Liszt, and Rubinstein among others, was an active musician in New York for more than fifty years. Besides assisting Gottschalk, he performed a similar service at Jenny Lind's American debut and at her subsequent concerts. Gottschalk dedicated *The Banjo* to him.

⁸ Jacob Grau and his nephew Maurice Grau (1849–1907) helped to make operatic history as impresarios in the United States.

my first concert in New York on my return from Europe in 1853 took place on February 11, decided to postpone my reappearance for some days so that it might take place on February 11, 1862—a memorable coincidence, of which the public (whom it did not interest the least in the world) was informed through all the newspapers.

A question by many of my friends: "Why do you say such things in your advertisements? Why don't you strike out such ambitious epithets in your placards?" Alas! Are you ignorant that the artist is merchandise that the impresario has purchased, the value of which he enhances as he chooses? You might as well reproach certain pseudo gold-mine companies for announcing dividends that they never will pay as to render an artist responsible for the lures of his contractor. A poor old Negress becomes, in the hands of the Jupiter of museums (Barnum), Washington's nurse. Why, then, do you think you should be astonished at the magnificent titles that are coupled with my name?

The artist, once thus sold, no longer belongs to himself, but becomes the property of the impresario, who endeavors as he sees fit, to heighten its value. His friends help him and shout that he is of good quality; his enemies that he is trumpery and worth nothing. The impresario being vulnerable only through the pocket, that is, through the artists whom he cries up, it is upon the latter that the blows fall; like coachmen who, every time they meet the horses of the rivals whom they hate, strike them with their whips, so it is upon us that the critics, who have quarreled with the impresario, take revenge.

Thus far the press of the United States has treated me with great kindness, with the exception of two newspaper writers, one of whom is an old minister who does not understand music, and the other an obscure writer who uses his pen in the service of his personal antipathies. If they had used one-hundredth of the efforts that they have employed to prove that I am a fool—the one in acquiring a knowledge of the art of which he pretends to be a luminary, the other in correcting one or two pieces for the piano which he has published—they might have succeeded in arriving at an honest mediocrity instead of remaining malicious nobodies.

In New York I met again the same kindness; time had not changed the old sympathies. Unfortunately the systematic ill will of some of my old detractors remained the same. Mr. H. continues to distill from his sourish little pen the personal spite that he pours out every week through his little musical drain, which, fortunately, has nothing to do with the musical world.

The *Murmures éoliens,* which I have just published, appears likely to have some successs. It is encored at all my concerts. *Pastorella e cavaliere* and *Ojos criollos* are always called for again. Apropos of *Murmures éoliens,* I am led by the chain of my recollections to measure the emptiness of human things. When, in 1853, I returned to the United States, which I had left eleven years before (at eleven years of age),[9] my reputation, wholly Parisian, had not, so to speak, crossed the Atlantic. Two or three hundred concerts, given in Belgium, Italy, France, Spain, Switzerland, etc., had given me a name, but this name, so young, was not yet acclimated in America. My first concert in New York was a success, but the receipts did not amount to half of the expenses. The second, given at Niblo's Theater, was a fiasco; in the two concerts I lost twenty-four hundred dollars. The excellent Wallace[1] had offered me, with that good-natured kindness which was so natural to him, to conduct the orchestra, and Hoffman, the admirable and conscientious pianist, whom at all times I have ever found ready to oblige me, played with me two pieces for two pianos. In these two concerts I then lost twenty-four hundred dollars. It was a decided failure. Barnum then wanted to engage me for a year, offering me twenty thousand dollars and expenses paid, but my father had his prejudices (unjust) against Barnum, in whom he obstinately insisted in seeing only a showman of learned beasts. I refused. We left, my father and I, for New Orleans, my native city. My fellow citizens received me in triumph. I was at that time the only American artist who had received the sanction of the European public, and, national self-love assisting, I was received with an indescribable enthusiasm by the Louisianians, less, without doubt, because I deserved it—I already have said that—but because I was first

[9] Gottschalk actually was thirteen when he left New Orleans for Paris.
[1] William Vincent Wallace (1813–65), Irish violinist, composer, world traveler, and adventurer, composed two successful operas—*Maritana* and *Lurline*—as well as much immensely popular piano music. He had known Gottschalk in 1842 before the boy's departure for Paris. See *The Adventures of Vincent Wallace in New Zealand,* which is the closing chapter of Berlioz's *Evenings with the Orchestra.*

celebrated in Paris under the name of the *"pianiste compositeur louisianais."*

From my birth I had always lived in affluence—thanks to the successful speculations entered into by my father. Certain of being able to rely upon him, I quietly permitted myself to follow those pursuits in which I anticipated only pleasure and enjoyment. Poorly prepared for the realities of American life by my long sojourn in the factitious and enervating atmosphere of Parisian salons (where I easily discounted the success that my youth, my independent position, the education I had received, and a certain originality in the compositions I already had published partly justified), I found myself taken unawares when one day, constrained by necessity and the death of my father, hastened by a series of financial disasters, I found myself without resources other than my talents to enable me to perform the sacred duties bequeathed to me by him. I was obliged to pay his debts, of which my concerts at New Orleans already had in part lightened the weight, and to sustain in Paris a numerous family, my mother and six brothers and sisters.

Of all misery, the saddest is not that which betrays itself by its rags. Poverty in a black coat, that poverty which, to save appearances, smiles with death at the heart, is certainly the most poignant; then I understood it. Nevertheless, my brilliant success in Europe was too recent for me not to perceive a near and easy escape from my sad troubles. I believed success still possible. I then undertook a tour in New England. At Boston my first receipts exceeded one hundred dollars; at the second concert I made forty-nine dollars. I have not related that an hour before I was to begin a concert in Boston a dispatch from one of my uncles apprised me that my father was in the pangs of death and had just blessed me—a singular and touching wandering of his great intelligence at the moment of his dissolution—in seven languages, which he spoke admirably. I cannot describe to you my despair, but let those who comprehend it add to it the terrible necessity of appearing in public at such a moment. I might have put off the concert, but the expenses had been incurred; the least delay would have augmented my loss. I thought of those to whom I had become the only prop; I drove back my depair and played! I do not know what I did on that evening. H—— thought it his duty, in view of my prostration, to make known to the public the circumstances in which I was placed. I need not say that Mr. X., who, from my first appearance, had not ceased to disparage me in his musical journal, continued to attack me after this concert, not permitting the great affliction that had overwhelmed me to disarm him. Another newspaper had the melancholy courage to say that doubtless it was unfortunate that I had lost my father, but that the public had paid a dollar for the purpose of receiving a dollar's worth of music, and had nothing to do with the personal affairs of Mr. Gottschalk—a logic more rigorous than Christian.

Throughout all New England (where, I am eager to say, some years later I found the most sympathetic reception), there was but a succession of losses; A.S., in a newspaper, devoted a whole column to my kid gloves; another to my handsome appearance and my French manners. At P., after my first concert, attended by seventeen persons, one editor gave a facetious account, in which he asserted that he hated music, but that mine was less insupportable to him because, in the noise that I drew from my piano, there was no music. Be it as it may, I lost sixteen hundred dollars in a few months.

Killed by the gross attacks of which I had been the object, discouraged by the injustice of self-styled musical judges, who denied me every species of merit; undeceived, disgusted with a career that even among my own countrymen did not promise the means of providing for the wants of my family and myself, I returned to New York.

My compositions continued to have a large sale in Paris. Then it was that I received a letter from one of my old friends and patrons, the respectable old Countess de Flavigny, who afterward was appointed lady in waiting to the Empress Eugénie. She exhorted me to return to Paris, and held out to me the probability of my soon being appointed pianist to the court. But I was held back by diffidence. It was painful to me to return to Paris, first theater of my great success, and confess that I had not succeeded in my own country, America, which at this time was the El Dorado, the dream of artists, especially as the exaggerated accounts of the money that Jenny Lind had made there rendered my ill success more striking.

I had composed a few pieces, one of them of a melancholy

character with which was connected a touching episide of my journey to Santiago, Cuba, and seemed to me to unite the conditions requisite for popularity. A publisher bought it from me for fifty dollars, advising me to endeavor to copy the style of the pianist Gockel, of whom a certain piece—how I do not know—had just obtained a great run.

At last one day I played some of my compositions for Mr. Hall, the publisher. "Why do you not give a concert to make them known?" he said to me. "*Ma foi*," I answered him, "it is a luxury that my means no longer permit me!" "Bah! I will pay you one hundred dollars for a piano concert at Dodsworth's Rooms."

Eight days later I played my new pieces in this small hall (whose proportions are such that I should never wish to see them exceeded, as they are such that make the piano heard advantageously before a select audience): *The Banjo*, the *Marche de nuit*, the *Jota aragonesa*, and *Le Chant du soldat*. Its success surpassed my most brilliant expectations. During five months I continued, without interruption, a series of weekly concerts for the piano only, in the same place, without being forsaken by the public favor. *The Banjo, La Marche*, and many other pieces bought by Hall were published and sold with a rapidity that left no doubt as to the final result of Hall's speculation, which time has only corroborated. Everybody knows of the enormous edition that was published of *Banjo*, and *Marche de nuit*. I then concluded a contract that assured to Hall the exclusive rights to all my compositions for the United States. As Hall wished to possess my works written before those he had just published, and having faith in my talent as a composer, he addressed the publisher of the melancholy piece I have already spoken of, for the purpose of buying it. "Willingly," was the reply. "It does not sell at all; pay me the fifty dollars it has cost me, and it is yours." This little piece was *Last Hope*, of which more than thirty-five thousand copies have been published in America, and which still produces yearly to its publisher, after a run of more than twelve years,[2] twenty times the amount that it cost him. I always have kept at the bottom of my heart a sentiment of gratitude for the house of Hall, who first discovered that I was worth something; and from that moment

---

[2] *The Last Hope*, revised version, had been published in 1855.

dates the friendship that unites me to his family, and that time has only ripened.

But my ill will toward those publishers who, when I stood in my most need of them, continued only to discourage me increased with my success. Returned today to New York after an absence of six years, and in a position that I have conquered inch by inch, I avenged myself by refusing all those who approached me, one to offer five hundred, another one thousand dollars for only one piece. One publisher, the one who had first bought *The Last Hope* (a gentleman, I must say, toward whom I bear no grudge), offered me one thousand dollars for my *Murmures éoliens*. This sum made me smile on comparing it with the thirty dollars at which I had offered my pieces in vain some years before. It then was gratifying to me to give a proof of my gratitude to General Hall, with whom my contract had expired. I sent to him *Murmures éoliens, Pastorella e cavaliere, Ojos criollos,* and many other pieces, asking him to fix the conditions of a new contract, which I was ready to sign.

◇◇◇◇◇◇◇◇◇

New York, February, 1862

What astonishes me is again to find New York in 1862 at least as brilliant as when I left it for the South in 1857.

The majority of foreign journals give so opinionated an account of the events of our war that it is impossible, at a distance, to form an exact idea of the state of the country. For a year I have constantly read *that the theaters are closed; that the public finances and private fortunes are exhausted; that the North is a prey to famine; that the terrorism of Robespierre is revived by the American republicans; that they kill each other in full daylight.* (I came near having a duel in Puerto Rico for having doubted this fact, which was asserted by a Spanish officer); *and that bands of incendiaries have laid waste all our large houses.*

"Can you think of giving concerts before a public that wants bread?" one of my friends asked me in Havana on learning that I had decided to return to New York, and, although my national pride did not permit me to admit that he was right, I acknowledge, between ourselves, that I thought the same thing myself.

Let no one tax me with exaggeration. I still have in my possession a newspaper in which a correspondent writes from the United States that the depreciation of our money is such that he has seen a workman dying of hunger offer a baker one dollar in paper to obtain a piece of bread. The number of these veracious correspondents increased in direct ratio to our prosperity and the umbrage that the enemies of our government took at it.

There are few governments not interested in the fall of the republican edifice. The least enlightened fear it; the more liberal are jealous of it. "It is a fine thing in theory, but it is a Utopia," a celebrated statesman said to me. Unfortunately for the adversaries of democratic principles the thing so far seems possible, whatever they may do. The truth, carefully sifted by the organs of their press, sometimes reaches the people by fugitive gleams that set them to thinking. One understands that, under such conditions, they [the adversaries] have profited by the clouds that have obscured our political horizon, and that they have availed themselves of as an irrefutable argument.

When we consider the political importance and the commerce of the United States, the facilities of communication, the numerous works written on the country, we can hardly comprehend or explain the ignorance in which so many foreigners remain who are relatively instructed on the value of the three or four of the greatest nations of the globe. Viscount Duquesne, a French admiral, asked me in Havana in 1854 if one might venture in the environs of St. Louis without fear of being attacked by Indians. For many the country remains the same as it was when Chateaubriand wrote *Les Natchez,* and saw "*paroquets*" in the branches of the trees carried by the majestic floods of the "Meschacébé" (Mississippi).

The father of a talented French pianist who resides in New York wrote from Paris to his son some years ago to learn if the *fur trade was exclusively carried on by Indians in New York!*

Her Highness the Grand Duchess of Russia asked me in 1849 if Barnum was not one of our great statesmen! A great French newspaper made an army march in a few hours from Richmond to Charleston. I know that all this is so absurd that it appears almost impossible, but I do not advance anything that is not true and that I cannot prove. There certainly is an intelligent class who read and who know the truth; but it is not the most numerous, nor that most interested in doing us justice. Proudhomme, that vast and luminous mind, who always fights for progress, sees in the pioneer of the West only a *heroic assassin*, and in all Americans *half-civilized savages*. From Talleyrand, who said that *"l'Amérique est un pays de sales cochons et de cochons sales"* (America is a country of dirty and filthy swine), to Zimmerman, director of the piano classes at the Paris Conservatoire, who without hearing me refused to receive me because *"l'Amérique n'était qu'un pays de machines à vapeur"* (America was only a country of steam engines), there is not an eminent man who has not spat his petty spite upon the Americans.[3] Perhaps it is not out of place to say here that *le petit Américain*, refused as a pupil in 1841,[4] was appointed in 1849 to sit as judge on the same bench as Zimmerman at the examination for prizes at the Conservatoire.

There is no doubt that there are immense lacunæ in certain details of our civilization. Our appreciation of the *beaux-arts* is not always enlightened, and we treat them like parasites occupying a usurped place. The wheels of our government are, like our manners, too new not to grate upon the ear sometimes. We perhaps worship a little too much the golden calf, and do not kill the fatted calf often enough to feast the elect of thought. Each of us thinks himself as good as (if not better than) any other man—an excellent faith that engenders self-respect but often leads us to wish to reduce to our own level those to whose level we cannot attain. These little faults happily are not national traits; they appertain to all young societies. We are, in a word, like the beautiful children of whom Montaigne speaks, who bite the nurse's breast, and whom the exuberance of health sometimes renders turbulent.

I heard Brignoli[5] last night in *Marta*. This favorite tenor still has his beautiful voice, and has preserved, notwithstanding the

---

[3] Eighteen years before, Cherubini had refused the thirteen-year-old Liszt admission to the Conservatoire because he was a foreigner. Zimmerman, incidentally, was the father-in-law of Gounod.

[4] The year 1842, not 1841.

[5] Pasquale Brignoli, "the silver-voiced tenor," was born in 1824 in Naples and died in 1884 in New York. He came to the United States in 1855, and

progress of an *embonpoint* that annoys him, the aristocratic elegance that, with his fine hair and his handsome white neck, has given him so much success with the ladies. Notwithstanding the defects with which his detractors reproach him, he is an artist whom I admire above all singers, who are all, for the most part, uncouth. He understands music and knows how to judge a musical work. His enemies will be much astonished to learn that he knows by heart Hummel's Concerto in A minor,[6] which he studied when, as a child, he thought of becoming a pianist, and which he still plays in a charming manner! He knows how to sing, and if it were not for his fear of the public, which paralyzes all his powers, he would be classed among the best singers of the age. Besides, he is careful of his grooming, which, among artists, is one of the rarest qualities, and which I place among the most brilliant of those possessed by Brignoli. I knew him in 1849 in Paris, at the period when, still quite young, he made his début under the amorous aegis of the beautiful Madame R.[7]

My companion in the wilderness of M[atouba], the poor maniac, has followed me to New York. He is wild in the midst of the bustle of a great city. He is an excellent man, a striking example of the part that circumstances have in the formation of what is called a man of genius. He is a great man spoiled. The stuff was in him, but fate had willed otherwise. Born at Guadeloupe of parents of whom one was a Negress, the other a European, he developed his taste for music at an early age. He played on the violin when only eight years old, and taught himself to play the piano and to read. He wrote verses and read Voltaire, Rousseau, and the philosophers. But, unfortunately for him, that was before 1848. Slavery still existed in the French colony, and

---

sang in *Il Trovatore* at the opening of Philadelphia's Academy of Music in 1857. At a New York concert in February 1862 he played a duet with Gottschalk.

[6] Johann Nepomuk Hummel (1778–1837), a pianist, composer, pupil of Mozart, Haydn, Salieri, Clementi, and Albrechtsberger, was a fellow-pupil of Beethoven and teacher of Czerny, Heller, Henselt, and Thalberg. When Liszt, as a boy of eleven, made his Viennese debut, he played, among other works, a concerto by Hummel.

[7] This entry, with modifications, appeared in the *Atlantic Monthly* for May 1865.

he soon learned that because of the prejudices of caste the sphere in which he must move became more restricted as soon as he tried to become free.[8]

[After Gottschalk's New York concert of February 11, 1862, he played frequently in New York, Brooklyn, Philadelphia, Newark, Baltimore, and Washington, sharing the program with a vocal company composed of Isabella Hinckley, Brignoli, Susini, and Mancusi, and directed by Max Maretzek. (The New Orleans Daily Picayune had this to say about Isabella Hinckley, October 7, 1860: "Signorina Inclini [why will she not be native and democratic enough to call herself plain Miss Hinckley.].") Sometimes he was the stellar attraction (Grand Gottschalk Gala Night, March 15, at the Academy of Music in Philadelphia); on other occasions he played a more subsidiary role.]

◇◇◇◇◇◇◇◇◇

March 5

My first concert at Washington given—great success. Audience varied! diplomats, generals, etc. In the first row I recognized General Herron, my old friend from New Granada.[9]

The porch of the hotel is always crowded. There are some thousands of soldiers, uniforms of every nation: German, French, Polish, Austrian, Croats, etc. I particularly remark a regiment from the West, I think, whose shako, a sort of monument, which has in back the appearance of a Tyrolese hat, and in front is ornamented with a visor and surmounted, not by a plume, but by a squirrel's tail, which twists around the felt crown and covers the top. This crowd, these diverse uniforms, these different idioms, which mingle in every way, remind me of a scene in Schiller's *Wallenstein.*

After the concert, a squint-eyed gentleman requested me, with a mysterious air, to grant him an interview for ten minutes to-morrow. He has come! I thought it was for the purpose of bleed-

---

[8] Gottschalk evidently is referring to Firmin Moras, who became his faithful valet and factotum.

[9] New Granada was the name given, at various times and under various conditions, to an area that included what is now Colombia, Venezuela, Ecuador, and Panama.

ing my purse, I am so accustomed to that. The number of fathers out of work, of orphans of tender age, and of widows without support is invariably singularly developed the morning after a concert, and my lodgings are generally overrun. But my squint-eyed professor is simply a professor of physiology at the university. He has remarked, he said, that I played more quickly than any other, and as he has seen that one of his confraternity, in a book just published, has affirmed that the number of percussions given by the human nerves could not transcend twenty-five in a second, he would be happy to prove the falsity of his rival's assertions. He dared to hope that I would confirm his observations. He gave me a long dissertation and repeated to me that he was happy to have known the pianist who could make more than twenty-five *percussions* in a second.

O Art! where art thou? I took on enormous proportions in his eyes by telling him that I play the *Perpetual Motion* by Weber in less than two minutes. What would you wish me to have said to this ignoramus? Could I descend from the pedestal on which he had placed me? Here I am, then, definitely classed by this squint-eyed gentleman among the most powerful of known motors.

Third concert tomorrow, March 8. Second, this evening, the seventh. Tomorrow I shall go to General Wadsworth's camp. Two young cavalry majors are to send us horses, the roads being so broken that it will be difficult, even with our hackneys, to get to the camp, which is on the other side of the Potomac. The government has done us the favor of sending us a safe-conduct.

Mr. Seward, the Secretary of State, desires to see me, not as an artist only, but also as a Louisianian remaining faithful to the Constitution.

The day before yesterday, the house of Baron Mercier, the French Minister, was burned. All the furniture and the wardrobe of Monsieur and Madame were lost to the extent that Madame the Baroness had to borrow stockings from Madame Rigo. Interesting details!

The city has the appearance of having just been taken by assault. Military everywhere. Soldiers on every side. An immense crowd.

I have solemnly taken the oath of allegiance to the government at Washington. My horror of slavery made me emancipate, ten years ago, three slaves that belonged to me. Although born in the South, I recognize but one principle—that of the Constitution. In a republic where universal suffrage is not a chimera, where the citizens are free and intelligent men and not servile machines, where the ambitious never separate their personal glory from that of their country, no honest and republican conscience ought to feel embarrassed. What timorous minds find in the Catholic dogma regarding doubtful points I find blindly in politics. I bow down before that interpretation made by the supreme authority with so much the more facility as having the conviction that those who rule the destinies of the country are truly the legitimate expression of the will of the greatest number, and I know that thus I fulfill the fundamental duties of the republican system.

Besides, the South—whose courage and heroism I honor, while deploring the blindness that has precipitated it into a war without issue—the South leans upon two political errors. In the nineteenth century, nationalities are no longer broken—the general movement tends to unification. No one fraction of the people has the right to reclaim its autonomy, if it does not carry with it greater guarantees of progress and civilization than those of the majority enslaving it. But the South in wishing to destroy one of the most beautiful political monuments of modern times—the American Union—carries with it only slavery. It is, indeed, unbecoming to my fellow-citizens of the South to ask for the liberty of reclaiming their independence, when this independence is to be made use of only for the conservation of the most odious of abuses and the most flagrant outrage upon liberty. I do not have any illusions regarding the Negro. I believe him very inferior morally to the white. No race so maltreated as this by chance has been could have remained as (Remaining part not found.)

~~~~~~~~

[In mid-March 1862, Gottschalk left for his first tour of the West, with the inevitable opera troupe, this time composed of the conductor Emanuele Muzio, Carlotta Patti (sister of Adelina), Pasquale Brignoli, the baritone Susini, and the basso Mancusi. After concerts in Cincinnati, Louisville, and St. Louis the musicians arrived at Chicago.]

Gottschalk as a very young man. Lithograph by Guglielmi after a painting by Luigi Rubio

Gottschalk as he looked on his return from Europe. From an early edition (William Hall & Son, New York) of Bamboula

Photograph of Gottschalk taken at *La Serena, Chile,*
north of *Valparaíso,* in 1867

Drawing referring to Gottschalk's first monster concert, performed by thirty-one pianists and two orchestras at the Theatro Lyrico Fluminense, Rio de Janeiro, October 5, 1869, from A Vida Fluminense, Rio de Janeiro, October 2, 1869

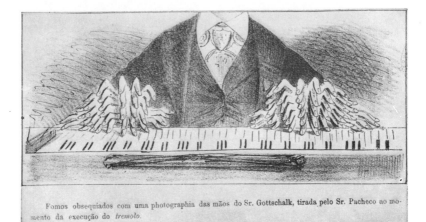

Fomos obsequiados com uma photographia das mãos do Sr. Gottschalk, tirada pelo Sr. Pacheco no momento da execução do *tremolo*.

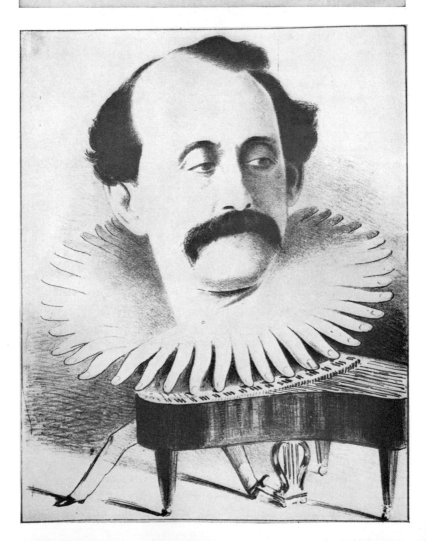

Caricature of Gottschalk (colored lithograph) by Joseph
Mill, from Ba-ta-clan, a French "Journal Satirique Illustré,"
Rio de Janeiro, June 19, 1869. The four-line verse reads:
"When on an ungrateful instrument/One knows as he
does how to express one's soul,/Why press so strongly/The
pedal of publicity?"

TOP: Caricature by Henrique Fleiuss, from A Semana Illustrada, Rio de
Janeiro, July 8, 1869. The caption reads: "We were presented with a
photograph of the hands of Mr. Gottschalk, taken by Sr. Pacheco at
the moment when he was playing Tremolo. J. F. Pacheco was the most
noted photographer in Rio during the second half of the reign of Dom
Pedro II.
BOTTOM: Drawing by Henrique Fleiuss, alluding to Gottschalk's virtuosity, from A Semana Illustrada, Rio de Janeiro, May 30, 1869

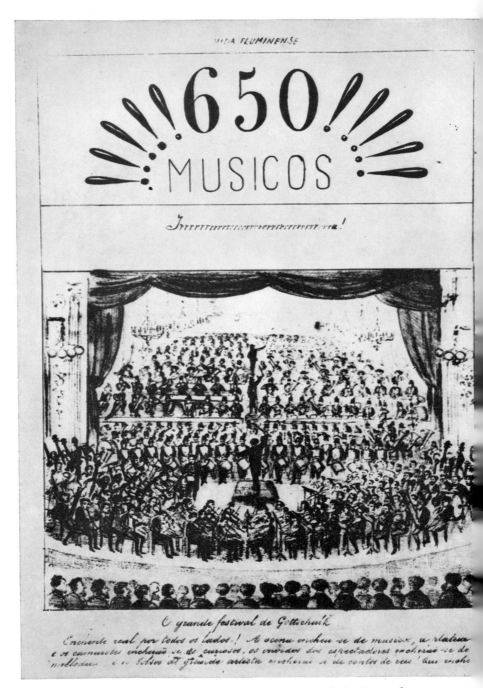

Drawing by Angelo Agostini of the great Gottschalk Festival,
his last public appearance, from A Vida Fluminense,
Rio de Janeiro, December 4, 1869

O Funeral de "Gottschalk."

O ultimo retrato de Gottschalk

feito (d'après nature) no salão da Philarmonica Fluminense no dia em que, depois de embalsamado pelo D.º Souza, o corpo do insigne pianista alli esteve exposto.

Gottschalk's funeral through the streets of Rio de Janeiro, December 19, 1869
BOTTOM: The last drawing of Gottschalk, by Angelo Agostini, made after the embalm-
Gottschalk's body in the salon of the Philharmonica Fluminense, Rio de Janeiro
(Both from A Vida Fluminense, Rio de Janeiro, December 25, 1869)

Bust of Gottschalk by Franceschi. Formerly the property
of Clara Gottschalk Peterson, in the Milton W. Latter Library, New Orlea

◇◇◇◇◇◇◇◇◇◇

Chicago, April 14

The corps of General Wallace arrived here last evening.

American industry is everywhere. The city of Chicago is almost on a level with Lake Michigan, and was flooded about five years ago. In certain quarters the yards of the houses had the appearance of little lakes. The whole city has been raised from ten to twelve feet. This has been done by means of immense steam machines that raise house, foundation, and edifice without shaking them. The Tremont Hotel, which occupies nine hundred square yards, of cut stone, and six stories high, was raised eleven feet without any of its inhabitants being aware of it. Not the least shake; only, in leaving the hotel, instead of descending five steps to the level of the pavement, it was necessary to descend a dozen. The city of Chicago alone has at this time in its storehouses one hundred thousand barrels of flour and five million bushels of grain. In a few days Lake Michigan will be navigated by more than one hundred strong vessels laden with the products of the West, destined for the seacoast.

◇◇◇◇◇◇◇◇◇◇

Milwaukee (State of Wisconsin), April 15, 1862

I have just seen, exposed in a tinsmith's shop, a trophy of the Indian War. It is the banner of Ma-na-wau-na-ma-kee—in English "Great Hole in the Day." This chief, who commanded the Sioux, became celebrated for his audacity, his astuteness, and his cruelty. (Since this was written, the Sioux have ranged the State of Minnesota and have massacred eight or nine hundred of the inhabitants.) I have seen the portrait of a warrior who had killed *two men, six women, and eighteen children.* One hundred of these miserable beings have been shot and forty of their chiefs hanged. The trophy I have spoken of is a long pole, terminated by a little ring that makes it resemble a butterfly net; over the ring is stretched, like a tambourine, the skin of the neck, of the head— all the scalp, in fact—of another chief, whom Ma-na-wau-na-ma-kee killed in battle. The hair of the vanquished, very long, and black as a crow, hung from the ring over the pole like the Turkish standards. The wind, shaking these long locks, caused the hundreds of copper and silver rings and the eagle feathers attached to them to jingle in a very sinister manner. Every ring indicates an enemy killed and scalped by Ma-na-wau-na-ma-kee. Frightful to behold are the ears, the nostrils, and the gaping holes of the eyes on this human skin, the wrong side of which is covered with brilliant red resin, which adds to the horror of this bloody spoil. I had a great desire to buy it, but I was asked eighteen hundred francs for it— three hundred and sixty dollars.

Milwaukee is one of those Western towns of the United States which, born but yesterday, are built as if by magic. Peopled principally by Germans (in a population of sixty thousand souls they number forty-five thousand), it promises—thanks to the industry of this economical, hard-working, and industrious race—to become one of the most flourishing depots for grain in the West.

It already possesses a Philharmonic Society, a theater, a concert hall, and a magnificent hotel. Do not forget that we are one thousand miles from New York and very close to the Indian territories. The cook of the hotel is a *bordelais*. The good man is wild with joy since our arrival. He had not spoken French for ten years. He had heard me, it appears, on my passage from Bordeaux in 1852, and absolutely insisted on giving me a dinner, to which I invited my traveling companions—Brignoli the tenor, Susini the baritone, and Maestro Muzio, the friend and pupil of Verdi.[1] If you have ever been to Bordeaux, you must retain the remembrance that they know how to eat there, and that the *cèpes à l'huile* and the *rognons au beurre frais* deserve to partake of the glory of the Château-Lafitte and St.-Émilion. I must add that our good *bordelais*, true artist that he is, made it a point of honor, and I declare that the *salmis* that he served up to us were

---

[1] Emanuele Muzio (1825–90) was Verdi's only pupil, and, from 1844 to 1847, his personal representative, editor, secretary, chronicler, and billiards partner. In 1848, a political refugee in Switzerland, he received financial aid from Verdi. Although he had to refuse Verdi's recommendation that he conduct the première of *Aïda* in Cairo in 1871, he conducted the Parisian première of *La Forza del Destino* in 1876. Verdi was inconsolable at the death of Muzio, his "sincere, devoted friend for about fifty years."

all incomparable. We have invited him (the proprietor cook) and his family to our concerts.

I had a shave before the concert. My barber, while scraping my chin, assured me, with an important air, that I must be upon my best behavior, for "we have here a gentleman amateur of great talent." Mercy on us! Who shall deliver us from these amateurs of great talent, whose species multiply and monopolize all the little villages of our planet?

Milwaukee is on the shores of Lake Michigan, which lake, by the by, is as large as the Black Sea and has swallowed up, during the stormy season this year, forty or fifty vessels.

◇◇◇◇◇◇◇◇◇

April 18 [*1862*]

My concerts are not very profitable. We are in Holy Week, and neither the Episcopalians nor the Catholics go to concerts in the second half of Lent.

At one of the stations, going from Chicago to Toledo, we found a convoy of wounded from the last battle—Pittsburg Landing. It is a heart-rending sight. All the ladies of the place are nursing them. The Miss Nightingales multiply here.

◇◇◇◇◇◇◇◇◇

April 20

Yesterday the ice finally broke in the strait between lakes Michigan and Huron, permitting the steamers of the Far West to return eastward. The West furnishes grain in abundance to the New and the Old Worlds.

◇◇◇◇◇◇◇◇◇

Toledo, April 20

The rage for conversion, the fever of proselytism, which constitutes one of the characteristic traits of Americans, is discovered at every step we travel. At the hotel we found framed placards in which the Reverend So-and-so very cordially invites his brother travelers to visit his church. Sermons every Sunday at 10:30 o'clock, 1 o'clock, and 7 o'clock in the evening. It is a great satisfaction to an American to take to church a friend whose faith is doubtful. To him the excellence of his own religion is so clear that he has no doubt about the conversion of anyone he takes to his church. It is a certain conquest, and he has saved his friend.

◇◇◇◇◇◇◇◇◇

Hamilton, Canada, April 23

English soldiers, jointed dolls all of a piece, very neat, but brutalized by the discipline and religious worship that the so-called liberal education inculcates in each Englishman for the hierarchy and the fictitious superiority of name and money.

The taste for music is not well developed. An officer very candidly said to me after the concert that the people were not satisfied. I ought to have played themes from the operas *La Sonnambula*, *Lucia*—in short, a London repertory. "That is," said he, "some real music. You should have played some themes without ornament."

Let us never listen to the public. We should hang ourselves in despair. At St. Louis the wife of a judge said to me that I was deficient in charm, that my music was too learned (I had just played a transcription of the *"Miserere"*), that I ought to play national airs—"Yankee Doodle," "Hail Columbia," "Dixie's Land," etc. At Havana, Count O'Reilley discovered that I played too loud. At New York, H—— said that I played too soft.

We took a carriage ride at Toledo with M——, Carlotta Patti, and a young German, a music seller. I gave him a cigar. At the moment I was least expecting it, he was taken with nausea, and, *ex abrupto*, he unintentionally besprinkled me.

◇◇◇◇◇◇◇◇◇

April 24

Composed a serenade for Simpson, on the words of a friend of Pond's.

◇◇◇◇◇◇◇◇◇

April 26

In the car I met Monsignor the Bishop of Chicago (Roman Catholic), who was on his way to New York to embark for Europe. Mlle Patti had already been to see him to obtain the release of her brother Carlito, whose name appeared in a list of prisoners from the South. The bishop lives in a beautiful building that overlooks the lake.

Return to New York from Lockport, a journey of seventeen and a half hours. Lockport will be a very pretty town, but for the present it is only a village, notwithstanding its eleven thousand inhabitants.

Concert of four hundred and fifty persons, who appeared never to have seen anything of the kind before.[2]

A short time ago, a young soldier of the Army of the Potomac was brought before a court-martial for having been found asleep while on duty. An example was necessary. Neither the age of the soldier, almost a youth, nor his previous good conduct could influence the judges. He was condemned to death. The President was informed of it and, taking into account the irreproachable character of the poor condemned one, immediately sent a telegraphic dispatch to the commanding general telling him that, by virtue of his power, he pardoned the young man.

---

[2] Gottschalk played in Lockport, New York, at Ringueberg Hall, on April 25, assisted by "Carlotta Patti, the charming cantatrice . . . Mr. Simpson, the distinguished English tenor; Signor Morino, the eminent baritone." Probably representing "the very elite of Lockport" at the "musical feast," the *Lockport Daily Journal and Courier* of April 26, while saying that "Mr. Gottschalk is a wonderful proficient on the piano," regretted "that the Anglo-Saxon tongue is not better adapted to the real spirit and soul of vocal music" and found it "not a little singular that music is never quite so witching as when it takes on a 'foreign air' . . . We still assert that the real power and soul of vocal music consists in elocution, and that distinctness of utterance is as much a part of good musical elocution, as it is a part of good reading. But the concert last evening was a very fine one. The reason that we could not understand the language was purely our own incompetency, and fault. We certainly enjoyed the musical sounds."

◇◇◇◇◇◇◇◇◇◇

April 27[3]

At a station on my journey back to New York, a crowd consisting of women, children, and a respectable old man in mourning, awaited the arrival of the train at the station. The old man frequently wiped his eyes with his handkerchief. The conductor informed us that he was the father of a young officer killed in the last battle (Pittsburg Landing), whose body was expected, and was about to be received by his family and friends. The coffin will not arrive this evening. The old man, with the singular stoicism of his kind, coldly asked the conductor for the time, and, when our train left, we saw him with his little company disappear behind a turn in the road. In the background we saw the principal houses of a pretty little village whose inhabitants all seemed to be in a state of excitement. What a sad thing is war! The sky is blue, the air bland, the verdure begins to appear! I never shall easily forget that poor old father who, with trembling lips and eyes red with tears, thought that he concealed his grief from us.

[During the following four weeks Gottschalk played frequently in New York, Brooklyn, and Philadelphia.]

◇◇◇◇◇◇◇◇◇◇

May 1862 [*Written in retrospect*]

St. Louis is the capital of Missouri and contains about two hundred thousand inhabitants. It is a dull and tiresome town. Like all American cities of French or Spanish origin, it is composed of heterogeneous elements that have not yet amalgamated. Society is divided into separate cliques. The Catholics (old French Creoles from Louisiana), who, as I have already said, went up the Mississippi at the end of the last century and founded St. Louis, are in the majority and are so much the more fervent because the Episcopalians (Anglo-Saxons), also very numerous, are animated

---

[3] Gottschalk and his colleagues had performed April 7–12 in St. Louis. The *Missouri Daily Democrat* noted that *The Union* was greeted with hostility by the "secesh" element (secessionists).

with the spirit of proselytism and make a bitter war on them, which the others return with interest. The Germans (they are numerous here, as throughout the West) have organized a Philharmonic Society, which performs the works of Beethoven, Mendelssohn, Schumann, and Wagner. I was introduced to an old German musician with uncombed hair, bushy beard, in constitution like a bear, in disposition the amenity of a boar at bay to a pack of hounds. I know this type; it is found everywhere. It is time that many great unknown musicians should be convinced that such carelessness is the maladroit imitation of the surly and misanthropic behavior of the great symphonist of Bonn, that it does not constitute a sufficient title to merit the admiration and respect of their contemporaries. Besides, soap is not incompatible with genius, and it is now proved that the daily use of a comb does not exercise any injurious influence on the lobes of the brain.

St. Louis is not a handsome city because so much is lacking. The streets are badly paved and its buildings are irregular, but it possesses an interest for me that none of the sumptuous new cities of our continent inspires in me. It recalls New Orleans to me.[4] The names, even, of the old families are familiar to my ears. Indeed, a great number of the old French inhabitants of Louisiana ascended the river and took up residence at St. Louis. I even see that the city was founded by an old Louisianian.

I too often have present in my memory one of those stupid remarks of Trollope in his book on the United States. Thus, when he speaks of Baltimore, which he loves, he found in it an English air and drank excellent Madeira there; but let me be permitted to say that to me St. Louis is a kind of relaxation from the noisy isolation (!) in which I live, thanks to my respectable friend Mr. B., at whose house I always find a homelike hospitality, and whose family circle always recalls to me the domestic hearth.

I have been to mass at Father Ryan's church. The music rather pleased me, notably a trio of men's voices without any accompaniment, in which, to my astonishment, the voices did not seem ardently to wish to shake off the yoke of the tune to run at random into independent regions. The tenor, a German, I be-

---

[4] Gottschalk's affection for his native city was shared by his brother and sisters, who dedicated *Notes of a Pianist* "To the City of New Orleans, the Birthplace of Louis Moreau Gottschalk."

lieve, reached B *flat* from the chest, which would have done honor to any artist.

Alas! why does the priest who chants the mass invariably think himself obliged to get out of key? Music is the attire in which the words are clothed to do more honor to God. It ought, so to speak, to perfume the thoughts. When shall we understand that to sing false and through the nose is unworthy of God? That which is unworthy of our ears is still more so of God. What torture it is for the faithful who have ears to hear the whole of the Gospel chanted a key lower than the organ accompaniment! The priest generally commences correctly but lowers his tone insensibly. In spite of the organist, who gives him the keynote, he soon passes to a lower one, and would descend insensibly into the cellar if the litany did not finish in time.

Why give to God the prerogative of bad music? What! shall we sing just and true in our concerts, and sing false and badly to God? Understand that in the church, I do not wish trilling or theatrical expressions, which shock me and destroy holy meditation, any more than I would permit wit or frivolous elegance of language in pulpit eloquence.

Noticed in the choir of the church a tablet with this inscription—

Donné par le roy de France, 1818.

At St. Louis they gave a serenade to General Halleck, who came out on the balcony and made a speech. He announced, in the midst of an enthusiasm impossible to describe, the capture of the island and the fort that for three weeks had resisted the flotilla of Commodore Foote and the army of General Pope. We have taken five thousand prisoners, one hundred twenty-five cannons of large caliber, ten thousand guns, three generals, etc., and at the same time the bloody battle of Corinth took place: twenty thousand dead and wounded—a sad victory!—and even sterile, as Beauregard has gone back, unhindered, to his entrenchments at Corinth, where he is protected by formidable works and an army of one hundred thousand men.

Last Sunday at St. Louis they expected, at six o'clock in the evening, the first arrival of the wounded from Pittsburg Landing (Corinth). Besides the ordinary hospitals, they have converted two or three of the most beautiful buildings in the city into hospitals for the same purpose.

At Cincinnati I saw a superb library and lecture hall of the Young Men's Mercantile Association. There are three hundred thousand volumes—all the French classics—I found there *Le Nord,* the *Gazette d'Augsburg,* the *Charivari, Figaro,* all the illustrated papers of Europe, and all the great newspapers of the world. The expenses of this establishment are thirty-seven thousand dollars per annum, which is defrayed by an annual contribution of three dollars from each of the members. I saw there a superb bust in white marble by our great sculptor, Hiram Powers.[5]

The commerce of Cincinnati is confined principally to lard and hams. Three or four million hams are shipped from this, the largest city of Ohio, to every part of America. I have visited the principal slaughterhouse and manufactory of hams. An ingenious and gigantic steam machine seizes the poor animals, kills them, scalds them, cuts them up, cleans them, washes and salts them. All this is done without interruption, and if you have the patience to go to watch the other end of the machine, you will see them come out of it in the form of a ham, ready to be eaten, from the poor innocent pig who entered the other side of the machine full of confidence. Nine hundred hogs are thus dispatched daily![6]

◇◇◇◇◇◇◇◇◇

May 26 [*Philadelphia*]

The news received yesterday, Sunday, of the defeat of Banks by Jackson has aroused patriotic enthusiasm, which the rapidly succeeding victories of the last two months had weakened by inspiring an exaggerated serenity. The Seventh New York Regiment, composed exclusively of young men belonging to the aristocracy of that metropolitan city, leaves tonight for Washington. It numbers twelve hundred able-bodied men. Seven other regiments leave New York tomorrow.

The State of Massachusetts will send ten or twelve thousand more in a few days. They fear that the Confederacy, taking the

[5] Hiram Powers was born in Woodstock, Vermont, in 1805. He was one of several American artists of the time who spent most of their lives in Italy; he died in Florence in 1873.

[6] Gottschalk was not the only traveler to comment on the abattoirs of Cincinnati. See Frederick Marryat, edited by S. W. Jackman: *A Diary in America, with Remarks on Its Institutions* (New York: Alfred A. Knopf; 1962), pp. 222, 223.

offensive, plans to march on Washington. There was a riot yesterday in Baltimore. The people wanted to hang a man who expressed secessionist sentiments. An imposing police force guards the streets.

A bad business for me, who ought to give a concert there in two days. I understand very well how to fill the hall, but it is dangerous. It would be to announce that I would play my piece called *The Union* and my variations on "Dixie's Land." In the first I intercalate "Yankee Doodle" and "Hail Columbia." The second is a Southern Negro air of which the Confederates, since the beginning of the war, have made a national air. It is to the music of "Dixie's Land" that Beauregard's troops invariably charge the soldiers of the North.[7] At the point at which men's minds are now the hall would be full of partisans of both sections, who certainly would come to blows. But I should make three or four thousand dollars. It is true that in the tumult I might be the first one choked.

Superb concert at the Academy in Philadelphia. The passengers who left today (this morning) for Washington have not been able to get farther than Baltimore, the trains having been taken entirely by the government for the purpose of transporting with the least delay the volunteers from the Northern states, who are pouring in from all parts and are burning to meet with the Confederates. Tonight all the generals, majors, brigadiers, and colonels of the troops from the State of Pennsylvania have received orders from the state government to alert their soldiers and leave in twenty-four hours. The State of Pennsylvania already has furnished one hundred thousand men; it will send eight thousand more from here in four days; the State of New York, one hundred thousand men.

I have played *The Union*. Unheard-of enthusiasm. Circumstances gave it a real interest, which has been the pretext for a noisy and patriotic demonstration by the audience. Recalls, encores, hurrahs, etc.!

---

[7] Dan Emmett (Daniel Decatur Emmett), a Northerner, wrote "Dixie" as a walk-around for Bryant's Minstrels in 1859. He acknowledged that in this kind of music he aimed always "to be true to the Negro peculiarities of song. . . ."

If I had played it in Baltimore at this time, when the excitement is at its height, I probably would have been knocked down.

◇◇◇◇◇◇◇◇◇

[*May*] *1862*

After having given fifteen concerts in New York, and eight in Philadelphia, I left for Baltimore and Washington. My impatience greatly increases as I approach the theater of war. I desire, above all, to see the Army of the Potomac. The advanced lines of the Confederates are but a few miles from the federal capital.

From Philadelphia to Baltimore the route presented nothing new to me. It only recalled a trip I made in 1856, from Washington to New York, during which myself and four or five hundred other travelers in the train were on the point of dying of cold and hunger. We were surprised by a great snowstorm, so furious that in a few hours the track was obstructed completely. We remained stationary the whole night. Our provision of wood and coal was exhausted, our food also. The cold became insupportable; the morning found us literally buried under the snow, masses of which were piled up above the doors of the cars. Our position was no longer tenable; our only hope was to see arrive, I think from Wilmington, the nearest town, a snowplow and a party of laborers. While we were waiting, hunger made its demands, children wept, the women cried lamentably, the conductor swore like an Irishman, and I myself shivered with cold. All this made a frightful tumult. Mounted on the roof of a car, I scanned the countryside, which, as far as the eye could see, presented the aspect of a gigantic cream cheese on which a few flies had been caught. The country was intersected with ditches and brooks; it was out of the question for us to venture through the snow, the depth of which seemed prodigious. At last I saw a man on a sled a quarter of a mile off. With my handkerchief and my arms I made a series of telegraphic signs so violent that the farmer who drove the sled stopped and motioned to me to come to him, pointing out the direction I must take to avoid falling in the holes or ditches hidden by the snow. After having disappeared twenty times, to be buried anew, on coming to the surface I arrived almost frozen at the sled. My man reached a road he knew. In two hours I arrived at Wilmington and forgot my sufferings before a huge fire and a slice of roast beef. As to my traveling companions, whom I left to get out the best way they could (I have many times accused myself for having abandoned them at a critical moment), they arrived hungry and angry at nightfall.

The winter of 1856 was one of the severest ever experienced in New York. The bay itself was frozen over. From New York to Albany the Hudson was frozen so hard that wheeled vehicles traveled the river for the distance of one hundred fifty-five miles. One night when I was returning from Brooklyn, where I had been to give a concert, our steamer was blocked by the ice at the falling of the tide, and I did not arrive in New York until six o'clock in the morning—that is to say, we had taken seven hours to cross what every day, under ordinary circumstances, takes only five or six minutes. The boats used for crossing in winter are of iron; the prow of each is armed with a blade of steel which cuts the ice and makes a channel through the solid surface.

At this moment the weather is beautiful. The sun floods the country joyfully. The green fields recall to me those of Escaut; there is not one irregularity. The Delaware River flows on peaceably. At every station I notice pickets of regulars. Every branch of the railroad line and every bridge are guarded by posts of volunteers. We reach the Chesapeake, the width of which is considerable in this place.

◇◇◇◇◇◇◇◇◇

Chesapeake

Crossed in going to Washington May 27, 1862. Springtime. Health below zero.

◇◇◇◇◇◇◇◇◇

Route to Washington

I still notice pickets of regulars at every station, at every branch of the road, and at every bridge. I just have another proof of that incessant activity of mind which torments the Yankee. We have in our car many individuals whom, by their appearance, I judge to be Western farmers. Our train stops to await the one from Washington; one of the farmers has profited by it to get out. From here I see him walking in a field alongside the road; he has dug a little hole with his heel, and he is about to study the nature of the ground. No doubt if he finds it rich he will think nothing of quitting his farm in the West to establish another in these latitudes.

The *adaptability* of the Yankee is wonderful. He is ready to set his hand to anything, to settle down anywhere if he sees the least chance of success. His imperturbable confidence in himself, an indomitable fund of energy, and, we also must say, a greediness for gain that too often extinguishes every other feeling explain his facility in adapting himself to all the circumstances of life. My music publisher, Hall, was first a lawyer; afterward, by turn, a dealer in furniture, manufacturer of guitars, music publisher, piano manufacturer, member of Congress, senator of the State of New York, general of militia, and today he is to be found in his music shop, busy at work, making bargains, and selling my compositions. I ought to add that through all these numerous changes he has merited the esteem of his fellow-citizens by the incorruptible honesty of his dealings and the uprightness of his mind.

◈◈◈◈◈◈◈◈◈

In the Cars going to Washington, May 27

Scarcely was the proclamation of the President published (in which he calls for reinforcements to defend Washington in case the Confederates take the offensive) when at once all the soldiers of the Northern states were on foot. In twenty-four hours five hundred thousand men were equipped, armed, and on the march for Washington. The federal army already amounts to nearly a million men; with the reinforcements they will receive from the National Guards not serving as national troops, they may number a million and a half.

Our train has a car, fitted like a kitchen for an excellent restaurant, which ocupies the head of the train. A servant comes to hand to each traveler the bill of fare for the day, which is, *ma foi*, very varied and tempting. At Philadelphia, as in all the large towns on the route that had to be traveled by the troops on the

way to the theater of war, the ladies and young gentlemen have
formed associations for the purpose of providing food for the
different divisions at each of the stages. In the city of Philadelphia
alone, the ladies have given two suppers and two dinners to three
hundred fifty thousand men.

Needless to say, these succors are spontaneous and voluntary,
as the government provides the ordinary rations for the troops.

In every village the ladies are enrolled as nurses, and I assure
you that, on seeing at St. Louis the white hands that dressed the
wounds of Halleck's soldiers wounded at Pittsburg Landing, I
have more than once regretted that my laborious profession did
not leave me the least hope of being thus, one day, the object of
these touching cares of our beautiful and charitable patriotic
ladies.

3 o'clock P.M. At a branch of the railway we are stopping to
let a train of soldiers pass us; it is the Fifth Volunteer Regiment
of New York Artillery going to Washington. They exchange
three enthusiastic cheers with us, and are out of sight, their train
being "an express."

The restaurant boys pass through the cars with glasses of lemonade, ice cream, and cake. Decidedly these Yankees are the only
true travelers in the world. At St. Louis I was struck with the
marvelous comfort of the sleeping cars, in which, for one dollar
more, a magnificent bed is prepared for you, with elastic mattress
and pillows. The cars are arranged to enable them to give every
family the number of beds it desires. As soon as day dawns, they
are again converted into ordinary cars. The mechanism by which
the beds are made is most ingenious and does honor to the inventive spirit of the Americans.

◇◇◇◇◇◇◇◇◇◇

Washington, May 30 [1862]

I was present at the rehearsal of a concert that is to take place
at the Convent of the Sisters of the Visitation during a fair for the
poor. The convent, which the mother superior invited me to visit,
comprises a small park, a monastery for the sisters, a concert hall,
magnificent halls for study and for the recreation of the scholars,
large gardens, a beautiful collection of philosophical equipment,
and spacious dormitories that hold one hundred beds.

The young girls who are receiving their education here at this time are nearly all from the South, and many of them have not heard from their relatives for nearly a year. A charity school and a home for the poor are attached to the convent. The kind reception that these good sisters gave me prevents me from expressing my opinion of their music under pain of being horribly ungrateful. It may suffice for you to know that the only professor of music in the convent is an *English sister*, seventy years old, who teaches the harp, the piano (I was about to say the harpsichord), and singing, and whose compositions constitute the whole repertoire of the pupils. One of the pupils, the daughter of General B[utler], who has taken New Orleans and occupies it at this moment, has made in my honor an incursion into profane music by playing for me in a stormy manner *L'Orage* [*The Storm*], a *fantasia* by Lacombe, and Ascher's fantasy on *Lucrezia*.

Two hundred most charming young girls were present at this preparatory rehearsal. Some of them who had been to my concerts knew me. I had requested the mother superior not to ask me to play, the fatigue of my journey and of my concerts forcing me to avoid all superfluous effort, but soon two of the sisters got up and, calling to their assistance two young girls, who introduced themselves to me as being the daughters of General W——, Governor of Louisiana, asked me as a compatriot to satisfy the whole community's desire to hear me play.

On my leaving, the mother superior presented me in the name of the scholars with a box containing some pieces of charming embroidery, which I take precious care of in remembrance of the pretty white and rosy little fingers that worked them.

The convent is in Georgetown, three miles from Washington, on an eminence overlooking the countryside. There is nothing more picturesque. In the chapel they made me take notice of a very fine tablet presented to the community by King Charles X. On entering the city we met a convoy of rebel prisoners and some wagons filled with wounded. This afternoon a regiment of volunteers from Rhode Island has made its entry. This regiment numbers one thousand two hundred men, and has answered, in three days, the call of the President, although they were five hundred miles away.

◇◇◇◇◇◇◇◇◇◇

Washington

There was at Washington a young English juggler, prestidigitator, and professor of the piano. His lessons not succeeding, he took to traveling as a virtuoso prestidigitator. His exhibitions of sleight-of-hand are embellished with pianoforte variations—to which the name he has given himself on changing his profession (of Palmer he has made Heller) gives a certain interest, many persons thinking that he is the author of *La Chasse*, while he has only become the rival of Robert Houdin.[8]

It is said that Titiens and Negrini are engaged by Ullman for next winter, also Ristori. The first two will certainly have great success. I have strong doubts about the last. Except in New York, Philadelphia, and Boston, where there are many foreigners, Italian is unintelligible, and a course in Japanese would do as well as the tragedies of Alfieri or of Pellico for an audience of honest Yankees. I hope Ristori may not be disappointed. The success of Rachel in the United States must not be considered as evidence of the taste of the Americans for foreign actors. Rachel had a name consecrated by a series of triumphs without parallel for twenty-five years. Her name had pierced the envelope of indifference to foreign art which is peculiar to Americans. Besides, everybody understands, or ought to understand, French, while Italian, which is not a commercial language—and for many Americans is of no use except as it serves to scan the melodies in the operas of Bellini and Verdi—is only a language de luxe and is not spoken. Except *"io t'amo,"* which is proverbial, I doubt if among one hundred thousand persons outside of New York, one hundred are to be found who can understand one phrase of what Madame Ristori is prepared to give them.[9]

---

[8] In 1854, Robert Heller played Beethoven's Piano Concerto No. 4 with the German Musical Society of Boston. His musical model was Stephen Heller (1815–88), a composer of light, facile piano music. By the 1860's, Robert Heller was billed as "Pianist and Illusionist . . . Salon Diabolique . . . EVENINGS OF MUSIC AND MYSTERY . . . embracing the Supernatural Vision and the Stupendous Suspension Feat."

Jean-Eugène-Robert Houdin (1805–71) was a French conjurer and mechanician, who in 1855 received a gold medal in Paris for applying electricity to clocks.

[9] The career of Adelaide Ristori (1822–1906), Italian tragic actress, was

◇◇◇◇◇◇◇◇◇◇

En route to Philadelphia

Midnight, May 30. The battalion of a regiment that was in the last battle is just entering the station, covered with dust; some wounded officers have to be supported. We have just picked up many wounded and sick at a station. They are generally young officers belonging to rich Northern families. I have never in my life seen a more heart-rending sight than the spectacle of these heroic victims of our monstrous war. Sweating from fever and shivering in spite of the temperature of June, a young officer whose features, naturally handsome, are disfigured by wasting enters the car supported by two soldiers; he is carried to his car. He is a living skeleton. I have since learned that the bursting of a bomb shattered his thigh. A convoy of wounded went through the town yesterday. The hospitals being full, they were sent to the naval arsenal. They were so feeble that many of them had to rest frequently along the road. They were escorted by an immense crowd of children, women, and citizens, all eager to show their sympathy. Boys in the street offered to carry their knapsacks and arms for them during their passage.

The opera house (Academy of Music) in Philadelphia is certainly one of the most beautiful in the world. It holds very nearly two thousand eight hundred persons, comfortably seated. Tonight the last act of [Donizetti's] *La Favorita*, with Brignoli, De Lussan, Susini and four choristers, and the second act of *Lucia* with Kellogg,[1] were given. The four choristers all Germans. What pronunciation!

At Washington I had the whole diplomatic corps at my concert. They were all placed together in the first rows of orchestra seats—Count Mercier, French minister; His Excellency M. de Tassera, a distinguished poet, Spanish minister; Baron Stockel,

---

eminently successful, especially in the United States, which she visited four times, beginning in 1866. She was noted for her psychological penetration in playing such roles as Mary Stuart, Phaedra, and Lady Macbeth.

[1] Clara Louise Kellogg (1842–1916) was the first American opera singer to win fame abroad. Her repertoire was prodigious, as were her efforts in behalf of producing operas in English.

Russian minister; Mr. Blondel, Belgian minister; Chevalier Berti-
nati, Italian minister.

I was to play *The Union*, a patriotic fantasia, in which I have
intercalated the American national airs. The idea came into my
mind to salute each of the gentlemen by playing to him the national air of the country he represented. This entered into the
conception of my piece, enlarging the whole, its title being, as I
have told you, *The Union*. I had the pleasure of seeing all these
official countenances brighten successively as fast as appeared
"Partant pour la Syrie," "La Marcha real," "Garibaldi's hymn,"
"God Save the Czar." Not knowing the Belgian hymn, I was
satisfied by playing Blondel's air, *"O Richard, ô mon roi,"*[2] as
counterpoint to *"Partant pour la Syrie."* Mr. Blondel, the minister
of Leopold—I was about to say the minstrel—whose taste for art
renders his mansion the rendezvous of all the artists who visit
Washington, found my impromptu to his taste and rewarded me
with some beautiful verses, which I intend to set to music.

LINCOLN

President Lincoln is the type of the American of the West.
His character answers but little to the idea that they have in
Europe of a nation's ruler. Tall, thin, his back bent, his chest
hollow, his arms excessively long, his crane-like legs, his enormous
feet, that long frame whose disproportioned joints give him the
appearance of a grapevine covered with clothes, make of him
something grotesque and strange, which would strike us in a disagreeable manner if the height of his forehead, the expression of
goodness, and something of honesty in his countenance did not
attract and cause his exterior to be forgotten.

Lincoln is eloquent in his own way. He can speak a long time
and utter no idle words. How many great public orators would be
embarrassed to do as much! He possesses the three qualities required in our popular government—an *inflexible firmness*, an *incorruptible honesty*, and *good sense*, which make him find the
natural solution to questions the most difficult in appearance.
Brilliant eloquence without good sense and honesty is not only
dangerous, but also of pernicious influence. Lincoln is essentially

---

[2] From Grétry's *Richard Coeur de Lion*.

good and benevolent. He loves to tell jokes and does it with a humor that is always very comical, but the salt is not always the *purest Attic*, if all the stories attributed to him are authentic.

◇◇◇◇◇◇◇◇◇

June 3

Gave a concert alone at Worcester (Massachusetts). Brignoli, Amodio, and Madame de Lussan are in Boston; they gave a concert there last night; the whole weight of the concert thus fell on my shoulders. Played the Prelude in D flat of Chopin, under the name of *Méditation religieuse, Last Hope, Banjo, Union, Trovatore*, and *Murmures éoliens*. Recalled several times. A crazy amateur, having a book of Beethoven's sonatas under his arm, came to seek me between the first and second parts of my performance, asking me to play an andante by Beethoven. I consented by playing that in A flat of the "*Sonata pathétique*." I had the satisfaction of seeing my amateur while I played, with his eyes fixed on the text, in the English style, to see if I made a mistake. Of all the absurdities practiced by the Anglo-Saxon race in matters of art, this is what makes me suffer the most. Their manner of playing music is wholly speculative; it is a play of the wits. They like to see such and such chords resolved. They delight in the *episodes* of a second repetition. "They comprehend music in their own way," you will tell me; but I doubt if it is a right one. Music is a thing eminently sensuous. Certain combinations move us, not because they are ingenious, but because they move our nervous system in a certain way. I have a horror of musical Puritans. They are arid natures, deprived of sensibility, generally hypocrites, incapable of understanding two phrases in music. They never judge until they are assured that it is proper, like those tasters who do not esteem a wine until they have seen the seal, and who can be made to drink execrable wine imperturbably, which they will pronounce excellent if it is served to them in a bottle powdered with age. These Tartuffes of sound often commit deplorable mistakes. It is the Englishman before a picture, his look perfectly indifferent; seeking the number in his little catalogue, he takes care not to compromise himself by an impromptu judgment. He admires only when he is perfectly sure. His catalogue says "chef-d'œuvre of Rubens"; he then lets go in all confidence the trigger of his false enthusiasm. He thinks, in good faith that he understands the chef-d'œuvre because it is placed under his notice by a consecrated judgment.

The Anglo-Saxon race lacks the pensive element so indispensable in the arts. Patience, perseverance, laborious effort excite their admiration. Then, again, they must find in music the stiff, starched gait that they like in themselves. This is the reason for their rage for oratorios. They discover an air of great respectability in this music, which they do not understand, but which they listen to with comic gravity; saying, as of those bitter drops of which they are devotees, "they are excessively bitter to swallow, but assuredly they are excellent for the stomach."

Chickering has just had constructed, in one of his magnificent warehouses, a music hall, a perfect gem, which he graciously places at the command of artists who visit Boston. The hall contains nearly four hundred parquet seats. It is decorated in exquisite taste, with gold and white. Caryatids support the ceiling, which is of metal. It is admirably adapted for sound.

In the battle before Richmond, which began on June 1, the aeronaut succeeded in maintaining his position for many hours above the scene of action. He had carried up with him an electro-telegraph apparatus, the wires of which were attached to the quarters of General McClellan in such a way that our generals were instantly informed of the enemy's movements.[3]

The Seventh Regiment of New York Volunteers, the most aristocratic corps of the United States, composed entirely of the sons of wealthy families, has taken with it, for a service of three months, its own band. This fancy of millionaire soldiers will cost them fifteen thousand dollars. It is a magnificent military band, numbering more than sixty persons, all good artists.

Mr. B., a furrier, who has made more than two hundred

---

[3] Gottschalk had more than just a casual interest in aeronautical feats. On March 31, 1855, from Congo Square, New Orleans, he made an ascent with the balloonist Godard, to the accompaniment of an earthbound orchestra. "No pen can describe it, no imagination can conceive it," he wrote to a Cuban friend of his sensation of release and exaltation. He resolved, he said, to take with him on a future flight a portable harmonium, on which he would improvise "en las regiones etéreas." His composition L'Extase was based on this experience.

thousand dollars by selling beaver skins from Canada and bearskins from the Rocky Mountains, has become almost a theatrical mono-maniac. He is forty-five years old, with a small, sourish voice. He has a daughter sixteen years old, pretty but singing false, and a wife forty years of age who sings badly. With these elements he has formed an Italian opera company, in which he is tenor *assoluto*, his daughter prima donna, and his wife contralto. It must be admitted that his operas are got up regardless of expense; but imagine *La Traviata* by a merchant of otter skins and his interesting family! Their début took place at the Academy of Music. The eccentricity of the thing had drawn an immense crowd; all the rabbitskin mer-chants strutted there. They applauded Mr. B., whose acting was adorable, and all won success in bursts of laughter. They were recalled. Miss B. managed to appear the same evening in four marvelous costumes, that cost, it is said, five thousand dollars. The father, B——, was dressed absurdly. In the first act he was muffled up in a troubadour's cloak and funnel-shaped boots that reached to his waist and gave him the appearance of a mock scavenger. Besides, he had not been willing to sacrifice, to the demands of the stage, a magnificent pair of whiskers. We are going to have *Il Trovatore* in a few days, Madame B. singing Azucena. I have known people less crazy who were sent to the madhouse.

June 5. Second concert at Providence. All my pieces encored. Recalled three times. After *Rigoletto* the public opened a sub-scription in order to persuade me to give a matinee on the 9th, for piano alone. I'll play six pieces announced in the program, and six others left to the choice of the audience.

Ullman has taken the Academy of Music for one week, intend-ing to give monster productions like those of Jullien in London.[4] Miss Kellogg, Madame Hermann (the wife of the prestidigitator),

---

[4] Louis Antoine Jullien (1812–60), French conductor and composer of dance music, was one of the most flamboyant showmen of the nineteenth century. Theodore Thomas called him "the charlatan of the ages." J. S. Dwight observed, however, that "he can play the best kind of music." In his own defense Jullien said that his aim was always to popularize music. Although he played works by the first American composer of grand opera, William Henry Fry, what stands out most conspicuously in American musical history is the night he led the orchestra in his own *Firemen's Quadrille*, with firemen entering the hall to put out a real fire. In France, toward 1860, Berlioz was noticing Jullien's growing inability to manage his own affairs. He died insane.

Madame Borchard, and Madame d'Angri, prima donna, are engaged; also, Brignoli, tenor; Amodio, baritone; Susini, bass. I shall play two or three pieces between the acts, and the evening will end with a séance of sleight-of-hand by Hermann, whose success in Spain ten years ago attained prodigious proportions. Hermann has just made a very profitable tour of the West; he is very adroit and, above all, understands the difficult art of attracting the public.[5] His wife sang at his performance.

I see by the papers that in Chicago, St. Louis, and Baltimore they gave *Les Noces de Jeannette* with some success.[6]

◇◇◇◇◇◇◇◇◇

Portsmouth, June 5

A charming little town; beautiful and clean. All the houses are of wood painted a virgin white. The streets are lined with trees whose foliage, meeting at the top, sifts the daylight and makes them look like an alley in a park. Every house has a little garden in front and a kitchen garden with large fruit trees in the rear. Our arrival was an event. A number of charming young girls passed before the hotel with the evident intention of seeing us and of being admired. They are very pretty, though a little provincial in their stiffness. At the station we met three or four hundred persons; there were numberless embraces. We learn that it is a couple just married and gone off on the consecrated tour.

Tonight a concert in Portsmouth. Extraordinary enthusiasm. All the pieces encored. The hall is used on Sunday as a church. It is an amphitheater. The "baby show" that Barnum has announced for many months takes place at the museum. The public crowds there.

---

[5] In February and March of the preceding year the Hermanns and Gottschalk had given performances together in Havana, Mrs. Hermann sometimes accompanying Gottschalk at a second piano.

[6] *Les Noces de Jeannette* was an extremely successful light opera in one act by the French composer Victor (Félix-Marie) Massé (1822–84). First performed at the Opéra-Comique, Paris, on February 4, 1853, it received its first performance in the United States in New Orleans in November 1854.

❖❖❖❖❖❖❖❖❖

Portland, Maine, June 6

A magnificent concert—the most beautiful I have had for many years. I played admirably. Encored; recalled. The hall contains twenty-five hundred persons and is one of the finest in the world for its acoustic properties. The public wants me to return and give another concert. Extraordinary enthusiasm.

❖❖❖❖❖❖❖❖❖

Salem, [Mass., 1862]

Concert, Saturday, June 7, Much success. A small town. Before the commercial development of Boston it had a large trade with India; now it is torpid. The old, rich merchants of Boston retire here. We remarked on our way to the hall a great number of young girls going and coming. It is the town library, and they go to exchange the books they have out for new ones. These libraries exist in all of the United States.

Leaving at 8 o'clock, we had the prospect of spending a Sunday in Salem. "Rather die!" said Susini. We hire a gigantic four-horse coach. It has the form of an English stage, and holds four inside and four outside. The weather is beautiful. The horses pace the road. We visit the naval arsenal at Charlestown. They work there by gaslight.

We arrive in the morning at 1½ o'clock.

"*Madamina*" from *Don Giovanni* is almost always encored at my concerts. Susini sings it with his beautiful voice. Is it the beauty of the music which is so sparkling that it attracts even Western audiences? "Yes, without doubt," the believers will answer me. How is it that every time he sings it without announcing it there has been a complete failure? Isn't that sufficiently convincing? How, then, do you explain the complete silence of the public every time Susini sings the barcarolle from Ricci's *Sulla poppa*? And one day that the program announced "*Madamina*," Susini sang by mistake the work by Ricci. Wild applause from the amateurs, who were transported in thinking that they heard the music of Mozart.[7]

❖❖❖❖❖❖❖❖❖

June 18

In the car, going to Providence, I found Mason, the pianist, who is about to give a concert at the Young Ladies' Academy.

The countryside is delicious: a little bay very near New Haven; the sea on the right; nice sailing parties riding at anchor; a cluster of trees behind a pretty village; and a church whose sharp steeple seems to pierce the sky.

❖❖❖❖❖❖❖❖❖

Springfield, Mass., June 28, 1862

Visited a large gun factory belonging to the Government, where as many as twelve hundred rifles are made daily by a machine. Three thousand workmen are employed here.

❖❖❖❖❖❖❖❖❖

Newark, June 30

MATINÉE

(State of New Jersey) Pop.: 70,000. A remarkably active manufacturing town. It reminds me of Holland, the country being little or not at all broken. The Passaic River meanders capriciously and unrolls itself in windings. The country is so flat that one might think the little sailboats were sailing on firm land among the tilled fields.

❖❖❖❖❖❖❖❖❖

Burlington, Vermont, July 3

A small town built on Lake Champlain. I have never seen in Switzerland anything more beautiful than the mountains that surround it. My concert had attracted many. Two steamers loaded

---

[7] In Boston, with Dwight as the target, Gottschalk is supposed to have switched the order of a Beethoven work and one of his own. Mr. Dwight reportedly did not notice the difference.

with people from St. Albans and a train from Jericho arrived expressly for the concert. Bishop Hopkins, of the Episcopal Church, was present. I played the Chopin prelude for him. After the concert he invited me home to take tea with him. The bishop is a charming man and also an excellent painter. I remarked at his house a copy of *La Vierge à la chaise*. His wife and his sons and grandsons are good musicians, and I found a good piano. Near his house, on a hill overlooking the lake, he has built a large boarding school and a chapel in Gothic style.

◇◇◇◇◇◇◇◇◇◇

En route to Montreal, July 4

I am happy to escape the noise of the Fourth of July. I smell Canada, or guess it to be ahead. At the station we pick up passengers who are recognized to be Canadians by their appearance, as also by the horrible French they speak. It is a mixture of old Norman with the expressions of Molière. The Canadians are behind the times and ignorant.

10 o'clock. Arrived at Montreal. The train stopped at the station opposite Montreal, which, as well as the river, opened magnificently to view. In the distance are splendid buildings, among which we must mention Notre Dame, a beautiful cathedral with very fine steeples. We cross the river on a steamboat. We are hardly ten hours in Canada, yet we have already met some specimens of that surly, conceited, egotistic type, of which only the English (fortunately) have the secret.

◇◇◇◇◇◇◇◇◇◇

From Montreal to Lachine, July 5

On the road I saw a tailor's sign, "*Hardes toute faites.*" It is old French. Arrived at Lachine. Opposite, on the other shore, we see the church of a village entirely inhabited by Indians converted to Catholicism. It is called Coylmawaggher. The church, whose small cupola is covered with copper, glistens in the sun like a minaret. The St. Lawrence is magnificent. We see some rafts descending the current; it is frightening to behold. They cut timber up the St. Lawrence, and, to avoid the expense of transportation, they attach the trunks of the trees together and thus let them float to Montreal. Two or three men with long poles direct this singular raft. It would make your hair stand on end to see these men guide it over the rapids of the river; the raft glances, rebounds, disappears in the foam, and passes the rapids like an arrow.

At the invitation of three officers of the Scots Guards we went in a canoe as far as Alvarge Island; two soldiers followed us in a boat with provisions. The daughter of Trobriand,[8] Madame Stevens, of Boston, Colonel Reid, and two Misses Reid accompanied us. We sang in chorus the quartet from *Rigoletto*. Large wild birds flew away, frightened by our harmonious accents. Kam is the life of the company, as are also Captain Blair and Lord Dunmore. The peasants wear buckles on their shoes.

◇◇◇◇◇◇◇◇◇◇

July 6

Arrived at Quebec. Citadel on the top of a cliff, four or five hundred feet high, that commands the harbor. The suburbs begin at the shore, but, properly speaking, the town is wholly on the top of the hill; it is reached by a crooked, narrow, silent street.

At Montreal, *L'Ange déchu* by Kalkbrenner[9] is the object of attraction. The blind pianist Letendale (French) is very polite to me. La Belle, the organist (the Canadian names are very singular; I will give a list of them hereafter), paid me very obsequious attention. Lord Paulett, general of the Guards, was present at the concert. The pieces played in English at the theater are translated from the French.

The cathedral is very handsome. The streets are crowded with priests, and Sulpician convents abound. There are sisters of every

---

[8] Count Philippe Régis de Trobriand (1816–97) was a French journalist and author who emigrated to the United States in 1841. He was editor and proprietor of the *Revue du Nouveau Monde*, New York, in 1849–50, and joint editor of the *Courrier des États-Unis* from 1854 to 1861. He then joined the United States Volunteer Service as colonel, becoming brigadier general in 1864. He was the author of *Quatre ans de campagnes à l'armée du Potomac* (1867).

[9] Friedrich Wilhelm Michael Kalkbrenner (1784–1849) went to Paris from Germany, manufactured pianos, and conquered the fashionable world as pianist, composer, and teacher.

sort, sisters gray, sisters blue, Sisters of the Visitation, of the Villa Marie, of St. Joseph, etc. The old noble Franco-Canadian families have preserved the word *"seigneur."* Is it simply the translation of the English word "Lord" or a vestige of the Middle Ages?

I improvised with great success, at my concert, on the air, "A *La Claire fontaine."* I heard them whistling several of my pieces in the streets.

The population is ugly and apathetic. Despised by the English, they retaliate with hatred and jealousy.

On the terrace at Quebec I am five hundred feet above the bay, and at my feet the country is stretched out, producing a singular optical effect. I see the steeple of a church; its spire is thirty feet below me. I can cast my eyes into the courts of all the houses and look into all the chimneys. On Sunday afternoon it is the main promenade of the city.

The commerce of Quebec, much reduced, consists of timber, the forests being immense. The garrison consists of two thousand men. The churches, as I have said, are very numerous and exercise a very great authority. Thus they prohibit the theater but permit traveling circuses, puppet shows, and magic lanterns. I leave you to judge the intellectual level under such a rule.

Everything reflects the sacristy in Quebec—dull countenances, sallow complexions, and thin women. The streets, the houses distill ennui. I see in the streets quite a number of young men in long blue frock coats with yellow piping and with a long green sash around their waists. They have a pretended air of seminarists, and the cut of the surtout, which is too large for them, and the bad sleeves recall the cassock. These are pupils of the college.

The pronunciation of the Canadians is ridiculous and pretentious, the more so as they think that they speak so well. Mr. Cauchon was the Minister of the Interior for some years. Those are called demagogues here who have not contributed to the subscriptions for the pope.

J'aparrçouais ein via (vieux) homme près du bouis (bois), (Canadian pronunciation). Mr. Cauchon laughs very much at the ridiculous pronunciation of the Parisians, *"Rachail surtout exagerait leu français et lui fésa régretta leu Canada."*

"Ses louais" (laws) are local; England has nothing to do with them.

◇◇◇◇◇◇◇◇◇

July 8 [*1862*]

Saw the interment of a sergeant of artillery who was killed by a soldier. A detachment of the Seventeenth Rifles of the artillery gunners and one hundred sergeants, with the staff officers, accompanied the body, which was placed on a gun carriage. The music was singular. The drummers beat a roll that lasted one bar; then a rest for one bar, and a blow of the bass drum on the weak part of the bar; then a harmony of eight bars in the minor mode, played by flutes in minor thirds. It was melancholy and mournful and filled you with profound emotion. I followed them for a quarter of an hour, not being able to tear myself away from the melancholy charm of this strange music. The sound of the bass drum in countertime, the rests alternating with this lugubrious roll, the plaintive melody of the flutes, and the slow rhythm marked by the tread of the soldiers produced an effect I had never before imagined.

◇◇◇◇◇◇◇◇◇

Quebec, July 9

Review on the Esplanade. The troops are superb and of fine appearance. The governor general walked in citizen's dress. The band is large, and played "Dixie," which is very popular here, not only on account of its melody, which is very original, but because, being the air adopted by the Confederates, they are delighted in being able by this means to prove their sympathy for the South. After the review, the band played "God Save the Queen" before the colors, which were escorted by a guard of honor and all the officers; afterward the national colors, accompanied by the band, playing "Rule Britannia," marched the whole front of the ranks, the soldiers presenting arms, the officers their swords. It was a magnificent sight. The immobility of the men was surprising.

Afternoon, 4 o'clock. Took the steamer to return to Montreal.

Obliged to play for the ladies; greatly applauded. A waiter, of whom I asked the time, answered me, "*Ouiturécor*" (8¼ o'clock).

◇◇◇◇◇◇◇◇◇

July 11

From Montreal by train to Ottawa.

CANADIAN NAMES OF PERSONS

Abraham l'épine	Lapin	La fontaine
Drôlet	Lelievre	Pain chaud (doctor)
Poulain	Pigeon (grain merchant)	Robineau
L'osier	Franche montagne	La chance
Le hardi	Rosier	Genaut
Casse grain	La voie	La vigueur (violinist)
Grenier	Poirier	Du charme (pianist)
Pas mal	Le rose	La belle (organist)
Canon (judge)	Pommier	L'arrivée
Beaupré	Le meilleur	

Lord Dunmore, a handsome fellow of twenty years, lieutenant of the Grenadier Guards, amused himself a month ago, on board the *Nesleville,* of rebel notoriety, by trying to run the blockade. At first he nearly was taken by the Yankees; afterward he was stopped near Charleston by the rebels and was not able to justify himself. He amused himself during his short captivity by making sketches. I have smoked excellent cigars with him. Kam, a charming and very amiable fellow, is another young officer in the Scots Fusiliers.

◇◇◇◇◇◇◇◇◇

July 11

Arrived at Ottawa. They are building a house of parliament here that, considering the narrowness of the town, and the number of deputies it is required to accommodate, gives it the appearance of Robinson Crusoe's canoe. As in Washington the dwellings are scattered. It is a city in prospect. From the station the convent of Gray Sisters, who educate young girls, can be seen. Its cathedral is handsome and possesses an organ made in England at the cost of £1700 sterling. The bishop is from Marseille—his name is Joseph Guyges. There is also a college for young men kept by the Oblate Fathers, a very numerous order in Canada.

❖❖❖❖❖❖❖❖❖

Ogdensburg, Sunday, July 13, 1862

I was walking on the shore of the St. Lawrence River, whose tumultuous waters rolled like the waves of the sea. The "Ballad to the Moon," by Alfred de Musset, was recalled to my mind on seeing the sun go down. Its deep red disk, drowned in the violet mist, appeared to hang balanced on the top of a church steeple of which I had a glimpse on the Canadian shore. The night drew on, the air had a delightful freshness, and the streets were over-shadowed by large trees whose thick foliage imparted an air of mystery to all the dwellings. A Protestant church concealed behind a cluster of trees attracted my attention. The sound of the organ and of a hymn sung by female voices rose above the silence and calm of the night. Nothing could be more beautiful than this hymn; in spite of myself I was melted to tears. It was Sunday's evening service.

❖❖❖❖❖❖❖❖❖

En route to Watertown, July 13

A crowd of soldiers was in the cars and some Irishmen *dans les vignes du seigneur* (drunk). Decidedly I do not like the Irish; they are a rude, ignorant, superstitious race. Watertown is a pretty spot. My concert has taken place—a great success—received some bouquets. There are many French people living here, so many that a French paper, *Le Phare des Lacs*, is published here.

At Watertown I found a singular type of Frenchman. He gives lessons in dancing, in French, singing, and in fencing, and now and then is an impresario and an agent for concerts. He has engaged Thalberg[1] for four months and has built a very handsome concert

---

[1] Sigismond Thalberg (1812–71) was a major figure in the pianistic world of his time. Born in Geneva, a natural son of Prince Moritz von Dietrichstein and Baroness von Wetzlar, he was a pupil of Hummel, Pixis, and Kalkbrenner. In 1834 he was appointed *Kammervirtuoso* to the Emperor of Austria. He toured Europe, Brazil, the West Indies, and the United States. A friendly rivalry existed between him and Liszt. In November and December 1856 and January 1857, Gottschalk and Thalberg often joined forces at two pianos in concert, dazzling the New York public with their combined virtuosity. At the instigation of Lowell Mason, Thalberg played for children in public schools at Boston, New York, and elsewhere.

hall. He also raises horses, has many fine trotters, and offered me a superb one in exchange for fifteen concerts in Canada, to be given for his benefit. I have declined.

❖❖❖❖❖❖❖❖❖

Kingston, Evening, July 15

A fine concert and very great enthusiasm.

17th. A pretty town more animated than most of the others in Canada. Much enthusiasm at my two concerts. To go from here to Toronto, we shall have to leave at 11 o'clock this evening by a special train, which the company had the goodness to arrange for me and my piano.

❖❖❖❖❖❖❖❖❖

Toronto, July 18

My first concert under the patronage of Major General Napier. Some officers who knew me in Paris were present. At the theater *The Marble Heart* was played, a translation from *les Filles de marbre*. Dion Boucicault, the prolific purveyor to the English theaters, is the most impudent plagiarist in the world. Not a comedy, not a French drama is published without his translating it and putting his name to it and thanks to some alterations they become his own works.

❖❖❖❖❖❖❖❖❖

Batavia, July 22

Charming little town.

❖❖❖❖❖❖❖❖❖

Rochester, July 22

Great enthusiasm. The musicians of the military band are playing under the balcony while waiting for me.

❖❖❖❖❖❖❖❖❖

Auburn, July 23

Here there is a state prison that contains eight hundred prisoners. Magnificent concert.

❖❖❖❖❖❖❖❖❖

Canandaigua, July 24

In the cars three people are reading *Les Misérables* in English. Everybody is reading it now. Canandaigua is a charming town on the borders of Lake Canandaigua, surrounded by mountains.

In the middle of the town is a beautiful green lawn in the center of which a large tree covers with dark shadows a rough stone under which an Indian, one of the last occupants of the country before the arrival of the whites, is interred. He was an Indian chief. Mr. Wood, who first settled at Canandaigua, was his friend. He was an old man when he died many years ago. He had never failed during his life to paint the tomb of his friend white every year.

❖❖❖❖❖❖❖❖❖

Geneva, July 25

Geneva is situated on the lake, which is forty miles long and three miles wide. Immense concert—an inundation of bouquets. The shores of the lake are exactly like those of Lake Geneva (Switzerland), and its water is so cold that persons drowned in it never rise to the surface. I spent the day at the house of the Rev. Mr. Reed, a very well-informed gentleman who keeps the college at Walnut Hill. He has a charming dwelling built of brown stone, covered with ivy and moss. I took a sail in a yacht on the lake.

❖❖❖❖❖❖❖❖❖

July 26 [*1862*]

On going from Geneva to the extremity of the lake (in a steamer) to take the train for Elmira, the most beautiful country in the world is seen. Young girls from a boarding school are on board;

each one has a basket filled with dainties. The mistress and her husband carry a basket filled with cold eatables. They were going on a picnic and left us at a charming little landing place. The thick, tufted trees threw their branches almost to the water at the edge of the lake. A white little church pierced the foliage of the hill. Shady ravines seemed to invite them to be seated. Decidedly these young girls have chosen a delicious place to pass a charming day and dine upon the grass.

◇◇◇◇◇◇◇◇◇◇

Elmira, July 26

Gave a concert, and (by the by) conducted myself badly toward the audience. It is true that the audience did not deserve better treatment.

◇◇◇◇◇◇◇◇◇◇

Oswego, July 29

Passed four hours at Syracuse on the road. A pretty good concert at Oswego. Found there the excellent Barry and his neat, pretty wife, as amiable as ever. Great enthusiasm. The commerce of Oswego consists of lumber for buildings and all sorts of grain. Near Oswego is probably the greatest flour mill in existence. Last year it ground 550,000 barrels of flour. I took a walk on the shores of Lake Ontario, which is a vast blue ocean. On my left a tongue of land covered with thick shade ran out into the blue mirror of the lake; on my right, Fort Oswego, with its wooden wharf. I was on a steep cliff, about one hundred feet high, that looked out on the country-side around me.

◇◇◇◇◇◇◇◇◇◇

Rome, July 30

Neat little village, but I will, nevertheless, never go there again.

〰〰〰〰〰〰〰

[At Rome only a few people attended Gottschalk's concert. At Utica he was assisted by local talent: Miss Kitty Foster, soprano, Mr. Joseph Sieboth, and Mr. William H. Dutton. "The echo, the

swell, the drum movement were produced with perfection and
mastery," a newspaper critic observed. Years before, the comment
on a Gottschalk concert had been: "Coming as an alternative after
a black deluge of minstrelsy . . . doubly refreshing."]

◇◇◇◇◇◇◇◇◇

Utica, July 31, 1862

A charming town of 27,000 inhabitants. All the houses have a
green grass plot in front. The streets are lined with trees, which
give a parklike appearance to the town. Ivy covers the houses, and
its festoons reach to the roofs, falling back gracefully over the
windows.

They say that McClellan, under the influence of his old sympathies and the memories of his comradeship with the Southern
generals, who, for the most part, were his friends and schoolfellows,
has not pushed the war as vigorously as they had a right to expect
from him. You must recollect that Jefferson Davis was Secretary of
War at the period of the Crimean War, and that it was he who
first discovered the merits of Captain McClellan and sent him to
Sebastopol, where he made himself known by the sagacity of his
observations and the depth of his judgment in the report that he
made to his government on that celebrated siege. Others say that
he is in favor of slavery and consequently less hostile to the South
than he is to the Republican party of the North, the party by
which, for some time, the President seems disposed to be influenced. It is said that treason lurks in the highest region of our
government, and that, obedient to the sympathies of the family,
McClellan has revealed, at many times, the federal plans before
Richmond. I know nothing about this. So many absurd and con-
tradictory things are said that it becomes necessary to renounce an
opinion founded on rumors and admit only those probabilities
which are approved by the strictest good sense and the most
rigorous moderation.

～･～･～･～･～

[In the intervening period of nearly four months Gottschalk
vacationed in August at Saratoga, New York, where he also gave
a concert for the benefit of wounded soldiers, a deed acknowledged
in a letter signed by ex-President Fillmore and others. He heard

eight-year-old Teresa Carreño play, and predicted her brilliant career. He gave a concert in New York on October 1, assisted by Theodore Thomas playing the violin, and gave a few lessons to the little Teresa. She fainted when he first played for her. One of her early compositions was called The Gottschalk Waltz. Around 1900, she wrote: "Everything that concerns Gottschalk is of the greatest interest to me."

A letter to Gottschalk's Cuban friend Espadero, dated November 19, 1862, reveals his schedule for early November: twenty-one concerts in twenty days in Philadelphia, New York, Yonkers, New Haven, Baltimore, Hartford, Portland, Portsmouth, Boston, Providence, and Springfield.]

❖❖❖❖❖❖❖❖❖

Cleveland, Sunday, November 23
It snows, it blows, the lake is furious; waves of muddy water rise up like mountains and roll and spread themselves in sheets of foam on the shore, on which they first break with a crash. I hear their roarings in my chamber. Nothing can give you an idea of the gloom with which this inspires me. Sunday is always a splenetic day in all Protestant countries, but in Cleveland it is enough to make you commit suicide. Lake Erie is dangerous at this season; like all the Great Lakes of America, it is a sea, plus tornadoes of wind and the dangers of the coast, which are multiplied in consequence of the proximity of the shores.

❖❖❖❖❖❖❖❖❖

November 24
In going from Cleveland to Detroit we met in the car Mrs. Stephen D[ouglas], wife of the famous senator who contested the presidency with Lincoln and made himself the leader of a great party. The beauty and elegance of Mrs. D[ouglas] have become proverbial, and are as celebrated as the eloquence of the senator, who has been dead for nearly a year.[2] She still possesses great beauty, appears to be about twenty-five years of age, although her intimate friends (alas! who doesn't have them?) claim that she is past thirty. Her

---

[2] In fact Douglas had been dead for more than a year and a half.

black costume, her bonnet, from which the widow's cap of white tulle peeps out, marvelously sets off the beauty of her complexion and the regularity of her features. She is a woman such as the Greeks doubtless imagined when they dedicated a worship to beauty. After having once seen her, it is more difficult to forget her than to have her always present in the imagination.

◇◇◇◇◇◇◇◇◇

Toledo, November 26, 1862

Nothing interesting. Audience stupid. In the Artist's Room this bill was attached to the wall: "If, before commencing a concert, the performers do not pay the rent of the hall, the porter has orders from the proprietors to turn off the gas." That does not give us a very high idea of the honest; of the artists who have performed before the Toledian public, or of the liberality of the amateurs of the town.

◇◇◇◇◇◇◇◇◇

November 27

Going from Toledo to Erie (Pennsylvania), on a seat near me in the smoking car, some farmer was playing the fife. He practiced conscientiously. His stock of music was limited to some Scottish and Irish airs. Only he played everything in F. I would have seen nothing amiss in that if he had not invariably taken it into his head to play B natural instead of B flat. At the beginning I was shocked, but after a while I was singularly pleased with it. The obliterated note once introduced, there was a fight between the C and F, which, by turns, seeming to dispute the possession of the singular, melancholy harmony, plunged me into a sleepy reverie. Without doubt I saw unfolded before my eyes all sorts of charming things, for they ravished me as long as my reverie lasted, but I was not able afterwards to recall them. The Scottish melodies are, according to my mind, those which have the most character; they are truly the music of the mountains and of fantastic legends. I discover in them the reflection of the Scottish character; mystical, exalted, very superstitious, poetic, dreamy, and wild. Their intervals of a fourth and frequent employment of the plagal chord, the

rhythm weakened by the absence of accentuated cadences powerfully contribute to give them their character of strange melancholy
and twilight poesy.[3]

◇◇◇◇◇◇◇◇◇

Erie, Pennsylvania, November 27

Three or four days ago, being at Cleveland at the Hotel Augier
(the most frightful, filthy eating house in the world), I was looking through the window and saw at some distance a small cemetery. A rector to whom I had been introduced that morning told
me, respecting this subject, that the cemetery for many days had
been the theme of conversation, that every night for a week past,
a ghost had been there and even had ventured into the streets.
Some women were said to have seen it. The story appeared foolish
to me, like all ghost stories. Nevertheless I read the following in a
Cleveland paper this evening: "Last night two Irish servants met
the ghost of the Erie Street cemetery. The fright that these poor
girls received has been such that one of them fainted, and the
other has had a nervous attack, which still continues and places
her life in danger."

◇◇◇◇◇◇◇◇◇

Sandusky, Ohio, December 4

Small town and very strange audience. The applause here consists
of whistling, which frightened Patti very much.

In the car where I have gone to smoke, I find myself in the
midst of a mountain of trunks. I end by squatting down among
them, and from there I hear the conductor say to his companion,
"I have two embalmed bodies there!" Imagine how I felt!

◇◇◇◇◇◇◇◇◇

Zanesville, Ohio, December 5

There were many soldiers in the audience. The hotel very passable,
and the landlord did all he could to be agreeable to us. I forgot to

---

[3] The relationships between folk tunes and scale patterns had not yet
engaged the attention of musicologists. Possibly Gottschalk was not aware
that the "Scottish and Irish airs" were in the Lydian mode.

mention a remarkable incident at Sandusky: during the concert a warrant of arrest for me because I had not paid the license to the town. "Very well! Let us pay the six dollars, and I'll not have to go to prison." These things are amusing and break the monotony of our existence. I had just finished *Murmures éoliens*, which the public had encored. I returned to the Artist's Room and found myself in the presence of the constable. Oh! the instability of human things. On the one side glory, on the other somber dungeons of Sandusky. The Capitol and the Tarpeian Rock! Strakosch, the new Decius, has offered himself up and, thanks to six dollars, has saved me from the horror of captivity.

◇◇◇◇◇◇◇◇◇

December 6 [1862]

Going from Zanesville to Columbus, after looking in vain for a seat in the smoking car, I found myself in a car filled with men who were badly clothed and had long beards. I thought at first that they were recruits, but learned that they were prisoners of war, and had no more doubt on the subject on hearing one of them whistle "Dixie." Not having a seat, I was invited by a young, handsome fellow of twenty to sit down beside him. He had an old torn hat and an old blanket on his shoulder. This young man was from Virginia and, judging from his refined manners, belonged to a good family. His behavior contrasted singularly with his tattered clothes. They were all under the guard of three or four officers and soldiers of the United States. This sight was heart-rending. One of the soldiers bought five cents' worth of popcorn and gave a handful to one of the prisoners, who shared it with two other companions. I wished also to give them somethnig, but was afraid of compromising myself. These poor unfortunates wore that air of indifference and stoicism which the miseries and sufferings of war unhappily have impressed on their countenances.

Is it not singular that Americans who seem to possess a clear and practical judgment and more than an ordinary power to understand principles, as soon as they enter into the domain of the aesthetics of art for the most part go astray and repeat absurdities that their good sense should make them reject? Lately I made these reflections on reading an article on Blind Tom in a magazine remarkable for the talent of its contributors and the general tone of its articles. I refer to the *Atlantic Monthly*. The author of this article, himself without doubt a talented writer, judging by his style, makes so many errors and commits so many blunders that it is impossible for those competent in the art to permit the continuance of the celebrity of Blind Tom, whose title to posterity as a musician is, I fear, as authentic as that of the old Negress of Barnum is to have been Washington's nurse. And first of all, what would you say of an audience that declared as correct a repetition, made from memory by a child, of five or six thousand words that it had heard but once? You certainly would say that an audience capable of verifying from memory such a long discourse would be altogether as phenomenal as the phenomenon itself. Nevertheless, my hypothesis is based upon a discourse that is in words familiar even to the ears of a child, on matters having relation to human passion, to its interest, its affections—that is to say, on things that all comprehend, know, and feel. But with Tom we have to deal with music— that is to say, an art whose subtlety must necessarily escape the layman. "Tom," says the author, "repeats the piece from memory." This is supposing what is not proved: that Tom had no knowledge of the piece. What was the piece? If it was simply one of those known melodies with its invariable dress of variations consecrated by long usage, I shall astonish no person by remarking that any child studying music and endowed with a good musical ability does as much every day. If the piece is difficult and complicated, I absolutely challenge the competency of the public to judge the accuracy of its reproduction. The writer of the article will pardon me for telling him that he recalls to me an audience that I saw assembled to witness a most extraordinary thing that a mathematical phenomenon was about to perform, which was to resolve the most complicated problems instantaneously from memory. Mr. Ampère of the Academy proposed a most difficult problem to him. The infant prodigy gave him an answer, and the audience applauded to the skies with confidence. He might have answered whatever he wished. The honest people did not know a word of algebra and ingenuously thought that what they heard was really marvelous. I will go farther and affirm that "Yankee Doodle" can be played in five hundred, six hundred, or even one thousand different ways, provided that the theme is generally preserved, without more than ten in the audience perceiving the least difference.

◇◇◇◇◇◇◇◇◇◇

December

Invariably at every concert a small, scribbled, note requests me to play *Last Hope*. The other day I received one composed as follows: "Would Mr. G. kindly please 36 young girls by playing *The Last Hope*, which they all play."

At Cleveland the cold is intense, the north wind blows, the lake roars. To complete our misfortune, we go down to the Augier House, where it appears that the old proprietor has sold out and the new one has not yet taken possession; we fall into an interregnum, that is to say, something that is not anarchy, but is not much better. Besides, the stoves are broken, and everywhere in the hotel we are frozen. The meals take place at such precise intervals and the discipline is so severe that you are always too soon for dinner or come in when it is over, unless you stand on guard in the passage and push your way in at a given moment. We ask for the wine card. An interminable list is handed to us, but it is not possible to obtain any of the wines. Nevertheless, we finally are given a bottle of Lafitte, but, not having any salad to dress, we think it more prudent not to drink it. The bills, to boot, are swollen in ratio to what we have suffered. On venturing a trivial remark we are insulted.

◇◇◇◇◇◇◇◇◇◇

Madison, Wisconsin, December 1862

This town is hardly more than twelve years old, and nevertheless is already remarkable. The cathedral (Catholic) and the marble capitol are superb.

◇◇◇◇◇◇◇◇◇◇

December 12, 1862 [*Cincinnati*]

Monsignor the Archbishop of Cincinnati last Sunday preached a sermon of which this is very near the tenor: he is not a formalist and voluntarily practices tolerance, seeing that he detests above everything the spirit of Puritanism, but the theater today is so scandalous that he can no longer close his eyes to the deplorable effects it produces upon the masses. He glorifies himself for never having put his foot in such a place, and for never having seen a theatrical play. He has never even read a play of Shakespeare, etc., and he ended by recalling to his audience how much Bossuet[4] condemned the theater. He also made allusion to the discussion of the Bishop of Meaux with an Italian monk. He recalled having heard that an actor who played the role of a bishop in a theatrical play was struck with paralysis in the right arm during the performance —"a judgment of God," he added.

Behold what is unfortunately the state of religion in the United States; it struggles with the convulsions of the Shakers, with the hysterical, with the Methodist shouters of camp meetings, with the Mormons, and with the superannuated thunders of ignorant Ultramontanes.[5] Since I have visited Canada and have been able to measure the degree of brutishness to which the absolute reign of faith as understood by the Marist fathers and the Sulpicians can lead a people, I tremble, on seeing the Irish immigration increased in a ratio that threatens to overrun the whole United States; it is the saddest of all on account of the ignorance, the brutal instincts, and the blind and ferocious superstition of all the Irish. However, I do not know which I should fear the more, the fanatics of the Bible or the fanatics of Rome. The Puritans are as rabid as the monks of the fifteenth century. They think only of proselytism and of the propagation, in spite of everything, of their faith. Like all other fanatical sects, they have forgotten the spirit to attach themselves to the mere letter. In 1856, in the State of New York, individual subscribers furnished more than one hundred thousand dollars for the purpose of printing Bibles! It is impossible to be serious in thinking on the results obtained by these immense efforts! Fifty thousand Bibles sent to China, six thousand Bibles to Chandernagor, five thousand little books to the coast of Africa— and in English. Is it not a monomania, and ought not this way of understanding religion be cured by cold-water baths?

---

[4] Jacques-Bénigne Bossuet (1627–1704) was a French theologian and historian who became Bishop of Meaux in 1681.
[5] Catholic extremists.

◇◇◇◇◇◇◇◇◇

Indianapolis, December 15

Next to my own room is that of a major who has been sick for two months. He is under an indictment for disobeying the orders of his superior. Four soldiers are on guard in the corridor, and two sentinels guard his door. The State of Indiana has a formidable party in favor of rebellion. One of the soldiers coughed horribly. I offered him a lozenge, of a type that cured me of a cold from which I suffered greatly for some days. He accepted it with thanks. At the moment of swallowing it, one of his comrades said to me distrustfully, "Ah, ha! aren't you a secessionist? We shall die soon enough without your coming to poison us." Poor unfortunates!

The snow has been let loose over the whole country that I have traveled through for the last two days (from Kentucky to Indiana). I think with breaking heart of the wretched men in the field; of thousands of men without shelter, sleeping on the snow, and not having even a blanket.

At Louisville I met an inspector of cavalry, an old lieutenant in the Belgian Guards. In the three months he has been in Kentucky, he has inspected fifteen new regiments of cavalry. The personnel and equipment, he told me, are magnificent. Our artillery also is immense, and I do not believe that finer could be found in Europe.

For four days the telegraph has been giving us eventful news of a great battle being fought at Fredericksburg. The whole force of two great armies is engaged. The result is still undecided. The carnage will be frightful.

What singular audiences I meet with! You can imagine what the population must be in little towns that, founded only seven or eight years ago, nevertheless give receipts of three or four hundred dollars, and sometimes more. The other evening before the concert, an honest farmer, pointing to my piano, asked me what that "big accordion was." He had seen square pianos and upright pianos, but the tail bothered him. Eight or ten days ago, at Zanesville, a charming young girl and her honorable mamma spent the whole concert watching my feet. They did not know the use of the pedals and saw in my movements only a kind of queer trembling and odd, rudimentary dance steps that for two hours and a quarter afforded them an inexhaustible source of amusement. They were on the front benches and greatly annoyed me.[6]

What I become accustomed to with difficulty is the whistling of some enthusiasts. Whistling here is applause carried to its highest point. Where the hands and the voice are insufficient, they have recourse to whistling. Another annoyance is the people who arrive late at the concert and cross the hall in the middle of a piece, marching as if they were marking time for a battalion of raw recruits. There are also those who talk during the concert, but as these are not found only in the concert hall, I merely speak of them by way of remembrance.

I live on the railroad—my home is somewhere between the baggage car and the last car of the train. Certain naturalists assert that insects reflect in their physiological conformation the peculiar characters of the vegetation upon which they live. According to that (if this peculiarity of insects extends as far as pianists), I ought to have the gait of a locomotive and the intelligence of a bandbox. All notions of time and space are effaced from my mind. Just like the drunkard who, when asked the distance between the Chaussée-d'Antin and the Porte St.-Denis, replied, "ten small glasses." If you ask me what time it is, I will reply, "It is time to close my trunk" or "It is time to play *The Banjo*" or "It is time to put on my black coat." These three events are very nearly the most memorable of my daily existence. I console myself by thinking that I am not the only one of my species.

◇◇◇◇◇◇◇◇◇◇

Chicago, December 20

I have just read in a Milwaukee (Wisconsin) paper that Richard Storrs Willis,[7] in his magazine *Once a Month*, announces that "Gottschalk is, it is said, about to marry a young lady—a million-

---

[6] Both the foregoing anecdotes appeared in a letter from Gottschalk published in the *Courrier des États-Unis* of March 17, 1863. He explained, however, that such occurrences were the exception, not the rule.

[7] Richard Storrs Willis (1819–1900), journalist, edited the *New York Musical World*, published volumes of church music, taught music, and contributed to the American edition of the 1865 *Life of Felix Mendelssohn-Bartholdy*. He was a younger brother of the poet Nathaniel Parker Willis.

airess—from New York." Permit me to assert that the news is not
true. Be assured of it, O my friends, with all the affliction I have in
giving it to you. No, alas! I have not at this moment the least
hope of ever attaining that oasis of life which is called marriage. I
have not yet arrived at that blessed haven where, after so many
storms and tempests, I might cast anchor, and my *fiancée opulente*
is a myth that becomes more and more fabulous as I advance along
the arid path of celibacy. Is it not sad? And are we not worthy of
pity—we old bachelors who, like stray travelers, see the fatal time
draw near when we shall remain alone on the road of life? We
must travel the desolate way that still separates us from the sovereign goal, without a holy love to partake our joys and our griefs, or
a friendly arm to sustain us in our last hours.

Not being able to do better, I console myself by thinking of
the muse, the eternal bride always young, always constant for those
who love her, whose chaste caresses defy the outrages of time. For
her there are no old bachelors, no wrinkles, no white hairs, no winter of life, but only the perpetual springtime of illusions. She sings
sweetly in my heart marvelous things that ravish, console, and
soothe my grief, and her seductions are as powerful at the close as
at the dawn.

But I perceive that I have become pathetic, and after having
carefully driven back the solitary tear that curiously hangs to the
balcony of one of my eyelashes, seeming to admire the lyrical sentence I have just written, *"je reviens à mes moutons."* My marriage
has been an old rumor for ten years, making its appearance periodically by changing, only to rejuvenate itself, the initials of the myth
to whom I am engaged.

Between South America and the United States it has so often
been said that I was married or dead that if only half of the deadly
and matrimonial events of which they have made me the hero
were realized I would have had the fortune of half-a-dozen
funereal shows, and would have been obliged long since to im-
migrate to Utah to avoid certain nice susceptibilities of our modern
legislation.

These apocryphal marriages recall to me the poor devil of a dervish in an Arab tale, who, with empty stomach and purse, was
invited to dine tête-à-tête with an opulent nobleman of capricious
disposition at Baghdad. The table was sumptuous, the crystal
sparkling, and vessels of gold and silver covered it in profusion. The

master of the house did the honors magnificently. "This ragout
of pheasant is delicious; permit me to offer you some. Taste this
wine of Shiraz; it is exquisite; these figs of Damascus are divine,"
the master of the feast repeated as he presented the plates and decanters to him.

Ragout of pheasant, Damascus figs, and Shiraz wine! The devil,
you will say, this lord of Baghdad prepared good things, and your
dervish is a fortunate fellow! Do not be too hasty in your judgment
and, above all, do not interrupt me again—on which I proceed.

Far from being fortunate my dervish is suffering the tortures
of Tantalus, seeing that the plates and decanters *contain nothing*,
a fact that does not prevent the host from pretending to taste the
one and relish the emptiness of the others. The dervish awaits
with anxiety the arrival of each new dish, hoping to be more fortunate, but the courses succeed each other in the midst of all the
usual ceremonies of a great feast without the shadow of any food
appearing, and the poor dervish leaves the table, his spirit saturated
with the gastronomic vapors of this imaginary repast, but with
empty stomach and hungrier than ever.

I am the dervish, and the newspapers that marry me to fanciful young heiresses are so many opulent noblemen of Baghdad,
and you will discover the moral at my cost without my assistance,
and as I shall be accused of writing without any reason what possesses as little substance as the repast offered to the dervish, I
hasten to speak about my concerts at Chicago, which have been
very substantial as to the receipts. I have given four concerts there
and must return there tomorrow to give the fifth and last. Chicago,
of all the Western cities, is the one that most resembles New York.
It is animated and flourishing; one feels that it is young, full of sap,
and asks nothing better than to enjoy life. It possesses taste and enthusiasm, I think, of a higher standard than the other cities in this
section of country. What I also prefer in it is that it is exempt
from that provincialism which one feels the more in proportion
as one leaves the intellectual focal point of the United States.

The ladies here wear beautiful furs. The commerce in furs is
considerable. They come by land from the Russian possessions in
America.[8] The ladies, who always possess a fertile, inventive genius

---

[8] In 1867, the Senate ratified the treaty of purchase of Alaska from
Russia.

about their clothing, have found means to render graceful the enormous fur bonnets in which they muffle themselves this winter. These hats remind me of the fur cap of a drum major, but are flatter and end in a kind of fox's tail that hangs over the neck.

The stores are immense. In one block alone I counted five fashionable stores each five stories high and each employing from eighty to one hundred clerks. The small merchants from the interior of the Mormon territories come here at the beginning of winter to make their purchases.

Milwaukee, Wisconsin, has 60,000 inhabitants, splendid residences, parks, marble fountains, etc. A female furrier paid me a visit. She is the daughter of the Comtesse de ——. However on learning that I knew the Grand Duchess Anna of Russia, she became more reserved, and I thought that she was afraid I might discover that her title, of which she makes a great display here, is not as legitimate as her Alsatian accent, which she sought in vain to conceal. It is remarkable that almost all the Russians in America are counts, just as almost all the musicians who abound in the United States are nephews of Spohr and Mendelssohn.

◇◇◇◇◇◇◇◇◇◇

New York, December 1862

I have just finished (it is hardly two hours since I have arrived in New York) my last tour of concerts for this season. I have given eighty-five concerts in four months and a half. I have traveled fifteen thousand miles by train. At St. Louis I gave seven concerts in six days; at Chicago, five in four days. A few weeks more in this way and I would have become an idiot! Eighteen hours a day on the railroad! Arrive at seven o'clock in the evening, eat with all speed, appear at eight o'clock before the public. The last note finished, rush quickly for my luggage, and en route until next day, always to the same thing! I have become stupid with it. I have the appearance of an automaton under the influence of a voltaic pile. My fingers move on the keyboard with feverish heat, and for the moment it is not possible for me to hear the music without experiencing something of the sensation of that hero of Alexandre Dumas *fils*, condemned for one month to eat nothing but pigeon. The sight of a piano sets my hair on end like the victim in the presence of the wheel on which he is about to be tortured. While my fingers are thus moving, my thoughts are elsewhere. Happier than my poor mechanism, it traverses the field and sees again those dear Antilles where I tranquilly gave a little concert every two or three months, comfortably and without fatiguing myself, where I slept for weeks the sleep of the spirit, so delicious, so poetical, in the midst of the voluptuous, enervating atmosphere of those happy lands of the *dolce far niente*, whose lazy breezes murmuring softly bear on their wings the languid, distant harmonies of the countryside, and whose quiet, dreamy birds seem never to rouse from the contemplation of all the marvels of this terrestrial paradise except to love and to sleep. What an awakening for me after five years of that tropical gypsy life!

The libertines please themselves by peopling their paradise with a crowd of imaginary houris. I do not imagine mine except as an express prohibition against giving a concert under the penalty of being precipitated into purgatory. By way of retaliation hell ought to be the general entrepôt for all the harpsichords little and great, past and future. This perspective freezes me with terror.[9]

I have taken some notes during the long hours of travel in the West. They are written *en courant*, and I myself shall have trouble in deciphering them from the leaves of my memorandum. The jolting of the train makes my lead pencil describe all sorts of fantastic figures; there are zigzags, hieroglyphics, and Gothic cathedral steeples.

For some time I had wished to give three concerts in one day (I already had done it at St. Louis, and I claim, in default of other merit, to be the first pianist who has accomplished this tour de force in America), but the question was of three concerts echeloned over a route of one hundred miles. Leaving New York in the morning, I arrived at Newark for a matinée announced at noon, and had there complete success. At one-thirty I took the train for Albany, where a second concert was to take place at half-past four. The third was to be at Troy, and was not to begin until eight o'clock at night. So far everything went well, but "man proposes and God disposes"! I had in the car for neighbors a charming young girl and her mother, both hampered with boxes, umbrellas, and other

[9] Parts of this entry up to this point were published in *L'Art musical*, Paris, on July 31, 1862 and June 16, 1864.

movable utensils, embarrassing, invading, calamitous, without
which no female having any respect for herself could ornament
the interior of a car. They stopped at Fishkill. On seeing them get
up, I did as much under the influence that two pretty eyes always
exercise, and rushed out, my heart in my mouth, my right arm
gracefully bent (the left carried a cage and a canary, another feminine article that I had forgotten to mention in the inventory of
these ladies, and that I had heroically seized). I offered my hand
to help them descend. Here my readers may interrupt me to say
that my story is not amusing and has nothing extraordinary in it.
Wait, then! *Que diable!*

Wait! alas! it is just what the locomotive did not do. In the
midst of the courtesies of my traveling companions and of the
little *consecrated* conversation that I owed to them, *felicitating
myself on the happy chance that . . . with hope that . . .*
and a thousand other pretty things of the same kind like knights-
errant who meet beautiful princesses, the whistle was blown, the
conductor had cried, "All aboard," and I only came to myself to
see the last car of my train disappear around a turn in the track!

Behold me upon the road without any baggage at Fishkill station, that is to say a half hour's walk from any habitation, and
with a concert to be given at Albany in an hour! "Frankly," you
say to me, "I only half pity you; you still have the two princesses!"
The two princesses! Bitter mockery! One of them, the mother, is
walking with her husband, who has come down to meet them at
the station. The other, the daughter, turns her back to me and,
hanging on the arm of a handsome fellow, one of her friends
(whom I thought frightful), gives him a thousand tender looks.
They all jump into a pretty phaeton (the young man's, without
doubt), which drives off rapidly, leaving me in the dust under a
sun like that of Arabia Petrea, a prey to the horrors of being left
alone, given up to corroding reflections on the inconvenience of
being too susceptible. I swear (a drunkard's oath) I never will be
caught again. Don Quixote after the fight with the windmill could
not have presented a sadder figure. Firmin (I was about to say
Sancho), whose life passes in packing, unpacking, and repacking
my trunks, and who seems from this intimacy to have contracted
a tender affection for them, thought of the telegraph office. It
was four o'clock. The hall at Albany probably was full. He sent

a dispatch to Strakosch commending to him his dear trunks and advising him of the accident. I, for myself, recalled to mind that Church,[1] our great, inimitable Church, the painter of Niagara, of the Andes, and of so many other beautiful pictures, had many times spoken to me of a marvelous property that he had purchased on the banks of the Hudson near Fishkill. A little lad was discovered just then whose father, a carpenter, worked for Church. I again took courage and, giving some money to the boy, made him conduct me to Church's residence, where I passed a charming afternoon.

~·~·~·~·~·~

[*The following observations on music appeared in Gottschalk's first article for the Atlantic Monthly, February 1865.*]

~·~·~·~·~·~

There is a class of individuals for whom the arts are only a fashionable luxury, and music, in particular, is an agreeable noise and elegant superfluity that at a soirée agreeably revives the conversation when it languishes, and commodiously serves to fill up the interval separating the time for lemonade from the time for supper. For them all philosophical discussions on the aesthetics of art are no more than puerilities, analogous to that of the fairy who occupied herself in weighing grains of dust in a scale of spider's web. The artists (to whom, through a prejudice that goes back to the barbarism of the Middle Ages, they persist in refusing a place in the higher sphere of social order) are for them only merchants of the lowest rank who trade in questionable products, most of the time awkwardly, as they rarely make a fortune.

Performers are for them mountebanks or jugglers who ply the agility of their hands, as dancers or acrobats that of their legs. The painter whose chefs-d'oeuvre decorate the walls of their salons figures in the budget of their expenses under the same heading as the upholsterer who has covered their floor with an Aubusson; and if they were left to themselves, they would value according to the price of the canvas and the oil the *Heart of the Andes,* by Church, or the *Le Marché aux chevaux,* by Rosa Bonheur. It is not for these, who are disinherited by thought, that I write, but there are

---

[1] The landscapes of Frederick Edwin Church (1826–1900) achieved wide popularity.

others—and it is to those that I address myself—who recognize in the artist the privileged instrument of a moral and civilizing influence, and who appreciate art because they draw from it pure and unspeakable enjoyment, who respect it, because it is the highest expression of human thought aspiring toward the Eternal Ideal and love it as the friend into whose bosom they pour their joys and their griefs, to find there a faithful echo of the emotions of their soul.

Lamartine rightly has said, "*La musique est la littérature du cœur, elle commence là où finit la parole.*"[2] Indeed, music is a psychophysical phenomenon. It is in essence a sensation, in its development an ideal. In order to understand or, at least, to perceive music, it suffices not to be deaf. Idiots and furious maniacs have submitted to its influence; not being confined to the precise and restricted meaning of a word, and expressing only the status of the soul, music has the advantage over literature that every one can assimilate it to his own passions, and adapt it to the feelings that dominate him. Its power, limited, in the intellectual order of things, to the imitative passions, is illimitable in that of the imagination. It answers to that innate, undefinable feeling which every one possesses, *the Ideal*. Literature is always objective; it speaks to our understanding and determines in us impressions in harmony with the limited sense that it expresses. Music, on the contrary, may be by turns objective and subjective, depending on our state of mind at the time we hear it. It is objective when, under the wholly physical sensation of sound, we listen passively and it suggests impressions to us. A warlike march, a waltz, the flute's imitation of a nightingale, the chromatic scales imitating the murmuring of the wind in the "Pastoral" Symphony are examples of it. It is subjective when, under the influence of a secret impression, we discover in its general character an agreement with our psychical state and assimilate it. It is then like a mirror in which we see reflected the emotions that agitate us, see them with a fidelity so much the more exact because we ourselves, without being aware of it, are the painters of the picture unfolded before the eyes of our imagination. I will explain myself: play a melancholy

---

[2] This quotation from Lamartine strikingly resembles Herman Melville's definition: "Where the deepest word ends, there music begins, with its supersensuous and all-confounding intimations."

passage to an exile thinking about his distant country, to an abandoned lover, to a mother mourning for her child, to a conquered warrior, and be assured that each one of these various griefs will appropriate these plaintive harmonies to itself and will recognize in them the voice of its own suffering.

Music in itself is still a mystery; we know that it is composed of three principles: the air, vibration, and rhythmical symmetry. Strike an object under the exhausted receiver of an air pump— there is no sound, because there is no air there. Touch a resounding glass—it becomes silent, because you have arrested the vibration. Take away the rhythm of the simplest air by changing the duration of each of the notes that compose it—you will render it unrecognizable and obsure because you have destroyed its symmetry.

But why, then, do not several hammers striking in cadence make music? They possess air, vibration, and rhythm. Why does the accord of a third tickle the ear so agreeably? Why is the minor mode suggestive of sadness? There is the mystery, there the inexplicable phenomenon. We do not hesitate to say that music, which, like speech, is perceived through the medium of the ear, does not, like the latter, call upon the brain for an explanation of the sensation produced by the vibration of the nerves. It addresses itself to a mysterious agent within us which is superior to the intelligence, being independent of it, and makes us feel what it can neither conceive nor explain. Let us examine the different attributes of musical phenomena.

1. *Music is a physical agent*; it impresses on the body shocks that shake the organs to their base. In churches the flames of the candles oscillate to the murmurings of the organ. A powerful orchestra near a sheet of water ruffles its surface. A learned traveler speaks of an iron ring that swings to the murmur of the falls of Tivoli. In Switzerland I excited at will—in a poor child afflicted with a frightful nervous malady—hysterical and cataleptic crises, by playing in the key of E-flat minor. The learned Dr. Bertier asserted that the sound of the drum gave him the colic. The sound of the trumpet, some physicians assert, quickens the pulse and excites, though most insensibly, perspiration. The sound of the bassoon is cold; that of the French horn at a distance and the remote harmonies of the harp are voluptuous. The flute, played

softly in the middle register, calms the nerves. The low notes of the piano frighten little children. I had a dog that would sleep on hearing music, but as soon as I played in a minor key would howl piteously. The dog of a celebrated singer whom I knew would moan bitterly and give signs of violent suffering when his mistress sang a chromatic scale. A certain chord produces on my nerve of hearing a sensation analogous to that which the heliotrope produces on my sense of smell and the pineapple on my sense of taste. Rachel's voice charmed by its ring before one had time to seize the sense of the phrase or to appreciate the purity of her diction.

We can affirm, then, that musical sound, rhythmical or not rhythmical, influences our whole being; it quickens the pulse, slightly excites perspiration, and produces a species of voluptuous and transient irritation in our nervous system.

2. *Music is a moral agent.* Through the medium of the nervous system it brings the superior faculties into play; its language is that of sentiment. Moreover, the ideas that have presided over the combinations of musical art establish relations between its composers and the soul. We sigh with Bellini in the finale of *La Sonnambula*; we shudder with Weber in the sublime phantasmagoria of *Der Freischütz.* The mystical inspirations of Palestrina, the Masses of Mozart transport us into the celestial regions toward which they rise like melodious incense.

Music awakens in us reminiscences, memories, associations. A celebrated pianist, a friend of mine, related to me that he knew a charming young girl in a city where he was giving concerts. He was twenty years old, with all the poetic illusions of that romantic age; she was sixteen. They loved each other without daring to confess it and perhaps without knowing it themselves. But the moment for parting came. He was passing his last evening at her house. Watched by the family, he could scarcely shake hands with her stealthily at the moment of bidding her adieu. Alas! the poem begun was arrested at its first page; he never saw her again!

Disheartened, frantic with grief, after having wandered at random through the dark streets, he found himself again, without knowing how, under her window, at two o'clock in the morning. She also was awake. Their thoughts, united by that divine tie which merits the name of love only in the morning of life, had met together, for she was playing softly in the solitude of her chamber the first notes of a mazurka that they had danced together. "My tears flowed," he said to me, "on hearing this music, which seemed to me sublime. It was the stifled plaint of her heart; it was her grief, which was exhaling from her fingers; it was the eternal farewell!

"For years I thought this mazurka a marvelous musical inspiration, and it was not until a long time afterward, when age had dispelled my illusions and effaced the adored image, that I discovered that it was only a vulgar, common composition. The gold had been transmuted into brass."

The old man, chilled by age, may remain insensible to the pathetic accents of Mozart and Rossini. Repeat to him the simple and artless song of his youth; the present vanishes and the illusions of the past return.

I was acquainted with an old Spanish general who hated music. One day I took it into my head to play to him my *Siege of Saragossa*, in which I introduce *La Marcha real* (the national hymn). He commenced crying like an infant; this air recalled to him the immortal defense of the heroic city behind whose fallen walls he had fought the French; it sounded, he said, like the voice of all the sacred affections that constitute home.

The mercenary Swiss troops formerly in France and Naples could not hear, without being affected, the *"Ranz des vaches,"* that air of old and rude Helvetia, when from mountain to mountain the signal of revolt summoned the three insurgent cantons to the cause of independence. The desertions caused by this air became so frequent that the government had to prohibit it.

The comical effect may be remembered which was produced on the French troops in the Crimea by the Highlanders marching to battle with the bagpipe, whose sharp, discordant sounds inflamed those brave mountaineers with warlike ardor by recalling to them their country and its heroic legends.

Napoleon III finds himself obliged to allow the Arabs, the spahis and Turks, whom he has incorporated into his army, to have their barbarous music of flutes and tam-tams, so that they will not revolt. The tam-tam enables these soldiers to make marches under which, without this powerful auxiliary, their strength would succumb.

Play to a Creole of the Antilles one of his dances, with its quaint rhythm, its plaintive and dreamy melody, and immediately you will see him filled with enthusiasm.

The *"Marseillaise"* contributed as much to the republican victories of 1793 against the invaders of France as the genius of Dumouriez.

3. *Music is a complex agent.* It acts at the same time on life, its forces, its instinct, its organism; it has a psychological action. The Negroes charm snakes by whistling to them. It is said that fawns permit themselves to be captured by a pretty voice; the pipe tames bears; canaries and sparrows love the flageolet; in the Antilles and South America lizards are hunted with the whistle; spiders have been seen not to leave a fiddler. In Switzerland the shepherds hang large bells to the necks of their finest cows, which are then so proud that they march at the head of the herd as long as they are permitted to wear them; they have been seen to refuse their pasture and to die after they have been taken away from them. In Andalusia the mules lose their strength and their power of endurance if the innumerable bells with which these intelligent animals are accustomed to be adorned are taken off of them. In the mountains of Scotland and Switzerland the flocks pasture best to the sound of the bagpipe; and in the Oberland the stray cows in the mountains rejoin their keeper at the sound of the horn.

Donizetti, a year before his death, had become an imbecile, owing to a softening of the spinal marrow. They endeavored by every means to revive a spark of that intellect once so vigorous. All of the doctors were baffled. Once he seemed to recover a gleam of intelligence, and this was on hearing one of his friends play to him the Sextet from his opera *Lucia.* "Poor Donizetti," he exclaimed, "what a pity that he died so soon!" and that was all.

In 1848, after the horrible battles of the insurrection that had made Paris an immense field of carnage, I hastened to conceal my sadness and disgust at the house of one of my friends who superintended the immense insanse asylum at Clermont-sur-oise. He had a small organ and sang pretty well. I composed a Mass, and we invited a few artists of Paris and also some of the most docile patients of the asylum to hear it. I was struck with the bearing of the latter, and I induced my friend to repeat the experiment and extend the number of the invitations. The result was so favorable that we were soon able to form in the chapel a choir of the insane of both sexes who rehearsed on Saturday the hymns and chants that they were to sing at Mass on Sunday. A raving lunatic, a priest, who became more intractable from day to day, and to whom the strait jacket was very often applied, noticed the periodical absence of some of his companions and showed some curiosity to know what they were doing. Once we admitted him into the chapel; he listened to the sacred music and appeared interested in it. The following Saturday, on seeing his fellow-patients prepared to go to the rehearsal, he asked to accompany them. The doctor told him that he would permit him to go if he would suffer himself to be shaved and decently dressed. This was the thorny point, for he never was willing to wash himself and became furious when he was required to dress. But to our great astonishment he quietly consented. Not only this time did he listen quietly to the music, but we further discovered him frequently trying to join his voice to those of the choir. When I left Clermont, my poor old priest had become one of the most assiduous at the rehearsals. He still had fits of raving madness, but they were less frequent, and when Sunday came, he was seen dressing himself neatly and awaiting impatiently the hour for going to chapel.

I will sum up: Music being a *physical agent*—that is to say, acting on the individual without the assistance of his intellect; a *moral agent*—that is to say, reviving his memory, exciting his imagination, developing his sentiment; and a *complex agent*—that is to say, having a psychological action upon the instinct, the organism, and the forces of man, I thence conclude that it is one of the most powerful means of ameliorating and ennobling the human mind, of elevating the morals, and, above all, of refining the manners of the people.

The truth is now so recognized in Europe that we see there the *orphéons*, or popular musical societies, increasing as if by magic under the powerful impulse that the government gives them. I do not speak, for instance, of Germany, where all sing and where an industrious, peaceful, and intelligent people always has associated choral music with its labors and its festivals. But I will more particularly mention France, which today has more than eight hundred *orphéons* composed of workingmen. How many of these latter, who spent their moments of leisure at the cabaret in drinking, now find a pleasant recreation in these meetings, where the spirit of association and of fraternity is engendered and developed; and, if we could get a comparative statistic of crimes, without doubt it would be discovered that they have diminished in proportion as musical societies have increased. In fact, you are better, your heart is in some way purified, when it is strongly impregnated with the noble harmonies of a fine chorus, and it becomes difficult not to trust as a brother him whose voice is blended with your own and whose heart is united with yours in a community of pure and joyful emotions.

If *orphéons* ever are established in America, be assured that the barrooms—the scourge of the country—and revolvers will cease to be national institutions.

◇◇◇◇◇◇◇◇◇◇

[Chicago] January 1863

I have been confined to my bed for four days by a severe attack of neuralgia in one eye and one side of my head. I have suffered very much, but thanks to the attention of Dr. Smith, the most amiable companion that a sick man could desire, and to the attentions of all connected with the Tremont House, the best hotel I know of (with the Continental in Philadelphia), I am greatly better and hope in a few days from this to begin my concertizing peregrinations again. I was alone in my room when a moment ago a friend brought me a journal of last month containing a letter from a lady in Indianapolis on my concert in that city.

It is 7 o'clock on New Year's Day! Magical time that, when we are children, excites in us a glow of indescribable felicity, and that as we grow old brings with it only the remembrance of lost happiness. I was recalling family joys and was measuring the extent of what we all lose as we advance in life. Each of these periodical festivals is like a milestone on the pathway of existence. We stop a moment to look behind; we count the empty spaces that have been made around us, and, what is sadder still, those which have been made in ourselves. What ruined illusions! What noble emotions extinguished! What friendships (which in the generous impulse of youth we thought eternal) we look back upon! Our heart contracts, and we understand that happiness is no longer in the future, but in the past, and we have let it escape us without knowing it.

These impressions, which we all experience, are perhaps more lively in me because the kind of life to which I am condemned causes me to dwell on them more. To be always only a musical abstraction, not to have the right of applying any of the sympathies accorded to the artist as an individual, to be inclosed within the walls of the concert room without the power of acquiring any of those strong affections which, independent of that prestige which celebrity bestows, ought (whether right or wrong) to belong to all and to no one in particular; to be a public thing that the first comer manipulates as he pleases—such is the sad reverse of the brilliant (?) career to which I am condemned. It was under the influence of these thoughts that I began to read the article from Indianapolis which my friend had sent me.

Let me, first of all, describe the pleasure that it gave me. I have often received praise in the course of my artistic life (and who has not? I say this that it may be understood that I am not convinced that I have merited it), but I do not think that I ever received anything that has so delightfully affected me. Had I been given only the approbation of this mother, I should think that I had not wasted time in writing the *Berceuse* (*Cradle Song*). Although I have not yet reached the dignity of marriage, my love for children makes me understand by intuition all the holy poetry that surrounds the cradle. Again I repeat it, no praise in my life has so much touched me as that of this mother recognizing in my poor little composition, humble as it is, a reflection of her affection for her little infant when, hanging over its cradle, she recalled to herself the *Berceuse*, which she had just heard at my concert.

"The cradle song—is it not a mother's heart set to music? Bending over my own little sleeping one, now, on coming home, I felt like blessing him who has thus given melodious utterance to the holiest of human feelings—a mother's love. A *good* man he must be—the composer of the *Berceuse*." (Indianapolis correspondent of the *Home Journal*, signed "Mrs. Frank Smith.")

Music, you know, is a mirror in which, according to our mood, we see a reflection of the images that engage us most. It is a sketch that we color with our own dominant passions. Its language being comparatively undefined, it has the advantage over written poetry of imposing no boundaries upon the hearer's thought, of opening infinite spaces wherein his soul may spread its wings to rove unmanacled. Thus a sweet and plaintive melody heard by a mother who has lost her babe, a lover who bewails his mistress, an exile who dreams of his far native land will appear to each of these sorrowing hearts the echo of its own proper grief and the reflection of its musings.

I was led to compose the *Berceuse* by memories of a younger sister of mine, dearly loved and brought up by me, whom I cradled in my arms during her infancy through a painful illness that threatened to take her away from us. Finally, thank God, she triumphed over it. I imagined her lying in her cradle as of old, and at the thought of losing her, all my youthful emotions, all my affections, ripened by age and strengthened by absence, sprang up afresh to be condensed into this little *morceau*, which, despite its trifling artistic value, I dearly love because it recalls to me a great sorrow once spared my heart.

[About this time Gottschalk received word from his sister Célestine in Paris that their brother Edward had contracted consumption. He made arrangements to have Edward sail for New York with their youngest brother, Gaston. Eighteen years younger than Moreau, L. Gaston Gottschalk was to become a well-known singer.]

◇◇◇◇◇◇◇◇◇

Springfield, Illinois, January 8, 1863

St. Nicholas Hotel (! ! ! !) Each one of these exclamation points, if it could speak, would tell you a story of tribulations, of all kinds of mortifications that should render the St. Nicholas Hotel, Springfield, forever celebrated! First, the legislature being in session, the house is full, which is the same as saying that the beefsteaks are leathery, the eggs too hard. Let him explain who can the affinity that exists between victuals and a crowd, and what makes one the consequence of the other; but its existence is the fact. (I have bitterly realized it at the Burnett House in Cincinnati. One of my agents had to share his chamber with three persons. One of them stole his gold watch, his chain, and his frock coat.) We are cooped up, six of us, in a little room hardly large enough to hold one bed comfortably. The water to wash with is as black as ink. The proprietor charges us for a supper that we have not eaten, and, upon a timid observation that we make respecting it, looks at us as if he wished to crush us and, addressing the porter, throws out this memorable phrase, which seems to me not to speak very highly in favor of the honesty of the travelers with whom he is in the habit of dealing: "Billy, take care that the trunks are not taken away before the bills are paid!"

O excellent Lincoln, Springfield has been your home, but that does not increase my admiration for its inhabitants!

[*Upon his return from the West this time Gottschalk remained in New York for several weeks. Edward and Gaston arrived. On April 7 the pianist began a series of successful concerts at Irving Hall, concluding with the inevitable "farewell concert." He resumed touring shortly before the following entry. Always popular in New York, he played there five times again in May.*]

◊◊◊◊◊◊◊◊◊

Alexandria, April 27 [*1863*]

I have for a long time wanted to see this little city on the northern boundary of Virginia; therefore, I came here from Washington. This city has played such a very important part in the war —occupied in turn by the Federalists and the Confederates and finally becoming the headquarters of the first—that I experienced on going there a little of that indefinable sentiment which seizes us when we find ourselves on an old field of battle, picturing in our thoughts the great victory of which it has been the theater. Besides, every inch of Virginian soil is American, for we find on it everywhere the footsteps of Washington.

We put up at the Marshall House Hotel, almost entirely occupied by officers. The Alexandria garrison amounts to from thirty to forty thousand men. The general hospital of the Army of the Potomac has been established at Alexandria; therefore, we meet invalids at every step. The sight of a mutilated soldier is always a sad spectacle; here it is heart-rending, almost all those whom I

meet being young men—some almost children. The Marshall
House is celebrated in the annals of this war. It was here that
Colonel Ellsworth, a young hero of nineteen years of age, was
killed. This Ellsworth, a new Charles XII, from his birth dreamed
only of wars and combats. Love, it is asserted, had never knocked
at his heart, and he died, it is said, a virgin.

As in the past, I continue to be whirled in space. This agitated
life is a distressing monotony. The Carthusians themselves have not
a rule more unpitiable and of more unchangeable rigidity than that
to which my destiny submits me. *Pianistomonambulist!* Everything
is foreseen, everything is marked out, everything is regulated in my
peregrinations. Thanks to the experience of my agent, I know in
advance, within a few dollars, the amount of the receipts in a town
of a given number of inhabitants. I know, with my eyes shut, every
one of the inextricable cross-threads that form the network of the
railroads with which New England is covered. The railroad conductors salute me familiarly as one of the employees. The young
girls at the refreshment room of the station, where five minutes are
given, select for me the best cut of ham, and sugar my tea with the
obliging smile that all well-taught tradespeople owe to their custo-
mers. In my black suit at 8 o'clock I salute my audience, and give
them *Il Trovatore*. At a quarter to nine they encore the *Murmures
éoliens*. At half-past nine they call again for the *Berceuse*, in the
midst of the enthusiasm of some young romantic virgins and some
papas slightly inclined in a semiconscious state to sleep, who find
the piece full of agreeable effects. At ten o'clock I carry off my
patriotic audience to the belligerent accents of *The Union* fantasia;
and at half-past ten I throw myself, exhausted and depoetized, into
the prosaic arms of the blessed Morpheus, whom I should be
tempted to canonize if I were pope, and if the good man (I speak
of Morpheus) had not chosen to live before the invention of canon-
ization.

Then morning, breakfast in a hurry, and, alas! five, six, seven,
eight, or ten hours of railroad, and always the same thing—the
crowd, and to be isolated! Isolation is certainly sometimes a sad
thing, but to be alone and find yourself surrounded—or be jostled
by the multitude and feel that, aside from the indirect relations of
the ticket office, no other tie attaches you to those who surround

you—is it not worse than ostracism or the desert? I indemnify myself by making observations about the faces of those I meet. I
classify individuals.

A book written by a talented observer on the physiognomy of
the public would be very interesting. Lavater,[3] if he had had the
great misfortune of being obliged to give concerts, certainly would
have studied the character of that collective being, that monster—
gentle and ferocious, satiated and famished, glutted and corrupted,
artless and capricious—which is called the public. You would not
believe how much there is that is interesting in the public (outside
of the receipts, which naturally are the most important of its
phases). Do you remember the story of the prisoner in the Bastille
who, amid the horrors of his captivity, found amusement in taming
a mouse—the only companion of his solitude; and of that other,
who beguiled the monotony of his time by hunting in the dark for
a pin that he threw at random? I am like them. The horrible
monotony of concerts, the invariable repetition of the same pieces,
the daily round of railroad cars, isolation in the midst of the
crowd (the saddest thing of all)—these force me to seek for dis-
traction in my torments themselves.

While I play, I study, not the faces, but the public. I propose
the following problems for solution: Why does the public on one
day applaud to the skies? Why does it remain cold on another? I
have got into the habit of feeling its pulse at my first appearance. I
understand by the sound of the applause if there is in the town a
professor favorable or hostile to me. I could, if required, tell you
by the general expression of the faces if they are German or Dutch
(I call German the countrymen of Schiller, Goethe, Mendelssohn,
and Beethoven; and Dutch those whose only characteristic traits
of their mother country are love of beer, a cordial hatred of every
person who combs his hair regularly, sometimes washes his hands,
and has the unpardonable weakness not to circumscribe his geographical notions by the Rhine or Danube).

I could, if necessary, even tell you if such and such a musical
journal has or has not many subscribers in my audience—if
Mason's Musical World, Dwight's Journal, or the *Home Journal*
is in the majority—by the warmth or coldness of the audience.

---

[3] Johann Kaspar Lavater (1741–1801), Swiss poet and theologian, was
the father of the so-called science of physiognomy.

I do not know what sorry jester said that there was only one
fantasia for the flute, alluding doubtless to the intolerable effect
of the tepid-water pipe upon all the lucubrations imprudently
confided to the perfidious instrument of Pan.

I have come, in the maze of the giddy whirl of concerts in which
I find myself, and thanks to the invariable periodicity that thrusts
me every evening upon the stage before the same piano, to
imagine that there is only one public. It is dangerous and capricious
in its humor, but I recognize its identity by invariable and characteristic signs.

First. The young girls from the boarding school (may I be
permitted to confess that it is the most interesting element of the
audience, and that upon which my attention most willingly rests).
Last Hope and *Pastorella*, the first, doubtless, on account of the
romantic tint of its title, the second, thanks to the small talk between the malicious and awkward young girl and the amorous
chevalier, generally have the privilege of awakening in an unequi-
vocal manner the notice of the pretty battalion on the left or right
wing. At one or the other extremity, like the guardian of the flock
who is charged with the care of keeping on the road the unruly
sheep, is generally found the local Beethoven, who is not celebrated, whose immaculate, delicate taste cannot be pleased with
the plain water gruel served up to the barbarous vulgar, and who
feeds only on the divine ambrosia emanating from the masters
(dead—this is important, and purified in the crucible consecrated
by opinion and by time); this is of the best tone, seeing that aristocracy is always conservative. The great dead! How many little
crimes are committed in their name! It is sweet to be able to crush
a living youth who incommodes you (and what way is more commodious and less compromising than to throw an old name at his
head?).

Chopin's genius has developed within the fifteen years since he
has rid his contemporaries of its perishable envelope. One could
scarcely believe how much his compositions have improved.

Thirty years ago he traveled in Germany, when his compositions
obtained only the disdainful criticisms of the worshipers of suns
that had set.

The form! O pagans of art! The form! When, then, will the
time come, routine fetish worshipers, when you will have the

courage or the talent to avow that there is more genius in the pretty waltzes of Strauss than in five hundred pages of schoolwork; in eight notes of genius, wholly without ornament, ignorant of their nakedness, but beautiful in their ignorance, than in a logarithmic problem?

There was a period in France, in Italy, and in Spain when *concetti* were the rage. The poetic mania in its licentiousness, deceiving itself in its devouring fervor, clung to a worship of material tours de force. The idea! What is it, then? It matters not what sensualists, endowed by God with the power of creation, can imagine it! But the form, the arrangement, the science, the meter —in this lies the difficulty.

Already under the lower empire the rhetoricians of Byzantium, in the midst of general decadence, were led astray in that labyrinth in which poetry was lost for so many centuries. The writers of *concetti* did better. Had they, for example, to write upon a cup, they set themselves to work to compose a kind of Chinese puzzle, of lines (the meaning of them being almost indifferent) whose different lengths should, in their ensemble, give to the eye the appearance of a superb cup! What patience, and above all what marvelous knowledge of all the combinations of the phrase! Others proposed to themselves to write a poem in which the letter A should be excluded; and for twelve thousand verses they promenaded the astonished reader on an ocean of metaphors without ever striking against the banished letter.

The self-made Aristarchus generally gives lessons on the piano. His hair is uncombed, as becomes all men of genius who respect themselves a little. He professes a particular esteem for beer, and seeks in it (without excluding other stimulants) his inspirations. Hoffmann[4] the fanciful has contributed in no small degree to the immoderate use of liquor. Since it has been asserted that Hoffmann got drunk to write his fantastic tales, no artist can truly worship art who does not drown his faith in the waves of the fecundating

---

[4] Ernst Theodor Amadeus Hoffmann (1776–1822), writer, musician, and jurist, was an important representative of the Romantic movement in Germany. His literary works, particularly those stressing the supernatural and the grotesque, influenced such widely divergent personalities as Schumann (*Kreisleriana*), Offenbach (*The Tales of Hoffmann*), and Poe (*The Fall of the House of Usher, William Wilson*).

liquid. Beethoven and Liszt have contributed to the advent of long hair.

There is within me a want of equilibrium between my aspirations and my aptitudes. The former desire to soar toward regions of incomparable sublimity; the latter tend toward the lowest depths of reality, fettering in some way the flight of my aspirations and keeping me prisoner. From that come my lack of confidence in myself and my irritability when I am criticized.

If I write, my imagination takes the wings of Iris, traverses space, and shows me fairylands. As soon as I want to put it down on paper, from being a butterfly it becomes a bat. The wings become weighty under the burden of my phrases and fall heavily. The mischievous thing tempts me, draws me on, intoxicates me, offers me a thousand encouragements to follow it. With pen in hand I try to give a form framed in my own words to the beauties she permits me to have a glimpse of, but, like the will-o'-the-wisp that the belated traveler pursues, it vanishes into the darkness at the moment when I think I have grasped it.

For fifteen months my existence has been that of a carpetbag. I certainly would become brutalized by this daily routine of railroad travel and of concerts if I had not set myself to work to find some possible way to combat the weariness and perils of the road, which threaten my intelligence. I have tried sleep, and have slept a great deal, but one cannot always sleep. I soon perceived that my temper was becoming soured by being, in the midst of a delicious dream, awakened with a start by the conductor striking me on the shoulder and decisively calling out, "Tickets, please."

I had to try some other means. I had read somewhere that the Arab of the desert, to appease his thirst, puts small pebbles into his mouth—the salivary glands, irritated by the foreign contact, dilate, and in feeling his mouth moistened, the poor traveler deludes himself into thinking that he has drunk (a German would not fail to call it a confusion between the objective and subjective). Here was a ray of light. Why, said I to myself, should I not try this means, and, by transferring the "hydro-lithic" process of the Arab from the physical to the moral order of things, obtain a similar result? And I commenced writing notes of my travels. Such is the monotony of my travels that I soon understood that what I wrote was much less the reflection of my surroundings than the expression of what took place within myself. But as that notion moistened my brain, constantly menaced with petrifaction, I did like the Arab, I accepted a saliv—salutary illusion by which I could traverse, without succumbing, the Sahara of concerts through which I have whirled for more than two years.

I am fond of my notebooks (I was about to say my pebbles); they never leave me. They are like an intimate companion for me, a mute confidant who has an immense advantage over all the railroad friends I ever have met, that of hearing me without my being obliged to strain my voice over the sharp summits of the highest note, as it listens to me and never interrupts me. It is discreet (of what friends could as much be said?) to the extent that, had you under your eyes the ten or twelve notebooks that I have filled from the Mississippi to the St. Lawrence, and from New York to the Mormon Desert, they would take great care to prevent you from discovering anything other than undecipherable hieroglyphics; every one of their pages looks like the side of an obelisk. The jolts of the road and the haste with which I write assist, it is true, marvelously in making them discreet. There are steeples, spirals, lozenges, rockets—what should I say?—but of writing, none. One sees in them everything and nothing, like flying clouds chased by the wind, in which everyone, as he fancies, sees a house, or a man on horseback, or a chain of mountains.

Decidedly I think that my notebooks would gain greatly by being translated into the vulgar language. Imagination might see in them charming things, which some readers, alas, will search for in vain at the end of my pen. I am only a pianist, do not forget it, and an American, which more than excuses me for my bungling style and awkward language.

❖❖❖❖❖❖❖❖❖

Elmira, New York, Sunday, June 14, 1863

I am convinced that one day some savant will discover that time is a fluid that expands and contracts as it is exposed to such and such moral atmospheres. No one ever will make me believe, for instance, that Sunday at Elmira is composed of twelve such hours as make up the other days of the week.

This morning, after breakfast, I took a nap. Then I went down into the parlor of the hotel, where I found two ladies with their Sunday faces on—that is, looking as dismal as possible. I also found there a large Bible. Everyone knows how strictly Sunday is observed in all puritanical countries. To judge from appearances, it is a day devoted to lamenting the irreparable affliction that God has inflicted on us by the gift of existence. It is to die of the spleen.

I do not know if God in his goodness ever thinks of us, but if he thinks of casting his eyes, on a Sunday, upon his creation in America, it is very doubtful whether he rejoices in his work on seeing so many disheartened faces. As to the Bible (like that I found in the parlor), I should not have remarked it except for its colossal proportions. The zeal of the Bible societies is such that you cannot find a hotel—what do I say?—a chamber in a hotel or steamer without one or more Bibles. The number of Old Testaments the Bible societies gratuitously dispose of amounts annually to two millions; two-thirds of the books are sent to the Malays, Chinese, Hindus, Kaffirs, Malagassies, and Siamese, who doubtless receive them joyfully and sell them to their grocers by weight. The remainder are distributed in the United States, especially among soldiers. I dare to assert that among them miscreants are to be found, regardless of the Hebrew epics, whose sacrilegious pipes are lighted with the erotic heat of the canticle of canticles of Solomon.

Besides the Bible societies, there are, in every town, tract societies, which rival the ardor of the first and whose mission is to scatter profusely all sorts of religious Bible stories, edifying anecdotes, miraculous conversions, parallels between infidels and Protestants, and the sectarian excellence of the —— sect (here place the name of one of the two or three hundred sects that flourish in the United States, each one of which aspires to govern the others). All this in pamphlets, flyers, etc., which rain upon the traveler in the steamer, in the hotels, in the railroad cars, in the streets, everywhere, finally, where the presence of a man gives promise of a soul to be saved and a recruit for the ranks of the phalanx, be it Universalist, Methodist, Calvinist, Puseyite, Baptist, Spiritualist, or something else. I recall a good man who was always found in the trains going from New York to Philadelphia, at seven o'clock on Sunday evening (the only train permitted on that day), and who strove to slip, whether welcome or no, into the travelers' pockets a little sermon on the nonobservance of the Sabbath day and the terrible punishments reserved for those who by traveling on Sunday committed the crime of high treason against the Divinity.

What could I do? No stores open, no carriages in the streets, not the least noise, not the least sign of life, except a few passers-by, who, gliding along like shadows rather than like living beings, were going to or returning from church, which makes it all dull, silent, desolate. The town appears as if it had been visited by the plague or cholera. Wearied to death, I opened the great Bible; after having "traversed the desert with Moses, been drowned in the sea with Pharaoh, and, having been present at one or two massacres of the Philistines," I felt inclined to meditate thereon, and went upstairs to my room to sleep.

O human inconsistency! The piano, which has been a torment to me all the week, possesses for me today an irresistible charm. It is the charm of forbidden fruit, for, although it is permitted (by going to the bar through the back door) to take an indefinite number of brandy, whiskey, or gin cocktails, to play on the piano, except under certain psalmodic restrictions, is positively prohibited. The harp perhaps might be tolerated—for David played the harp —but the piano, fie!

About seven years ago, one Sunday at Cape May, I sat down in my room to practice a polka—the *Forest Glade*—which I was then composing. Just as I began, a violent thunderstorm burst over the hotel, and at the first flash of lightning several ladies and a clergyman, seeing in the storm an unmistakable sign of divine wrath, came rapping at my door, imploring me to stop my profane, though anything but tempestuous, music. I now remember the scandalized countenances of those worthy people too distinctly to venture again on any such experiment.

Fortunately the gong (which is no respecter of the Sabbath or any other day) sounded for dinner. Somebody had appropriated my hat, doubtless involuntarily, as I found another in its place; but somehow in all such cases, by a phenomenon that I cannot undertake to explain, the hat left in place of yours invariably is an old one.

This reminds me of an incident connected with the Princess de Salm. This charming and accomplished woman (she was only a countess by right, though people persisted in calling her princess, probably on account of her problematic relationship with the Emperor Napoleon) was, in 1851, the time at which I was presented to her, merely a delicious little creature, full of wit, who was trying her wings in Paris before attempting to soar, but whom, under some absurd pretense, official and other stupid circles refused to receive. The gossips pretended, though I never believed a word of it, that she had taken out her letters of naturalization in the Cytherean Valley that extends along the heights of Notre-Dame-de-Lorette.[5]

Baden-Baden was at this time only the rendezvous of hypochondriacs, wealthy do-nothings, and gamblers. Berlioz had not yet thought of fledging his operas there, nor Octave Feuillet[6] his comedies, nor, in fine, Madame de Salm her *Proverbs*, to which, along with her beautiful eyes, she was indebted for her ascendancy in certain literary and gallant coteries.

You know that she was married again, some months ago, to the Chevalier Ratazzi, the celebrated minister of the King of Italy. At the period of which I speak, her beauty was certainly ravishing and her wit sparkling, but she had two defects. One, that she was deaf (alas! she still is); the other that she had Monsieur de Salm for a husband—Monsieur de Salm, whom society, with that instinctive perception which is the infallible characteristic of the masses, never called other than the "husband of Madame de Salm." He is dead, now, poor man! and without ever having seen the Chevalier Ratazzi, his successor. I think I may boldly affirm that she has lost nothing by the change.

One evening at the house of the Marchioness of Salcedo (she is said to have been a particular friend of Ferdinand VII, King of Spain, who also was visited frequently at the time by Mademoiselle de Montijo, now the empress), I found in place of my hat, which was new, one so old and of such singular shape that despite my good nature I could not keep from protesting loudly against the change. One of my friends heard me and, touched by my misfortune, proceeded to examine the fossil chapeau I had in my hands. "Why that," said he, "is the hat of the husband of Madame de

---

[5] Notre-Dame-de-Lorette: a quarter of Paris. Larousse defines *lorette* as: "*Jeune femme élégante et de moeurs faciles.*" "Cytherean Valley" alludes to the isle of Cythera, where Aphrodite emerged from the sea.

[6] Octave Feuillet (1821–90), a French novelist and playwright.

Salm." I recognized it at once; nobody but he wore such old hats. Whereupon I approached the count, and, sure enough, he had my hat under his arm. He made me a thousand excuses—for, after all, he was a gentleman—and to our mutual satisfaction we entered once more into possession of our legitimate coiffures.

We leave tomorrow for Williamsport, Pennsylvania. This week I have given ten concerts in six days in ten different towns.

I might have gone this evening to hear the Rev. Mr. Beecher, who has a church here, but I was told that he is but a copy—minus the eloquence and talent—of his brother, another minister, whose congregation is considered to be the most aristocratic and the richest in New York or Brooklyn. The Beechers, father and sons, are ministers, and all very distinguished. The present generation reckons five brothers, all ministers, and one sister, Madame Beecher Stowe, the celebrated author of *Uncle Tom's Cabin*. The Reverend Henry Ward Beecher has acquired great notoriety outside of his evangelical jurisdiction by the impassioned enthusiasm with which he combats slavery. He is the idol of his congregation to such an extent that lately it has offered to pay all the expenses of a five-month trip to Europe besides his ordinary salary. He has accepted the offer, and at this time is visiting England before going to Paris, where he cannot fail to distinguish himself.

◇◇◇◇◇◇◇◇◇◇

Williamsport, Pa., Monday, June 15, 1863

Left Elmira this morning at 4 o'clock. Arrived at Williamsport after a journey of seven hours. Williamsport is a very pretty town containing about five thousand inhabitants. On a *modiste's* sign I saw the words "Ice Cream." This hybrid business reminded me of the island of St. Thomas, where the publisher of the *Tidende* (a Danish newspaper) is a manufacturer of bathtubs, and where tobacconists sell preserves and patent medicines. The milliner has a very pretty little boudoir in the rear of her shop; it is the sanctum sanctorum, where she probably tries on the dresses. A small marble-top table makes one suspect that it is also the refreshment saloon. In the window I see baskets of strawberries and straw hats, the former looking like bonnets *full*, and the latter like baskets *empty*. The music seller is a clockmaker. There is an air of ease, simplicity, and cheerfulness about the place which reminds me of the Swiss villages.

4 P.M. The town is all in commotion. A dispatch has been received announcing the invasion of the state by three columns of Rebels marching on the capital. The dispatch is placarded on all the street corners. You may easily imagine the agitation caused by this news. For myself, I am less surprised at it than worried. The apparent inactivity of General Lee had too much the appearance of a feint not to lead us to suspect him of appearing unexpectedly at one of the weak frontier points of Maryland or Pennsylvania.

Do not be in a hurry to accuse the Federal commanding general of want of skill. Do not forget (as the European journals have forgotten) that our war embraces an extent of territory equal to the whole of Europe, Russia excepted. What army of observation could flatter itself with preventing an incursion of the enemy on a frontier whose extent, on the north, should be hundreds of miles, at one end of which should be placed a capital to be defended from another formidable army, always ready and eager to pounce upon it?

Remember, also, that friends and enemies, loyal and disloyal, Federal and Confederate, speak the same language, have the same manners, the same faces or nearly so, and almost the same uniforms; circumstances that, by facilitating espionage, at the same time neutralize the services they might otherwise render. The people themselves—Secessionists tonight, Unionists tomorrow, and vice versa, as the vicissitudes of war make them fall into the power of one or the other party—offer many embarrassments to the Federal general, who feels the imprudence of listening to the information he receives, not knowing whether the source from which it emanates is worthy or to be suspected. This will explain the state of things at Yorktown, with its Quaker guns and a few pieces of veritable artillery, holding the army of General McClellan in check little more than a year ago while the Confederate artillery had been transported, unknown to the Federalists, beyond the Chickahominy.* The front of Lee's army threatening Washington was

---

* That General McClellan could not have been aware of the true state of things, with all the resources of the Federal Government at his back, and with the most daring and intelligent men under his command, is not to be conceived of by anyone of ordinary intelligence [translator's note].

formidable for three weeks, and apparently menaced it, but the Confederate general had filed off the flank of his best divisions, and, thanks to the cooperation of the inhabitants, his maneuvers were not discovered until his first columns had been in the Cumberland Valley for two days.

Besides, Pennsylvania is a mountainous country, covered with impenetrable forests, intersected by rivers and brooks, with immense spaces of uncultivated ground—that is to say, with all the elements fitted to complicate or render inefficient the vigilance of an army of observation. Finally, Lee is a great general, judging from the testimony of General Scott, who before the rebellion considered him the best strategist in America. Again, it must not be forgotten that the Federals have had to attack the Confederates on their own ground; they defended themselves; and as an old Spanish proverb says: *"Es tan fuerte un hombre en su casa que aun cuando muerto se necessitan cuatro para llevarlo"* (A man is so strong in his own house that, even when he is dead, four men are needed to carry him out).

5 P.M. Another dispatch from the Governor of Pennsylvania, calling all able-bodied citizens to arms. The Confederates, says the dispatch, have seized Martinsburg and are making forced marches on Hagerstown. This last town is only forty-five miles from the state capital.

I go out into the streets. The crowds multiply and increase every moment. I pass again before the shop of the fruit milliner: her hats full of strawberries and her beribboned baskets still are there, but the poor woman appears terribly frightened.

A voluntary military band (the only one in Williamsport) draws up in battle array on the principal square; is it necessary for me to say that it is composed of Germans (all the musicians in the United States are Germans)? There are five of them: A *cornet à piston* with a broken-down constitution (I speak of the instrument), a cavernous trombone, an ophicleide too low, a clarinet too high, a sour-looking fifer—all of an independent and irascible temper, but united for the moment by their hatred of keeping time and their vigorous desire to cast off its yoke. I must confess that they succeeded to such an extent that I am doubtful whether they played in a major or minor key.

Fresh dispatches received excite the greatest consternation. The

Confederates are marching on Harrisburg. The crowd is stirred up; patriotic meetings are organized. An old gentleman in black clothes, with a large officer's scarf around his waist, harangues many of his friends from the porch of the hotel. The band strikes up and marches through the streets, filling the people with military spirit, thanks to the strains, more noisy than harmonious, of this performing cohort.

With all this, the chances for the concert this evening are rather dubious. The receipts, which promised famously this morning, suddenly are paralyzed.

11 P.M. I played this evening, after all, before a very respectable audience, which listened with marked interest and a more sustained attention than I always meet with in the audiences of small towns. My little piece entitled *The Union*, was much applauded; it suited the moment.

Madame Strakosch (sister of Adelina Patti and wife of Maurice Strakosch) also was very much applauded. She possesses a very agreeable contralto voice, an attractive appearance, and a popular name, three conditions of success, enhanced, in her case, by distinguished manners and a private life that the tongue of slander never has assailed. The family of the Pattis is truly a dynasty of distinguished singers. The father, Salvatore Patti, was still an excellent tenor *di forza* twenty years ago. His wife (the mother of Adelina), a fiery lyric tragic actress of the name of Barili (she was first married to Signor Barili), is still celebrated in Portugal, Spain, and Naples, where she achieved some great triumphs. I said that she was a fiery actress. She sometimes had transports not connected with art and, it is reported, several times allowed herself to be carried away into violent apostrophes against the audience for not listening to her with all the attention and respect owing to her talent. A very worthy woman otherwise. These freaks were readily forgiven, thanks to her fine voice and to her large black eyes, which Adelina has inherited.

Her eldest daughter, Clotilde Barili (deceased some four or five years ago), was eminently successful in New York and all Spanish America, particularly at Lima and San Francisco. Her sons, Ettore Barili, a distinguished baritone, Antonio, a *basso profundo*, and Nicola Barili, *basso cantante*, bravely maintained the reputation of the family. The children of the second marriage (Patti) are Amalia Patti, married to Maurice Strakosch, a very distinguished pianist, whose charming compositions deserve to be better known; Carlotta, whose extraordinary voice and marvelous agility have set the United States wild and just now are exciting in London a second edition of the enthusiasm that Adelina has gained there. After Carlotta come Carlo and Adelina; Europe already is acquainted with the latter; as to Carlo, he is a fine fellow, rather bohemian, as his adventurous temper has led him to California and Mexico (where he played the violin in a very remarkable manner), to New York, where he sang, married, and divorced (he was then seventeen years of age); to Memphis, where, after having been the hero of gallant adventures, he remarried, it is said, enlisted as a private in the Southern army, became a musical leader, was killed and resuscitated in many battle bulletins, and is as well today as all the other Pattis, who to so many privileges add that of never being sick. What a family! Do you know as many in art whose coats-of-arms are worth as much as those I have just enumerated?[7]

◇◇◇◇◇◇◇◇◇

Williamsport, Midnight, June 15, 1863

I suggested to Strakosch that the concert announced for tomorrow at Harrisburg had better be given up. It is evident that people who expect every moment to be bombarded are not in the state of mind to hear *Cradle Songs, Aeolian Murmurs*, etc., to say nothing of the risk we might run by rushing into the lion's den. But the prospect of a good house and the probability that the rumors of invasion were exaggerated made him turn a deaf ear to me.

At the concert this evening, I noticed a young man who, having occasion to cross the hall, did so on tiptoe, not seeming to share the general opinion in this country that in such cases it is best to make as much noise as possible. Incomparable young man! How I regret not being able to inscribe thy name on my tablets or have it engraved in letters of gold, in order that it may be handed down to the admiration of posterity!

---

[7] This history of the Patti family also appeared in a letter from Gottschalk, dated June 15, 1863, to *L'Art musical* (Herman Klein: *The Reign of Patti*. [New York: The Century Company; 1920], p. 430).

I leave tomorrow morning for Harrisburg.

Making all allowance for exaggeration, there is no longer any doubt that the rebels are advancing toward the capital, and I begin to think that, unless it be a part of the plan of Strakosch to make me play before General Jenkins and his staff, our concert tomorrow will hardly come off.

Another division, or rather army corps, of which the command of Jenkins is only the advance, is already at Carlisle, in the valley of the Cumberland. It is commanded by Ewell, the general whom Stonewall Jackson recommended on his deathbed and designated as worthy of succeeding him in the command of the famous Stonewall Brigade. This General Ewell has become famous for his rare courage. He has a wooden leg, which he has fastened to his saddle on the day of battle.

Stuart, the cavalry general of Lee's army, is young, handsome, brave, and generous. The last information having been given me by a Baltimore belle strongly attached to the Secessionists, as are almost all the ladies of Maryland, I cannot guarantee its accuracy. A woman's imagination is a deceitful prism through which she sees everything rose-colored or everything black, according as she loves or hates the object reflected. This would furnish matter, if I knew how to write, for a very long chapter, in which, acknowledging that it is the privilege of women to inspire in us our noblest actions and to be the source of all our poesy, I would deplore the influence that they so fatally exert over our conduct. But for the women, our civil war would long ago have been ended. Through their imprudent zeal and the intemperance of their opinions, which, in politics as in other things, carry them beyond their mark, they have on both sides contributed to foment the discord and to envenom the strife. Quevedo, the great satirist, was accustomed to cry out when any event, catastrophe, or crime was related to him, "*Quién es ella?*" (Who is she?). Indeed, women are found at the bottom of every social revolution and in all the little incidents of social life.

Imbued with prejudices, they execrate or adore a principle, a law, a race, as their rancors or their personal affections drive them in this or that direction; nervous and irritable, they become heroic without suspecting it, like Monsieur Jourdain, who spoke prose without knowing it; passionate and unreflecting, they commit with innocent frankness monstrous cruelties at which their tender natures would revolt if the blindness of their passion did not almost always prevent them from seeing rationally and soberly. Without giving entire faith to the stories of jewelry made from bones gathered on the battlefields, I will cite that woman of the South who burst into laughter on seeing pass by the funeral procession of a young Federal officer killed near Baton Rouge and that young madwoman of the North, A—— D——, unfortunately endowed with eloquence, who, for some time has gone about lecturing, preaching with ferocious simplicity the massacre of all classes in the South; and the "strong-minded women" of New England who demand the annihilation of the McClellan party, because it is too moderate toward the Rebels and the women. What do I say? The ladies of Baltimore, Nashville, and St. Louis, crying, as loud as they can bawl, "Hurrah for Jefferson Davis!" in the presence of wounded Federals, wrapping up their children in Confederate flags, and making them sing every time an officer of the United States passes by, "My Maryland" or "Dixie," for the purpose of drawing on themselves the prosecution of the government or of rendering plausible the reproaches that the enemies of the latter make—that it attacks women and children; and my beautiful female fellow-citizens in New Orleans, provoking the officers of Butler so far as to render indispensable the regrettable measures which that general thought it his duty to take, seeing a conflict becoming imminent on account of their incessant hostile acts. Here is what a young officer, a friend of mind, wrote to me on this subject: "On arriving at New Orleans, I flattered myself that I was above such little annoyances; I had made up my mind to consider them as childish behavior; but soon, I admit, the contortions, the grimaces, the sneers of the women whom I met, the insulting care with which they placed their handkerchiefs to their noses when they met me or wiped their dresses if they had touched me in passing, the affectation with which they walked in the mud in the middle of the street rather than to walk on the pavement where I happened to be—all these little pinpoint annoyances, to a well-educated man who was disposed to accord them his protection and to respect them, triumphed over my philosophy and caused me a sort of painful humiliation that you cannot imagine; and nevertheless these insults are nothing in comparison with those which many of my companions have suffered!" However, without undertaking to make an apology for all the acts of Butler, I do not easily understand the indignation caused in Europe by his famous order of the day, which says that "Every woman who shall insult an officer or soldier in the streets will be considered as a common woman." I have no need of Butler to arrive at the same conclusion, and the proof of it is in the answer of Beauregard's sister, whose opinion was asked respecting this "infamous edict." I have none, said she, seeing that it does not concern me. Is it difficult to judge by this answer that she was a lady, and consequently had nothing to fear because Butler's order did not justify the insults of an officer or soldier to her?

I do not like war, and military glory affects me but slightly when it is not justified by a great principle: the Italian war and the War of Independence in the United States, for example. Strong-minded women are ridiculous, and they become odious as soon as their mission ceases to be that of tenderness, charity, and devotion. The lady of Forli of whom Machiavelli speaks was an unnatural mother, an indecent virago; Charlotte Corday, a romantic and probably amorous fool; and all the women of the South and North who place themselves on their balconies in festal garments when the coffin of an officer of the enemy passes by, and who thus insult the august majesty of death by displaying ridiculous emblems fill me with horror!

It is one o'clock in the morning. They are beating the "to arms" in the streets. I leave at daylight for Harrisburg, for, no matter what I say, Strakosch turns a deaf ear to me.

◇◇◇◇◇◇◇◇◇◇

Williamsport, June 16, 4 o'clock in the morning

A fresh telegram from the governor orders the National Guard to hurry to the defense of the State capital.

One of my cousins [Leonard Myers], a member of Congress and a major in the Home Guard of Philadelphia, has informed me that he is leaving for Harrisburg with his regiment. Another of my cousins is an officer in the Southern army. Sad war! Both nearly of the same age and bound to each other by fraternal affection, but the hazards of this terrible strife might place them face to face with weapons in their hands!

◇◇◇◇◇◇◇◇◇◇

In the cars on the road to Harrisburg

Hagerstown definitely is in possession of the Confederates. The governor asks the people to put before their doors all the empty barrels that they may have to dispose of; they will use them on the fortifications to be thrown up at Harrisburg. All along the road we see farmers under arms, in battle array and doing military drill. They all seem to want to obey the command of the governor, who orders all able-bodied men to the field to meet the enemy, and to take the Susquehanna as the line for battle.

A traveler we picked up at the last station assures us that the Confederate Army is not more than thirty miles from Harrisburg. Everybody is frightened. Strakosch begins to see his mistake.

It is ten o'clock in the morning. The train continues to advance at full speed toward Harrisburg—that is to say, toward Jenkins, for the city must be attacked tonight, if it is not taken already. What shall we do? As for the concert, it is out of the question; but ourselves, our trunks—my pianos—what is to become of us in all this confusion?

1 P.M. A mile this side of Harrisburg the road is completely obstructed by freight trains, wagons of all sorts, and in fine by all the immense mass of merchandise, etc., which for the last twelve hours has been concentrated near the town to avoid its capture or burning by the rebels. The train stops at the middle of the bridge over the Susquehanna—why? The anxiety increases. Can you conceive anything more terrible than the expectation of some vague, unknown danger? Some passengers have sat upon the floor so as to be sheltered from bullets in case the train should be fired upon.

One hour of anxiety, during which all the women, while pretending to be dead with fright, do not cease talking and making the most absurd conjectures. I myself am only slightly comforted, and the idea of a journey to the South at this time is not at all attractive. But the train standing in the middle of the bridge, the silence, the unknown, the solitude that surrounds us, the river whose deep and tremulous waves murmur beneath our feet, and,

above all, our ignorance of what is taking place in front and what
awaits us at the station—is not all this enough to worry us?

Tired of this suspense, I decide to get out of the car. Strakosch,
Madame Amalia Patti, and I go toward the station, which we are
assured is only a walk of twenty minutes. We find at the entrance
to the depot piles, no, mountains of trunks blocking the way. One
of the mountains has been tunneled by a frightened locomotive.
Disemboweled trunks disgorge their contents, which charitable
souls gather up with a zeal more or less disinterested. The conductor points out to me a pickpocket, an elegantly dressed young
man moving quietly around with his hands behind his back.

What luck! I have just caught a glimpse of my two pianos—
the cowardly mastodons—(Chickering forgive me!) snugly lying
in a corner and in perfect health. These two mastodons, which
Chickering made expressly for me, follow me in all my peregrinations. The tails of these monster pianos measure three feet in
width. Their length is ten feet; they have seven and a half octaves,
and despite all this formidable appearance possess a charming and
obedient docility to the least movement of my fingers. The Chickering sons (Chickering, the father, founder of this great house,
has been dead for some years) have given, by their labor and con-
structive talent, for some time past a great impetus to the manu-
facture of pianos. Their factories at Boston turn out forty-two
pianos a week! Five hundred workmen are employed in them constantly. The later instruments, constructed on new models of their
own invention, rival, if they do not surpass, the finest European
pianos.

I acknowledge that my heart beat at the idea of leaving these
two brave companions of my life exposed to the chances of a
bombardment or an attack by assault. Poor pianos! Perhaps tomorrow you will have lived! You will probably serve to feed the fine
bivouac fire of some obscure Confederate soldier, who will see
your harmonious bowels consumed with an indifferent eye, having
no regard for the three hundred concerts that you have survived
and the fidelity with which you have followed me in my Western
campaigns.

The city expects to be attacked at any moment. Three thousand
people are at work on entrenchments. The clergy (many hundred
persons), in a meeting that took place on this subject, have placed

themselves at the disposition of the governor, to be used for the defense of the city. Priests, pastors, rectors, ministers of all denominations are at this moment engaged in wheeling barrows full of earth and in digging pits for the sharpshooters. This evening, the State of New Jersey is to send two or three regiments of militia. New York also furnishes her contingent. The Seventh Regiment of the National Guard is already on the way. This regiment, whose fine discipline Prince Napoleon so much admired, is composed of young men of the aristocracy of the Empire City. Many other regiments of volunteers are to follow soon. Everybody here except women and children appears disposed to fight. The discharged officers and men of the last nine months' levies have met and reformed their old regiments.

2 P.M. A battery of artillery passes at full gallop. We are crushed in the midst of the crowd. Jones's Hotel is a quarter of a mile away. Many groups stand before the telegraph office. The rebels, the dispatches announce, are eighteen miles away. All the shops are closed, and most of the houses from garret to cellar.

"Decidedly our concert is done for!" exclaims in a piteous voice my poor Strakosch, who has just returned from a voyage of discovery. The reflection is a rather late one and proves that my excellent friend and agent is a hopeful youth and trusts to the last, like Micawber, that something will "turn up."

The hotel is overrun by a noisy crowd, in which I recognize many New York reporters sent in haste by the great newspapers in the hope of furnishing their readers with sensational news. Sensational news is a new synonym for "a canard." The three pretended captures of Charleston and that of Vicksburg, a year ago, the death of Jefferson Davis, and so many other canards have been very ingenious combinations by the newspapers, thanks to which, by causing the sale of many millions of "bulletins," they have realized enormous profits. Unfortunately everything wears out in this world, and credulity is so deadened that now everything is doubted. I hear some people around me who assert that the rebels never have stirred from their headquarters on the Potomac. This is going too far. A rich merchant of the city who was riding out this morning in his equipage, drawn by two splendid horses, was made prisoner by the Confederate advance scouts. His horses and carriage were seized, and he was not released until he had sworn not to tell what he had seen in the rebel camp. I have just spoken to him. The newspapers have told the truth for once.

"Dinner, gentlemen!" A general rush to the dining room. The hotel now is literally invaded. I succeed with great difficulty in finding a place at the table. The faces of the people about me are filled with alarm. Outside, rumors are repeated in a low voice. The poor blacks who wait upon us look so sad and suppliant that it would seem to me laughable if I did not know the horrors of slavery and the fate reserved for the free Negroes of the North who fall into the power of the Confederates. "The rebels!" These words sound to them like a funeral knell. The clamors of the crowd which come to us through the open windows make them tremble all over. The countenance of the darkest of them (an old man) seems to be changing from the blackness of ebony to the grayness of the badger, which all know is the case when a Negro becomes pale.

A long file of laborers and workmen, preceded by a drum, passes under my windows; they are going to the arsenal to obtain arms. The governor, by a proclamation, has promised them to all citizens who present themselves. In the condition in which the city is at present, if the rebels think of advancing, they will take it without its being able to make the least resistance. It is true that all the citizens are under arms or working upon the fortifications, but these fortifications, thrown up in a few hours, are incapable of sustaining any real attack, and in any case will not be of any use unless the Confederates give time for the defense to be organized.

I see all along the river great clouds of dust; it is from the herds of cattle which the frightened farmers are driving toward the mountains in hopes of hiding them from the rebels. The report spreads that a spy has just been arrested. A young man who was working on the fortifications was killed a moment ago by falling from an embankment twenty-four feet high. Great consternation! General Milroy, commanding the advance guard of the Federal army, has been defeated; his equipment is in the possession of the enemy, his force routed. The officers of his staff have just arrived.

A thousand absurd rumors are in circulation. The great news for the moment is that McClellan, who is the idol of the army, particularly since the President has removed him from command, arrives this evening to place himself at the head of the Pennsylvania Militia, to crush Lee and proclaim. . . . . But I know McClellan; he is thoughtful, profound, and prudent and will take good care not to risk, by a hazardous move, the almost certain chances he has of reaching the presidential chair after Lincoln.

Old men, women, and children are leaving the city. A train left this morning carrying off many thousand refugees. In a few hours our position has become very critical. We cannot advance, and I fear that our retreat will be cut off. A militia regiment passes at quickstep; it is going to the front. They are, for the most part, young men from fourteen to eighteen years old. They murmur greatly against Philadelphia, which, being the principal city in the state (numbering six hundred thousand inhabitants), has not yet sent one regiment of its National Guard to defend the seat of government, while the distant states of New Jersey, New York, and even Rhode Island already have fifteen or twenty thousand men on the road to Harrisburg and the valley of the Cumberland.

A train being announced to leave for Philadelphia in an hour, we run to the station. Strakosch will remain behind to search for our trunks, which have been missing these two hours. My tuner has lost his head; the two mastodons of Chickering's have disappeared, and the express company declines to be responsible for them. Too obstinate Strakosch, why in the world did he make us come to Harrisburg?

◇◇◇◇◇◇◇◇◇

Harrisburg, June 16

I have learned lately from an ex-officer of Beauregard's (now retired from the army) that the latter has for his barber and factotum a young Spaniard who is attached to him and follows him everywhere. By the most singular coincidence, this is none other than Ramón, the little gypsy I adopted in Spain when he was a child. Some of my friends will remember having seen him in his picturesque Andalusian dress when he arrived with me in New York some years ago.

I met him in 1851 running half naked through the streets of Valladolid and making little wax figures. He was dying of hunger and, not wishing to ask alms, he offered to the passers-by the simple products of his art. He was seven years old. Abandoned, he said, by his parents, the poor child had forgotten even the name of the town in which he was born, and remembered only the harsh treatment that he had suffered from his father, a gypsy like himself. Attracted by his intelligent look, I adopted him. At the end of some weeks, Ramón was transformed, thanks to a complete *majo* costume that I had made for him, and thanks also to that happy thoughtlessness of childhood which forgets the troubles of the evening and conceals with a golden veil the darkness of the morrow. He accompanied me for eighteen months through all my travels in Spain. Ramón soon became celebrated. His grace, his Andalusian wit, his embroidered leggings, and the history of his adoption made a little hero of him. The queen asked to see him, and, as a faithful hidalgo, he had the honor of presenting to Her Majesty his chef-d'oeuvre, a little wax bull in which he had displayed all the resources of his talent, and which dazzled less by the exactitude of its contour than by the originality of its pose. I even think that I remember that this bull was grotesque, but as Ramón had the faith that saves in art as in other things, I presided gravely at the presentation to his sovereign of the work of my protégé, and perhaps the poor boy still flatters himself every morning, on shaving his general, with the intoxicating illusion that his bull ornaments one of the galleries of the Alcázar Real.

Recalled to France, I embarked at Cádiz for Marseille. The vessel putting in at Almería, we landed, Ramón and I. When we arrived at the Plaza de Armas, my attention was attracted by a gypsy who persevered in following us for some time, attentively observing Monsieur Ramón. All at once they flew into each other's arms: "*¡Dios mío!*" "*¡Virgen María!*" It is my brother! It is you!— just as at the theater, and there they are, still embracing. "*Señor,*" Ramón said to me with an expression that did little honor to his patriotic feelings and in which I saw less of tenderness than of fear. "*Señor,* I know the houses; it is here where my father beat me so much." The crowd, drawn by this touching scene, commented with that kindness for strangers which characterizes the people of Andalusia, murmuring loudly against "My Lord" (everything in Andalusia which is not Spanish is English or French) who wished to separate a child from its lawful guardians.

They made Ramón understand that he had nothing to fear, that he was at home, that I had no more right over him, but the poor little fellow, little reassured by the idea of finding the paternal tent again, and frightened at the prospect of the enchantments of nomad life, forgotten memories of which now were opening before his eyes with menacing brightness, the poor little fellow said, clinging to me, more dead than alive: *"Señor, por Dios, no me deje volver"* (For the love of God, sir, do not let me return).

That did not appear to be the wish of the crowd, as the cries "Let us call the mayor; to prison with the kidnaper of children!" made themselves heard. I tried to make an explanation. "No—to the jail!" I must refer it to the decision of the *Señor corregidor,*[8] and here we are on the way, I at the head, Ramón hanging onto my greatcoat, and the crowd pressing on my heels. Fortunately the *corregidor* was an honest man. He had heard me in Madrid. "*Ma foi,*" he said to me, "I can do nothing in this matter. The child has a father; it is for him to decide." His father, after having been a horse dealer at fairs, some years before had joined the armed smugglers *con amore.*

Having, at the moment when he had brought one of his commercial operations to a happy conclusion, met a refractory customhouse officer, he had very neatly dispatched him with a blow of a knife.

The knife was found near the corpse. Papa Ramón was arrested, confessed, and had just been condemned to be garroted, that is to say strangled (the punishment still used in Spain). He was in a cell on the ground floor of the public jail. Without taking the trouble of entering the prison, the *corregidor*, who had wished me well, took charge of the negotiation. (Ramón, myself, and the crowd—now the entire town—had followed.) He explained the state of affairs to him. The windows of the cell were walled up to the height of six feet, terminated by an iron grating that, while it permitted the light to enter, prevented the prisoner from seeing out or being seen. "A rich Englishman," (!?) the *corregidor* shouted to him, "has adopted your son Ramón. Will you authorize him to take him with him into his own country?"

Soon a doleful voice was heard: "My son Ramón, the child of

---

[8] The magistrate.

my bowels! *¡Jesús María! ¡Virgen del Carmen!* Abandon him to an Englishman? You cannot think of it, *señor corregidor!*" "He is right," the crowd said, and I avow that I did not know what to answer. I looked at Ramón; he had such a pitiful countenance, so eloquent a look, that I felt willing to make a last attempt. I desired the *corregidor* to drive away the crowd and permit me to speak privately (save the walled window between us) with Papa Ramón. In short, the result of the consultation was that at the end of five minutes, the pacified crowd could see two hands issue between the bars of the window (just as in the fine picture of Paul Delaroche representing Lord Stafford when he receives the benediction of . . . in which we perceive only the hands). I got upon a stone, I cautiously placed three dollars in one of the extended hands, and I led away Ramón, whom his father declared he had abandoned to me as my entire property. The people applauded, felicitated Ramón, still blue from fright, cried out, "*¡Viva el inglés!*" conducted me as far as the vessel, and would have carried me in triumph if my natural modesty and my impatient desire to be rid of my new friends had not been opposed to it.

◇◇◇◇◇◇◇◇◇

Harrisburg, June 16, 4 P.M.

The alarm sounds, the drums beat a call to arms. Military bands parade the streets, playing national airs; the national flag is borne amid cheers and produces indescribable enthusiasm. I detest war, but at this moment I feel that I should love to be a soldier. Good God! What does military enthusiasm amount to? A little music, a great deal of noise, arms that glitter in the sun, and the crowd that looks on! Admirable simplicity of means, which would appear providential to me if I did not remember that both sides possess the same elements of enthusiasm, crowd, sun, and noise, and consequently the same sources of heroism.

On which side is the truth? Which are the martyrs? Which are the executioners? Jefferson Davis decrees thanksgiving to the Almighty for the manifest protection that He gives to the Confederate arms; Lincoln orders public prayers to ask of God continuance of His favor to the glorious starry flag, symbol of justice and of civilization; it is in the name of outraged liberty that the government at

Richmond demands the national independence of the South and inflames the ardor of its troops in the name of the same liberty that at Washington electrifies the population of the North and puts on foot an army of a million men to repulse the pretensions of the South. Both, penetrated by the sanctity of their cause, cut each other's throats in emulation of one another and die like heroes! Moral: man is a machine more nervous than thoughtful, a voltaic pile clothed like flesh, which gives off sparks and shocks when we know how to heat it. It is not for me to touch these great questions here in order to answer them, or to mix myself in the troubles that disturb my unhappy country. I have my opinions, but they matter little. What was I thinking of, to go and throw myself among the briers of politics? When I give my pen license, it runs at random and does a thousand foolish things, like a female parrot let loose in a guava tree.

One train leaves at five o'clock; another left at two o'clock. I doubt the one promised us can accommodate the constantly increasing crowd of four or five thousand persons which presses into and around the station. Litters are provided for the sick; many are occupied by wounded soldiers who will not be left here. Immense trains of merchandise continue to arrive. The panic increases. It is no longer a flight, it is a flood,—a general *sauve qui peut*. It would seem, in view of the speed with which the inhabitants abandon their city, that the rebels already were in sight. Trunks, boxes, bundles of clothes, furniture, mattresses, kitchen utensils, and even pianos are piled pell-mell on the road.

Carriages, carts, chariots, indeed all the vehicles in the city, have been put in requisition. The poor are moving in wheelbarrows. A trader has attached to his omnibus, already full, a long file of spring carts, trucks, and buggies, whose owners probably had no horses, and drags them along to the great displeasure of his team, which sweats, froths, and falls under the increased weight of the load. A long convoy comes in, with ten locomotives in front. It brings cannons, caissons, and many steam engines under construction, which have been sent to Harrisburg to prevent their falling into the hands of the enemy. The confusion is at its height. Cattle bellowing, frightened mules, prancing horses, the noisy crowd, the whistling locomotives, the blinding dust, the burning sun. "V*oyez-vous d'ici le tableau?*" (Do you see the picture here?) as Valsin said in *Ma* *tante Aurore.* Ah, imprudent Strakosch, what business had you in this cursed place?

The station is full of locomotives. I have counted thirty at a time. They look frightened like the people around them. Puffing, out of breath, rushing forward, striking and bellowing at each other —I seem to see a horrible troop of antediluvian animals flying before a geological flood.

The train leaves in a few moments; it consists of eight or nine cars in which are piled at least two thousand persons. We are like herrings in a barrel. The women are sitting on one another, the men all standing, and the children everywhere: not one inch of room is unoccupied. We are dying from thirst; the heat is intolerable. Remember that today I already have made a journey of seven hours and a half, and that from here to Philadelphia there is as much more, and you may understand how I curse my gallantry, which has just led me to give my seat—which by force of perseverance and audacity I had succeeded in capturing—to a young lady. She (the young lady) did not even look at me; obeying in this an error widespread in the United States among ladies (not one of my female friends ever has been willing to acknowledge it), which consists in believing themselves exempt from all humane considerations toward a person not introduced to them, and regards as an inalienable right what, taken altogether, is only the result of voluntary homage. Of the thousand ladies to whom in my travels I have given my place, or for whom I have lowered a window, paid the conductor, or offered my hand to help down, I have set down in my notebook that seven-eighths of them have abstained prudently from thanking me. Up to the time when I read Trollope on the United States, I had attributed this reserve to an exception made in my disfavor, and I cursed my evil star, which had condemned me to the deprivation of the charming smile that is the ordinary reward the weaker sex pays to the ruder. The little marks of deference of which I have just spoken, I have since learned from Trollope, are the same prerogatives that all my brothers of the ruder sex enjoy.

Gallantry, the ladies should not forget, no longer grows on earth as in the days of chivalry; it is the last vestige of an epoch when many things were believed in that now are dead; it is today a delicate flower, a hothouse plant that would die if it refused the fecundating rays of their smiles. But it is two o'clock in the morning. We are in Philadelphia. Fifteen hours and a half of railroad in one day, not to mention our emotions!

The devil take the poets who dare to sing the pleasures of an artist's life.

❖❖❖❖❖❖❖❖

June 17, 1863

Left Philadelphia at 6 P.M. for New Brunswick. We are stopped on the road for three hours; it is eleven and a half o'clock. We are standing still. The road having only one line, we are obliged to wait at a turnout for a convoy of soldiers who left New York at six o'clock and are to pass us at this station. An accident probably has happened to it. In the meantime, it looks as if we are to pass the night here. Our locomotive has left us on a voyage of discovery.

⸙⸙⸙⸙⸙⸙⸙

[*Two weeks later: the Battle of Gettysburg. Strakosch, nothing daunted by the war, sent the troupe on a tour of New England; it did not last very long.*]

❖❖❖❖❖❖❖❖

July 13

Concert at New London today. The drawing for recruits has begun. That which was feared is now being realized: the lower class—the Irish—resist. The telegraph has just announced to us that they have set fire to the buildings where the drawings take place. They are armed. The authorities have ordered out the regular troops now encamped at Morris's Island to march to New York immediately. Blood will flow. The insurgents having taken up the rails on the railroad for several miles, communications are interrupted.

❖❖❖❖❖❖❖❖

July 14

The railroad bridge at Harlem has been burned by the rioters. The news travels a long way around to reach us: The *Tribune* office has been burned to the foundations; the artillery is in the streets.

◇◇◇◇◇◇◇◇◇

July 14

I found on my piano (as always at every concert) a charming basket of flowers. Almost all my pieces were encored. After the last piece an old gentleman came forward and made a speech, thanking me in the name of the audience for the pleasure I had given them. He offered me a serenade by the military band of the fort, which he commands.

◇◇◇◇◇◇◇◇◇

Fitchburg, [Mass.] July 15

Charming country, surrounded by mountains. The houses are built on steep slopes. The hotel is called Fitchburg House. At the hour for beginning the concert, the heavens, which had been cloudy all day, opened and poured down cataracts of rain; the streets were a foot deep in mud. In spite of this we had a respectable audience, and I was enthusiastically encored.

◇◇◇◇◇◇◇◇◇

Nashua, [N. H.], July 16

Pretty little town, like all the towns in New England, hidden like a nest in the midst of the verdure of its gardens and of its tall trees. At four o'clock the news of the taking of Port Hudson [Louisiana] was received with all kinds of joyful demonstrations. Bells ring, explosions are heard, etc. etc. A certain Mr. F. sent me some verses in which he compares me to Apollo.

Met in the street three little boarding-school girls in a buggy, who threw me kisses.

◇◇◇◇◇◇◇◇◇

Manchester, July 17

Manufacturing town, in which there is nothing remarkable. Only sixteen tickets sold, which forces me to give up the concert, more particularly as Madame Strakosch has just telegraphed me that she dare not leave her children in New York while the riots continue. Tomorrow I was to give a concert at Portsmouth, but the telegraph has just transmitted the news of a riot. I definitely will return by way of Boston to New York.

~~~~~~~~~

[*Gottschalk took his brother Edward to Saratoga, New York. After the middle of August, Edward's condition worsened. "The doctor tells me . . . that at any moment he may—I cannot write the dreadful word", Gottschalk wrote to a friend. They returned to New York City, where Edward died on September 28, 1863, at the age of twenty-six. He had accompanied Moreau to Cuba in 1854, assisting him as auxiliary pianist.*

During October and November, Gottschalk and his pupil Harry Sanderson were soloists in a series of orchestra concerts conducted by Theodore Thomas at Irving Hall, New York. Following several appearances in Philadelphia, Hartford, and elsewhere, the pianist was poised for another extended tour.]

❖❖❖❖❖❖❖❖

[New York] December, 1863

We are in town. My company consists of Mademoiselle Cordier, prima donna; Brignoli, tenor; Carlo Patti, violinist; Behrens, accompanist; and myself. Also Max Strakosch, agent and impresario; Ashforth, tuner, to whom is entrusted the duty of overseeing the packing and unpacking of my pianos; Marie, lady's maid to Mademoiselle Cordier; Emile, Brignoli's valet; and Firmin, my confidential servant, valet, major-domo, secretary, and factotum, who has been my alter ego for many years and who tyrannizes over me with that good-natured familiarity which all servants think they have a right to exercise over those they have willingly taken care of for many years.

Such is the list of names of our "Concert Troupe." I now come to the members of it. Mademoiselle Cordier is not pretty, but she is French, that is to say, has all the piquant graces that appear to belong to her countrywomen. She has a flexible voice, which she uses with much art. She was educated at the Paris Conservatoire, where she took a first prize. An excellent musician (*rara avis*), she can read what she sings, and does not possess the gift accorded to almost all Italian singers, of not learning until after having been taught for many years like a canary bird on the bird organ. Her maid is a young, thin, sentimental German who paints flowers, is always asleep, is very ugly, and professes an absolute indifference to her personal appearance.

Brignoli is, as you already know, one of the most seductive tenors that can be imagined. His voice, which reminds me of Mario's,[9] has marvelous purity. His servant Emile is an old sailor who reads Renan's Life of Jesus and is enraptured with the beauties of its style. Behrens is a young German from Hamburg who wears spectacles, is a good musician, and has a good heart. He has two weaknesses (who doesn't have them?). The first, I have to tell you, is to make puns. He is constantly thinking (his notebook and pencil in hand) during the concert, in the carriage, morning, evening, and after dinner, how he may distort a word to make a pun on it. His second is being a fervent disciple of Brillat-Savarin. In every small place, he finds means to have delicacies prepared for him. We have made him superintendent of provisions, and he oversees the preparation of our meals when we arrive at a hotel. Ashforth, a tall, phlegmatic American, looks after the pianos with the love with which an English coachman looks after his horses. He is the best tuner I know.

Strakosch, my agent, impresario, and friend, a fine fellow, is active as he alone can be. De Vivo, second agent, a Neapolitan, is goodhearted and is devoted to me; and, finally, there is Levy, a young Englishman, third agent, with a very large nose—a good fellow, a worker, poor but honest, and on the road to become a first-class agent.

We are a blessing to hotel proprietors, whose purses we fill, and for whom we are also an excellent advertisement, as the newspapers never fail to mention the hotel where we stay.

❖❖❖❖❖❖❖❖❖

December 28

A SNOWSTORM

After having given two concerts in Chicago, I left for Rockford (five hours by train from Chicago), where I am to give a concert

---

[9] Mario, Marchese di Candia (1810–83), has been characterized as the greatest operatic tenor of his generation. Of the Italian nobility, he established his career, which developed comparatively late, in Paris, London, and St. Petersburg. He married the very famous prima donna Giulia Grisi.

by myself this evening. I had sent the rest of my company to Racine (four hours by train from Chicago) to give a concert without me. My name being powerful enough at Rockford to enable me to attract an audience without the aid of my companions, I take advantage of it. On their part, they cannot fail to draw the crowd, and thanks to this strategic maneuver I'll have a double financial gain without increasing my expenses or losing time. Tomorrow I must leave Rockford, and they Racine, in order for us to join each other at Milwaukee (Wisconsin), where a concert is to be given in the evening by our whole company. The cold is excessive. At Rockford the snow, which has been falling uninterrupted for two days, is a foot and a half deep in the streets. The sky at this moment is clear, the air pure. The thermometer, which up to now has stood at about eighteen degrees below zero, begins to go down.

Rockford (Illinois) is a very pretty town of one thousand souls, flourishing like all the Western towns. It possesses three seminaries for young ladies, which I think ought to furnish this evening's concert with a contingent of five hundred persons. Young ladies' seminaries in all the small towns of the West are the soul of a certain class of concerts. The desire for cultivating the mind and purifying the taste is an imperative necessity among American women; I never have found it in so high a degree in any other people. The liberty that they enjoy in the United States, and that would frighten European mothers, far from injuring the development of those exquisite qualities which characterize their sex, on the contrary, adds to the allures of beauty and vests a fund of confidence in their own strength and a maturity of intelligence which guard them more infallibly than the anxious, suspicious solicitude with which a European education surrounds them. Here they are the sole guardians of their innocence and safety; and while I am far from thinking that they do not slip at times from abuse of it (perfection is not of this world), I do not hesitate to prefer our system. Our young ladies are responsible to their conscience and enter into marriage fortified by a practical sense that, in taking from them a little of the unhealthy and sickly sentimentality of young European girls, prepares them for the realities of life. The young European girl—ignorant of everything, and not made accountable by the long childish tutelage imposed upon her—slips, stumbles, falls, without knowing it; if she escapes the perilous passages, she offers to her husband a frivolous companion, a *"Dora,"* that is to say, a pretty plaything, but certainly a wife incapable of assisting and sustaining him in his troubles.

The snow has stopped falling. I sink into it knee-deep. The town pianist, a professor, has just offered me his services and proposes a sleigh ride. I confess that the sleigh ride in itself is very pleasant, and I would be very fond of this kind of locomotion if it could be used in summer, but winter being a condition *sine qua non* for sleighing, I cannot find any compensation in it for the cruel sensations that I suffer from the wind, which cuts my fingers, nose, and lips, and leaves me just enough heat to enable me to feel my suffering.

The cold freezes me, soul and body. The snow reminds me of death. Besides the wind, the sharp particles of snow that stick into the skin—is it not terrible? Does not even Nature herself die in the presence of winter? Toward evening, with their naked branches, cutting the distant horizon, the leafless trees affect me like a band of skeletons, that begins a macabre dance. Where are the birds? Where are the flowers? Where is the sun? I hate winter, for it gives me pain, but it is the true season for inspiration. When at night the house trembles to its foundation, as the hail strikes the windows like a flock of funereal birds that want to get in—then is the hour of inspiration. Some find fantastic hallucinations then; then I hear the echo of an indefinite, secret grief, found in the depths of the soul of all men. True poesy is found only in revery, in the midst of grief, under an inclement sky. I get irritated reading those poets who, full-throated, sing good wine, their radiant sun, their satisfied amours, and whose listless music is contented with some——

I should be very glad to decline the sleigh ride. But the good professor would be offended, and I sacrifice myself. His vehicle is worthy of notice; it is original, a small square box placed on a buggy frame, for the wheels of which two iron runners have been substituted. It is primitive, scarcely solid. We accommodate ourselves as well as we can in this little machine and set out. The wind increases, the cold also. My neighbor's nose is blue. As for mine, I no longer feel it; our horse, animated by the noise of the bells, flies rather than runs. We devour space, we have passed through the town like a hurricane and enter a wide road at a tremendous pace. At every turn of the road our little box and its contents fly from the ground and describe a quarter of a circle in the air. Luckily it falls flat again, and we stick to it as well as we can. An old blind mule has stopped in the middle of the road. Our speed is so great we cannot turn in time, and we strike against the poor beast, which sends a pair of heels at us without striking us. Half of our box remains behind, but there is still enough to hold onto. The horse no longer obeys the reins. I begin to understand that our pleasure ride will end by our being thrown into a ditch. Our destination is a seminary for young girls, of which I begin to see the roof and trees at the end of the road.

We arrive at the seminary. An old, dried-up lady receives us. I am introduced to her; she is the directress of the establishment. Miss So-and-so, Mr. Gottschalk. We go into the parlor. A gentleman with disheveled hair is walking up and down, declaiming "a lecture" that he has to give to the young girls this afternoon. Uncombed head (I speak of his exterior), beard unshaved; type, genus unknown—gold spectacles. He is a German professor of literature, French, and philosophy—was it necessary to tell you that he wore gold spectacles? Do not all the Germans—musicians and savants—wear them?

This is a point of transcendental physiology which I leave to the investigations of the learned—to wit, whether the Germans who are to become musicians are born with little gold spectacles, just as others are born with a wart on the nose, or whether this parasite is developed and grows in proportion as they plunge into the depths of the science of harmony. Or again, whether this appendage is an honorable badge and symbol awarded to those who have penetrated all the secrets hidden from vulgar eyes. Finally, are the gold spectacles of the musical Germans like the cane of the Spanish alcalde or the switch of the English soldier in walking, without which neither one nor the other of these immutable and invariable types considers itself complete?

I visit the seminary. The pupils are engaged in their studies, but in the halls, on the staircase, in the dormitory, we meet young girls who, under their little air of fright or indifference, badly conceal their unruly curiosity. It is plain that they know who I am, and I foresee that I shall have to play for these very pretty, rude little things before leaving. A piano groans in an adjoining room! It is the *Maiden's Prayer*. How far will this virginal prayer pursue me? We get back into our square little box, and after another fantastic and giddy ride, I find myself again (God be praised!) before my hotel, where the waiters (*garçons*) are girls; I mean to say that the servants are of the weaker sex. These young girls are, for the most part, ugly and dirty; I suspect that they are princesses in disguise; their squeamish looks and the air of offended dignity with which they give me a very small piece of roast beef make me divine their illustrious origin, and fill me with confusion. The silly Abigails!

◇◇◇◇◇◇◇◇◇

[Harvard, Ill.] December 31

We are again pursuing our journey. It continues to snow, and from certain signs the farmers say it will have drifted, and will certainly have obstructed the road. Here we are stopped. We must get out. Harvard is the name of the place where the conductor tells us we must get out. It is a small village of five hundred inhabitants. It would be dangerous to proceed farther while the storm continues. The thermometer has gone down to twenty-five degrees below zero. We might have been overtaken by the tempest in the midst of the prairies, where we would have been buried under the snow, ourselves and the whole train in a few hours. We have escaped a great danger by being able to reach a station. We must now try to find lodgings for the few hours that we remain here. The storm will doubtless pass over in the afternoon, at least the conductor leads us to hope so. A tavern is at the side of the road. "Harvard Hotel, Cayer, proprietor." The idea of passing a day at the Harvard Hotel has nothing seductive in it. What kind of rooms, and, above all, what kind of dinner, will they give us?

Agreeable surprise! The landlord, a stout man whom his friends call Judge—who has never had such luck before—conducts me to my room; it is very comfortably furnished and warmed. A mahogany table covered with tapestry of needlework, an album with *cartes de visite* and photographs, and gilt-edged books in the prairies of the extreme West! One thousand miles from New York!! O civilization! Gilt-edge books and French lithographs

(Moses defending I know not what woman, after a picture by Schopin), the monuments of Paris, and a large volume of maps on the Crimean War, written by the commissioners sent out in 1855 by His Excellency Jefferson Davis, then Secretary of War of the United States, which commission was composed of Colonel Delafield and Captain McClellan of the Engineers. These names thus associated have a singular effect! What a contrast, and what events since the illustrious traitor occupied himself with so much solicitude to perfect the military science of the Federal army officers, and chose for this purpose little Captain McClellan. I would have remained a long time meditating on the instability of human affairs, and on the mysteries that the future conceals, if the gong for dinner had not just called me to the reality of things, which is much more pleasant than reverie, seeing that I am very hungry and that the dinner, whatever it may be, will be very welcome. I do not suppose that the Harvard Hotel dinner will be a Belshazzar's feast. Again a rash judgment and an agreeable surprise. After having disagreeably speculated upon what might be the ordinary of this poor little tavern at a village of the extreme West, and found a resigned consolation in my hunger, I went down into the dining room and found it very clean. The thick linen tablecloths are white, the dishes and plates large, but scrupulously clean, the servants pretty, courteous, and not at all princesses. The bill of fare for dinner would make the mouths water of the pseudo-hunters of the plain of St. Denis, who are condemned not to taste venison save under the equivocal and apocryphal form of steaks called roebuck, which the industry of the Parisian restaurateur has enabled him to make out of lamb kept preserved in vinegar until it gets the taste of venison. Here they served up to us a quarter of true roebuck marvelously roasted with its juice; some broiled venison, wild ducks, and prairie chickens. A large pudding and a glass of excellent ale ended this festival of Belshazzar.

Decidedly I submit to my fate. I get again into the train. One hour, two hours glide by, and we do not start. There are two stoves in the car, yet nevertheless the cold increases until Strakosch's ears are nearly frozen. The wind increases, the snow falls in avalanches, we must spend the night at Harvard. Unfortunately, counting on leaving, I paid my bill after dinner, and consequently have renounced all my rights to the room I have occupied part of the day—it has been immediately taken. The hotel being too small to hold all the passengers of the train, a place was first provided for the women and children. Not being able to get in under either of these categories, I have the sad perspective of passing the night on the floor, at a temperature of twenty-six degrees below zero. There are fifty or sixty of us in the same place. The society is not, as you will understand, very select. It is composed of sick and discharged soldiers, of pioneers from the Indian frontiers, peddlers, of horse-traders, and ragged immigrants. I fastened my money in my fob, and also my watch chain. Two or three persons who from their dress appeared to belong to the well-to-do class approached me and acquaintances were instinctively made. In a moment this colony was divided into distinct groups, into little clans that without being hostile to each other, showed nevertheless that if occasion required they would know how to defend themselves against the aggression of their neighbors. I begin to think of my corner for the night. The storm roars outside. If you have never experienced a storm at sea you cannot form any idea of this upturning of nature. My thoughts turn to the poor travelers who will have been surprised on the prairies. They will find certain death there. The house creaks on its foundations. The wind whistles lamentably. Do you know anything more mournful than those ascending and descending chromatic scales that you hear when the wind whistles through the cordage of a vessel? It seems to me that I am on board. Two firemen have just entered with their hands frozen; with great trouble we succeed in restoring their circulation. It is the first time that I see for myself what I have so often read of in the history of voyages to the North Pole. I have had to give up reaching the train where our trunks are, which is only some hundred paces off. Flung back at every step, blind and suffocated by the snow, which strikes the face furiously, I was forced to return in about five minutes almost frozen. They are about to put guards on the locomotive; they will relieve each other every half hour, to keep up the fire, under penalty of seeing the water freeze in the boiler, and then adieu to leaving tomorrow. The countryside, which I see in the twilight through the windows obscured by the ice, is frightfully sad. A limitless meadow that in summer is doubtless an ocean of verdure but now presents to the eye only a desert of snow that is lost in the distant horizon. The hardened snow, masses of which fall with a dull rumbling noise from the roof of the house, and the roaring of the storm drive one to despair with sadness. I write my journal to combat sad thoughts that besiege me.

Poor Strakosch, after two hours of superhuman effort, has come back from the telegraph station, whence he sent a dispatch to Milwaukee, explaining our position; I doubt if it arrives at its destination. Before an hour the wind and snow will have torn down and buried all the telegraph wires under ten feet of snow. The thermometer is still going down. The cold is insupportable, notwithstanding our immense stove, getting red-hot, its jaws flaming with trunks of trees. A cattle train is stopped some distance from the hotel. We hear the bellowing of the poor beasts in the midst of the snow. They will probably perish from the cold tonight.

Max, by virtue of begging, has obtained a bed at the postmaster's, the house separated from ours only by a small garden. It is seven o'clock in the evening. We have just supped on venison and a cup of tea. I wanted to go to my lodgings, but the storm is so violent I have not been able to make the twenty-five paces that separate the house from the post office. The darkness is profound. Assisted by Firmin and Strakosch, I again venture to go out. Supporting each other, thrown down at every step by the wind, covered with snow, and almost paralyzed with cold, we reach the house of the postmaster. The postmaster, a tall, thin, phlegmatic American with a beard turning gray, bids us welcome. The teakettle sings on the lighted stove. A half-open closet reveals the plates and preserves of the family. A large Bible on a white wooden table, a pretty white cat that purrs on her mistress's lap, a little girl of ten years, a daughter of the postmaster, knitting stockings next to her mother, while the latter washes the plates used for supper—all form a picture of neatness, decency, and peacefulness. It is poverty but not want. It comforts and does not sadden. In Europe you cannot understand or comprehend the character of the American farmers. The orderly and respectable habits that characterize them are too incompatible with the gross turbulence and brutalizing ignorance of European peasants to enable you to find an equivalent to the laboring class of American farmers. We talk politics with the postmaster (all Americans of every class understand in their minutest details the political history of the United States). The storm increases every moment; I shall never be able to sleep tonight. The cold is so intense that our clothes are stiff and creak as if they were paper. I wish you good night. I go to shiver until tomorrow morning.

January 1, 1864

SNOWSTORM (THE SEQUEL)

Although I had spent the night with all my clothes on, with a woolen comforter around my neck and a fur cap on my head, and though I had constantly lain drawn up under my mountain of bedclothes, on awaking I found my mustache covered with hoarfrost. The thermometer thirty-two degrees below zero! Our shoes are frozen, likewise our hats, and we are obliged to put them under the stove to thaw them. An old trapper assures us that it will be a very rough winter. The muskrats on the Indian frontier have built their cabins two stories high, he tells us, and all the trout have forsaken the rivers to reach the deep water of the lakes. These are signs that infallibly announce extraordinary cold weather.

We had with us in our car a sick young soldier. I am anxious to learn how he got through the night. I carefully wrap myself up in furs and, accompanied by a guide, I seek the car to learn if we could do anything to comfort this poor man. He is very feeble and young. He is returning to his family. I look for someone in the village who can take care of him until he is well. Poor young man! Will he ever again see his family? By the mercy of God there are noble hearts in this world of dollars and cents. I have found a young farmer who undertakes to take care of him gratuitously.

The cattle have bravely endured this terrible night. Only one horse is extended on the ground, to all appearance frozen! They rub him, he is getting up again, he will probably recover. The engineers and firemen have suffered most. They had to remain on the engines all night to keep up the fire, or the water in the boilers would certainly have frozen. No probability of being able to start today. Milwaukee is impossible. I cannot even return to

Chicago, although the wind blows in that direction and consequently would help us in getting along; before us the snow is piled up into immense drifts that render the journey impossible. We breakfast. Before the dining-room stove an enormous deer is stretched out, killed last night at our request; it will be for our dinner. It has the handsomest head I have seen. We also have quail. They cost sixty cents per dozen here and are almost as large as pigeons. The ladies, I am told, spent the night in dancing. Someone found a fiddler in the village. Fortunately there is no piano. But for that I would have had to play.

◇◇◇◇◇◇◇◇◇

Adrian, Michigan, January 8, 1864

Infamous concert. Seventy-eight dollars!! The people say that they prefer "a good Negro show." They are furious at the price for admission—one dollar.

A singular American characteristic! They insult us as if we forced them to pay.

In the cars a gentleman and a lady are talking: "Those people are those who performed last evening." "No, they belong to the panorama, which, by the way, must be a very handsome affair, judging from the price of admission—one dollar" (this is spoken with a dissatisfied air).

One dollar admission! It is the universal theme. Everybody talks about it, and, singularly, it is with animosity, as if the fact of putting on the handbills one dollar were sufficient to take the price of admission out of their pocket. It is monstrous!

◇◇◇◇◇◇◇◇◇

February 22

After having rested in New York for three weeks, I have begun a new series of concerts today (the anniversary of Washington's birth). After having visited the large towns of the East, I think of going to the extreme West. I'll go as far as the Indian territories. I count particularly on working in Minnesota and will push on as far as Mankato, the principal town of the state, which was the theater of the massacres committed by the Indians two years ago.

I was much applauded by the public this evening. After an encore I played my fantasia *The Union*, which called forth the most patriotic enthusiasm; it arose from the circumstance that it was the birthday of Washington, the founder and father of our great republic.

◇◇◇◇◇◇◇◇◇

Bridgeport [Conn.], February 23

A pretty little town, two hours by train from New York, the birthplace of Tom Thumb and of Barnum.

◇◇◇◇◇◇◇◇◇

February 24

Concert at New York. Crowded. It is the ninety-fifth or ninety-sixth concert that I have given in the city of New York within the last year and a half, without counting at least one hundred and fifty that I gave before my voyage to the Antilles.

◇◇◇◇◇◇◇◇◇

Hartford, February 25

A handsome town in Connecticut, four and a half hours from New York. While I was in a music store I heard the following conversation:

First lady—"Are you going to Gottschalk's concert?"

Second lady—"Yes, if I can find a place in the front row."

First lady—"Is it too near, the sound is not so pure as at a distance."

Second lady—"I do not care about hearing. I want to see his fingers. I know all his pieces."

First lady—"Ah! You play the piano?"

Second lady—"No! But I have a friend who plays them all on the guitar."

(The truth.)

◇◇◇◇◇◇◇◇◇◇

February 26 [*1864*]

Concert at Boston. Very fine concert. Boston, by a singular anomaly, is the city that has contributed the most to shake off the yoke of the metropolis, and that has retained the most English appearance. It is par excellence the aristocratic city. It pretends to be the most intellectual in the United States. It is not to be denied that it has made enormous progress in the sciences and arts. The university at Cambridge is the most celebrated in the United States. Her poets are known the world over. She has for eight years possessed the largest organ in America. (It cost sixty thousand dollars in Germany.) A musical amateur (Mr. Perkins)[1] has presented to the city a statue of Beethoven that cost twelve thousand dollars. It is a beautiful work of art. Boston has six theaters and three concert halls, two of which can seat thirty-five hundred persons. It is in one of these, the Tremont, that I gave my concerts. It is in my opinion the best for hearing and the most magnificent concert hall in the world.

◇◇◇◇◇◇◇◇◇◇

Providence, February 27

Two hours from Boston. An aristocratic city, and one of the oldest in the United States. It was founded by one of the Puritan pilgrims who emigrated under the Catholic King James II, and still preserves the rigidity of its founders.[2] I have a large audience. It is the first concert without rain that I have given in Providence.

Near Providence (at Newport) is the United States Naval School, and a naval station of great importance. The State of Rhode Island is the smallest of the Union.

---

[1] Charles Callahan Perkins (1823–86) was an eminent Bostonian whose interests shifted between art and music. After being graduated from Harvard in 1843, he went to Rome to study painting. In 1850 he became president of the Handel and Haydn Society in Boston; a year later he was studying piano with Moscheles at the Leipzig Conservatory. He became a well-known art critic.

[2] Gottschalk's history is somewhat askew. James II ascended the British throne in 1685. Providence was founded in 1636 by the Rev. Roger Williams, whose liberal convictions made him a refugee from Boston.

◇◇◇◇◇◇◇◇◇◇

Sunday, February 28

Return at night to Boston. Sunday—a day of mortal ennui!! Marked progress nevertheless. One can now smoke in the streets, and carriages can be driven. Two Sunday papers, even, are published. Hardly fifteen years ago these three things would have appeared like monstrosities to the puritanical inhabitants of Boston.

An excellent musician, distinguished violinist, and graceful composer has resided for some years at Boston—Julius Eichberg.[3] He is leader of the orchestra at the museum and has composed some comic operas that have been successful.

This evening—hall overflowing—all my pieces have been encored. Played for the first time on Mason's new organs, which are quite good. He manufactures one hundred weekly.

◇◇◇◇◇◇◇◇◇◇

February 29

Received an invitation from the Institution for the Blind, Deaf and Dumb. These poor creatures have had a great affection for me, since I invited them to come to all my concerts. They have never missed one. Two days ago they sent me some articles made by them, baskets of pearl and filigree work, and a letter written by a young girl *deaf, dumb, and blind,* Miss Laura Bridgman. The poor girl has written, "Grace be with you." I have been really touched by this gift.

---

[3] A native of Düsseldorf, Germany, Julius Eichberg (1824–93), while still a boy, was highly praised by Mendelssohn and later was associated with Schumann. Writing as critic in a Geneva newspaper in October 1850, he called Gottschalk "a marvelous composer and pianist, the meteor of last winter's season in Paris." In 1859, Eichberg settled in Boston, where he remained until his death. He directed the orchestra at the Boston Museum for seven years, founded the Boston Conservatory of Music in 1867, and was director of music in the public schools. His best-known works were an operetta, *The Doctor of Alcantara* and a patriotic chorus, "To Thee, O Country."

❖❖❖❖❖❖❖❖❖

March 1

I start in two hours for Springfield, three hours from Boston. A concert there tonight. The snow is falling, and it is very unpleasant. Small audience. The stage is slanting and the floor waxed, owing to which, during the finale of *Jerusalem*, my chair slipped and slid as far as the footlights, which left my hands fingering the air! To get backstage, we pass through a cul-de-sac, then a low door, a passage, then a ladder staircase that ends at a trap door that we raise up, and we arrive at a little room where a tailor and his daughter are sewing. Leave at midnight for New York, where we arrive at eight o'clock in the morning.

❖❖❖❖❖❖❖❖❖

March 2

Last evening, Miss Harris, a young American prima donna, made her début in *Lucia*. Success: voice a little weak, but much intelligence and great facility. This evening, concert at Niblo's. I play the Quartet in E Flat by Beethoven.[4] The Andante (which recalls, in the first bars, the *"Batti"* from *Don Giovanni*) is one of the sweetest, tenderest, and brightest inspirations of the giant of Bonn.

❖❖❖❖❖❖❖❖❖

March 3

Left for New Haven. A charming city, where the celebrated university, Yale College, is situated. The students number six hundred. They confer degrees as high as Doctor of Sciences. Large audience at the concert. Decidedly, the puritanism of New England is rapidly disappearing. The majority of my audience this evening is composed of Episcopalians, even though we are in Lent! ! !

---

[4] Probably Gottschalk is referring to Beethoven's piano quartet in E-flat major, arranged from the grand quintet for piano, oboe, clarinet, bassoon and French horn, Opus 16.

◊◊◊◊◊◊◊◊◊◊

March 4

Left this morning for Stamford, where I play this evening. Arrived at half past eleven A.M. It is a pretty town. There are two large colleges for young girls, who, without fail, will be at the concert. My tickets are sold at the post office.

Brignoli, after an absence from the stage of nearly a year, has made his reappearance at the Academy of Music, now under the direction of Maretzek. The opera selected by this charming tenor was *I Puritani.*

Brignoli has been the tenor par excellence of New York City for eight years. Of all the singers who have appeared for twenty-five years on our first lyric stage, he is the only one who has succeeded in triumphing over the insatiable avidity of our people for novelty and change. Mirate, Mario were greatly applauded when they came, but hardly had they left when they were forgotten, and the public has turned again to Brignoli with more enthusiasm than ever. One of the most charming of the lady admirers of Brignoli exclaimed, on hearing Mario one evening, that the latter had been less adroit than ordinary in concealing by his art and talents the changes that time had made on him! "Decidedly, the Brignoli stocks have gone up fifty per cent. since they have run opposition to him." This is characteristic, and makes us understand the importance of the reappearance of the tenor after an absence of two seasons,—during which Mazzolini, the tenor engaged by Maretzek in 1862, gained ground in public estimation and created a powerful party among the enemies Brignoli's success had raised against him. Mazzolini is a tenor *di forza;* his voice is hard, hoarse, and sometimes of doubtful pitch; but he is a very good actor and, when it is necessary, screams loud and for a long time, which always pleases the bulk of the public, who want it for their money and are concerned more with quantity than quality. Ten apples are worth more *than one pineapple.* They are right from their point of view; ten apples take up more space in the stomach, and filling it is probably the first object they have in view when they eat.

Ione, the detestable opera by Petrella, has had an unheard-of success, due in part to the play and to the acting of Mazzolini. Maretzek, an adroit manager, has fathomed public sentiment and engaged Brignoli. Sides were immediately taken. The first evening, the Academy was full from top to bottom. Unfortunately Brignoli, whose last trip with me to the West had fatigued him a little, was confused. His natural timidity before the public was increased by the sight of his rival, Mazzolini, who from the hall was looking at him through enormous glasses! Thus it was that my Brignoli became paralyzed and did not sing as he can sing—that is to say, in the most charming manner in the world. At the second performance they gave *Sonnambula*, and Brignoli became indisposed after the second act; they were forced to replace him with Lotti, a young German tenor, who is still a substitute but will soon become a distinguished star. It may be said without contradiction that the entire audience, almost all opponents of Brignoli, profited by the occasion to make an ovation for Lotti. These small events have given the New York exquisites exercise for a week—human passions are so hasty and easily find a pretext to show themselves. The evil-disposed have taken advantage of the stag's head and of the horns, which Brignoli always carries with him, to assert that his confusion and disorder have been caused by a baritone of his enemies, whom our tenor insists on believing to be an *evil eye*, and whom he sees as he comes upon the stage, wickedly sitting in the first box in the balcony.

The concert was deplorable this evening. Complete silence. I correct myself. Silence when I entered and when I went out, but animated conversation all the time I was playing. But happily we conducted things briskly, and dispatched over eight pieces in twenty-five minutes.

It is not half-past eight, and I have already put my overcoat on again. "Short and sweet," said a charming girl going out. "A great deal shorter than sweet," grumblingly answered her beau. This is the only concert where no piece has been encored. I saw on the wall of the artist's saloon the ornamental signatures of musical celebrities who have preceded me. "*Sam*" *something* (the name was not legible), "the best dancer in wooden shoes in the whole world." It was he who wrote it. "Charley So-an-so, a first-rate drummer, who can't be beat."

There are anomalies in the credulity of Americans which proceed less from a bad disposition than from candid ignorance. For example, a child or a young girl asks her father for something at the table, and takes good care not to add, "If you please"; when she is served, it is very rare to hear her say, "Thank you." As for the men, it is useless ever to ask them to make use of these puerile formulas. They are too *manly*. This again appears in the order of ideas which makes them walk on their heels, and make as much noise as possible, when they have to cross an auditorium. At all my concerts I have a chance to observe this. They would be ashamed to walk on tiptoe; it would not be worthy of a strong mind; but what do they call "manly"? Is it, when you tread on your neighbor's feet, to look at him with a menacing air, as if saying to him, if you are not satisfied I will knock you down? All this is "manly"! *Manly* comes from man, and, man being superior to the brute through his intelligence and not through his force, should this not be rather called brutishness? An artist appears before the public, he salutes you; do you not feel something that tells you that you ought to welcome him in return for his salute, by the only means in your power, by applauding him? And if he is celebrated is it not the duty of politeness to show him that you are disposed to hear him with pleasure, prepossessed as you are in his favor through his good reputation? Then after a piece has pleased you, you applaud, in order that he may play it again (which is, take notice, a gratuitous favor). No sooner does he reappear to show that he is about to accede to your wishes than the applause ceases, as if you said, "Now that I have what I want, I laugh at you." It is the child asking for something and giving no thanks for it. You tell me these are puerilities. Agreed. But these trifles—"if you please," "thank you," "I ask pardon"—when you are accustomed to them through constant discipline, are like so many little canals through which your sentiments of amenity and politeness are accustomed to flow outwardly. A man who treads upon my corns, and quickly turns around to express to me his regret, is certainly more likely to become my friend than my enemy. But if, besides the pain he has just caused me, I must also endure his insolent indifference, I suffer doubly. If these trifles were more rooted in our early education, we would have fewer disgusting fights, less shameful degradation, drunkenness, etc.

◇◇◇◇◇◇◇◇◇◇

March 5 [1864]

Matinee at New York, large audience, although the opera (*Faust*) took place at the same hour, a remarkable opposition. Broadway is full of inquisitive people. What is going on? It is the departure of the first Negro regiment for the war. Reached Paterson by rail in one hour. My tuner goes to the music seller who disposes of my tickets. He has sold nine. New Jersey is the poorest place to give concerts in the whole world except Central Africa. Here is as much as my memory enables me to give, as a sketch of the results obtained at different times that I have given concerts there: Elizabeth, eighty persons. Orange, no concert, the public's fault. Trenton, the first time I visited it in 1856 with Madame Bostwick, gave a result of forty-five dollars gross receipts, expenses forty dollars, profit five dollars to divide among the artists. I had the imprudence to try once more at Trenton, some months ago. Result, forty-nine dollars gross receipts; audience icy, the premises going to ruin. I could not even succeed in making them applaud me. The only manifestation that I obtained was a blast of a whistle which a facetious Trentonian lanced at me after *Murmures éoliens*. After the concert a gentleman came to ask me if I stow "Acolian effects" in my piano. New Jersey is incurable. Concerts will never take there. Harry Sanderson himself also took a chance at New Brunswick (take notice that it is the most liberal place of all in New Jersey for concerts), gross receipts, first concert seventeen dollars, second concert twelve dollars. I must nevertheless say that the Negro minstrel performances always draw the crowd.

Observation—A man said to my tuner, "The people here are down on Gottschalk because the last time he was here he was so drunk he could not play." To those who know my habits this will appear less ignoble than ludicrous. Decidedly, that French philosopher who said with great gravity, *"Plus je connais l'homme, plus je préfère le chien"* (The better I know men, the more I prefer dogs.), did not after all say anything very horrible. I am not aware that dogs tear each other to pieces with as much avidity as men do.

◇◇◇◇◇◇◇◇◇◇

March 7

Left New York at ten o'clock for Philadelphia, where I am to give a concert tonight. Last night the concert for the benefit of Harrison took place. The orchestra performed the overture of an opera, *Bourgeois gentilhomme,* composed by Fradelle. The German opera is broken up for want of money.

◇◇◇◇◇◇◇◇◇◇

March 8

Fine concert at Philadelphia. The liberal movement making way against Puritan bigotry is gaining ground every day. The Protestant clergy at this moment is taking measures to prevent the running of cars on Sunday. They have called a meeting to which they have invited all those who are in favor of observing the Sabbath. None but the "reverends" were at the meeting. I played at the concert the *Tannhäuser* march for four pianos.

◇◇◇◇◇◇◇◇◇◇

Return to New York, Wednesday, March 9

Played with Sanderson, a young American pianist who has a great deal of talent, of which I am proud for more than one reason, having been his principal master and most constant friend.

◇◇◇◇◇◇◇◇◇◇

March 9

Left for Norwalk. In every quarter "sanitary fairs" are prosecuted with enthusiasm. Chicago, the first, produced $100,000; Cincinnati $310,000; Boston $200,000; Brooklyn $500,000; New York, probably $1,200,000; without counting all the small towns. They will probably make in all twenty millions.[5]

---

[5] The United States Sanitary Commission was created by the government in June 1861. Its purpose was to assist in the care of sick and wounded soldiers and of their families. It was supported mainly by private contributions, churches and "sanitary fairs," a species of commercial expositions. Only a few days later, probably in Boston, Gottschalk took part in an event under its auspices.

Norwalk is a pretty town, in a picturesque location. It is ten miles from the town to the station, properly speaking. The road is wide and shaded with trees in summer, behind which the pretty white wooden houses with green shutters are concealed.

Again, this unfortunate prejudice! A hackman, who had at once offered me his services with an almost agreeable air (I say almost, because no hack driver is forced to be polite, through certain laws of which you and I are ignorant, but which doubtless are dictated to him by some authority), no sooner saw Carlo's unlucky violin than he discovered the error he was about to commit in taking us for slightly respectable gentlemen, and his question, "where are you going, you people?" proved to me that he appreciated us at our value, or at that which the public opinion of my dear country gives us.

The concert takes place in one of the handsomest little halls I have yet seen in the United States. My audience, without doubt the same that I had here last year, is one of those for whom I am disposed to repeat as many pieces as they want me to. An amiable audience, warm, intelligent, elegant, the majority composed of young girls whose charming faces are made to turn the heads of pianists, present and future, who venture (less prudent than Ulysses) to cast their eyes upon their auditory. Dear Norwalk! I love you whom I have done nothing for, both for the warm sympathy that you show me and for having escaped the icy influence of your neighbor, Stamford, whose remembrance, without being so dear, will last as long as yours. Bad impressions, alas! engrave themselves as deeply on the memory as the good, and often the latter even are effaced while the others still remain.

Half an hour after the concert I was again on the railroad for Boston. One word more. Norwalk (it is with regret that I state this) has no good cigars. The one I have just smoked, bought at the hotel, is veritable poison. Arrived at Boston at seven o'clock. The railway porter has forgotten to put our trunks in the car, and, happier than we, they remain tranquilly behind. If they do not arrive in time, we shall have to put off the concert this evening. I am assured that I can sue the railroad company, but I know by heart the fable of the iron pot and the earthen pot, and have learned to my cost that lawsuits are a bad business for those who attack others stronger than themselves.

◇◇◇◇◇◇◇◇◇◇

Boston, March 11

Unpleasant weather. I play badly—too much fatigued, and have the influenza. Madam Anna Bishop also gives a concert this evening. She is at least fifty years old, but thanks to her name, rendered illustrious by her first husband, Sir Henry Bishop, the composer of "Home, Sweet Home," and also to the great popularity she enjoys in the United States, which she has acquired by singing English ballads, she still succeeds in making good receipts. Her voice is still agreeable, and she uses it with art. She has married, for the third time, Mr. Schultze, an American, who has nothing to do with art. Her second husband was Bochsa, the celebrated harpist of the First Empire.

Second concert. Eichberg gives an orchestral concert.

◇◇◇◇◇◇◇◇◇◇

Sunday, March 13

Ennui—ennui—ennui.

◇◇◇◇◇◇◇◇◇◇

March 14

Left at eight in the morning for Norwich (Connecticut). In the car a neighbor introduced himself to me as one of the brotherhood. He is a traveling music master, whose species is known only in the United States. They go from village to village and organize classes, which they teach collectively—religious hymns, national songs, etc. There are collections of little airs published for this purpose.

Superb weather. A dazzling sun. The snow sparkles under the rays of light. At every village on the road we take up young girls from the seminaries who are going to Norwich to be present at the concert.

Arrived at Norwich: Professor Whittleny introduced himself to me. He is a singular personage who deserves to be described to you. Small, fat, a large bust, short and crooked legs, heavy black eyebrows, from beneath which appears a roll of oily, ruddy flesh. The professor in a basso-profundo voice informed me that he has been the founder, director, headmaster, professor, and proprietor for forty years of a normal college of music for young girls who intend to teach. "All pretty, sir, never less than fourteen or more than twenty years of age. In good health—and I have the satisfaction of being able to say that during the forty years that I have been the head of Music Vale" (the name which he has given to his colony, situated in the middle of a picturesque and lonely valley) *"there has not been one death.* The principals have come with me today to go to your concert. But I desire particularly to introduce you to my pupils. I only teach theory, and I make them work it out by practicing on three harps, which cost me eight hundred dollars, the first in 1825; and I have besides twenty-five pianos, but they are a little old" (judging from the harps which are from 1825). Every time the professor gets up he looks as if about to take wings to fly away. I gave him seats for himself and his school. After the concert he came and grasped my hand warmly; "never, no never, have I heard anything so touching." His enthusiasm knew no bounds; he embraced me, and I am convinced from making acquaintance with his breath of what I had already suspected—that is to say, the worthy professor of Music Vale is a much greater amateur of whiskey than of music; and after having been introduced to his pupils, I discovered that Apollo has less to do at the seminary than his mother.

◇◇◇◇◇◇◇◇◇◇

New London [Conn., April 15]

Arrived at half-past eleven A.M. Walked through the town in springlike weather. The churches are in the ratio of one for every ten dwellings. I noticed one dwelling, surrounded by gardens, which its proprietor has had the questionable taste of painting canary yellow. From the garden pales to the roof, including the shutters, all is yellow. Another, at some distance, is painted a delicate lilac.

◇◇◇◇◇◇◇◇◇◇

March 21

Set out again from Philadelphia for Baltimore. It is superb weather. I have engaged Madame Variani, an American soprano, for a week. She is married to Edward Hoffman, a talented pianist and brother to Richard Hoffman.

Behrens is reading one of "Dwight's papers." I turned hastily away, having resolved never to read that paper again. An honest press, enlightened criticism, never wounds me, even when they notice my weaknesses and my defects; but "Dwight's paper" is the reservoir of every little bilious envy, of every irritating impertinence, of all sickly spleen, which, under the form of anonymous correspondence, gives the writers the small comfort of injuring all those who give umbrage to their mediocrity, and enable them to conceal themselves behind the column of the chief editor, D., waiting for the passage of the object of their envy, and then hurling at him with an edifying uniformity their little bladders filled with gall. Their spite increases from the small effect of their bombardment. The doctor offers something analogous in his mode of cure. When the blood is vitiated, is corrupted, when matter has accumulated, he makes an opening for the bad humors by means of cauteries and blistering. The musical profession, under the influence of the bad effects of vanity and envy, has need of this instrument to turn aside its bad humors. The need of it was generally felt, and "Dwight's paper" has been just the thing.

En route to Baltimore. Our car is filled with very noisy soldiers who sing songs, smelling also of the eternal whisky. At first we do not pay any attention to it, but they begin to be very disagreeable. One begins to smoke, then a second—a third imitates him. We ask them please to abstain from it on account of Madame Variani and a young lady who accompanies her, to whom the smoke is disagreeable. They hasten to let us know, with a crowd of epithets taken from the blackguard's dictionary, that we are no gentlemen, that these are no ladies, that, being soldiers, they have a right to do as they please, and they would prove it to us. After this speech—more remarkable for its vulgarity than its logic —all the soldiers in the car commenced whistling, screaming, and howling, after the manner of the Chinese, or of savages when they wish to show their indomitable courage. An officer present prudently abstained from interfering—for many reasons. His first (which I consider bad, he gave us when we appealed to him) is that they are soldiers on furlough, and that he hardly had a right to control them. The second (which he did not give us, but which I confide in secret as being good) that the whiskey bottle, which for two hours has gone around in the vicious circle of our heroes, has made many drinking stations on his lips, and that an officer would be unwelcome to reclaim an authority which is drowned in a flood of spirits.

"We will do whatever we please"; these words sound in my ears. I acknowledge that I was choked with anger— a disagreeable anger, because it had to be mute, like right before brute force. To be obliged quietly to submit, when you know that you are right, is the hardest thing in the world, and I experienced it at that moment.

Concert at Baltimore. The hall hardly holds five or six hundred persons. I love Baltimore. I love its people. I am assured that they are Secessionists, but I don't want to know anything about it, and have no right to speak but of what they have let me know— the warmth of their friendship and the constancy with which they keep their appreciation of me as an artist. Besides at Baltimore they love the arts. They sing more there, and better, than in many of the large cities of the United States. The professorship of the piano is represented there by artists of great talent, who love me (*O rara avis!*) and whom I love. O Baltimoreans, my friends, may you someday forget our misfortunes! !

◇◇◇◇◇◇◇◇◇

March 22 [*1864*]
Concert at Washington. On the front row, my friend the Swedish minister, Count Pieper.

◇◇◇◇◇◇◇◇◇

March 23
Been by carriage to Alexandria. Roads cut up. Desolation everywhere. I have obtained a permit from the provost marshal to go and return the same evening by the Virginia shore. Concert at Alexandria; quieter than the last; many sentinels stand guard in the passages, and have even sat down with the audience, to suppress the noise should there be any. We set out again immediately after the concert. In the first carriage with myself were Madame

Variani, Hoffman, and his mother. In the second carriage came Strakosch, Behrens, Carlo Patti, and Firmin. Then all at once these words, "Halt! Who goes there?" The password! And the click of a gun reached us with a clearness of sound which was increased by the darkness surrounding us, striking us with an emotion (I must confess it) not a little disagreeable. We show our safe-conduct and, after some parley, we proceed. A half hour glides by. The weather is superb, the sky starry, and the atmosphere almost warm. The moon lightens the two banks of the Potomac, on which the angular lines of the fortifications are visible. "Halt!" Again that devilish click. Decidedly, I do not like traveling in the midst of the advance posts. We show our papers—they are all right. We proceed. The officer in command of the post keeps our safe-conducts, assuring us that they are no longer necessary, as in half an hour we will be at the bridge that crosses the Potomac (a bridge three-quarters of a mile long); it leads into Washington. At the middle of the bridge we are stopped by an untimely sentinel. Unfortunately our safe-conducts remain behind us. The chief of the post arrives. Impossible to pass. "It is our orders." We shall have to return to Alexandria, but the situation on that side is scarcely more favorable. We have no permission to enter Alexandria by night, and we shall be obliged to remain on the road until daylight.

Max Strakosch, who has got out and has gone on ahead to confer with the commander of the post, losing patience at this piece of obstinacy, let escape an energetic exclamation in the language of the *Vaterland*. O good luck! The sergeant is a German. He loves music perhaps, and the end of Carlo's violin case that sticks outside the coach door convinces him of our innocence and peacefulness. He jabbers in German with his compatriot Strakosch, and the end of it is that we pass, after (for form only) the brave warrior has examined our countenances by placing his lantern under our noses.

❖❖❖❖❖❖❖❖❖

March 24

Concert at Washington. The President of the United States and his lady are to be there. I have reserved seats for them in the first row. The Secretary of State, Mr. Seward, accompanies them. Mrs. Lincoln has a very ordinary countenance. Lincoln is remarkably ugly, but has an intelligent air, and his eyes have a remarkable expression of goodness and mildness. After an encore I played my fantasia, *The Union*, in the midst of great enthusiasm. Lincoln does not wear gloves. I played very badly and was furious with myself, which, however, did not prevent many of my friends from coming to congratulate me on my success. One of them who was present at the first concert (at which, by the way, I played very well) said to me, "Well and good, you are in the vein tonight, for at the first concert one saw that you were badly prepared."

◇◇◇◇◇◇◇◇◇

Good Friday, March 25

Took the railroad to return to Baltimore, and met there my excellent and constant friends Mrs. B—— and her daughter.

◇◇◇◇◇◇◇◇◇

March 26

Concert at Washington. Crowded from top to bottom—every place taken. Lieutenant General Grant and all his staff were present. Grant, the most fortunate of all our generals, is a small man, of ordinary appearance, slender, modest. He has taken more than one hundred thousand prisoners and captured five hundred cannons in two years and a half. The title of lieutenant general, which has just been decreed to him by the government, is at the least equivalent to marshal (of France). We have only had three lieutenant generals: the first was Washington, the second Scott, after his fortunate Mexican campaign, and the third Grant.

Madame Variani sang "The Star-Spangled Banner," each stanza of which was applauded to the skies and encored. The enthusiasm nevertheless is confined to the gallery filled with soldiers; the parterre, the boxes, and orchestra seats abstain from demonstration. You are not ignorant that Washington is of very doubtful loyalty and that her most influential families sympathize with the South.

◇◇◇◇◇◇◇◇◇◇

Easter Sunday, March 27

It is most beautiful weather. I set out again for Baltimore at half-past seven P.M. and arrived at the house of my good friends, the Curletts, at ten o'clock.

◇◇◇◇◇◇◇◇◇◇

March 28

Left for Harrisburg. For seven years I have tried eight or ten times to give a concert in Harrisburg, and every time I have been prevented by some unforeseen circumstance. You will perhaps recollect that last year the Confederates invaded Pennsylvania at the time announced for my concerts, and that on the day I arrived in Harrisburg, the advance guard of the Secessionists was only a few hours from the city, and the concert was put off indefinitely.

◇◇◇◇◇◇◇◇◇◇

Harrisburg, March 28

Capital (seat of government of Pennsylvania). Well populated, particularly by the Germans. It has preserved their customs. Its houses and pavements of brick are clean. The names of the streets, like all others in Pennsylvania, are borrowed from the vegetable kingdom—Cherry Street, Almond Street, Walnut Street, etc. The capitol, where there are two large halls for the legislative bodies, is a niggardly monument of cut stone and bricks, surmounted by a cupola; its elevated position in the middle of a green lawn gives it a certain air of grandeur.

The concert takes place in the courthouse. My tuner wants to install the piano on the platform about four o'clock, but the court is in session, and the judge has sent word to him to wait an hour. The hall is pretty, and my piano is just below the judge's bench. The audience is charming. I observe in it some of those rose and lily complexions of which our ladies have the privilege, and which I denounce to the artists who follow me as being those

which trouble the soul while you are playing. They make you play
false notes and give a suppressed sigh every time your imagination
evokes their charming images. The hotel is excellent.

◇◇◇◇◇◇◇◇◇

March 29 [1864]

I just woke up, calling for help. Civilization is outraged by a
barbarous custom to which we submit through that kind of cowardice which we exhibit in regard to all ancient usages—an abominable custom which lacerates the ear—I speak of the gong. What!
I am of my own free will in a hotel to enjoy all the privileges of
hospitality, and I must submit to this unmerciful discipline that
condemns me, by a barbarous fashion, to be deprived of my
sleep.

A regiment of veterans is passing under my windows. I am told
that for three days they have been fighting in front of the Army
of the Potomac. Yesterday I noticed at a station some fortifications, improvised with trunks of trees, and a blockhouse, built
since the invasion of last year. I took a walk through the streets
and recognized the charming young girl who applauded me so
much last evening.

The world behind the scenes is all in a flurry on account of
an adventure of which Mademoiselle Vestvali, "the superb," as
the playbills announce her, has been the heroine, I was going to
say the victim, if the buxom proportions and masculine character
of the celebrated contralto did not render it impossible that she
should ever play that role. She has smartly chastised the two
fools who got scotched by her rich attractions.[6]

"He plays only his own music." Of all the criticisms of which
I am the object on the part of the impotent and jealous who, like
thorns and barren bushes, encumber every avenue of art in America, I avow that this is the one that I am the least disposed to
accept. If I had never been able to compose, no doubt the poorest
of musical pretenders who had manufactured a polka or a valse
would have thrown it in my face that I played only the music of

---

[6] A full account of the incident can be found in the New York *Times,*
March 26, 1864. Vestvali was the first to sing the role of Azucena in New
York, at the Academy of Music in 1855.

others. If my compositions had failed in originality, "They are copies" would not have failed to be said; but I compose, and what I compose is unfortunately my own, and, further, the public seems to like my music; hence their rage. I understand it, but what I cannot understand is that, after taking a great deal of trouble to find fault with me, they make into a crime what in me really is a merit. It is the cunning of the fox—unfortunately one of that animal's ancestors was guilty of the same thing with a vine of our acquaintance, and since then we have held him in slight estimation.

Sometimes, in my moments of discouragement, I feel what the white man felt in the midst of Negroes, when he was disconsolate because he was white and had not a flat nose. I begin to regret having received from God the afflicting gift of being able to create. Why cannot I enjoy in all the plenitude of its glorious privilege the right of criticism, and of being able to bark at those who compose? Criticism in these cases is so much sweeter. If Thackeray were lecturing to you, would you complain that he gave you Thackeray, and would it not be absurd if he recounted to you the passages of *Hamlet* or *Othello* which any actor could recite to you? Perhaps they could recite it better than Thackeray; would you conclude, from that, that Thackeray had less talent? No, certainly, because a vulgar mind, possessing no peculiar physiognomy, no strongly marked character, can accommodate itself to every fashion, while he who has been cast in an original mold cannot abdicate his individuality, or that which gives him superiority, in order to reduce himself to the level of the first comer who knows how to read and has a voice loud enough to make himself heard. Do you insinuate that the classics are superior to all we accomplish? Granted, but besides reserving the right to ask you what you understand by the classics—this convenient club with which you knock on the head all those who annoy you—I should like to know if, because the apple is a fruit less delicate than the pineapple, you would wish that there should be no apples? Berlioz told me that the originality, the subtle refinement of a special talent, could be appreciated only in very old societies. If we are yet to proclaim an art and to form our taste, then I understand that you would like better a tame interpretation of consecrated chefs-d'œuvre than an original that is not yet consecrated and whose place in art you dare not yet designate. I continue the comparison I began. The consecrated chefs-d'œuvre are the roast beef, *les grosses pièces de résistance,* on which the people who begin to feed at the banquet of civilization must be nourished. But wherefore, when they are sufficiently fortified, should you refuse them the little dainties of the dessert, particularly if, instead of being insipid and indigestible, they seem to stimulate your taste and refresh your palate dulled and overheated by too rich food? Have you complained that Rachel was great only in the tragedies of Corneille and Racine? Have you denied her talent because she avoids comedy? We all know that Shakespeare is superior to Mr. de Cordova; nevertheless, none of those who listens to the charming lectures of this witty artist conceives that it is a crime in him to give us his own instead of permitting himself to be taken in tow by a great name embalmed by the glory of two or three centuries. The question is reduced to this: "all apples must have the taste of pineapples." If this be the case, "your humble servant," is not the man for you. I do not understand that art is like a uniform in which all of us must be aligned and drilled like Prussian sergeants.

There are some individuals who like only dried fruit; they even like it a little moldy, and if they find dust in it they are transported. The fruit in flower, the perfume that opens to the sun and betrays a young and vigorous growth, "Fie, then, pooh!" and every fool who knows no better cries out, Fie! pooh! and all the envious and impotent, who in their conscience know better, join in the chorus, so well that the poor apple tree that innocently opens its flowers to the sun, leaving to Nature—who had made it a tree and not a bush—the ripening of its fruit, finds itself wholly interdicted and would let itself dry up with chagrin, if it did not feel within a conscience stronger than the clamoring of the fool, the envious, and the ignorant.

◇◇◇◇◇◇◇◇◇

Lancaster, March 30

The concert was very good last night. The hotel is like all the other Pennsylvania houses, of brick with white windows; and a low and narrow door. In the parlor there is invariably placed horizontally on the mantelpiece one of those oblong looking-glasses, divided into three compartments, which date from the beginning of this century. We see around us old family portraits, badly painted but interesting from the simplicity of their details and their costumes, which belong to the last century. One fact to be noticed is the remarkable fecundity of the families. In Pennsylvania the carriages, the waiting rooms at the stations are filled with chubby-faced children. The population, although American, has preserved all the characteristic traits of the Germanic provinces: the large shoes, the immense round hats, and green vests with double rows of gilt buttons, and their blue or yellowish overcoats with enormous skirts, which the German peasants have the exclusive privilege of wearing, abound here. The women have their waists under the arms; some wear an iron-gray horizontal bonnet, like that with which the Quakeresses muffle up their heads under an affectation of Christian humility. We noticed at the station an immigrant with three pairs of twins.

Their manners are generally gentler and simpler than those of the other states I have visited. There is less luxury and a kind of patriarchal simplicity.

◇◇◇◇◇◇◇◇◇

March 30

Leave at eleven o'clock for Harrisburg.

After having had a foretaste of spring we are again precipitated amid the regions of winter. During the whole week the atmosphere was warm and everything green was sprouting in the sun, and now the rain, the snow, the hail, and the whole desolate train of a season in which, despite all that the Northerners say of it, I have not yet been able to find any charm, but in which, on the contrary, I constantly discover fresh enemies. At the concert this evening the governor and the secretary of state were present. Tomorrow morning I leave at eight o'clock for Bethlehem, where I give a concert in the evening.

Observation! I am bound to state that here, instead of saying "man," they say "gentleman." The young clerk at the desk, in pointing us out to the boy, said, "Show these gentlemen their rooms." In the West they invariably say "man." The driver no more speaks to us as "fellows," and I have not yet heard anyone say "show" in speaking of our concerts.

Decidedly, although a little backward, Pennsylvania is more polite than some of her brilliant sisters.

◇◇◇◇◇◇◇◇◇

March 31

Left for Bethlehem at eight o'clock in the morning. Behrens, who is always hungry, buys a dozen oranges. He complains that fruit is not nourishing, and that it is two hours since he breakfasted, and what a breakfast! ! We arrive at Bethlehem in an hour; it is a very picturesque village. The principal street runs uphill and, like all the interior towns of Pennsylvania, it looks oldish and quiet. The houses are low, the windows and doors narrow. We finally found the village hotel. What most strikes the intelligent tourist who visits the United States to seek something other than his fortune is the absence of all tradition; everything is new; everything glitters like new-made furniture. We look in vain for anything that speaks to the imagination, carrying it back of the present generation. The villages are towns in miniature. The farmers' wives and daughters wear crinoline and bonnets with flowers. Here, at least, I find one of those good old taverns such as existed in the last century. The master and mistress of the hotel (two good old people) come to receive us on the porch. "You are welcome," they say to us.

Magnificent concert. The hall full. The whole village was present. The seminary was represented by two hundred-odd pretty young girls. The population is wholly German, and the government Moravian.[7] After the concert a dance at the hotel. (Charming young girl!)

---

[7] Gottschalk's definition of the government as Moravian is not so incongruous as might be supposed. Bethlehem was settled in 1741 by a group of the Moravian Brethren, the oldest Protestant sect, with roots in fifteenth-century Bohemia. Their leader, Count Nikolaus Ludwig von Zinzendorf, established a tightly knit, self-sufficient community. By the time Gottschalk arrived in Bethlehem, the noble works of its own eighteenth-century composers had been forgotten—a familiar phenomenon of nineteenth-century America. But the musical heritage remained. Since 1900 Bethlehem has become famous through its annual Bach Festival.

Carlo is decidedly the spoiled child of the boarding schools. All the young girls dote on him. He is besides a charming fellow. I have to write my autograph hundreds of times.

I have forgotten to mention the Moravian church, in whose interior are found the portraits of the founders of the colony, which have countenances impossible to describe—all Germans. At the concert I noticed a man in spectacles and his wife, who laughed all the time and never once applauded. I wager a hundred to one that he is the professor of the place! I have visited the seminary, which is superb. There are two hundred twenty students, divided into twenty families of ten, who each have their halls for study, their supervisors, and their dormitories, so disposed that they are constantly under the eye of the master. There is a large pool of running water in which they can swim in summer. I have heard less swearing in Bethlehem than in any other place in the United States, and I have seen fewer drunkards there. This gives it a place in my memory—a privileged place, the horror which I have for drunkenness not being equaled except by that which Mr. D[wight] has for my music. Another thing to state—although I have walked all over the town, I have not even heard once *The Maiden's Prayer*. Decidedly, "Bethlehem, you wish to make a conquest of me! ! !"

◇◇◇◇◇◇◇◇◇

Left at six o'clock, accompanied by the ladies at the hotel. We arrived at Easton (twenty-eight miles) at seven o'clock. They fought to get into the concert room. The hall has only four hundred seats, and they have sold six hundred tickets. I join the ranks to get in. The aisles are blocked by those who came late and have to stand during the concert. Although they have requisitioned all the chairs of the neighborhood, mine, which was at the piano, has been taken by a gentleman who is determined to keep it without wishing to be convinced that he should not. A piece of old theater curtain hung crosswise on one side of the platform conceals us from the audience when we do not have to appear. It is the Artist's Room.

We have returned to Bethlehem with the ladies and gentlemen. In the train the whole company started to sing my "Cradle

Song," Patti singing a high tenor. One couple who were sleeping sent us and our "Cradle Song" to all the devils. We found everybody up at the hotel waiting for us; and the young girls from the seminary having obtained permission to spend the night with their relatives at the hotel, they danced till a late hour.

◇◇◇◇◇◇◇◇◇

April 2, 1864

Left Bethlehem. The professor of the place and some young people escorted us to the station. The whole seminary is at the windows; there is nothing to be seen but waving handkerchiefs; as we descend the hill the young ladies ascend to the upper stories; the dormer windows are soon invaded. The road makes a turn; again a last look cast behind. I perceive a very small white point that waves above the tops of the roofs. I wave my handkerchief in answer to this unknown little friend (may God bless her); no more—nothing more.

At the station we saw the local contingent of conscripts leave. A sad sight! Some of these poor young men blustered and sang, while others found in their flask the necessary courage for separation. The greatest number, those who have sisters, a mother, children, a wife, whom they leave behind them with a vague and very distant hope of seeing again, betray, in spite of American stoicism, their emotions by a "God bless you," "Do not cry," "One more kiss." Some veterans, bayonets on their guns, surround the detachment. A German conscript obtains leave to remain a few paces behind, and murmurs words of consolation in the ear of his poor wife, and his little daughter stretches herself up on tiptoe, while crying, to kiss him. He rejoins the detachment, and I see him smoking his pipe with a swagger; he seems thoughtless. The train starts; the poor man leans out the door to see his wife once more. Adieu to all bragging! Nature at the last moment has asserted her rights. "Dear Catherine," said he with broken voice, "God—God bless thee!" A large tear coursed down his cheek. He can laugh no more, nor these his companions. Wiff—wiff—wiff— the engine has started. The crowd gives three hurrahs! I found, on returning to the hotel, poor Catherine weeping in a corner, her head hidden in her apron, with her little daughter. "How

many children have you?" I asked her. "Four," she gently answered
me. God knows if my heart did not bleed at the picture of grief
and pain I foresaw for this poor family. I slipped some money
into the child's hand and stole away without looking behind me,
thinking of the undeniable right those fatherless families have
upon us all who are in possession of the superfluities of life, thanks
to the position in which it has pleased God to place us.

Arrived at Baltimore. I am with my good friends the Curletts.
Sunday I was at High Mass and heard a delicious "Agnus Dei" of
Marschner sung by Mrs. B——. The religious music of Weber
resembles some of the opera airs of Rossini. The sermon is poor
and the preacher has a most pronounced Irish accent. An old
maid, Miss H. (nearly a saint), who in the choir does police duty
over those in attendance and casts, especially on the young girls,
withering looks, sleeps behind a soprano part that she holds in
her hand. She suddenly wakes and puts on a majestic air, pucker-
ing her lips. She has caught Mary G., the old choirmaster's
daughter (who sings the alto in a style that dates from remote
generations), staring—a mischievous girl who never keeps time,
and always comes with two or three twenty-year-old scapegraces
hooked to her petticoats. "Scapegraces!" Spoken with a grimace
that smells of half a century of virginal bitterness, and in a tone
as sour as the green grapes of the fable.

Embark on board the *Morgan*. Arrive at Fortress Monroe
April 4. We land, our steamer not going any farther, and an oath
of allegiance to the government must be taken by all those who
leave here for Norfolk. Fortress Monroe has only warehouses for
military stores, and sheds under which millions of balls are piled
up. In the office of the provost marshal we are placed before a
desk behind which three clerks are seated. One of them reads the
formula, another makes us raise our hands together, and the
matter is finished.

◇◇◇◇◇◇◇◇◇◇

Norfolk, Va., April 4

Monday. I wanted to buy a notebook, and for this purpose entered
a shoestore, in the window of which I saw some stationery. Found
my notebook. At the end of the store are some bundles of music

piled up on a table; this shoemaker stationer sells music also, and he gives me a small written catalogue. I find in it *La Californienne*, by Herz, *La Carlotta Crisi* (probably Grisi) polka, *Last Hope*, by myself, *Les Cloches du monastère*, and all the mawkish American songs developed by the war—"Do They Think of Me at Home?" "Mother, Do Not Weep," etc. All these conceptions in themselves are touching, but the melodies adapted to them are absurd; they produce in one the same effect that the *Venus of Milo* would dressed up like Punch. I trembled for a moment, thinking that I had read the words *The Maiden's Prayer*; it was only a false alarm. Norfolk, which six years ago had its population more than decimated by yellow fever; Norfolk, which has successively been taken by Federal and Confederate armies; Norfolk, ruined finally, deserves to be spared, and for once, at least, it escapes the plague of *The Maiden's Prayer*.

"The Battle Cry of Freedom." I am accustomed to judge things for myself and to give myself but little trouble about the date or signature of a piece of music. I am aware that in doing so I show my perfect ignorance of the rules of respect that one owes to oneself, and that the great art prophets will shrug their shoulders with pity on reading this confession, which I make without blushing, hardened sinner that I am, but what do you want? I love better to discover in my chance wanderings a little unknown flower, humbly concealed at the foot of a thorny bush, than to be the infinitesimal fraction of a legion whom tradition makes bear arms on the great road of routine before the banner of a miserable chef-d'œuvre consecrated by many generations of blind admirers influenced by prejudice.

"The Battle Cry of Freedom" is this obscure flower I have discovered on the heap of dirt that the poetasters and the *musicasters* have raised at the foot of their country's altar since the war began. I know that many will tell me that my pretensions are not well founded, "The Battle Cry of Freedom" being very popular; and to those I shall reply that, as their admiration extends to a crowd of other trifles possessing neither poetry nor melody, they should not suppose that their suffrages can be flattering to an author.

He who drinks whiskey with pleasure should not venture his opinion on Tokay wine.

"The Battle Cry of Freedom" ought to become our national

air; it has animation, its harmonies are distinguished, it has tune, rhythm, and I discover in it a kind of epic coloring, something sadly heroic, which a battle song should have.[8]

The judgment of certain persons is like slow, sluggish waters, which would stagnate and grow thick with mud if canals that they have not the force to make for themselves were not opened for them. The judgment of these people is at the mercy of fashionable prejudices, of routine, and particularly of ideas consecrated by time. It is from among these docile supernumeraries that the rogues, the ambitious, and the envious recruit the forces of which they dispose. "Brignoli has lost his voice," and all those envious of his talents repeat with a clumsy hypothetical air: "Poor Brignoli, it appears, has lost his voice." How delightful it is to be able to crush a man whom you envy! False news propagates itself with a rapidity that I have never understood, particularly when it can be disagreeable to those whom we do not like. If it is simply a scandal, it falls of itself, but when it is a calumny, ah! what a windfall! The jealous nurse it and water it like a hot house plant. They put it under glass, watch over it with tender solicitude, and see with greedy joy its flowers open and exhale their poisonous perfume! What a good thing to avenge oneself! Only it sometimes happens to these horticulturists of venomous thoughts what happened to I know not what personage, whose glass mask fell off at the moment he was preparing a potion that would kill one of his enemies, and he died poisoned—a victim of his own machinations. In the language of the Spaniards "Le salió el tiro por la culata."[9]

Brignoli has returned from Boston and has sung again in New York. He sang as he always sings when he is not ill or the audience not repugnant to him; and the immense army of disinterested persons Brignoli has, all pulling very quietly the thread to cut off

---

[8] The composer of "The Battle Cry of Freedom" was George F. Root (1820–95), a disciple of Lowell Mason, and a popular song writer ("Tramp, Tramp, Tramp, The Boys are Marching," "Just Before the Battle, Mother," "The Vacant Chair"). Gottschalk played his own arrangement of "The Battle Cry of Freedom" under the title, Le Cri de délivrance, dedicating it to Root. It was printed by several publishers. Root heard Gottschalk play in Paris in 1851. See George F. Root: The Story of a Musical Life (Cincinnati: The John Church Company; 1891), p. 65.
[9] "The shot backfired."

the neck of Mazzolini, on discovering that Brignoli could sing as he used to, has made an ovation for him. The envious, wholly discomfited, crawl again into their crevices.

Beethoven, taken as a symphonist, is the most inspired among composers, and the one who composes best for the orchestra. The instrumental effects he combines on paper are always realized in the orchestra as he has conceived them. As a composer for the piano he falls below mediocrity—the least pianist of any intelligence, in our days, writes infinitely better than Beethoven ever did. "Hue and cry on the robber!!" are you all about to exclaim? You brawlers will never attain that height of admiration which I have for Beethoven when he is great, and it is through this admiration that I am forced to see his feebleness. I will explain: The piano is an instrument that Beethoven knew but imperfectly, and that at the period he wrote was but the embryo of the piano made by modern manufacturers. The instrumentation of the piano is a special matter. The point in question is not only to have ideas, but to know how to adapt them to the piano, and this is what Beethoven only imperfectly knew. The ideas so beautifully and so marvelously clothed in all the splendor or all the tenderness that the orchestra affords him in his profoundest originality are clumsy and often tame when he adapts them to the piano. The number of formulae he prepared for the piano was extraordinarily limited, and in many passages we feel what he has wished by perceiving that he has not attained it. Many of the effects he combined from his knowledge of the orchestra have failed on the piano, from not knowing how to translate them into the peculiar language of this instrument.

Imagine Raphael engraving his pictures himself after having painted them. The lines, the contours, the design of them would always be pure, the first conception always inspired, but the execution, the details, the tints, the shadows, the lights, the life, finally —do you think he would have obtained them? The poorest engraver would have succeeded better.[1]

Behrens, my accompanist, has just gone on a tour of discovery in the town. He has made the acquaintance of the leader of the

---

[1] This opinion of Beethoven's piano music was by no means confined to Gottschalk, and can be heard even today.

orchestra. The poor man is in distress; he wanted to make his performers play, in my honor, an overture the public had never yet heard, but he has had to give it up, his orchestra being composed of five musicians, one of which is a kettle drummer!! The poor man was distressed at the idea of having to accompany me in Weber's Concerto.

◇◇◇◇◇◇◇◇◇

Tuesday, April 5

There happened to me yesterday the most singular, the most incomprehensible, most disagreeable thing that has happened to me for many years. After dinner I went down to play billiards. A boy came to tell me that a gentleman wished to speak to me at the office. I told him to tell the gentleman to come in, but he soon returned, saying that the gentleman did not wish to come in, and was waiting for me. I went out, and found myself in the presence of a gentleman with a large mustache, in ordinary dress, who said to me, "I am Captain Clark, and when I asked for you it was your duty to come. I am Captain Clark, I tell you, and I will teach you to come when I send for you." All this was said to me, putting his fist under my nose, and with the amenity of a Prussian sergeant reprimanding a conscript. The emphasis he used in mentioning his name and grade made me suppose that he was one of the authorities, perhaps the mayor of the town, and that we had committed unwittingly some serious offense. I humbly requested him to tell me what was the matter. "You have just insulted a lady in the dining room, and I wish to punish you for it." The accusation was so absurd, and so unlikely, from the fact that I had dined alone at a separate table with Mr. and Mrs. Behrens, that I did not know what to reply, and the only thought that came to my mind was that Captain Clark had thought himself a knight-errant at the bottom of a bottle of whiskey, and that the lady I had insulted was as imaginary as the armies put to flight by Don Quixote when he fought against the windmills. Captain Clark, supported by many other valiant warriors, his friends, said to me that I was only a "strummer on the piano," that the place for all of us was (pointing with his finger to a closed door), that he would punish me, etc. A colonel, anxious to show himself, added in the voice of a cross hippopotamus, "I will throw him and his company out of the window." I assured the captain that I had not seen any lady at the table, and that besides I was not in the habit of insulting ladies. I gave him my word for it. "Your word of honor is not worth much. I do not believe you. I have known you for twenty years! !" What could I do? If I had had the least chance of crushing the captain I would have jumped on him, but all the probabilities of crushing were on his side, and it would have been more than absurd to risk my life to avenge myself for an unmerited insult, grossly offered by an unknown person whose esteem was indifferent to me, and whose moral value I was wholly ignorant of. In the meantime I must say that where soldiers rule is not a good place for civilians, particularly if they have the misfortune to pass for being polite and men of the world. There is nothing of which we are more jealous than those qualities we hear praised in others, and which we do not ourselves possess. The Captain Clarks are numerous, and he is not the first of the species I have met with, although I am pleased to say that no one has yet equaled him in brutality and rudeness. However, I have since learned that it was a plot got up beforehand to start a quarrel with me and make me commit some excess that might cause me to be arrested and driven from the territory.

Played in the evening. Poor hall, frightful weather, and not a carriage at any price if there was one in the whole town. Soldiers, soldiers, soldiers, *corps de garde!* The city is nothing but a vast *corps de garde.* Conquered country! Oh, the sword!

◇◇◇◇◇◇◇◇◇◇

April 6

Third concert, not the worst in the world and tolerably applauded. Patti is evidently the favorite here, and I am not astonished at it; it is not that he plays better than usual (we are all too much put out and bewildered in this *corps de garde* to play well), but because I never in my life played so badly. I am irritated, I feel my heart swelling with indignation at the unjustifiable attack made upon me, and the impossibility of justifying myself from the position in which I am placed renders me miserable. To add to it,

the stage box is occupied by Captain Clark and by Colonel
Giant Killer, who wished to throw us out of the window. Ah,
poor Muse, what business had you in this *corps de garde?*

◇◇◇◇◇◇◇◇◇

April 7

Superb weather. The elements seem to be appeased now that we
are going away. At eleven o'clock we take the steamer that is to
carry us to Fortress Monroe in an hour and a half. My friend
Major Darling waits for me at the wharf in an ambulance with
eight seats. We have arrived at the fort. The ditches are one
hundred eighty feet broad and nine feet deep. The garrison now
numbers three thousand men, the maximum is six thousand. The
interior of the fort is a small town. We pass before the quarters
inhabited by General Butler and his family. The officers have
formed a club, which meets in a small yellow one-story house
opposite the powder magazine. There are nearly thirty women
inside the fort. Opposite is an artificial island on which they have
built a fort mounting one hundred fifty cannons.

◇◇◇◇◇◇◇◇◇

April 8

Arrived at Baltimore, where the evening concert has been very
good. Always the same charming public.

◇◇◇◇◇◇◇◇◇

April 9

Was present at a concert given by a society of amateurs whose
aim is to encourage a love for music, to elevate the taste, and
to promote charity. Every month they give a concert for some
charitable work. The orchestra and chorus executed several fragments of Haydn's *Creation* and Beethoven's oratorio *Mount of
Olives,* and although not perfect the execution was very satisfactory.

◇◇◇◇◇◇◇◇◇◇

Sunday, April 10

Was at High Mass and have heard some excellent music. The choir, composed exclusively of amateurs, was excellent. A delicious "Ave Maria" by Marschner was sung most exquisitely by Madame B——.

Left Baltimore at half-past nine o'clock in the morning and arrived at Philadelphia at two P.M., where I did not even stop for dinner, but took the train for Reading. The concert has been good. The last time I played here the gas went out in the middle of one of my pieces and I had to finish it in the dark. If I were to judge by the applause my performance did not suffer from the absence of light. I like to think that it was to that I owed the applause. A shoemaker of the town, an amateur, had offered to play a fantasia on the flute. He did it to his own satisfaction and that of the audience.

Reading has played quite an important role, thanks to the Knights of the Golden Circle. These Knights are conspirators whose purpose was or is (for I am assured that the members are very numerous and the chiefs still at liberty) to resist the Government by force, and to offer peace to the South by accepting its conditions. The Knights of the Golden Circle availed themselves of the pretext of the arrival of Federal officers delegated to preside at the conscription, to make a levy of shields. The attempt failed through the adroitness of a secret agent of police who had become a member and denounced the conspirators.

◇◇◇◇◇◇◇◇◇◇

April 12

Left for Williamsport. Pennsylvania is the richest of the states by reason of its coal mines. The country is mountainous, woody, and intersected by brooks and rivers. We crossed on viaducts over many valleys whose depths, seen from the car door, made me dizzy. I had not dined, and, beginning to feel hungry, I succeeded in buying a herring and some bread at a station. I never ate a herring that tasted so delicious (hunger was cook). Behrens groaned and made the tears come to our eyes and our mouths water by painting for us a picture of the horrors of hunger and telling us what he would eat were he at Delmonico's. Arrived at Williamsport at eight o'clock. I had sent a dispatch to Strakosch telling of our delay. He immediately put up playbills announcing that the concert would not begin until nine instead of eight o'clock. My piano traveled with me on the train. Arrived at half-past eight o'clock at the hotel, took in a hurry a cup of bad tea, and away to business. One herring for dinner! Nine hours on the train! And, in spite of everything, five hundred persons who have paid that you may give them two hours of poesy, passion, and inspiration. I will confess to you secretly that they certainly will be cheated this evening.

◇◇◇◇◇◇◇◇◇◇

April 13

Elmira. Good concert. A great deal of enthusiasm.

◇◇◇◇◇◇◇◇◇◇

April 14

Owego. Every train brings reinforcements to our audience. A dozen have come from Towanda (thirty-six miles from Owego). The concert was charming. Every piece encored.

◇◇◇◇◇◇◇◇◇◇

April 15

We leave for Scranton. Arrive at noon at Great Bend Station, and must remain for ten hours, the train for Scranton not leaving until half-past two o'clock. Great Bend is not even a hamlet. The trains going to the West from New York pass here. The village is composed of five hotels. Travelers breakfast and dine here. A telegraph dispatch just now informs us that the train that comes from Scranton has run off the line, and, a bridge being broken, we shall probably not be able to get there tonight. A sad perspective, that of remaining in this desert for twenty-four hours. It is also a very considerable pecuniary loss, since, besides the receipts, which ought to be three hundred dollars, I shall have to pay the expenses of the concert and the salary of my company the same as if the concert had taken place.[2]

Decidedly, I shall not be able to get to Scranton today. The road is obstructed and cannot be cleared before night. I have telegraphed to Strakosch, who has been in Scranton since this morning, that I shall go back and stop at Binghamton, where I am to give a concert tomorrow.

The telegraph office is opposite the hotel. I make the acquaintance of the agent. What is to be done? After having examined the horizon to the right and seen dusky mountains, I look to the left and see there the same dusky mountains. Before me a green and gently undulating plain. The sky is blue. The landlord of the hotel, a white-haired old man, is sitting before the door caressing a pretty little girl who calls him Grandfather. A drunken Irishman is telling him how his companions at the mine (we are in the richest coal-mining district) wanted to resist the conscription. "When will Irishmen and whiskey cease to be indissolubly connected?" Answer: When the employees of the New York railroad shall become polite. When Mr. D[wight], of Boston, shall attain a clear comprehension of music and shall cease to adore the music of the future. When my countrymen shall walk on tiptoe in a concert room. When hack drivers shall be governed by a tariff to prevent them from cheating travelers and from insulting them if they timidly protest against this delicate operation.

In the telegraph office I found two other travelers, companions of ennui, and we entered into conversation. One of them I found to be Mr. Catlin, the brother of the historiographical Indian-painter who visited Paris some twenty years ago. I called to mind that Catlin then had very great success from curiosity!—thanks to the novelty of his subject he had treated (with a very inexperienced pencil). Théophile Gautier even devoted to him a long art critique. *Sic transit gloria mundi!* What has become of Mr. Catlin, and where are all his painted warriors? After having rambled all over Paris, perhaps they have returned to their own country, at the

---

[2] We can deduce from this that Gottschalk was paid a flat sum by his manager, out of which he was expected to pay his colleagues who assisted him and other expenses—at least on this tour.

bottom of some valley in the Far West, where of an evening they fill their wigwams with stories about the marvelous childishness and indecent vivacity of the palefaces upon the other side of the great salt lake.[3]

The electric apparatus, it appears, is getting impatient; for five minutes it has not ceased working. The operator announces to me that Strakosch is at the telegraph at Scranton and wants to speak to me.

(Conversation, one hundred miles apart.)

"Dress for the concert. The inspector of the line will dispatch a special train that will arrive at Great Bend at six o'clock, and you can reach here at nine o'clock, when a carriage will await you at the station and take you to the concert hall."

Answer (ten minutes afterward): "We are ready."

At six o'clock the train arrived, at nine o'clock I was at Scranton, got into the carriage, reached the hall and crossed it amid the applause of the public. The audience for an hour had been kept in hope by a telegraphic dispatch that was sent as fast as I arrived at a station and at five minutes after nine I was playing the *Overture to Guillaume Tell*. Every piece was encored. At eleven o'clock I took supper (I had great need of it) at the excellent hotel, Wyoming House.

◇◇◇◇◇◇◇◇◇

April 16

Concert at Binghamton. Very small but charming audience; the concert (unremunerative as it was) will leave a remembrance not less agreeable than that of last year, although that of last year was crowded.

◇◇◇◇◇◇◇◇◇

Sunday, April 17

Arrived after twelve hours of railroad at New York. Leave New York again for Newburgh at three o'clock on April 18. Repetition of my *Marche de Faust* for four pianos. O pianists who enter into

---

[3] Time has not upheld Gottschalk's derogatory opinion of Catlin.

the profession, be distrustful of amateurs! They are never frightened at anything, finding everything that is given them to play too easy, and are offended if requested to study it; in the presence of the audience they stick in the mud, embarrassed, and leave you to extricate yourself as well as you can.

Above all, remember that you alone will be held responsible, and as to them they know not how it happens that they made a mistake.

Three hours of railroad and we are at Newburgh. The station is at Fishkill. Newburgh is on the opposite side of the Hudson. Seen at a distance, the town of Newburgh presents a very pretty *coup d'œil*; its white houses, half concealed by verdure, seem to scale the side of a steep hill. It has the appearance of a toy village in painted wood. Its streets are quiet. The Hudson, seen from the heights of the town, rolls on majestically, and the setting sun at this moment is empurpling the village of Fishkill.

Do not trust to appearances. Newburgh, so peaceful, was last year the theater of a frightful tragedy, whose details will affright you. An unfortunate Negro, accused of having violated an Irish girl, was lynched and executed by the people. Some miserable wretches through their hatred for the Negroes excited the people. They broke open the doors of the prison in which the Negro was incarcerated awaiting his trial. In vain a courageous Irish priest (the most inveterate enemies of the blacks in the United States are the Irish) endeavored to appease them; these madmen seized the unfortunate black, drew him into the prison yard, mutilated him, and then broke his skull with a hammer. They dragged out his dead body by the heels and hung it head downward. What adds still more to the horror of the crime is that a few days later it was discovered that the Negro was innocent.

Not eighty persons at the concert. Pretext: that, the concert having been repeatedly announced, and not having taken place, the public was not willing to be disappointed again. There is no reason to give for it. There are no good or bad days. There is only a public willing or not willing to go to a concert.

I knew a town in France where a concert never succeeded, and it was always a source of amusement to see the ingenuity with which the inhabitants found an excuse for it. Sometimes it was that one of the most influential families had just lost its chief member. Sometimes a lady who was just dying. Sometimes it was too late in the season, sometimes too early.

My piano is in the hall; they have not had time to erect a platform. I am surrounded by a balustrade that entirely conceals me from public view, only my head is above it, and I imagine the very amusing effect this head must have.

It may be said undoubtedly that the audience is enthusiastic. Axiom: the enthusiasm of the audience is always in inverse ratio to the receipts. If the latter are very ordinary, the applause is great. If it is profitable the audience is cold. What is the cause of this anomaly?

I understand that the few amateurs who come to our concerts experience a sort of compassionate sympathy for the artist who must play before empty benches, and try to make him forget it by the cordial reception they give him. But what reason can be given for the icy restraint of provincial audiences when there is a crowd. Why is it that the public does not applaud when a piece finishes softly? Does it want to be astonished and not charmed? Primitive audiences are carried along by the eyes. My *Cradle Song*, which finishes with a long diminuendo that is gradually extinguished, is applauded on account of its fetching title, *Chant d'une mère au berceau de son enfant*, which is suggestive. The imagination of the Anglo-Saxons is not active enough to embroider, for itself, a poem upon the music to which they are listening, nor have they yet been able to find anything else in music but an agreeable noise, so that one is obliged to give them a detailed explanation of it, upon which they then build their little poem. This is so true that when it has happened that I played the *Berceuse* under another name, by which it was not known, it was a failure.

We left Newburgh at nine o'clock. I met a Bloomer. The Bloomers are the disciples of a sect founded by Mrs. Bloomer, the champion of woman's rights. We have many female lawyers and doctors in the United States. I do not believe in women who assert their rights. I shall be converted when I meet one who is young and pretty. All those I have yet seen are perfect frights. They are generally virgins who wish to free themselves from the odious bondage of men for the same reason that the fox found the grapes too sour. Oh, this arbor! What sour grapes it produces! My fellow-countrymen who laugh at my ribbon and fasten to their own buttonholes all sorts of baubles that at a distance resemble decorations—sour grapes! And the Democrats, who thunder in Congress against the European aristocracy and cause themselves to be called judges, colonels, generals—sour grapes! And pianists, noncomposers, who disdain to play any other than classical music, and the musicians of the future who have a horror of limpid melodies—sour grapes! And the horrible demoralization of European society, thanks to which you cannot find among twenty married women a faithful wife (this was said to me by a virtuous American, who loved her husband moderately)—sour grapes!

Since Liszt has given the word of command to the Germans, Chopin has all at once become classical. His forms, which before they regarded—without understanding them—as whimsical, his harmonics, so worked up, have become so many perfect models. I do not complain for my part, having been one of the old Chopinists, but what I deplore is the frightful abuse that is made of Chopin's formulas. There is not a small pianist-composer who does not think himself called upon to make Chopin mazurkas, Chopin nocturnes, Chopin polonaises—it has become an epidemic in the United States. They have become masters of Chopin's processes and employ them without discernment in the most trivial melodies. This recalls to me Madame F., who composed music à la Haydn.

❖❖❖❖❖❖❖❖

Schenectady, April 19

Detestable concert, hardly seventy-five persons, who applauded at random with a free and easy frankness that was very amusing.

❖❖❖❖❖❖❖❖

April 20

Left for Troy, where I have had a very poor concert. Why should I be so popular in certain towns and not at all in others?

Thursday. I started for New York at five o'clock in the morning. Concert in the evening at the Academy of Music, Brooklyn—superb audience. A young lady amateur, full of pretensions, like all amateurs, after insisting upon being placed upon the posters refused to play when her turn came, on the pretext that she could play only upon her Steinway. I played in her place, and all my pieces were encored. Steinway and Chickering, Guelphs and Ghibellines of the musicians, are divided into two factions—the Germans are for Steinway.

◇◇◇◇◇◇◇◇◇◇

April 22

Set out at three o'clock from New York for Poughkeepsie—charming place and charming concert. One of the papers, for the finale of *Sonnambula,* has put "female!" This brings to my mind a program printed in Bordeaux in which I played the *Bananier* and the *Savane,* which were printed the *Savanier* and the *Banane.*[4]

Poughkeepsie has several large boarding schools for young ladies and one or two large colleges. One of them, College Hill, is situated on a hill that overlooks the town. From the college porch (whose architecture almost resembles that of a temple of Diana) we see the Catskill Mountains, and the Hudson rolling on in all its majesty. This College Hill was, only three or four years ago, a simple boarding school. Its proprietor sold it, not being able to meet his expenses. His successor, an intelligent Yankee, began by studying the manners of the town, and found out that it was aristocratic but slow. Innovations there are like exotic plants planted in the open air; they wither and die. A boarding school under the name of academy had only had moderate success up to that time; he baptized it with the name of college, introduced new branches of instruction, a military uniform, and behold, soon a transformation took place, pupils flowed in from all quarters, and College Hill became what it now is.

◇◇◇◇◇◇◇◇◇◇

April 23

Left Poughkeepsie at ten o'clock. We arrive at Rutland at half-past four P.M., stopping ten minutes at Troy. Behrens, whose appetite increases with the fatigues of the journey, rushes into the

---

⁴ Gottschalk was also highly amused when his *Last Hope* nearly emerged in print as *The Latest Hops.*

buffet, but the bill of fare offers only tea and cold pies. Behrens, who is a philosopher, consoles himself by making puns that grow worse and worse and that, to spare his self esteem, I blame on his gastronomic disappointment.

Concert at Rutland very fine. The young girls of the town have asked me to play *Last Hope.*

◇◇◇◇◇◇◇◇◇◇

April 24

Superb weather. The mountains, from which the state takes its name (Vermont), undulating in the sun. Near the village are the celebrated marble quarries, known under the name of Rutland Quarries. The white marble is so abundant here that we notice white marble pavements, enclosure walls, brims of wells, and milestones on the road of the same material. We have taken a carriage ride to see the quarries. The workmen have, like all Northern workmen, struck for an increase of wages, proportioned to the progressive advance in price of all articles of prime necessity at the North.

The countryside is splendid. A waterfall rushes over, and, its spray sifting the sun's rays, forms a true rainbow. A fertile valley spreads out before us, its emerald hue alternating with the deep blue of a little stream that winds along slowly at random.

The dark mountains on the horizon still preserve the snows of winter at their summits. Behind us the village of Rutland, with its five or six steeples piercing the blue sky, the quarries of white marble, the blocks of which, already detached, sparkle like diamonds in the sun, and all around us the green fields of Vermont, the cloudless sky—all of this forms a picture that I do not know how to describe.

Behrens has had the unlucky idea of hiring a buggy, and, as he knows no more how to drive a horse than I know how to earn the good will of Mr. D[wight], the result is that he found himself in too direct contact with another carriage. His has come out of the encounter with a slight scar, which the owner of the carriage has generously estimated at twenty-five dollars. I doubt if the country of Vermont will leave as agreeable an impression upon him as upon myself.

Behrens was awakened this morning by the sheriff, who had been sent to him by the owner of the carriages, as Behrens had neglected to pay the twenty-five dollars. The affair is settled, but Behrens looks rather sheepish. He makes up for his discomfiture this morning by redoubling his appetite and emphasizing his puns more than usual. On guard! We leave in two hours for Burlington, where I give a concert this evening.

Arrived at the hotel in Burlington, we discovered that Carlo Patti was missing. Max returned to the station, and at the end of half an hour we saw Carlo coming, followed by Strakosch, his ears hanging down, like a refractory sheep that the watchful shepherd is leading back to the fold. Poor Patti slept the sleep of innocence and did not awaken until after the departure of the train from where he ought to have got out. As soon as he saw his mishap, he had the train stopped.

Very brilliant concert. The public warmly applauded us as soon as we made our appearance, and listened to us with attention. Result: We were forced to do our best, feeling ourselves at ease. O public! You who complain of the coldness of some artists find the reason for it in your own indifference. The artist generally reflects the humor of his audience; if the latter is cold, distracted, indifferent, talkative, and ill-bred, the artist, you may be sure, will not become warm, and inspiration will fail him. This spark, which ought to warm you, will not be struck from him when he feels that it would be extinguished amid the indolent impatience of those who listen and yawn.

How many times have I heard this in a small town the morning after a concert: "He has not been kind, and has not even repeated one of his pieces"—when the audience had hardly applauded me. Could I repeat what no one had asked to be encored?

◇◇◇◇◇◇◇◇◇◇

April 26

I set out in a few moments for Plattsburgh, on the other side of the lake. We go in a steamer.

Lake Champlain is like a mirror. The silhouettes of the mountains that surround it are reflected by it in grand shadows of a dark blue.

My friend, the Bishop of Burlington, has just published a book to prove that slavery is a divine institution, and draws his arguments from the Bible itself. Poor Bible! One of the great objections I have to the free interpretation of the Bible, as the Protestants understand it, is that everyone can make it speak whatever he wants, according to his prejudices. Bishop Potter, of Pennsylvania, *proves* by the Bible that slavery is abominable. The Bishop of Burlington *proves* by the Bible that slavery is a divine law, whence I conclude that the Bible in the hands of these gentlemen proves nothing unless it be that we have an odd spirit, and that the most absurd and odious doctrines always find something to sustain them.

Children and young girls constantly read the Old Testament, not expurgated holy history, but the Bible, such as it is in the original, with its crudities of language, its concupiscent images, its coarseness, its monstrous corruptions. Children do not see in it much to interest them, but young girls feed on it constantly, and nevertheless they preserve (or pretend to preserve) the purity of their imagination.

These same maidens who remain impassable in reading the Canticle of Canticles or the history of Lot, are troubled at the word "pantaloon," blushing to the ears if you pronounce the word "legs," and look upon you as ill-bred when, inquiring of you news of your mother, you tell them that she has given you a little brother. Fie, then! You may say that she had a bad headache. It is the only illness admitted in society. Puritanical anatomy recognizes only the feet and the head, and in some cases the arms, but nothing above the elbow. What is most delightful is that they understand very well, notwithstanding all this.

So if you wish to say that a danseuse has pretty legs, you say that she has charming ankles. You want to say that your wife is confined to bed, you say that she is obliged to keep to her chamber for some time. These expressions are consecrated and express absolutely the same thing. Oh, human hypocrisy! You easily accommodate yourself to these little subterfuges.

The journey across the lake is charming. Plattsburgh, where we are going, has only four or five thousand inhabitants. A speculator in the village has engaged us for a concert for three hundred and twenty dollars. A traveler has just assured me that every seat is taken, and that they come from twenty-five miles around to be present at this grand fête. A concert like ours is a real innovation for a village.

Arrived at Plattsburgh at one P.M. Excellent Hotel Fouguet, situated on the edge of a bluff that overlooks Lake Champlain. This lake freezes in winter; they then use boats on runners, spread their sails, and are carried by the wind. I am told that this kind of traveling is as rapid as it is agreeable, the rate being at an average, when the wind is favorable, of two-thirds of a mile every three or four minutes.

The concert has been magnificent, very crowded, and a great deal of enthusiasm. I should not like to say that it was not through human respect that they applauded.

We left again on April 27. I saw that we were approaching Canada, by the miserable aspect of the country and of the farms. The railway cars are narrow, comfortless, and roughly built. I just heard a neighbor speak to the conductor with that French accent which does not authorize the caustic rage with which the Canadians laugh at *"parler parisien"* (Parisian pronunciation). *"Je n'ponse poo"* (*je ne pense pas*), answers my neighbor to a question of the conductor. The train itself participates in that apathetic somnolency which appears to be the character of the Canadian. We stop every ten minutes and make only ten miles an hour. Arrived at a cottage on the banks of the St. Lawrence, we embark on the *Iroquois*, a steamer that will carry us to the other side of the river. On the poop of the steamer I notice two squaws (Indian women) who sell small articles worked with colored beads; one of them has such remarkably small feet that she attracts the attention of everyone, although smallness of the feet among the Indians is one of the traits of their race.

◇◇◇◇◇◇◇◇◇◇

Montreal

Patti, who went to take a walk, has already met some friends, good Secessionists, who cannot be gainsaid. Thanks to the noise that the rash enterprise at Buffalo has made (I speak of the attack of which he has been the subject in a paper, respecting his stay in the South and of his service in the Confederate Army), Patti has become a sort of hero. At St. Louis, where unionism is more than doubtful, he was applauded to the skies everytime he played. In every town he found unknown friends who welcomed him, congratulating him on his political opinions, and it seems that a sort of Freemasonry connects all these conspirators whose machinations, happily, are limited to hypocritically deploring the ruin of the North, and in making sterile vows for the triumph of the South. I know nothing more odious than this kind of hybrid patriot, who with arms crossed protests his devotion to the republic and remains neuter, except when by his clamors he tries to fetter the efforts of the Government. I admire and respect those of the South who fight and sacrifice themselves for what they think a just cause. I do not share their convictions, but I have only contempt for these *politicasters* of the North who wish peace at any price, without thinking that plastering up a few cracks is of no use when the foundation of the edifice is giving way, and that in the social body, no more than in the individual, an eating wound does not cease its ravages because it is concealed under an anodyne plaster.

"The Constitution as it was"—such is their cry. Fools that you are! The Constitution is a chimera, and the veneration you have for the broken pact is at least unseasonable. The Constitution today has become impossible. It would be as unreasonable to require that a man should always wear the clothes of his boyhood and have his limbs shortened in order to accommodate them to his clothes, now become too small, rather than enlarge them in proportion to his growth.

Behrens, who is the best fellow in the world, and whose humor is of a quality that has been able to resist the melancholy influence of the piano (I say melancholy, because I have remarked that those who make a trade of a thing are generally those who use it the least; witness the distillers, who hardly ever drink spirits, and the disciples of harmony who are never able to establish it among themselves)—Behrens, I say, after my parenthesis, has become morose for the last two or three days. The bad cheer has taken effect upon his placid and benevolent nature. This enters into the theory of one of my friends, a mad materialist, who believes that the celebrated elegiacs, poets, and musicians were so only because they had bad stomachs, and that a few pills discreetly and opportunely swallowed would have relieved them. Let us rejoice that they were not like my friend. For my part, I have always believed that the artist was a victim, fatally destined in spite of himself to be an instrument through which Providence breathes on the world certain expressions, certain ideas.

In Alsace, they scoop the eyes out of ducks and geese, and suspend them by the feet, head downward. In this position, little favorable to digestion, they feed them plenteously. The liver under this regime becomes fat, and it is from these livers that the famous *pâtés de foie gras* are made. Thus, artists who have never done great things, but when they were dying of hunger, or were consumptive, or amorous, or without hope, seem to me to be the geese and the ducks that Providence has condemned to the costly privilege of exhaling, at the price of their existence, harmonious thoughts which the *bons vivants* of mind taste tranquilly at the banquet of life.

A truce to poor jokes. Art is too pure, its source too elevated, its enjoyments too refined, its influence too noble, its essence, in one word, too divine for me to participate in the gastronomical beliefs of my skeptical friend. Art is the ardent aspiration for the beautiful. It is voluptuousness sublimed by the spirit; it is an irresistible transport that makes us burst the bonds of material space, through the ideal, and transports us to the celestial spheres.

This long digression into which I have been drawn has separated me from Behrens, and from the influence over him of the eternal "ham and eggs," this refuge of tavernkeepers taken unawares, and that punishment to which our disorderly life condemns us. As he who looks down on a country loses all idea of its perfection, so the stomachs of a vagabond company lose all notions of a regular appetite, which well-brought-up stomachs ought to have. We dine sometimes at eleven o'clock at night, sometimes at noon. Sometimes breakfast precedes the dinner a half hour, and sometimes it is separated from it by two hundred miles of railway. After this, do you wonder that my good Mr. B., who, because he has an excellent stomach, is not of an elegiac nature, has become sad for the last three or four days from our feasting at absurd hours on ham and eggs and stale sandwiches! Fortunately the St. Lawrence Hotel has an excellent table, and Behrens, who has made three festivals of Belshazzar today, feels in a merry humor and lets fly at me, when I least expect it, a broadside of puns of high Germanic flavor.

◇◇◇◇◇◇◇◇◇◇

[*Montreal*]

I am back from the concert. The rain, which has not stopped
falling since this morning, increased toward eight o'clock, which
evidently ought to have diminished the receipts. The hall nevertheless was well filled, and the ladies, elegantly dressed, produced
a beautiful effect as seen from the stage. The parterre is generally
occupied by those who care less for being seen than for listening
to the music. They applauded with enthusiasm, and listened with
an attention that singularly contrasted with the noise made by
some elegant English officers, who were determined to attract
attention to their blond whiskers, their convex chests, and to their
white gloves, which they held at a foot's distance outside of the
box. Their conversation, which with noble condescension they
made in a loud voice in order to permit the whole hall to enjoy
their high-flown humor, was disagreeably interrupted from time to
time by my piano, which I willingly would have taken away from
the program, these gentlemen replacing me in a very advantageous
manner, if I had not thought that, perhaps, the public, accustomed as it must be to them, would have much preferred me.

I know nothing more ill-bred than a fashionable Englishman,
unless it be *two* fashionable Englishmen.

In the box in question, there were three, and they worthily
sustained their reputation.

◇◇◇◇◇◇◇◇◇◇

April 28

Thursday evening. Second concert. As much as I had played without pleasure the other evening, so much I have excelled myself
today. All my pieces have been encored. I leave tomorrow for
Ogdensburg.

◇◇◇◇◇◇◇◇◇◇

April 29

Set out from Montreal at seven o'clock. In the car, Carlo Patti
—"Sunshine Patti," as I call him, because of the happy thought-

lessness of his character—has made a conquest. A young and pretty woman has made advances to him, and they are talking together. She was at the concert last night.

A Seidlitz powder or two drams of rhubarb seasonably administered and Petrarch becomes a Boccaccio, Lamartine a Paul de Kock, and Mr. D[wight] might become an amiable man. What a beautiful thing medicine is, and how unfortunate it is that I have not the recipe for those marvelous pills.

Arrive at Prescott, a small Canadian village on the left bank of the St. Lawrence. Opposite to it, Ogdensburg, on the American shore, seems to rise out of the water. The waves of this majestic river move slowly along. The sun makes them sparkle like myriads of little pearls. We cross in a ferryboat. Ogdensburg is a large town, very rich on account of its geographical position.

Seven or eight years ago I gave a concert here in company with Madam de Lagrange.[5] I remember that at that time I received a perfumed letter, in very small writing, in which someone invited me to come to the town of —— "to take lunch." The name was unknown to me. Nevertheless, I accepted. The house was concealed in the midst of a shady park, surrounded by high walls, thus defying the curiosity of the indiscreet. No noise from outside could disturb the quiet of this mysterious abode. I should have thought myself in the interior of a convent if an old servant had not come to receive me to tell me that his mistress wished me to wait for her in the conservatory adjoining the drawingroom. The residence was sumptuous. French albums, Parisian engravings, and a crowd of those elegant little trifles and superfluities which are found only in French salons and which the morose and traditional taste of the Anglo-Saxons excludes from their parlors, at once told me that the mistress of the house was or had been pretty, that she had taste, and yearned for Paris.

The mistress of the enchanted house soon entered. She was a

---

[5] Anna de Lagrange, Countess de Stankowitch, was born at Paris in 1825. An able singer, she made her debut in Italy. She arrived in New York in 1853 and made an extremely successful tour with Gottschalk in 1856. Punctilious in her dealings with managers and colleagues, she nevertheless allowed herself the idiosyncrasy of traveling with "quite a menagerie, including three dogs, a parrot, a mockingbird, and a husband, all docile and well trained." Upton, *ibid.*, p. 101.

woman of from forty to forty-five years old who must have been very pretty. She told me her name, and that celebrated name then recalled to me a youthful impression that had engraved on my memory the confused image of a splendid young girl, of pale complexion, superb form, and a wealth of undulating ebony hair, whom I saw one evening, on the balcony of the St. Louis Hotel in New Orleans, saluting, with the gesture of a queen, the crowd assembled to see her. A black velvet tunic boldly slanting on the shoulders caused to be appreciated the admirable complexion of a bosom too slightly concealed. Doubtless counting more upon the legitimate beauty of her charms than on that of her pretensions, she came to claim, as granddaughter of Vespuccius, a dowry from the American people. Congress, while composed of men who were individually capable of admiring the charms of the beautiful Genoese, judged apropos (and I congratulate them on it) to send back to the country where they build castles in the air the claims of the descendant of the godfather of our country. The beautiful adventuress was much pitied, much loved by the men, much hated by the women (the one is the consequence of the other), passed through every phase of celebrity—that is to say, that the former placed her upon a pedestal, and the latter tried to upset it into the mud. Like the stars, she had her zenith and her setting, and she was soon forgotten. America Vespucci, tossed during twenty years by the chances of fortune, became stranded some years ago on the banks of the St. Lawrence, where an old millionaire offered to her, as indemnity, I suppose, for the injustice of the legislators of his country, the sovereignty of the magnificent mansion where she concealed herself.

She had me visit the park, the aviary, the library, the marble baths. I was dazzled with all the splendors of this little Eden, hidden like a nest in the moss. "Paris," she said to me, sighing, "Paris!—without my fortune and twenty years less!"

The poor recluse gave me to understand that the honest Ogdensburgers did not treat her with respect. Envious of her taste, her travels, her fortune, and her power over a rich old fellow, whom, without any doubt, the provident mothers destined *in petto* to the honor of being their son-in-law, and angry that a stranger had dared to monopolize all this fortune, and that, by treading underfoot all the laws of that dead morality which we are all so happy to invoke when we are not able to crush those we do not like—the honest people of Ogdensburg had raised little by little around her one of those insurmountable walls made up of hatred, jealousy, and of secret malice cemented by that sour virtue of small towns. She never went out, saw nobody, and wept alone under the beautiful trees of her park, while the birds warbled on the branches.

I conversed a long time with her about Rubini,[6] whom she had known well at the salon of Madame Merlin,[7] where she frequently visited.

I asked today what had become of her. She left again one fine morning for Paris, said some—she is dead, said others.

Concert this evening. Not a large audience but sympathetic. I do not know how I was able to play; I am enfeebled. All the pieces encored.

◇◇◇◇◇◇◇◇◇◇

April 30

A constable has come to arrest me, by order of the president of the village (it is thus the mayor calls himself) for not having taken out a license, and I am condemned to pay a fine of fifty dollars. I go with the constable to the justice of the peace, and here is the exposition of the affair such as the justice of the peace gave it with admirable candor. "Mister, it is true that it is the custom for us to send in advance to collect the five dollars for the license, but as the mayor said that the constable whom he had sent last year made known to him that you had then refused to pay and had insulted the authorities, he has proposed to punish you for it by letting you give your concert without forewarning you that a license was necessary, in order to be able to fine you fifty dollars."

Admirable simplicity! And behold here justice well administered. Here am I condemned to pay fifty dollars because a constable who does not know me and confounds perhaps Jones

---

[6] Giovanni Battista Rubini (1795–1854) was a celebrated Italian tenor. He toured briefly with Liszt and was successful in England and on the Continent, especially in Russia. He amassed a fortune and retired in 1844.

[7] At the salon of Countess de las Mercedes Merlin, a native of Cuba, Gottschalk frequently played the music of Bach under her encouragement.

(who has insulted him) with Gottschalk (whom he has never seen) makes a false statement to a despotic mayor who avenges himself on me by laying a snare!

Fortunately, I got out of it.

◇◇◇◇◇◇◇◇◇◇

Sunday, May 1, 1864

Spleen! spleen!! spleen!!! The streets are deserted—I see the crowds returning from religious service. Young, irreproachable, singularly neat, after the filthiness of our soldiers, this appears to me so much the more extraordinary.

We embark at five o'clock on the *Ottawa*, a small steamer that crosses from Kingston to Cape St. Vincent in two hours. We shall sleep there and then set out for Watertown. The wind blows furiously and our poor little boat rocks dreadfuly. Mr. Strakosch, who is not a good sailor, and who a few moments ago became pale, seeks the solitude of the captain's cabin. I go up on deck. We come alongside a pretty schooner of which we see only the prow. She capsized five days ago in one of those storms so suddent and so terrible on Lake Ontario. She presented a most singular effect, lying on her side with her sails spread, her anchor down, her hull exposed, and her masts beating like the legs of some gigantic animal struggling convulsively. This recalled to my mind the painful impression that the death of a horse always makes in the bullfights. There is particularly at the end of his agony a mechanical movement of the feet, which act distractedly, as if they wished to walk in the air. It makes me sick just to think of it.

We enter into a narrow canal that leads to Cape St. Vincent. The boat lands at a spruce little hotel on the shore of the lake. A tall old man gives us a welcome, the more assiduous, as his hotel is at this moment empty, and we are nine.

His daughters, charming young persons, pink and white, wait upon us at table. Excellent supper. Fried trout, caught in the lake.

◇◇◇◇◇◇◇◇◇◇

May 2

Slept badly. The rats have feasted all night under one of the feet of my bed and have kept me awake.

We start at six o'clock for Watertown. Reach there at eight o'clock in the morning. We give a concert today at seven o'clock, because the workmen, I do not know of what factory, give a ball in the same hall, which is to begin at nine o'clock. Audience kind and very enthusiastic. Unfortunately we are tired out. The want of sleep gives me a buzzing in the ears, and from the first notes I feel that I shall hardly be able to play to the end of the program. This week we have slept, on an average, five hours in the twenty-four, and traveled every day.

◇◇◇◇◇◇◇◇◇◇

May 3 [1864]

Left Watertown for Utica.

The population of Utica is from thirty to forty thousand souls. There are some beautiful churches, Trinity Church, among others, in which I saw an excellent organ, built by a musical instrument maker of the town. Some of the streets are lined by trees whose thick foliage forms a delicious shade. But what particularly attracts the attention of travelers in Utica is its asylum for the insane, which is one of the most complete establishments on the American continent. The head physician of the hospital is one of our friends. He is hardly more sane on the subject of music than his patients.[8]

It pours rain, and I fear that the receipts of the concert this evening will be very poor.

Very warm audience. Utica has always received me well. I am always listened to with kindness there, and always warmly applauded.

The doctor takes me to sleep at the hospital for the insane. The doctors and attendants inhabit the façade of the immense quadrangle that the hospital occupies. It is eleven o'clock. The doctor invites me up into his chamber to smoke, he his pipe, I my cigar. Our conversation at first languishes as when given up en-

---

[8] The head physician was Dr. J. P. Gray. The program this time was shared by Carlo Patti and Behrens. Gottschalk played an *andante* by Beethoven, a *valse brilliante* by his Cuban friend Espadero, *Galop di Bravura* by Quidant, and Espadero's arrangement of the finale of Bellini's *Sonnambula*.

tirely to the pleasure of having nothing to do, and the spirit follows with profound solicitude the spirals of cigar smoke as it unrolls in the air and displays its forms before disappearing. I asked the doctor if he had ever occupied himself with spiritual manifestations, which for the last fifteen years have troubled the United States, and which at certain periods acquire new life by the appearance of some extraordinary phenomenon. The New York papers for some days have been full of the extraordinary things done by the Davenport brothers. I myself saw them at St. Louis, and will tell you hereafter the facts I have witnessed. The doctor said to me what all staid people candidly tell me here, "I do not know what to think." There is certainly one or some phenomena that evade science, and are connected with some unknown principle, from which electricity, and all the phenomena of second sight, of somnambulism, of mesmerism probably proceed.[9]

As to believing in the intervention of spirits, and making a new revelation of it, that is simply absurd. "I was (it is the doctor who speaks) at Port Hope some time ago. One of my friends, appointed by the government to do some work for the establishment of a railroad, had to live in a large stonehouse that had been placed at his disposition. The house had belonged to an old fur trader who had frequently committed acts of violence during his life, and had made himself particularly hated by the Indians who sold their peltry to him; he had robbed many of them, said someone, who added in a low voice that he had killed some of them. Whether or not merited, the bad reputation of the fur trader had become proverbial, and since his death the house, some said, was haunted, and afterward the inhabitants told me that every night the ghost of X. stalked through all the chambers." The doctor and his friend slept on the second story. The invisible ghost (no one had ever seen it, but it had been heard breathing, walking, coughing) always made itself heard the first night the new occupant spent in the house. Before going to bed the doctor and his friend went over the house from the cellar to the garret. They

---

[9] "We live in an age of magic. Professors of the black art descend on our City like soot from a burning chimney . . . we have had the Davenport Brothers, who pretend to have the Old Gentleman in a box . . . The immortals never come alone." The New York *Times*, May 2, 1864.

shut up all the servants in their chambers, and minutely examined the large lower hall, paved with stone, situated exactly under the apartment where they were to sleep, and in which the spirit preferred to make himself heard. All the doors leading into the hall were bolted, except that which led to the second story. Retired to their chambers, the two strangers waited. The hours passed on— nothing was heard save the noise of their breathing—and at last, tired of waiting for nothing, they went to bed, certain of having once more put an end to chimerical fears, and more than ever convinced that ghosts only exist in imaginations diseased or fond of invention.

At the hotel (Bagg's), an excellent hotel by the way, the servant came to tell me that two persons wished to see me. They introduced themselves—they are two young men who look like a farmer's sons—with the ease of Americans, who are never embarrassed, and told me that they had come twenty miles in a carriage to be at the concert, and that, learning that I was there, they profited by it for the purpose of seeing me. They are members of a community that has founded a village near Oneida. To my question whether they belong to a sect recognized by the government, they replied that theirs only dated from six years ago.[1] They cultivate strawberries, of which they have fifteen hundred acres, drink no strong liquors, and use no tobacco. They eat no meat, but only vegetables. They have formed an orchestra of thirty musicians, and in the evening on returning from the strawberry fields, the family assembles, a prayer is made, and a little concert is given. The chief of the community directed them to offer me their hospitality during the summer. Perhaps I shall accept; I am curious to see these new Arcadians at work.

◇◇◇◇◇◇◇◇◇

Syracuse, May 4

Of Syracuse I know only the two pavements close to the hotel, which is itself at the railroad station (bad hotel, by the way), where the cook tries to make uneatable the good things that the bill of fare announces. The trains arrive, leave, cross each other

---

[1] The Oneida Community actually had been in existence for sixteen years.

without ceasing and that in the midst of the town, and, crossing at right angles the most popular street of Syracuse, cause me an inexhaustible wonder. How is it that two or three hundred are not killed in the midst of this confusion? You cross the street and look to the right, "Take care!" cries a man to you. It is the tail of an immense train that backs and threatens from behind the horses, which take fright. If there is a Providence for children, drunkards, and the blind, be well assured that there is one for the American railways, for more independent enterprises no one could ever find.

Audience quite numerous and very dilettante.

Syracuse, without being different from some small towns I have visited, always gives me a good audience. However, I know nobody, or nearly so, and have no personal friends there.

◇◇◇◇◇◇◇◇◇◇

May 5, 1864

Leave again for Oswego at half-past two P.M. Arrive at five o'clock.

Oswego is remarkable for its picturesque location. The concert has been charming. I always play with pleasure at Oswego. They listen to me with attention; I am always enthusiastically applauded there. Do not hasten to conclude that because I always go back there with pleasure the receipts are good, for with me the one is not the consequence of the other. There are some towns where I always make money and that I do not like, and others where I make nothing and yet like to go. I know that this is absurd, that reasonable men will shrug their shoulders at it, but you know that artists understand but little about business and have but little foresight. There is one thing that money cannot rule: it is the inspiration of the artist.

◇◇◇◇◇◇◇◇◇◇

Friday, May 6

Set out again from Oswego at half-past seven A.M. for Geneva, where we arrived at four o'clock. We traveled since the morning through a succession of lakes with which the State of New York abounds. The smallest of these lakes is as large as Lake Neufchâtel. I have counted as many as forty-three in the State of New York alone. Geneva possesses a medical school, an Episcopal seminary, an independent college, and several boarding schools for young ladies. I have met here a dyspeptic English musician who, with the greatest faith in the world, maintains that England has produced the best musicians and the best composers in the world! Concert passable, and audience very kind.

◇◇◇◇◇◇◇◇◇

Saturday morning, May 7

Left again for Auburn. Concert magnificent, all the pieces encored. In the hall a charming battalion of young girls, those who cause false notes, and the remembrance of whom is accompanied with a deep sigh heaved by the old bachelors who have the pleasure or the misfortune of meeting them on their way.

Lately a gentleman among the audience did not cease repeating during the whole concert, "When are they going to play a tune?" And after three pieces sung by Madame S[trakosch], after those of Carlo Patti, after my five or six solos, he repeated, "I have not yet heard one tune," and he went away perfectly disgusted. You would be astonished to learn how many millions of men are like him. A general, whom you and I know, loves to repeat to his friends that he can recognize on hearing them but two tunes—one is "Yankee Doodle," and the other is not![2] One of my friends lately told me that at one of my concerts he was seated in front of two ladies who consoled themselves for the total absence of "tunes" by seeing that in the third part I must play "Home, Sweet Home" with variations. They waited patiently. The concert went on, "Home, Sweet Home" was encored, which did not prevent the good women from saying, "But when is he going to play 'Home, Sweet Home'?" and on leaving they complained bitterly that I had announced a piece that I did not play. The ears of many people are so little exercised that they understand only two or three songs that they continually hear from birth. "Yankee

2 General Ulysses S. Grant said this to Lincoln when the President commented favorably on a military band conducted by George E. Ives, father of the composer Charles E. Ives.

Doodle," for example, the hideous "John Brown," and the "Last Rose of Summer" (even this last is already too learned), and thus there must be only the melody, without harmony, without variations, absolutely naked, as a fifer would play it, for them to recognize it. The least artifice, the least ornament, they lose the thread, are confused, and the complaints begin that there is no melody.

A good enough concert at Auburn. I heard a lady going out say, "What a deafening racket he makes with his piano. There is no music at all in it." I have often heard others speak of it, who said that I always played too softly and that I did not make enough noise. O critics! you would be very annoying if you were not so amusing!

❧❧❧❧❧❧❧❧❧❧

Sunday, May 8

Been to Catholic church and heard Mass. Execrable music! Organ played by a young girl who made impossible harmonies. Sermon very long. The preacher screamed loud enough to tire his lungs. The congregation was affected.

❧❧❧❧❧❧❧❧❧❧❧

May 9

Set out again from Auburn at seven o'clock in the morning for Rochester, where I arrived at a quarter-past eleven o'clock. Charming town; one of the neatest, most animated, and most civilized of the West. My concerts here are always profitable and my audience always well disposed. Concert this evening excellent. I should like to transport in a lump, for the edification of Europe, some of the audiences that come under my notice.

The feminine type in the United States is undoubtedly superior to that of Europe. Pretty young girls are a majority in American audiences, while in Europe they are an exception. Besides the education of women, taken on an average, is more complete here. American women, with their delicate sentiments and the intelligence that our system of education develops, united to the native elegance of their sex, will do more than all the legislators in the world to polish men, and to circumscribe within reasonable limits the turbulent effervescence found at the surface of all new societies. Without them, whiskey and the revolver would completely overrun us. By their soft but powerful influence, our manners, little by little, become softened, and I foresee the day when a drunkard will be treated according to his habits, that is to say, like a brute, and when those who are always ready to draw their revolver will be punished as murderers.

At Rochester I have seen some of the most charming types of women that have ever crossed the dreams of an old bachelor! Outside of my exceptional position of pianist and old bachelor, this is the element I dread the most in my concerts—it gives me absence of mind, and a wrong note is very quickly struck! Suppose I have to make a leap to reach a black key at the extremity of my keyboard. I take my measure well, but the Capitoline is close to the Tarpeian; my finger, not well assured, because my eyes are on my audience and my spirit traverses the field, slips, and from the Capitoline summit—D sharp, for example—is ignominiously precipitated into the Tarpeian depths of E natural—to my consternation, and to the joy of the *pianisticules* whose subtlety for scenting out defects could never be equaled but by their bad will in discovering accomplishments. It would be well for all of us who criticize without mercy the works of our neighbor to make a sum in the rule of three for our own use. Let us suppose that Mr. X., who has never been able to play the music of others, or his own, for the double reason that the latter is still in a projected state (never to be realized) and beyond his powers—let us suppose that he falls with all his might upon some unfortunate pianist —upon myself, for example—do you think he would show himself moderate? Not at all. *Dernière espérance.* How as to that? Good for little girls! *Banjo.* A melody for the Negroes! Pooh! Lacks execution, without taking into account the old tricks!

Thus always the same song: "He does not play classical music." And when the ordinary run of mortals applaud, he shrugs his shoulders. But, wretched man, be prudent then! The more you belittle me, the more you bemire yourself in the dark mud in which your venomous impertinence stagnates. I am nothing, but I am more than you. What, then, are you?

Some of his friends, hidden by the lion's skin, cause themselves sometimes to be taken for the lion by only scratching without roaring. The more merciless they are in their judgments, the more talent is conceded to them. One who is nothing always displays skill by attacking those who are something. *"Audaces fortuna,"* etc. One has nothing to lose, and fools are easily caught. A Mr. Monte Mayer, a vulgar physician, has become celebrated in Spain by giving a course of lectures in which he proves that Newton was a fool. But these counterfeit lions cause fear because they never forget themselves and conceal their voices, but, by dint of playing the part of the king of the forest, they end by persuading themselves that they are really so—they wish to roar. It is then that we hear a hee! haw! bursting out—the fraud is discovered, and everybody laughs. They themselves never perceive it, and continue gravely to shake their asses' ears over their manes. I know an ass well, who, after having devoted his pen for ten years in proving to the artistic world that my compositions were detestable, was advised, miserable wretch, to publish in an unlucky day one of the lucubrations of his pen and of his gall-filled brain. I confess that, until the moment that this happy composition fell into my hands, I had thought myself killed by the attacks of this severe Aristarchus; but, after having read it, I consoled myself by addressing to him *in petto* this apostrophe, which I borrowed from Voltaire: "Sir: I pardon your criticisms because nobody reads them, but I shall never pardon your compositions because I have been obliged to read them, and they are too bad for me ever to forget them."

◇◇◇◇◇◇◇◇◇

May 10 [1864]

Set out again from Rochester.

I recommend Congress Hall to all travelers who attach any importance to an excellent table, prompt attention, and an affable and attentive welcome from a landlord.

Arrived at Lockport at two o'clock. It pours rain—the streets are lakes of mud—every gutter is a cataract. I confess that if I were the public I would pay double what one of my tickets costs not to go to the concert this evening.

Few at the concert, but those who have braved the inclemency of such weather are evidently musical amateurs, and I did my best. My principle is: the smaller the audience the more I apply myself. Artists in general act differently under the same circumstances. If the receipts are small, you see them assume an indifferent air, play or sing by halves, cut down their pieces, shorten their programs; and in acting thus they are ungrateful, illogical, unjust, dishonest, and unworthy of the name of artists. Ungrateful, because they make their bad humor bear upon those who justly have a right to their favor. Unjust, because those who are present should not be responsible for the absent. Illogical, because one might bet everything that those who, to go to a concert, brave the obstacles that have prevented the majority from going are true judges of music, who understand it, and to whom the artist, certain of being appreciated, should try to present himself in his best light. Dishonest, because the person who has paid for his ticket has a right to demand all that is promised on the program; and, finally, they are unworthy of their profession, because the love of lucre is with them greater than that of art, and he is not a true artist who measures the sum of emotions and inspirations that flow from his soul by the sum of dollars and cents that have entered into his coffer. Inspiration is not commanded, I know it. The public could not command it for its money. The program does not lead them to think so, but, to be true to themselves, artists should do what they ought to do. As to inspiration, it is independent of the will. It has happened to me to play horribly before crowded halls and before intelligent audiences; and on the contrary to play in villages, and before audiences who hardly understood it, in such a way as to please myself—a very difficult thing!

◇◇◇◇◇◇◇◇◇

Wednesday, May 11

Set out again from Lockport for Toronto (Canada).

Awakened at six o'clock this morning by that cursed gong. Is it possible that in this nineteenth century, in the midst of a republic, in a civilized society, this last vestige of barbarism should not yet be abolished? What! I am in a hotel. I pay for the purpose of finding there board and lodging, which includes sleep. I am neither collegian nor galley slave, nor slave, much less a soldier—

that is to say, I am not obliged to be subjected to discipline; and
nevertheless an autocratic landlord, whom I pay in order to promote my comfort, shall have the right violently to destroy my
sleep and brutally draw me from my repose at any hour that shall
please him, as if I were his property. And you and I support this
barbarous tyranny? Not one of those around me murmurs. Custom
is everything with the Anglo-Saxon. The empire of routine holds
him in leading strings. That the proprietor of a hotel should
think of ordering that his guests not drink more than a certain
quantity daily—would you not revolt at it? Is it not nevertheless
as despotic to require that you should be awakened at six o'clock
in the morning? But as from time immemorial, hotelkeepers have
arrogated to themselves the right of not permitting us to sleep
after a certain hour, we quietly submit to it.

It pours rain. The heavens are like lead, and it is cold; decidedly this spring is hostile to us; for one month, out of twenty
soirées, sixteen at least have been with a pouring rain. There goes
again another leaf torn from the tree of my illusions. This beautiful month of May, so poetical, so much sung by the poets, is a
myth.

Last Sunday at Mass the preacher took for the subject of his
sermon the worship that the Catholic Church gives to the Virgin
Mary. "The beautiful month of May has been especially consecrated to her," and, the occasion offering itself to make use of a
little rhetoric, he began by presenting to us nature awakening in
the spring, the buds first becoming green, the flowers exhaling
their perfumes to the breeze. "The sun," etc. etc. etc. Here, the
sky, which has been cloudy since the morning, opened to let pass
(a ray of sunlight, you will say)—no! lightning, after a clap of
thunder, followed by a deluge of rain, mingled with hail. The
poor priest, who had prepared his sermon in prospect of a month
of May, like all others, was completely taken aback, and com-
prehending that the breeze, perfumed by the flowers, and the sun
no longer agreed with a dull, rainy month, full of storms, tornadoes, and of bad designs, resigned himself to making a sacrifice
of his rhetoric, and soon finished his sermon.

One hour of detention at Hamilton en route to Toronto.
Some days ago, on arriving at a small place, a local paper fell into
our hands, and we read in it a diatribe of one hundred lines against

fashionable music, the Italians, the Germans, in one word, against every species of art that is not so elevated as the music of the Christy Minstrels. Our agent had neglected to give this Athenian my announcement, and he avenged himself for it after the manner of angry children, who beat themselves with their fists. Our man by this proceeding showed himself in all his folly. Our concert took place the same evening, and the good man with infernal malice finished his article by letting a poisoned arrow fly at us. "This was written many days ago, but we did not publish it, because we did not wish to do harm to the concerts that were about to take place. Having examined our columns, and assured ourselves that no concert was about to take place, we have decided to publish it." Max, who is patience itself provided no one touches his interests, became red with rage on reading the article. He saw only the last paragraph, "that there was no concert about to take place," which was calculated to keep away many of our audience. He called on the editor, and with the most agreeable air in the world, introduced himself.

Max. "I am your servant, sir. My name is Strakosch."

Editor. "Ah!"

Max. "I regret that you thought proper to publish that article."

Editor (with a stiff air). "Those, sir, are my opinions."

Max. "I am sorry for it (with a gracious air), but perhaps you will come to the concert?"

Editor (enchanted, but not wishing it to be seen). "Hem!"

Max. "Have you a family?"

Editor. "My stars, yes! I think that four or five tickets would do."

Max. "I am delighted! You will find them, sir, at your disposal at the music store, where they will cost you only seventy-five cents each."

And he returned charmed with his revenge. I figure to myself the discomfiture of the editor. But the consequences! Poor Strakosch! The editor will have his revenge, and if you ever return here (which probably you will have the good sense never to do) you may expect to receive his broadsides. I pity you, or rather I pity the artists for whom you will be the impresario, for it will be on them, as being the only vulnerable point of the impresario, that the blows will fall, like those coachmen who strike the horses of their rivals with heavy blows of their whips whenever they meet them.

Last month, June, I gave thirty-three concerts in twenty-six days. In fourteen months (during which I have remained idle only fifty days) I have given more than four hundred concerts and traveled more than forty thousand miles by railroad. This reminds me of the story by the son of Alexandre Dumas, where his hero laid a wager to live a whole month exclusively on pigeon! The first eight days did very well. The second week this insipid flesh began to disgust him. The twentieth day he had a horror of it, and on the thirtieth (for he heroically won his bet) even the sight of a pigeon's feather gave him a fever and seasickness! I am the same with my concerts; the sight of an audience gives me a nausea, and every evening in sitting down in front of the audience, to the keyboard, to which pitiless fate has devoted me, I experience the pangs of the thirtieth day of pigeon in Dumas's story. I am pleased to think that beyond the tomb concerts exist only in the memory, like the nightmare that we recall to ourselves confusedly in the morning and that has painfully disturbed our sleep.

The Orientals people their paradise with marvelous houris; the Indians fill theirs with prairies full of game where the chase is eternal. I love to imagine that in the paradise where I shall go (?) the local laws strictly prohibit ever playing music in public for money, under the penalty of listening twenty times successively to "*La Rêverie de Rosellen.*" On the other side I represent hell to myself as being the general *entrepôt* of all pianos—square, grand, upright, and oblique—an infernal Botany Bay for the practice of hardened pianists, in which an audience of the damned listen to an eternal "*Rêverie de Rosellen,*" played to the consummation of the ages by pianists, inhabitants of the somber empire! Ha! What do you say to it? It makes one shudder only to think of it, and Dante, had he known of the piano, would he have failed, do you think, to have made it take a part of that frightful torment in his *Inferno?* No, certainly, and if to the "*Rêverie de Rosellen*" he had added the "*Donna è mobile,*" and *The Maiden's Prayer,* of Miss Barda-zewska, I do not doubt that Ugolino[3] himself would have been

---

[3] Ugolino della Gherardesca was an Italian political leader in Pisa during the thirteenth century. His tragic story forms an episode in Dante's *Inferno.*

comparatively happy in not belonging to this honorable artistic corporation.

Sometimes I find myself delayed on the road by some accident or unforeseen event. I then dispatch a telegram to my agent and the hour for the concert is postponed; but it also happens sometimes that the telegram arrives too late for him to publish it. The audience already assembled in the hall becomes agitated and restless at not seeing the artist appear. My telegraphic dispatch arrives, and Strakosch reads it to the audience, offering to return the money to those who don't have the patience to await my arrival. A telegram from Strakosch in answer to mine, which I generally receive at the next station, makes me aware of the audience's decision. Then, if it is willing to wait for me, I send, from station to station, a telegram, which my agent reads to the audience to keep it patient. This calms it. Soon there is established between us a sympathetic tie. It becomes interested in the unknown traveler whose thought traverses space to communicate with that of the crowd anxious to see him. Every one converses with his neighbor; the young girls flirt with their beaux; the papas sleep or talk of Erie or of American gold; the hall is transformed into a vast, friendly *tertulia*.[4] As the telegraphic dispatches follow each other, the enthusiasm increases. I am seen approaching more than twenty miles, no more than ten miles off, the last stations are generally passed amid the expectant enthusiasm of the whole hall. The excitement becomes so great they almost embrace each other.

(N.B.) If I were one of the audience, by the way, I would not have the least objection in yielding (with discrimination) to this affectionate demonstration.

Strakosch then appears and with tremulous voice says, wiping his forehead as if he had just pulled the train, so impatiently awaited, more than fifty miles (or rather like an impresario who after having thought that his receipts were shipwrecked sees them riding at anchor at the bottom of his coffers), these solemn words, which the audience receives with a tattoo of hurrahs: "Ladies and gentlemen, I have the honor of announcing to you that Mr. Gottschalk has just arrived." I then make my entrance upon the scene, and the tattoo of the audience goes on increasing, swells, and takes

---

[4] In Spanish, a social club meeting or evening party.

such boisterous proportions that I should not know how to give you an idea of it unless you have heard the finale of *Ione*, by Maestro Petrella, or that of *Medea*, by Maestro Pacini, which, to my notion, are the two most deafening musical abominations that have ever been committed, since the invention of the bass drum, the cymbals, and the whole kitchen battery of modern instrumentation. I designedly enlarge upon this, because it is characteristic of an American audience, and a novel and wholly local phase in the psychology of concerts in the United States.

Nothing, lately, worthy of notice in my concerts unless it is a few lines giving an account of one of the last (favorably, I am bound to acknowledge), mentioning that "Mr. Gottschalk played his *Cradle Song*, for two pianos, with Mr. L——, and with magnificent effect." The *Cradle Song* for two pianos! I pity the poor baby who should be condemned to be cradled under the magnificent effect of two pianos. This brings to my mind by contrast the March from Meyerbeer's *Prophète*, which I saw at Havana arranged for the clarinet with guitar accompaniment! It is probable that the chronicler of this concert, having gone to sleep after dinner (without the aid of the two pianos in question), may have taken on faith the program and the probabilities, but that his pen still benumbed, confounded *La Fantaisie Triomphale* on *Trovatore* for two pianos with the *Cradle Song*, which the program announced for the same evening.

In the paragraph extracted from my last letter to the *Home Journal* the editor committed an error that many of the other papers reproduced and that I wish to rectify. "Gottschalk, it is said, has given in the United States nearly one thousand concerts and has travelled by rail and steamboat nearly eight thousand miles." It should read, not eight thousand, but eighty thousand miles. Eight thousand miles in two years are simply a trifle that the smallest learned animal, giant, dwarf, phenomenon, or traveling pianist who has speculated on the country can boast having done, and the rights I demand as the champion of concerts and of perambulation on railroads would be as doubtful as those of the King of Sardinia to the Kingdom of Jerusalem, or of those of Richard Wagner to the coming world, if I had only a credit on the ledger of posterity for eight thousand miserable little miles! ! But it is *eighty thousand miles* I have traveled in less than two years, giving, on an average, three concerts every two days. It is almost as notable as Dr. (?) Winship, of Boston, who lifts four thousand pounds, or the young Connecticut girl that Barnum exhibits who weighs six hundred pounds. My detractors can deny me everything in the future, I care little about it. They can say that I play only my own music, and that it is bad; *that I wear gloves* at my concerts (how horrible!); that I wipe my fingers before commencing to play, with my handkerchief *which I take from my pocket* (what a shame!): all these things form the subject of a widely extended, anonymous correspondence with which a crowd of austere lovers of art gratify me every morning, whose bilious little spite is alleviated by telling me confidentially the most disagreeable things in the world.

From the height of my eighty thousand miles I defy the whole world, and if my enemies, after having dislodged me from so many other positions, attempt to dispute with me the possession of this last bulwark. I solemnly declare to them that I shall defend it with the energy of despair.

ANECDOTES ABOUT KALKBRENNER AND OTHERS

Kalkbrenner, who by his didactic works is recommended to the respect of artists, but whose compositions by their vacuity are condemned never to be played, had a cold, neat, limpid execution and a pure but superficial and tedious style. The perfect elegance of his manners, his cultivated intelligence, and his talent gave him great success in society, but his extreme vanity, which had become proverbial, had in time rendered him insupportable. He thought himself infallible in everything, and had said forcibly, like a celebrated dancer of the last century, Vestris, I think, "there are in Europe three great men—Voltaire, Frederick, and myself." His best pupil, Stamaty, a fellow-scholar with Osborne, the fortunate fellow-laborer of De Bériot in one hundred duos for the piano and violin, was my teacher for seven years. In 1844,[5] then very young, I gave in Paris a soirée to which all the illustrious pianists of the period were invited, among others Kalkbrenner. I played Chopin's Concerto in E Minor, Thalberg's Fantasia on *Semiramide*, and

---

[5] It was 1845.

that of Liszt's on *Robert le Diable*. The next day I went to thank Kalkbrenner for having come to hear me. This attention softened a little the generally sour disposition of the old pianist, who did not forgive the new school for knowing something; he took my hand and said to me with an air of majestic condescension, "The style is good; as for the rest there is nothing astonishing; you are my grand-child (alluding to Stamaty, who was his pupil), but, for God's sake, who advised you to play such music? Chopin! I hardly pardon you; but Liszt and Thalberg, what rhapsodies! Why did you not play one of my pieces? they are beautiful, please everybody, and are classical!"

Kalkbrenner had a son whom he hoped to make the inheritor of his glory, but who, after having been a child prodigy, aborted and became a prodigious nullity. One night after having boasted before the French court of the improvisations of his child, then eight years old, the king expressed his desire to hear one of these marvelous inspirations. The child placed himself at the piano and played for some minutes, then, stopping all at once, he turned toward his father and artlessly said to him, "Papa, I have for-gotten—"

Kalkbrenner lived, when I was introduced to him, in the quarter of Paris called Cité d'Orléans. This Cité d'Orléans was a kind of artists' hive. You reached it through a narrow alley that opened into an interior court around which many elegant pavilions were clustered.

The first that met the eye was occupied on the ground floor by Zimmerman, the director of the piano classes at the Paris Con-servatoire. A wearisome pianist, a pedantic and ordinary composer, he was nevertheless an excellent professor, and it was he who formed Prudent, Goria, and all the pianists of the French school. On my arrival at Paris he had refused me admission to the Con-servatoire, saying that "America was the country of railroads but not of musicians."

On the first floor was the atelier of Dantan, the celebrated sculptor who has made the busts of every illustrious artist of this century. The pavilion alongside was occupied by Georges Sand when she was in Paris, and next to hers came that of Chopin. Op-posite, Count ——, an old amateur who speculated on his reputa-tion as a man of influence to gather to his house all the artists in

vogue to play and sing without its ever costing him a penny (this
species of Count de —— is often found), next to him lived Kalkbrenner.

Orfila, the great chemist,[6] was the friend of Kalkbrenner, whose
whims he ridiculed unmercifully. I heard him relate the following
anecdote one day that I dined with him, and a salad was served for
which Kalkbrenner had invented the seasoning. Among other
pretensions he boasted that he entertained better than anybody
else, and as to etiquette many sovereigns had taken counsel of his
knowledge in delicate situations.

"I gave a dinner to the chiefs of the Academy of Sciences and
Medicine, of which I was dean." (It is Orfila who speaks.) "The
French princes were also invited, and many other illustrious persons. The number of my servants not being sufficient, I engaged
some more; whether it was owing to ignorance of their duty, or
that they were frightened at the sight of such an imposing as-
sembly, one of them handed a plate to Kalkbrenner on his right
side. Kalkbrenner, finding himself eclipsed by the presence of so
many great names, and suffering impatiently from being relegated
to an inferior place, took care, as you may well suppose, to seize the
occasion to make himself noticed. 'My friend,' said he, in an assumed manner to the unfortunate servant, 'when anyone has the
honor of waiting on guests as distinguished as we are, he ought not
to be ignorant that plates are to be handed *on the left.*' And on
this he bridled up and, the servant having changed his position, he
helped himself plenteously from the dish. Some time after this,
Kalkbrenner also gave a dinner. It so happened that one of the
servants, in taking a dish off the table, upset the sauce on my
head," and on saying this Orfila showed us his head, on which
there was no longer a hair. " 'My friend,' I said to the poor servant,
stupefied by his awkwardness, 'when anyone has the honor of
waiting on such distinguished guests as we are, he ought not to be
ignorant that he must not upset sauce on their heads.' Kalkbrenner
understood the lesson, and found it so much the more bitter as he
liked, as I have said, to entertain, and boasted that everything at

---

[6] Matthieu Joseph Bonaventure Orfila (1787–1853), a native of the
Spanish island of Minorca, became a great figure in French medicine, medical
jurisprudence, and chemistry. An accomplished musician, he took a personal
interest in Gottschalk, often presenting him at his soirées.

his house followed the rules of court etiquette, of which he had instituted himself grand master."

Orfila gave a dinner to his friends every Thursday. It was at
the period of the cholera: twelve hundred persons died daily of this
horrible disease. All the doctors ordered a rigorous diet. "They are
asses," said Orfila, laughing; and he continued to give his friends
(who nevertheless found themselves no worse for it) everything
that was then considered as tending to engender the prevailing
disease—salads, ice creams, and fruit. "They are asses, and the
proof is that, after having killed me eighteen years ago, they were
not able to discover that I was not dead." Indeed, in a terrible
illness he had, he fell into a cataleptic state that gave such appearances of death that the physicians were deceived for many hours.
He was present, without being able to move, at the preparations
for his burial, and heard the conversations of the doctors who relieved each other, near him, and made their observations on the
deceased. "It is since my death that I have become disgusted with
life," said he with a comic seriousness, which leads us to suppose
that the dean of the Academy had been but moderately satisfied
with the funeral orations he heard made.

It was at these dinners that I became acquainted with the most
celebrated doctors and surgeons of the time. Trousseau, who began
to make himself known, and at that time devoted his leisure to a
pretty American; Boyer, the venerable chief of chemistry at the
Hôtel Dieu; Ricord, the artists' doctor; Pasquier, the doctor for
children and of King Louis-Philippe; Maisonneuve, who was
already planning his marvelous operations; Nélaton, the surgeon
who cured Garibaldi; and many others whose names escape me.

Orfila, notwithstanding the gravity of his labors and the aus-
terity of his manners, took delight in music, and sang (he was sixty
years old) with much spirit Italian *buffa* music.

◇◇◇◇◇◇◇◇◇

May 11, 1864

Arrived in Toronto at five o'clock P.M. Toronto is the oldest city
in Canada. Smaller than Montreal, it has the advantage of being
more animated. Its society is more hospitable and European.

A superb concert. We play and sing our best, and, to judge

from the enthusiasm of the audience, who encored from the first to the last piece, we succeed. I will mention an improvement over our concerts at Montreal, which is that conversation, if there was any, took place in an undertone that permitted the music to be heard. No young officers making themselves insupportable to their neighbors by their unseasonable talking, but, on the contrary, real English gentlemen who did not think themselves bound to show their ennui by acting in a manner annoying to the audience.

My *amour propre* for my musical progeny has experienced a rude shock this evening. Madame Strakosch, having been encored, took it into her head to sing my *Cradle Song*, which was not on the program. A charming woman asked me the name of that *"frightful piece,"* and who was the composer of it? And this is so much the more vexatious as I have not even the consolation of supposing that my pretty interrogator was one of my enemies and chose this mode of proving it. She had, the perfidious one, just cast a dart at me, and my vanity, which she had thus sharpened, rendered the candid opinion that she had expressed about my latest-born more painful to my paternity. It is salutary that, from time to time, we should be recalled to the reality of things—that is to say, that, amid the factitious atmosphere of biased opinions from interested flatterers, in the midst of whom we are pampered, the truth should reach us from without.

◇◇◇◇◇◇◇◇◇

May 12

I went out at eleven o'clock to dine at Mr. G.'s, a Pole by birth, whom long association with English society has rendered English. An engineer of great talent, he has almost wholly constructed the Grand Trunk Railway. His elegant mansion is a model of taste and of comfort. It is, in one word, what the house ought to be of such a man as he, who can offer and knows how to bestow the most courteous hospitality.

I have visited the barracks of the six batteries of artillery placed in garrison at Toronto. Those who are not with English soldiers will with difficulty form an idea of the admirable order and neatness that prevail there. The horses, all of Canadian stock, are magnificent animals, treated with a solicitude and care that struck me so much the more as I have still present in my memory the brutal, cruel, and improvident manner with which I have seen our cavalry horses treated. One of the officers, through whose politeness I was able to visit in detail all the barracks, introduced me into the mess-room where the officers take their meals. A piano in one corner, two oratorios of Handel, and, lying in another corner, as if it was ashamed of being found in such good company, my humble *Cradle Song.*

In the coach houses where all the harness was, I was astonished at the care with which every bit of leather is polished, every steel buckle cleaned; and nevertheless a great deal of the harness is ten years old, and has been used in the Crimea, having been in service at Alma, Inkerman, and the Malakoff. In spite of all this they look new. Heard in a music store the Fantasia on *La Muette,* played by a charming young girl, Miss C., an amateur, with most remarkable strength and clearness. I record this fact because it is the first case of native talent I have met with in Canada.

Second concert. A great deal of enthusiasm; nevertheless we neither played nor sang so well as yesterday.

◆◆◆◆◆◇◇◇◇

May 13

Left Toronto at half past twelve for St. Catherine, where we arrived at half-past four o'clock in the afternoon, It poured rain. The pretty month of May continues to hold its own. I have heard said that St. Catherine is picturesque! I seek in vain to discover the beauties of a country that I have heard spoken of so highly. As well seek the beauty of a woman in spring dress who should have accidentally fallen into the water and whom somebody has just drawn out. The water filters through the door and roof of the diligence. The streets are lakes; the trees, the houses, the hedges are vaguely defined through the compact lines made in the atmosphere by the drops of rain driven by the wind. The only inhabitants we meet are a young lad and an old blind horse, the one carried by the other and wading and splashing furiously to get under shelter.

We shall not make our fortune here. Behrens, who undertakes, ad interim, the functions of agent, having gone to the office for the sale of tickets, in a part of which he sees my portrait, inquires "Is

it here that tickets are sold?" The proprietor facetiously answers
him (unkind man), "You wish to say where tickets *should* be sold,
for we have not yet sold one."

Seated before the store, I am reading *John Marchmont's Legacy*
(another novel where lawyers and chicanery form the subject of
the book). When will the time come that English novelists shall
cease to explore the Court of Chancery, and the *Police Gazette?*
It is sad to see money, money, and always money, the moving
spring of all novels from beyond the sea. A will, a change of heirs,
a false heir, a fraudulent will; no heirs, no will; and you have *Orley
Farm, No Name, Woman in White, Aurora Floyd,* etc. Take away
the money and chicanery of the modern English school, and see
what remains. You will reply to me that French novels, which
speak only of love, are immoral. Granted. I do not like novels, but
if I must choose between the two passions, in view of the effects
they produce I should choose that which at least awakens in us
noble ideas, gives birth to noble sacrifices and self-denial. But then
I was reading before the stove, and Max was meditating, after
having read the latest news announcing a fresh Federal victory, a
plan for a joint campaign against the South, when a bass voice
requested to speak to the agent of Mr. Gottschoff (why are they so
obstinate in making my name Russian?). The new arrival is a pompous, fat, short, apoplectic individual who had no need of announcing himself as "collector of Her Majesty's customs" for me
to know that I had the honor of seeing before me an officer of the
British Government. The collector of Her Majesty has the important and dignified air of a judge who is just pronouncing a
severe sentence. He addresses Strakosch with that horrid tone of
perfidious politeness with which the attorney general examines a
culprit whom he wishes to make contradict himself. "You have
two pianos? Ha! I say, *Two* pianos, both yours, and only *one* on
the permit."

"Yes, we have one piano we have not declared, not desiring to
pay duty, since we remain only two days in Canada."

"Ah yes, I see, certainly. Has not Mr. Gottschoff played with
great success at Toronto? I have heard particular mention made of
a piece for two pianos which electrified the audience!"

"Yes, sir," answered Strakosch, "the Grand March from *Faust.*"

Her Majesty's officer. "For two pianos?"

Strakosch. "Yes, sir."

Contracting his brow, and in the attitude of the lawyer of the opposite party who has just discovered something injurious, the officer said, "Two pianos, sir, and you have paid duty only on one. The queen, sir, cannot thus be robbed, and you will have to pay the duty. The queen, sir, will collect the duty."

Strakosch, vexed and beginning to get tired of the character of inquisitor which this old imbecile assumed. "But, sir, this is absurd. You might as well collect a duty on the clothes which I wear and seize them!"

The officer, indignant and red with offended dignity. "Seize your clothes, sir! The queen, sir, would not do such a thing. This language is very indecent. I shall be obliged, to my great regret, to prevent you from using this instrument this evening. Seize your clothes!"

A dispatch arrives next day. He has seized my piano! Decidedly, this would have undeceived me if I had ever believed what my Spanish sonnets told me when they compared me to Orpheus taming the wild beasts. I have not been able to tame this collector.

Concert, notwithstanding the rain. There were fifty persons who applauded like five hundred, and for whom we played as if, in place of thirty dollars of receipts, we had received three hundred.

Excellent hotel. I forget—among the audience, in the first row, sat my collector.

Set out from St. Catherine for Buffalo.

Americans have a practical and utilitarian spirit that makes them reject all speculative theories, and they arrive at solutions of social problems which in Europe would frighten the greatest economists. The system of exchanges adopted by the teachers of music in America, for instance, offers me an example. At Philadelphia, one of my friends, a professor of music, gives lessons on the piano to two daughters of a tailor, who in return furnishes him with clothes the whole year! At New Orleans, a dentist offered, if I would give him tickets for him and his children, to attend me professionally for an operation of which I stood in need.

We are just crossing that audacious marvel of science, that incomparable monument of human genius which is called the Niagara Suspension Bridge. My last visit to Niagara was in December with Madamoiselle Cordier (to speak of it in detail).

The country is inundated. A traveler who was at Buffalo this morning assures me that the lower quarter of the town is completely submerged, and that they are navigating it on rafts. "Pretty month of May!" The rain seems to increase every minute.

Was I not right in saying that it was we who would pay for Strakosch's wit with the country editor? Here is, among other things, what his bile has suggested on my account: "Gottschalk has played in the most abominable, banging, screeching manner, torturing his piano and drawing from it the most inhuman sounds." Ah, Strakosch! May this critic enlighten you. And let us hope that, after having thus cast upon me all his venom, this terrible editor may peaceably return to his daily duty without persisting any further in his subversive and Corkonian theories of music. For my own part, I ask no more of him; and I admit that, if I had had as much to complain of from one of his employees as he had of Strakosch, I would have been still more severe on his prose than he has been on my music, and perhaps neither of us would have done wrong.

Brilliant concert in Buffalo.

I have taken a multitude of notes on Canada. What a frightful country! It is enough to let you know that it is essentially Catholic —Irish and French (what French? Low Normans of the seventeenth century) vying with each other in fervent rage, that is, as to which shall have the most churches, sermons, monks, and of white, black, and gray nuns. The Oblate Fathers, who promenade Quebec in their filthy cassocks, are only hypocritical forms outrageously rubicund and oily, or ignobly emaciated and famished. The pulpit is a throne; the confessional a citadel. I despair of humanity. Quebec exhales the enfeebling bigotry of a population preserved in ignorance and brutishness. The children are weakly, and there are many idiots and deformed. The skilled native pianists balance between *La Violette* by Herz and *L'Ange déchu* by Kalkbrenner. The Chevalier Gouanère is a genius, La Harpe the first French poet.[7] The old French families who own property are called *"Les Sagneurs de St. Herem, de la Montagne, ou de St. Maurice."* The population of Lower Canada—base, lazy, slavish, and superstitious—is despised by the English. It retaliates in jealous hatred.

[7] Jean-François de La Harpe (1739–1803) was a minor French critic and poet.

Every Sunday in the sermon at High Mass this phrase invariably re-
appears: "Above all, my children, do not sully yourselves by entering the threshold of those dens of perdition called theaters." They
permit magic lanterns, the circus, and puppet shows.

The polka is forbidden; the waltz prohibited; the lancers is
tolerated. Judge the intellectual level of this régime! The women
are thin, with sallow complexions. The walls, the houses, the streets
distill ennui. Every moment young men are seen in long blue
surtouts (the old Levite) with yellow edging (!) and green scarves
wound around their waists. These are the college students, who,
needless to say, are directed by the priests. Bossuet is the greatest of
philosphers; Voltaire is a blackguard whose crimes they pardon on
account of his miserable death and his return *in extremis* to eternal
truth (?).

The pope is a martyr, and Garibaldi a highway robber. They
have made (for the pope) a magnificent subscription. They brand
with the name of demagogues, lukewarm and hardened, those who
have not contributed to St. Peter's pence. Not one music store. In
the window of a bookseller, who sells the complete works of
Monseigneur Dupanloup, a copy of "Home, Sweet Home," arranged by Thalberg and *Last Hope* by Gottschalk, constitute the
whole profane catalogue. On the other hand, a great number of
hymns to Mary.

In politics, they still play, whistle, and sing "Dixie." The
audience calls to the orchestra every evening (*tous les souars*)
for "Dixie" as in '48 at Paris they called for the "Marseillaise."[8]

Names in Lower Canada have this peculiarity about them that
they always signify something. Do they not seem to be taken from
a chapter of Paul de Kock?[9] Reflecting upon them a little, we
easily find their origin in the seventeenth and eighteenth centuries.
The French soldiers were known, not by their names, but only by
their nicknames. They were almost the only colonists of Lower
Canada, and from them probably all these singular names are
derived.

---

[8] Gottschalk stubbornly refused to accede to their clamor for "Dixie."
[9] Charles-Paul de Kock (1794–1871) was a popular French novelist and
dramatist whose works abounded in descriptions of lower-middle-class Paris
life.

◇◇◇◇◇◇◇◇◇

November 1, 1864

Here I am again traveling after a long rest, if I may call rest four months without concerts, but filled in with three weeks of laborious idleness at Saratoga, followed by many others devoted to correcting proofs, scribbling an article for the *Atlantic Monthly*, writing ten or twelve letters daily, composing five new contraband pieces that are to be published under the ægis of a borrowed paternity,* and five or six pieces, which if not good are pure Gottschalk lucubrations that are just about to be launched into the serene eternity of oblivion, or into the ocean of criticism and malevolence.

I appeared once in public, a month ago, in a charity concert organized by some ladies. God protect you from charity concerts and from lady patronesses! Both are above all an abuse, and the public cares little if the artist has or has not *given* his services. (Here speak of the ferocious public.) To relate the concert of Wollenhaupt. Hissed outrageously.

I met here, day before yesterday, the Associated Company of Artists—Testa and his wife, the tenor Stefani, Amodio, and Madame Lorini, the maestro ——, and Behrens, of gastronomic and punning memory. It is the Neapolitan De Vivo who manages the whole thing. This troupe proudly calls itself on the playbills "Grand Italian Opera Company." Their list of attractions consists of *Trovatore, Lucia, Lucrezia,* and many other operas. Certain malevolent spirits might perhaps remark that the absence of choruses and of orchestra, of décor and of *basso profundo* was injurious to the effect, but on the other hand, the performance, not being impeded by these accessories, gains singularly in vivacity. *Lucrezia, I Puritani,* and *Trovatore* can all be played the same evening!—the whole in two hours and a half, and for fifty cents!

In Bellevue (Canada) the "Grand Italian Opera Company" gave *Lucrezia.* In the supper scene, when Madame Testa comes

---

* The author composed under the nom de plume of "7 Octaves" some charming little pieces, easier of execution than his usual ones [translator's note].

to the "Vaso d'oro," she says that the gold and silver vase of the
Borgia amounted to a blue china pitcher of water and two tum-
blers. The Canadian audience, who did not understand a bit of
Italian, nor of the opera, put up with the glass for the "Vaso d'oro"
(cup of gold), but Madame Testa, on seeing the Brindisi sung with
this singular cup, was taken with a fit of laughter that was caught
by Orsini and Gennaro. The audience, thinking that the laughter
was part of the opera, thought the scene marvelously played, and
laughed till they cried, and the opera of Lucrezia ended amid the
applause of the hall.

In another place Leonora (Trovatore) was forewarned that she
must not die; and why? "Because you will be obliged after falling
dead to get up and go out before the audience, since there is no
curtain."

In Quebec, an English corporal, endowed with a superb tenor
voice, he said, offered to sing the chorus in the "Miserere" of
Trovatore, behind the scenes. The Count di Luna and Azucena
accepted his assistance with so much the more eagerness, as it was
upon them that the task of singing this lamentable accompaniment
devolved. (The clock of the altar struck the hour.) The corporal
began, to his great satisfaction and to the consternation of the
orchestra (Behrens), and of the choristers (the Count di Luna and
Azucena), the worthy man having imperturbably struck a tone
higher than they. His success was unanimous. The *esprit de corps*
was connected with it. His friends, the corporals of the regiment,
and all their subordinates, the soldiers, were there on purpose to
applaud him. Intoxicated by his success, he followed next day the
Grand Company, who were going to give Trovatore in Montreal.
He offered himself for the "Miserere" with some other soldiers
who had practiced together, and took charge of the chorus. The
Count di Luna and Azucena accepted them eagerly, but at the
critical moment they escaped into their room, washing their hands
of what was about to take place. The orchestra (Behrens) assures
me that the effect was impossible to describe. Poor Behrens! He
seems to long for the time when he was the merry companion of
my company. This is perhaps the result of the affection he has for
me, but I think it must be also added that, his companions not
speaking either English or German, Behrens can perpetrate puns
no more.

◇◇◇◇◇◇◇◇◇◇

November 29

Concert in Providence, poor enough. Providence is decidedly trailing behind.

◇◇◇◇◇◇◇◇◇◇

November 30

Concert in Boston. Very great success. Morelli sings remarkably well. He belongs, although young, to the old school of singing, that is to say, he appears to be ignorant of the axiom of the Verdistas that you must scream to be a consummate vocalist.

◇◇◇◇◇◇◇◇◇◇

December 1

Hartford. Fine concert. Kind audience. *Faces to make one play false notes* in the front row. I got along, nevertheless, passably.

◇◇◇◇◇◇◇◇◇◇

December 2

Concert in Boston. Great success.

◇◇◇◇◇◇◇◇◇◇

December 3

Matinée in the Music Hall with the grand organ. L—— plays remarkably.

◇◇◇◇◇◇◇◇◇◇

December 4

Adieu, Boston! You are stiff, pedantic, exclusive (Mr. D. is its oracle)! Your enemies say that you are cold and morose. For myself, I say that you are intelligent, literary, polished; that your pedantry, if you have any, would be excusable if it had produced only the grand organ of the Music Hall, that glorious monument.

I should have much liked to know Longfellow personally, but his habitual melancholy and the burden of his afflictions keep him at a distance from the world. He called on me at my hotel, but I was absent, and my regrets are so much the more bitter and profound, as it is probably the only occasion that I might have had of seeing our greatest poet.

We have no traditions in America. Archæology, the worship of the past, could not exist in a society born but yesterday, that has not yet had time to think of resting in order to dream, occupied as it still is with providing for its material requirements. We are all, more or less, like that American who found Rome very *shattered*. To look back at the past is the business of a satiated and idle man; it is a luxury that only old societies satiated with civilization, and discounting the future, can indulge in. Our churches and our landscapes strike our senses but do not appeal to our imagination. I have never been profoundly moved by a very large landscape. My emotion is dissipated by the multiplicity of things. I desire to bind together the details, but the string breaks. I remain cold. A very small brook softly murmuring at the bottom of an obscure and shady glade sets me to dreaming. All my emotions are awakened by it.

I have been to Ticknor & Fields—the veteran publishers of America. It is delicious in our epoch of palatial stores to find again one of those old shops, dusty, somber, concealing under their antiquity that poetic perfume which always is associated with the past. Here Hawthorne's first essays were published. Longfellow here submitted his first verses to them. Whittier, the melodious Quaker, did the same. Invited by Fields to spend the evening with him, I met there the intelligent aristocracy of Boston. Hunt, the picturesque genre painter, Holmes, the amusing and inspired author of *The Autocrat of the Breakfast-Table,* and many others. The generous hospitality that Mrs. Fields offers to her guests is worthy of the reputation she bears, and answers to the idea one forms voluntarily of the culture and urbanity of the society of the modern Athens. I saw in her parlor a portrait of Longfellow and his wife, two admirable heads. The latter was well calculated to inspire the melodious verse of *Hyperion.* The head of Longfellow answers the ideal that we form of a great poet. Nothing can be more noble than the contour of his face, more harmonious than the calm it breathes, half veiled in the depths of the immense worlds in which he has plunged.

Opposite to Longfellow was a portrait that from a distance I took for one of some Italian of the Renaissance. I approached it and read at the bottom the lithographed verses of the *Bugle Call*, signed in a nervous but legible hand, "Tennyson." The head, not so handsome, not so striking as that of Longfellow, is superb. The swollen and half-closed eyelid (his enemies say the effect of opium) conceals an eagle's eye, which worthily crowns a heroic nose.

Mr. Fields, whose collection of autographs is very rich, showed me an entire chapter of Dickens' manuscript. It resembles fruitless efforts at sky, smoke, and foliage, done by some artless draftsman; after an attentive examination I discovered that the spirals that looked like smoke amid the rings I had taken for clouds were the author's method of erasure. As to the foliage it was Dickens' manner of writing. I must acknowledge that there was much more of smoke and clouds in it than of foliage, which proves to the admirers of the flowing and charming style of Dickens that it is not without polishing, filing, soldering, and hammering, sweat and trouble, that perfection and simplicity are arrived at, and that in literature, as in mineralogy, the diamond does not sparkle until after it has been polished.

Boston possesses what New York has not yet obtained: two concert halls, which are in no way inferior to any of the largest concert halls in the world, and which, as to acoustics, I consider superior to the best of this continent and of the Old World (Tremont Hall and Music Hall). Besides I love pedantry and vanity when they engender such results as the great organ and the bronze statue of Beethoven in the library. O Mæcenac New Yorkers, who boast of the golden patronage you accord to art, what are your titles? Is it perchance that usurious enterprise which is called the Academy of Music, by which you will draw from the impresario a double tax under the form of exorbitant rent and gratuitous admission? You kill the opera at New York, you face the impresario with this dilemma: to be honest, that is to say, become bankrupt, or to prosper, that is to say, rob his creditors. In view of the ultimatum we are not astonished at the little hesitation with which the greater part have chosen the latter alternative, and we consider that you are responsible for the ruinous deception practiced upon the poor artists who have not been paid.

◇◇◇◇◇◇◇◇◇

December 5

Concert in Harrisburg. Charming audience.

◇◇◇◇◇◇◇◇◇

December 6

Brilliant concert in Pittsburgh. They take here decidedly. I have never given a concert here that did not pay me. I played upon a square piano, my grand not having arrived in time. On commencing I cast a look of pity on it. "Poor little thing, thou dost not know what awaits thee." But the valiant little piano did not flinch, and sustained the assault without losing a string or a hammer.

◇◇◇◇◇◇◇◇◇

We traveled from Harrisburg to Pittsburgh by night; not a sleeping car, the worst weather in the world, cold and rainy, and fourteen hours among soldiers, smoking, singing, swearing, and doing all night, for their own pleasure, everything that could be most disagreeable to others.

Our civilization has some singular deficiencies. The comforts we possess in the interior of our houses and in our hotels disappear as soon as we travel. Might we not have many seats so arranged that by paying a little more a lady and gentleman might be certain of finding during their journey the security and repose that the laws of our country give us a right to demand? Is it proper that your daughter, your sister, should be exposed without end to the gross and profane language and to the obscene songs of a mixed society that the want of a division of seats forces you to submit to? You will tell me that our republican institutions are opposed to these divisions. I do not think so. You would have as much right to force all citizens to have their hands callous and not to wear gloves. Besides, have you not first- and second-class hotels? Have you not places suited to all purses at theaters? One can be a republican and not like the society of those who drink every five minutes, pick their teeth with their penknife, use their fingers for handkerchiefs, and eat sausage and keep you in remembrance of it through its odor a long time after the sausage has disappeared. Do not make a mistake as to what I think. I am far from claiming an aristocratic privilege in favor of the rich (of all aristocracies this is the most absurd and the least logical), but I demand in the name of civilization an end of some kind to the abuse that unruly and gross majorities exercise toward intelligent and polished minorities, whether it be in railroad cars or in the field of politics. I do not intend to say that because a man can pay more for a seat he must consequently behave in it more decently than a poor man (far from that, for the contrary theory, alas! might be proved victoriously). But undoubtedly with wealth, particularly in a new society, being generally the proof of social position, we shall be less exposed to and shall more rarely find neighbors who would tread upon our toes, spit over us, smoke under our nose, swear, and take a singular pleasure in disturbing us when we wish to sleep, under the protest that we live in a republic and that consequently everyone has a right to do what he pleases, and that one man is as good as another; he who does not wear gloves having the right to make another who does, understand that he is at least his equal if he is not his superior. All this is absurd and unworthy of us. In fifty years this will have disappeared, and our children will pity us for having so long tolerated such an abuse.

Again, another thing. In order, undoubtedly, that ladies may be able to avoid bad company, there are railroad cars, called "ladies' cars," to which men by themselves are not admitted. You may imagine the logic that has presided over this marvelous invention when you see a greasy immigrant and his "wife," or your coachman and his wife, or your cook, who have the right to pass the gates of paradise, which are forbidden to you if perchance you belong to the disinherited category of bachelors. Then, again, the insolence of the subaltern employees! Trollope has perfectly seized this national trait. If you are well dressed, the man in tatters, whom circumstances accidentally give a superiority over you, embraces it with avidity; he reclaims his dignity, which he thinks compromised in the presence of your gentlemanly appearance, and crushes you with all his plebeian insolence.

A conductor in the West will never say, in speaking of you, "this gentleman," but "this man," particularly if, by your dress and polite manners, he recognizes in you your superiority over him.

We accuse travelers who do not speak of us advantageously of exaggeration and taking sides, and we hate them so much the more as we ourselves well know that they have spoken the truth; and we pardon with difficulty those who discover our weaknesses and our oddities. Would it not be more reasonable for us to correct ourselves?

Pittsburgh is the Birmingham of the United States. The oil wells have given an extraordinary impetus to its already great prosperity. It has today forty or fifty large factories and two hundred oil refineries, all powered by steam; many cannon foundries, one of which, the most considerable, has cast large cannons weighing thousands of pounds each, and twenty-eight feet long. The speculations in oil are unheard of. A young Englishman of my acquaintance placed his capital, one thousand dollars, which he had with difficulty amassed in a small trade, in a petroleum company. In fifteen months his one thousand dollars had gained him seventy-five thousand!! A German tailor whom I know bought, three years ago, a piece of ground in Pennsylvania which cost him five thousand dollars. The nature of the soil gave promise of oil wells. He divided his ground into sixteen lots, and formed a company for exploring it. They dug—the oil flew out. He sold twelve-sixteenths at the rate of thirty thousand dollars each, that is to say, for three hundred sixty thousand dollars, and at the latest date the four-sixteenths he had reserved was producing for him seven hundred dollars per day!

◇◇◇◇◇◇◇◇◇◇

Wednesday, December 7

Second concert in Pittsburgh. An immense crowd. All my pieces encored. Spent the remainder of the evening at H. with Mr. M., music publisher, and two charming French gentlemen, G. and T., professors of singing.

Set out again from Pittsburgh at two o'clock in the morning. Night cold and endless. No sleeping car! Could anyone in the East imagine a railway company without a sleeping car!

◇◇◇◇◇◇◇◇◇

Thursday, December 8

Arrived at half past ten o'clock in the morning at Cleveland. It is bitter cold. The north wind blows; the lake rolls its great brown waves. The sky is wan. Some assert that Cleveland is charming. I have always found it extremely dull. Besides, the hotels there are so bad that you have to feed on bread and eggs rather than perish with hunger. I am assured that the old hotel has been replaced on the same site by a new one in the same style as those in the East.

Decidedly, the die is cast. Cleveland is devoted to bad hotels, the bill of fare ostentatiously containing an interminable list of dishes, not one of which is eatable. The fish is not fresh, the soup greasy water, the butter rancid, the turkey tough; the ox has had to work too long before he came to give battle to our jaws. I am helped to a preserve of such detestable taste that I give up eating. The tea tastes of camomile and hay. Everything is so dirty—so badly prepared! I hurry to get to Chicago; it is really the only city in the West that has attained the material civilization of New York. No one can form an idea of the importance a good hotel has for us. We arrive benumbed with cold, fatigued by a long ride, and hungry. Let anyone think of the disappointment, may I not say despair, in not finding fire, repose, or good beds.

The concert this evening will be full. All the seats are already taken this morning.

Splendid concert; we have given a double program—every piece having been encored. My *Cradle Song*, which I played to satisfy a private request that reached me under the form of a note, appears to have given satisfaction. I took notice that silence continued the whole time, no conversation annoyed me while I played, and the attention of the audience was not distracted for a single moment.

I am daily astonished at the rapidity with which the taste for music is developed and is developing in the United States. At the time of my first return from Europe I was constantly deploring the want of public interest for pieces purely sentimental; the public listened with indifference; in order to interest it, it became necessary to astound it; grand movements, tours de force, and noise had alone the privilege in piano music, not of pleasing, but of making it patient with it. I was the *first* American pianist, not by my artistic worth, but in chronological order. Before me, there were no piano concerts except in peculiar cases—that is to say, when a very great name arriving from Europe placed itself by its celebrity before the public, which, willing or unwilling, through curiosity and fashion rather than from taste, made it a duty to go and see the lion. Now piano concerts are chronic, they have even become epidemic: like all good things they are abused. From whatever cause the American taste is becoming purer, and with that remarkable rapidity we cite through our whole progress. For ten years a whole generation of young girls has played my pieces. *Last Hope, Marche de nuit, Murmuras éoliens, Pastorelle et cavalier, Cradle Song,* have become so popular that it is difficult for me to find an audience indisposed to listen to me with interest, since the majority has played or studied the pieces that compose the program.

We should all, however narrow may be our sphere of action, bear our part in the progressive movement of civilization, and I cannot help feeling a pride in having contributed within the modest limits of my powers in extending through our country the knowledge of music.

But Cleveland ought to have a better hotel. Besides, I have a theory about this, which is that, in the same way that nations have the political institutions they deserve, cities ought to have the hotels they deserve. If Cleveland, like me, detested rancid butter, stringy meat, and greasy soup, doubtless the hotel would become bankrupt. If, on the contrary, it prospers, it is because my tastes are not like those of the majority. The hotel is right; it is I who am wrong.

The aptitude of the American for commerce of all kinds is marvelous. It is, however, less the fertility of his mind than the sickly thirst for making money. To make money is the end of all his efforts. This aptitude is very useful in a society that forms itself and that requires everyone to contribute to the common well-being, but it destroys all individuality. The individual is absorbed in the collective whole. Benvenuto Cellini, if born in the United States, would certainly never have thrown his vessel of gold into the furnace to save the great statue of Perseus. "Lamartine is poor," I said one day to one of my friends. "What!" he replied. "I always thought he was so smart." The United States is the only country where they give a sort of public recognition to a rich man. Not only do they admire him, they honor him; still more, they think that he has rendered a service to the community in which he lives. For a long time I have considered this an anomaly, but I have ended by explaining it in the following manner: They think it kind of him to have fixed in the country the capital that augments its prosperity. It is always utility. It is this idea that inspires the newspapers in small towns when, on the occasion of concerts given by great artists on their travels, they oppose these invasions and recommend only the patronizing of local concerts, because then the money does not leave the locality. It is understanding civilization after the manner of the Chinese.

◇◇◇◇◇◇◇◇◇◇

Sandusky, Friday

Concert quite good. Recalled after each piece. The audience encored us all. Some officers who are at the hotel speak of the "show," and a man came to the ticket office for a ticket to the "panorama"!

Excellent little hotel. The bill of fare is less ambitious than that of Cleveland but more real, and we dine very comfortably. The name of the fish attracts the attention of Morelli, who, poorly understanding English, is astonished at the length of the name on the bill of fare. He passes it to us and we see on it, "Fish could not be had in the market today." Nevertheless Morelli asks for it many times without getting it, and complains that they place on the bill of fare what they cannot give. "Why do they announce this fish whose name is so long?"

◇◇◇◇◇◇◇◇◇◇

Saturday, December 10

Awoke at five o'clock this morning. The snow is five inches deep in the street. The hotel omnibus is full—we are piled up in it. We set out, but the wheels are soon in a rut. The horses pull; the traces break; the horses chafe, and leave the carriage in the road. Time presses; we walk as far as the station through the snow up to our knees.

On the road. Opposite Sandusky, on the lake, we are approaching Johnson's Island, where twenty-five hundred Southern prisoners are confined.

Left at six o'clock, we must stop at Clyde, a small village three miles from Sandusky, to await the train that goes to Toledo, where we have to wait again for two hours for the train that arrives in Detroit at half-past six o'clock tonight. In the car I found myself next to a Swiss who has been living for four years in Sandusky. He has planted three acres of vines, and his harvest this year amounts to twenty-five hundred dollars. His wine, which I have tasted, is a little sour yet, but, without any doubt, in a few years will be as good as any in Ohio.

We reach Clyde. It is a hamlet composed of warehouses for the railroad, a hotel, and twenty houses. The parlor of the hotel is very comfortable. We find in it a handsome stove, a sofa, tables, and a portrait of Grant. Grant, I believe, was born in Sandusky, and very naturally is the pride of the state.

After breakfast we assembled in the lower hall of the hotel around an immense cast-iron stove that reddens and sings gaily to the flame of the tree trunks that are thrown into it every quarter of an hour.

I have been talking to an old man who has the appearance of a poor farmer. We are talking—poetry! The United States presents to strangers this remarkable condition of things, that it is impossible for them to conjecture from appearances the rank or position of those they meet on their travels. If they meet some who sparkle with diamonds and blow their noses with their fingers, they will meet, just as well, superior and cultivated minds concealed under the fur-skin greatcoat of the pioneer of the Far West. My companion is well versed in the literature of the Bible. He loves poetry and evidently understands it. He speaks to me with enthusiasm of the poetry of David. M. de Lamartine, who has analyzed with the whole force of his style the splendor of the Psalms, would have been delighted in listening to my old companion.

The weather is superb. The dazzling snow scintillates under the rays of a bright sun. The train has arrived—we set out for

Toledo; I manage with great trouble to find a seat. There are more than eight hundred passengers. The general aspect and faces of the people one meets in the West offer a striking contrast to those of the East. Nearly everybody here lets his beard grow. Their clothes are coarse without being poor. Everything announces a great contempt for fashion, and neatness (which is one of the peculiar traits of the Yankee) has not much to do with their dress.

Detroit—population, French Canadian. The accent of these Bas Bretons of America is frightful. I met here a Frenchman who, after having for a long time sustained a lawsuit against the Government of the United States concerning a grant of land made by Louis XV to one of his ancestors, has just obtained a judgment that gives him, besides the land in question, damages to the amount of fifteen thousand dollars.

The Canadian shore lies opposite Detroit, from which it is only separated by the river. It is a dangerous neighborhood and obliges the citizens to keep up constant patrols, the rebels infesting the Canadian frontiers and threatening for many weeks to make a descent here in order to burn the town.

◇◇◇◇◇◇◇◇◇

Sunday, December 11

Arrived in Chicago from Detroit after nineteen hours of railroad. The snow is so thick that in many places it has drifted to a height of three or four feet and has obstructed the road.

Chicago is always *the* city of the West. We are to inaugurate Moore & Smith's new hall. The tickets are all sold in advance. Excellent hotel, Tremont House.

◇◇◇◇◇◇◇◇◇

Monday, December 12

Concert, hall crammed but the audience cold. I have noticed that an audience that inaugurates a hall is generally cold. Thus also I have never found any enthusiasm where there were high expectations in advance.

◇◇◇◇◇◇◇◇◇

Tuesday, December 13

Second concert. Audience very large and very brilliant. A great deal of enthusiasm. I saw there the richest farmer in Illinois. He owns seventy-three thousand acres of arable ground; in one of his farms alone there are twenty-one thousand acres. Lately he sold twenty thousand head of cattle in one lot.

They talk of making a gigantic canal from the Atlantic coast, connecting the great central lakes, and ending at Chicago, which will thus enable European vessels to land directly at Chicago, eleven hundred miles in the interior of the country.[1]

Fifteen hundred houses are at this moment being built. The new Academy of Music, which a very young man by the name of Crosby is building at his own expense (his colossal fortune of two million dollars having been made in two years from speculations in whiskey), will be inaugurated on the seventeenth of next May by the Italian Opera Company, which is at this moment in New York. The new hall will hold comfortably three thousand persons, and rivals that of New York in richness of ornamentation. The people of Chicago intend to establish a permanent Italian Opera Company in the West. Notice to artists without engagements!

Nothing can give you any idea of the feverish enterprise that exists here; everything is done in grand style. The stores are palaces, the hotels towns.

A newspaper attacks me because I play exclusively on Chickering's pianos, and thinks it shocking that I place the maker's name on a plate that decorates the side exposed to public view. He adds facetiously that it is said I intend to wear, suspended from my neck, a placard upon which will be inscribed the name of my favorite maker. This honest editor who does not appear to be *au fait* in the matter of concerts, ought to know that no piano, here or in Europe, is placed upon the platform without having on it the name of its maker. Then he also should know that Thalberg, for the twenty-five years that he has given concerts in Europe, has never played but upon Erard's pianos. That Chopin never laid his fingers upon

---

[1] In 1959 this plan became a reality: the St. Lawrence Seaway.

any others than those of Pleyel. That Liszt, in France, in Switzerland, in England, in Italy, in Germany, in Turkey, has always played Erard's to the exclusion of all other pianos. The reason for it is not what this honest editor thinks it to be, a commercial transaction between the maker and the artist (no pecuniary compensation could induce an artist to sacrifice his reputation by playing on an instrument he does not like), but simply because the nature of the different talents of those I have spoken of is better adapted to that of the different pianos they use exclusively.

Erard's, whose tone is robust, strong, heroic, slightly metallic, is adapted exclusively to the powerful action of Liszt. Pleyel's, less sonorous but poetical and, so to speak, languishing and feminine, corresponds to the elegiac style and frail organization of Chopin. There are very many excellent makes in America and my opinion is that ours are equal to the best pianos of Europe. I play Chickering's, not because all others are bad, but because I like their tone, fine and delicate, tender and poetic, because I can obtain, in the modifications of their sound, tints more varied than those of other instruments. The sound is in the execution of the pianist what colors are in painting. We often see fine pictures admirably drawn that nevertheless appear cold to us. They are wanting in color. Many pianists whose thundering execution astonishes us still do not move us; they are ignorant of sound. Drawing and execution are acquired by labor. Color and sound are born in us, and are the outward expressions of our sensibility and of our souls.

◇◇◇◇◇◇◇◇◇

Wednesday, December 14

En route to Peoria from Chicago. In the second-class car where I have gone to smoke, I have conversed with a Frenchman who, with his monkey, is returning from Oregon and Idaho. The former is a handsome jovial fellow with black beard and resolute mien. He was in Illinois for ten years, and he worked to improve his farm. Oregon and Idaho, with their inexhaustible golden riches, tempted him. He went there four years ago. He related to me his adventures among the mines; they are very curious.

Idaho is a vast gold mine; the precious metal is as plenty as pebbles, but *there is no water*, and nearly all the adventurers who were able to get there are dead. My Frenchman, who had for many months held on with four other companions, abandoned the territory. They had three wagons and for three months traveled through the desert fighting every night with the Indians who harassed them incessantly. No rain had fallen for two years, and our adventurers had to put up with drinking whiskey. They were constantly coming upon the bones or carcasses of other immigrants less fortunate than themselves, who had died from thirst or been massacred by the Indians. At night they intrenched themselves behind their wagons, which they arranged in the form of a triangle, and from behind which they repulsed these nocturnal attacks. Arrived at San Francisco, my Frenchman embarked on a vessel, on which there were already four hundred miners returning from the Eldorado with fewer illusions and perhaps fewer dollars than when they set out for it.

The poor little monkey is shivering with cold and squats sadly in a corner. Morelli has taken it into his arms, and the poor little being has put its arms around his neck and like a sick child is sleeping. The monkey is a very pretty little animal, less ugly than many Negroes I know (and whites also), and its intelligence much surpasses that of many a bimane without tails that I am acquainted with.

✦✦✦✦✦✦✦✦✦

Thursday, December 15

Concert tonight in Peoria. A very ugly place. The houses are mean and for the most part two-story. The streets are badly laid out. The concert hall offers one peculiarity; the platform, which is like a theater, is so high that it gives me the vertigo to look down upon the audience; we all fear to approach the edge lest we should be drawn into the abyss. It slopes so much that it gives one a sensation analogous to that of an inexperienced person upon a roof.

Audience numerous and enthusiastic. Hotel passable. Snow has fallen during the night. The river is frozen and is covered with hundreds of skaters, but few pretty women. Their costumes are indescribable. I forgot to say that at the hotel the waiters are girls. Besieged fortresses!

I have read in a newspaper that the immigration to the West

is so great that it is estimated that two hundred fifty thousand immigrants have gone to the Rocky mountains and the Pacific Coast within the last six years. Nevertheless this region is so vast that this access of population has not even been felt.

The greater part of these immigrants have established themselves in the gold-bearing territories of Colorado, Nevada, Utah, Idaho, and Montana. Oregon, Washington, New Mexico, and Arizona have comparatively few immigrants, and Nebraska, Kansas, and Dakota have probably lost the few they had, gold having more attraction than the richness of the soil.

◇◇◇◇◇◇◇◇◇◇

December 20

In Cincinnati. The Burnett House is an immense caravansary, very dirty and very dear, where what you eat is in inverse ratio to what you pay—that is to say, is very little. It is at the eating hours at the Burnett House that one can best form an idea of the appearance of the Western people. What is most striking is the free and easy behavior of the men and women. The farmers wear flat felt hats, covering badly cultivated heads. Their laughter particularly has something wild in it; it is a shrill sound, which recalls the neighing of a horse rather than the jocosity of a polished man.

I was playing at the concert the "Kreutzer" Sonata by Beethoven. The audience had greatly the appearance of going to sleep. The next morning a newspaper says: "We could ourselves have done very well without the long piece for the piano and violin." It was the same paper that last year complained that we did not give classical music.

Play at Mozart Hall. It is a very large theater; remarkable for your being obliged to go up three stories to get to it. While I was playing I recalled to mind the experience of the Swedish doctor, I think it was, who tried to suspend life, gradually lessening the temperature of the atmosphere in which he placed his subject until it froze like a sherbet, and which he thus preserved in an ice house *ad hoc* to make it revive some years later. I became frightened on feeling the cold waves of icy air that freely circulated around the hyperborean scene of Mozart Hall, which gradually abated the circulation of my blood; I began to fear that I might pass into the condition of a frozen mummy. I know of only two places in which I have suffered as much cold: Mont Blanc and the Young Men's Association in Detroit, which I have always suspected of being an ice depot.

◇◇◇◇◇◇◇◇◇◇

St. Louis

Arrived, December 22, after twenty-two hours' journey. I do not remember ever having traveled on this road without meeting with eight to ten hours' detention. At Richmond, a village in Indiana, we waited for four hours, as the road was blocked, a train having gone off the rails. The plausible reason was that three poor cows got on the track; they paid for their imprudence with their lives, and their corpses are still in the snow; but for those who see the broken rails and the bad condition of the road, it is impossible not to admit that to travel here is a perilous and rash enterprise.

Arrived at six o'clock on the banks of the Mississippi opposite St. Louis. The cold is intense. The station, instead of being opposite the wharf where the boat lands, is a quarter of a mile off, which we must walk on foot in a north wind that cuts our faces. Arrived at the steamboat, whose saloon(?) is already filled with soldiers, workmen, dirty women, and dirty children packed together. Crowded, suffocated, we manage to force ourselves into the midst of this crowd, but the atmosphere is soon so charged with the exhalations of those crammed into so small a space that we prefer the risk of being frozen to that of being poisoned. St. Louis is a sad-looking city. Poor in appearance, the shops are mean, and the street richest in large stores hardly compares with the poorest quarters of the Bowery. In the largest street the curbs of the pavements are broken, and we recognize the *same* holes we saw last winter.

The Lindell House is probably, as to its exterior, the most beautiful building of the kind to be found in America. Unluckily, it recalls to me a certain adage I cannot express better than by saying that I should like it better if there were fewer columns in the corridors and more chambers, less rose work on the ceiling, more tender beefsteaks, and the corridors kept heated at a temperature which did not recall the horrors of Captain Franklin and his heroic companions. At breakfast, our first meal (for the last two days we have lived on cold pies and apples), we literally froze. The walls and ceiling are painted in fresco, but the furnaces throw out no heat.

The waiter tends us with a listless nonchalance; he also brings us the plates ten minutes later. In summer iced coffee and frozen beefsteaks are perhaps acceptable—but in winter!

The result is that Morelli and I began a search through the streets for a restaurant. We discover a Frenchman, formerly from New Orleans, who gives us a genuine *beef*steak, and not a *cow*steak, and relates to us all his mishaps while waiting on us.

There is a class of persons who want to learn what the artist's intention is. The artist is an instrument through which God inspires good things to men. He is passive. You might as well ask of the sun his intention in producing marvelous effects of light and shade in a landscape. The inspired artist is like a keyboard that sounds correctly under the tremor that agitates it. We, all of us, have in us a fingerboard, but some have broken the cords of their soul in such a way that the fingerboard no longer produces a sound. Others sound false, although feeling everything deeply. These are generally those artists who, having a lively conception of the beautiful, and a thirst to express it, are not endowed with the faculty of formulating what they feel. Sometimes by dint of slow and patient researches, assisted by their insatiable desire to express what they experience, they attain to creating something that approaches to genius, but the effort and the labor are apparent, two shackles that genius does not know.

◇◇◇◇◇◇◇◇◇

Springfield, Illinois, December 26, 1864[2]

Concert tonight. This time the audience listens to us. Last time

[2] The entry was mistakenly dated December 20. "As for Gottschalk, if there was on his previous concert in this city, any dissatisfaction, it was all disipated [*sic*] by his apparent effort to please last evening. His playing was unusually brilliant and inspiriting, and we were more than ever convinced of his superiority over all other pianists we have heard, in touch and delicacy of style. But while we would give him credit as a superior artist, we must say, that we did not altogether like the programme; it fell below our ex-

private conversations completely masked the music. The audience seems disposed to enjoy what we give them, but it is too late! The impression that after two visits Springfield leaves upon me is very disagreeable. I have tried hard to exert myself, I cannot warm up, and I play like a warm-water spigot. Besides, the hall is horrible: a little, narrow, dirty staircase leads to a kind of mansard six feet square, filled with old and dirty objects. It is the Artist's Room. The small hall is bad for hearing. You go on to the stage by stairs that are like a ladder. Döhler plays "Yankee Doodle" and *Carnival of Venice*, two pieces that never fail in exciting the enthusiasm of the audience, but that invariably next day bring out a severe lecture from the newspapers. Fortunately we know what to think of it. It is only to save appearances that these gentlemen protest. They like this trivial music secretly, but, like all those who are conscious of their inferiority, they wish to conceal it by openly affecting to despise what secretly they love. O hypocrisy and vanity!

SERMON AT ST. LOUIS

The preacher was evidently intent on emitting the greatest number of words with the smallest possible number of ideas—like Hahnemann, who pretended to distil the ten-thousandth part of a grain of belladonna into Lake Leman, and to increase its power in the ratio of its *infinitesimability*. This good preacher was engaged for two hours in drowning in an ocean of empty phrases, one or two ounces of stale ideas. Besides, improvisation, as soon as it becomes a trade, has in it what is wearisome—that the preacher is accustomed to have upon all subjects a collection of formulas of which he avails himself as soon as he loses his ideas or has need to collect his thoughts in order to find them; the tongue knows and repeats these formulas mechanically, while the mind is occupied elsewhere. When one has launched out into a tortuous phrase, and begins to lose sight of port, and knows no longer where to land, he casts anchor on amplifications and synonyms; this keeps him in his position, and gives him time to get back again. This proceeding is like that of the milkmen of London, Paris, and of every other

---

pectations; it was not up to the standard we had set for his audience. The performance was brilliant, but the music fell sparkling and as cold as ice-crystals—it lacked warmth." *Illinois State Journal*, December 27, 1864.

place in the world where there are milkmen and water, who out of one vessel of milk make ten or twelve by adding water to it.

"Yes, my dear brother"—it is the preacher who speaks—"man is weaker than you can possibly conceive; more feeble than all"— a little water—"weaker than all other feeble creatures"—a little more water—"weak because he cannot resist temptations"—a good pint of water—"and weak because he yields instead of conquering" —hem! The vessel of milk is full. He stops here to put the full vessel to one side, and to begin at another, and so on, to the end of the sermon.

◇◇◇◇◇◇◇◇◇

Bloomington (Illinois)

I am warming myself in the concert hall before we begin. Hidden in the midst of the crowd, I look like an amateur who has come to listen. A little fellow who sells photographs of Carlotta Patti and myself in the hall offers me one, saying, "Do you want a portrait of Chuckle and his wife?" Who is Chuckle? I asked him. "What! He is the man who plays the piano." Where is he? "That is he who passed me," said the little monster, pointing out to me a fat man who came into the hall.

Good audience—much applauded.

We set out again after the concert, the cold being intense. Passed six hours in suffering, like Tantalus, falling asleep and not being able to sleep for want of room to rest. We ought to be four hours in going, but as it appears impossible for any train in the whole West to arrive at the proper time, we are six hours on the road. On our arrival we took an omnibus, and after a quarter of an hour's jolting we got to a little hotel, benumbed with cold and with broken backs. Our companions in misfortune are two poor nuns, who, motionless and silent, draped in their large black veils, look like two lugubrious statues of penitence and resignation. Next to them are two pretty girls who laugh, and a young mother with her baby. After having waited in the lower hall of the hotel, the landlord announces to us that all the rooms are taken! General consternation! Morelli complained in all the exhuberance of the Italian language; I kept quiet, which one might take for stoicism, but which was only the apathy of despair. Daybreak will not take place for an hour. We have succeeded in finding some wood. The fire is flaming. Morelli and I lie down upon the floor with our heads resting on our traveling bags. Roasted on one side by the fire, and frozen on the other by a draft of wind, which comes traitorously in from outside under the door, we turn from side to side every ten minutes, like a beefsteak in process of being cooked. "Ah, my good friends in New York! Would you could see me at this moment, and all of you, you young harebrains, who only perceive in an artistic career a road embroidered with roses and paved with dollars, meditate on this episode and   . . ." At ten o'clock they offer me a bed. I sleep for several hours.

Joliet is a pretty, picturesque, and flourishing little town. Last year it was the scene of a great scandal. A reverend gentleman, a Protestant minister, received a cowhiding from two outraged husbands. An inquiry was made which was followed by a meeting of bishops and Protestant ministers to try the unfortunate Lovelace. The result was that the two outraged husbands were not the only ones who had a right to complain of the minister, and the number of his feminine conquests was so great that half the population of Joliet would have had the right to give him a good thrashing.

To make a victorious tour of concerts in the West is for an artist to gain his chevrons. Bad hotels, snow, mud, railroad accidents, delays, setting out at three o'clock in the morning, etc. It requires an iron constitution and a flinty will to succeed at it. I am tempted to have inscribed at the head of my program: "G. has made the tour of the West three times," as the French legions inscribe "Arcole, Marengo, Austerlitz" on their standards.

Very fair concert at Joliet. While Döhler plays the *Carnival of Venice*, a man in the audience (without doubt to show that he knows the tune) whistles the theme in unison. After the last piece on the program, a woman, agitated and palpitating with emotion, rushed into the artists' room and asked to see the *actor* who played on the violin. We guessed by her description that she spoke of Döhler. "He has already left," someone answered, "and you will find him at the hotel." Upon this she tells with a choking voice that Döhler is her cousin, that she recognized him as soon as he appeared on the platform, although she had not seen him for ten years, that he had always been her favorite, that at the age of ten years he already showed—a singular aptitude in catching mice— that he kept them in a cage—all this with tears of joy interrupted by the exclamations of the crowd who listen: "Is is possible?" "That's so." (There are always some people ready to say, "That's so," without knowing why, or what the matter is.) The episode is interesting and breaks the prosaic monotonoy of our daily life.

The most interesting and pleasant part of the thing is that on our return to the hotel Döhler tells us about his interview with his cousin, who began by throwing herself into his arms, giving him the most tender names; the first part of the interview finished, the explanation began.

"I recognized you as soon as you appeared. Do you remember your mice? Why did you leave your paternal mansion to roam over the world?"—(I suspect she was going to say to play the actor with a violin, but she thought it would be cruel on this joyful evening to recall to his feelings his present degradation.)

"Dear Arenburg," she continued, and she prepared herself to spring at his neck; when Döhler, who is full of modesty (seeing that she was ugly and old), said to her, "I am not called Arenburg, Madam."

"How, unhappy one, have you changed your name?"

"My name is Döhler."

"Miserable one! Are you ashamed of it? Your name is Arenburg."

"Madam, I assure you that you are mistaken; I was never here before."

"Ingrate, don't you know me? And the little mice?"

"I do not know," replied Döhler. "I am a German, and I have never had anything to do with mice."

The good woman, not willing to lose her right of relationship, said to him with a tone of bitter reproach, and making use of the last argument, "But, miserable one, we are rich, do not fear" (this last remark gave me a high opinion of the lady's knowledge of human feelings); but Döhler, who is probity itself, magnanimously refused this bait of opulence and persisted in denying that he had ever played with a little white mouse.

Set out again Thursday, at four o'clock in the morning. Cold as Siberia. It snowed yesterday, and today we have hail. The streets look like a series of little avalanches. Stopped at a station at seven o'clock for breakfast—fallacious pretext—which the sole appearance of a leathery beefsteak and the smell of the coffee rendered simply absurd.

I read on a large placard on the wall: "Caution. Police officers and all good citizens are warned not to trust two young girls of doubtful reputation, who for some time have frequented the most fashionable streets of Chicago from ten o'clock in the morning till four in the afternoon. They are pretty and elegantly dressed. One of them generally wears a pink silk hat and a cloak trimmed with fur. It is hoped that the vigilance of the police and the zeal of good citizens will not be relaxed, and that these two adventurers will soon be arrested in the very act of persecution against —the Christy Minstrels whom they have followed for a long time around the world and who at this moment are attracting the crowd to Poyant Hall." What do you think of the advertisement? Is it ingenious enough? The American lure is a science and an art. Lately an omnibus horse fell down on Broadway, New York. He died in a few moments. It was near the city hall, where the great artery contracts and where consequently the always encumbered circulation becomes more difficult. At the end of a quarter of an hour the street cart carried off the poor animal, who was already covered with placards. On his belly you saw "Buy your hats from Knox."

The Buckley Serenaders[3] have invented a miniature handbill. They are miniature programs that you find stuck on your back, your hat, your gloves, by mysterious, indefatigable, and unseen hands. The Dutch tonic of Dr. H— is advertised in gigantic letters painted on the rocks that overlook the falls of the Genesee River. It makes one dizzy to read these big letters that seem to look with true Dutch *sang-froid* into the roaring gulf that opens beneath them. One shivers to think of the danger the person ran who painted this advertisement. It is the lure heroic.

Arrived at Kalamazoo at noon, Thursday. Excellent hotel, quite new. Charming concert and respectable audience. No cries, or

---

[3] A minstrel show troupe. Sample of the Serenaders' wit: "How do you feel tonight, Johnson?" "I feel high." "How high?" "Shanghai." Jane Marlin, compiler and arranger: *Reminiscences of Morris Steinert* (New York and London: G. P. Putnam's Sons; 1900), p. 109.

whistling. All the pieces are encored. The appearance of the audience offers a singular contrast to that of Joliet.

◇◇◇◇◇◇◇◇◇

December 30 [*Friday*]

Quit Kalamazoo for Ann Arbor, Michigan. Arrived at five o'clock. (Train delayed.) A flourishing little village that owes its importance particularly to the state university, which at this time numbers eight hundred fifty students. They confer degrees here as high as Doctor of Science, of Law, and of Divinity. The university studies last four years, and cost for the whole fifteen dollars. This sum is purely nominal, and is only a pretext in order that the students may not appear to receive state charity.

Today in the train a man said to his neighbor, who asked him if he knew the famous singer Goodstock, "Yes, very well, there he is," pointing to Muzio, who was sitting opposite.

Saturday, arrived in London (Canada) after a journey of eight hours. Small town. Concert tonight. Canadian receipts! Thirty-one persons including my servants and tuner, who from *esprit de corps* are sitting in the public seats in order to increase the number. It must be acknowledged that the applause was in the inverse ratio of the number. That is to say, that the audience is warm and I know really glad to have come, and I played my best before these twenty-one heroes (I deduct what does not belong to the audience) to thank them for their goodwill.

◇◇◇◇◇◇◇◇◇

[*London, Canada*] *New Year, 1865*

These words, which sound so delicious to the ear during our childhood, awaken in me only the echo of vanished joys and dissipated illusions. One more step made toward the goal! The time is past in which the years glided away too slowly for me. It flies now; and I see the sweet images that I found on my road when I began my march disappearing far behind me.

Dined with Mr. Edward Harris, whose wife I knew in Toronto with Miss McC———. A charming family, the aged mother receiving that respectful and tender affection which is the blessed harvest that parents reap who have known how to bring up their children. I am particularly struck by all this. We talk politics. The married daughter is naturally in favor of the South. It is not difficult, when in the company of Englishmen, to understand that their sympathy for the South is less the result of their sympathy for the people of the South than their antipathy for the North. They do not easily pardon the boasting of our newspapers, and the absurd and useless bravado that our editors have made use of for so many years when speaking of England.

◇◇◇◇◇◇◇◇◇

Ann Arbor

A little note is delivered between the first and second parts of the concert to Mademoiselle Simons, our soprano, requesting her to sing "Di Provenza il mar" from *Traviata*![4]

At London, this morning, the newspaper bestowed great praise on our baritone, Morelli, and his beautiful style. The joke of the matter is that Morelli left us two days ago to return to New York.

◇◇◇◇◇◇◇◇◇

Toronto, January 3

Between the first and second parts of the concert a telegram is sent me that reads thus: "—— will run away within three days if you do not have him arrested."

This —— is a French hairdresser who calls himself Dr. and Chevalier de St. Stanislas de Russie. He has speculated on shares with a sharper. While they gained, all went very well. Losses came, and with them disputes. The sharper claimed eighteen thousand dollars. The knight of the razor had not a red cent. They were about to arrest him. His wife and children came and threw themselves at my feet, begging me to go bail for thirty thousand dollars, which would keep him out of prison until the affair was tried. I consented to it.

I leave you to judge the effect this telegram had on me. The concert is interrupted. I leave for New York by the first train to-

---

[4] "Di Provenza il mar" is a baritone aria.

morrow morning. Unfortunately, the Secretary of the Interior decided, two days ago, that no one can enter into the United States across the Canadian border without passports countersigned by the American authorities. This measure has been taken to prevent the incursion of rebel emigrants from Canada. Lately twelve of these adventurers entered the village of St. Albans, on the border, and robbed the bank of three or four hundred thousand dollars.

◇◇◇◇◇◇◇◇◇◇

Harrisburg, January 28

Small audience, consequently great enthusiasm. The concert takes place in the court house. That artists' room is generally the witnesses' chamber, but the porter informs us that he has not been able to light a fire in it, and he has put us in the jurors' room, which is on the second floor. The cold is intense. We have to cross Siberian passages and go up a steep staircase forty steps to get to our den. The concert hall is below. After every piece I put on my greatcoat, my fur gloves, and go down forty steps. After my piece I again put on my furs, left at the door, and go up the forty steps. The program half over, I have already two hundred steps in my legs.

◇◇◇◇◇◇◇◇◇◇

Dayton, Ohio

Excellent audience—sympathetic and warm. Hotel, Siberian! High ceilings; immense, dark, and damp corridors; a total absence of heaters. My Swedish doctor, of whom I have already had occasion to speak, ought to come here and establish himself in one of the halls of Phillips's Hotel. Besides, the young man at the desk offers a fine example of the influence of cold on human nature. His behavior and politeness are those of an arctic polar bear.

◇◇◇◇◇◇◇◇◇◇

Toledo, Oliver House [*February 11, 1864*]

One of the best hotels in the United States. The complaisance of the waiter goes to our heart, and fills it with warm gratitude, like the rays of the unclouded sun, which melts the last crust of snow and makes the first green shoots appear. A very striking contrast to the insolence of the man at D——.

◇◇◇◇◇◇◇◇◇

February 14

Lately, in Bethlehem, a letter was written to the proprietor of the hotel which he made me read. I transcribe it for you; it will give you an idea of the small amount of dignity that is accorded to art, and the free and easy way in which its disciples are treated:

"I was not able to go to Gottschalk's concert last eve ning; but I understand that he is at your hotel. Ask him if he is willing to come and play for us, this morning, two or three of his pieces. Of course, I will pay him.
"Signed ——."

Three years ago I gave a concert in Wilmington (the only one, thank God, that I ever gave there). Our company consisted of Brignoli, Susini, Miss Hinckley, Morensi,[5] Behrens, and myself, under the managerial baton of Strakosch. The receipts were twenty-five dollars. The applause 0. Delaware and New Jersey are twin brothers in politics as in music, and the only two states in which musical art is in its first state of design. Muzio persisted a week ago in trying again with me his fortune at Wilmington. I told him my experience, but he would not believe me. The concert is announced eight days in advance. We arrive at six o'clock. We go to the hotel, which would be hardly decent in a New England village. Muzio visits the music store. He comes back in a few minutes. His astonished countenance tells me well enough that the Wilmington of 1865 likes concerts no better than that of 1862. There are eight tickets for the concert sold, and it is six o'clock in the evening.

Muzio, ten minutes later, gravely informs the music seller that I am taken with a violent headache, which will not permit me to appear this evening before the eight amateurs of Wilmington. We spend the evening at the hotel (?). I receive through the

---

[5] Advertised sometimes as Mme Morensi, other times as Mlle Montmorency, the contralto's real name was Kate Duckworth.

medium of a gentleman a letter in a feminine hand which I transcribe for the edification of my readers:

"We are very dissappointed in not hearing you. We are many ladies now at the music store; will you be so kind as to come and play something for us? We will pay you the price of the tickets." No signature. Can it be, madame or miss, that the innate delicacy of woman, and particularly of American woman—can it be that the music you must love, since you will spend the evening at the music store awaiting my coming to play, has not suggested to you that it was unworthy of you to speak of the *price of the tickets?*

This recalls to me two stories that represent your action under two aspects. One grotesque, the other uncouth, according as I look at them from the point of view of my pocket, or of my heart.

A certain Gascon—was he a Gascon? The French say a Gascon, the English would say an Irishman, the Italians a Neapolitan, the Spaniards an Andalusian, each nation having its type of clown— all are identical. Let us say Gascon. A Gascon then saw at an inn a beautiful parrot. He had never tasted a tropical bird. He was seized with a desire to taste it. "If the taste is equal to its plumage this must be the pheasant of the American forests!"

"How much for your parrot?" "One hundred francs," answered his host.

"Very well, cook it." The innkeeper knew his trade. He wrung the neck of the poor bird and put it immediately on the spit. "Now," said the Gascon, "give me five francs' worth."

This is for the *price of the tickets.*

Now for the second story.

I was traveling in Switzerland giving concerts. I was then very young. Without doubt, thanks to this circumstance more than to my talent, there was at Lausanne a great desire to see and hear me. My first concert attracted an immense crowd. I heard one day an old lady spoken of, who had lost her fortune, who adored music, but whose poverty and infirmities prevented her from going to hear me. She had expressed her regrets by saying that she had never so cruelly felt the loss of her fortune as in seeing herself deprived of listening to music.

I inquired where she lived, and introduced myself to her. She was a paralytic lady, very distinguished by her tastes and her venerable appearance, and I shall never forget the tender emotion

I felt at the bottom of my heart on seeing two tears from her eyes when I offered to spend the evening with her, to play for her alone everything she would be pleased to ask me. The next morning after this, to me, delicious evening, I received from an Englishman (O my charming but indelicate Wilmington correspondents, I then thought that only an Englishman could be capable of such a thing) the following letter:

"Sir, I hear that you have been playing for Madame ——. My wife also is ill, and for a number of years has not left her chamber. She desires to hear you. I offer you ten dollars to play two pieces to her!"

My answer to the Englishman applies equally well to my Wilmington correspondents.

"I have received the letter in which you do me the honor of making me the offer of ten dollars to play two pieces to your wife. I might forget the want of delicacy and tact which your request shows, if it was not for the vexation it gives me which prevents me, by its uncouthness, from acceding to the desire of an invalid."

❖❖❖❖❖❖❖❖❖

New York

Three years ago I wrote this: "Heard yesterday, for the first time, Miss Kellogg; a charming artist, a great deal of distinction in her deportment and in her intelligence." Since then Miss Kellogg's talent has only increased. Her singing of Marguerite in *Faust* is in everyone's memory and will not be easily effaced.

Is it not a subject to be proud of, to think that we, who yesterday were not able to count, so to speak, one artist, can today claim as ours talents like Powers, Palmer, Miss Stebbins, Church, Bierstadt, etc.? I recall the astonishment with which they read in Europe the tales of Poe, whose success in France, England, and Germany was already secured long before his fellow-countrymen wanted to accord him any merit. "What! An American?" and the people were amazed that a nation of merchants could produce a poet. They knew our literature only through Cooper, whose works are translated into every tongue. Washington Irving himself, although his name is known, has never had any literary success outside the United States, except in England.

But the *Americanophobes* also say: Poe has never been understood in his own country. Whence has come the great opposition of that clique of imbecile, jealous, and sterile pedants who, like thistles and thorns, always encumber the avenues of all the arts, and dispute their place in the sun with the generous and vivacious plants who, instead of thorns, present to the sight flowers and fruit? How many scratches and wounds for the man of talent before he *gets rid of* these impertinent brambles? "He had immoral principles." Ah! That is the great word. When, then, will you separate the man from the writer, the instrument from the thought? Will you find the virgins of Raphael lacking in purity because Raphael loved Fornarina? Do you deny the perfume of attar of roses because the Chinese inclose it in jars of stone instead of vases of gold? By this reckoning villainous verses made by a virtuous writer ought to be read in preference to the poetry of Byron, who was far from being a vessel of election!

Let me be understood. I lament that the man of genius is, sometimes, from his private character unworthy of the sentiments that his writings inspire, but do not forget that he dies, while his works live. His neighbors only are interested in knowing that he gets drunk, or that he is not a believer. But his works! They pass through the ages, luminous and immaculate. They ennoble and purify coming generations of civilized nations, and are the only source of human perfectibility. What does it matter to me that Raphael was not married to Fornarina? The *Madonna of the Chair*, in which the divine child looks on us, is not less admired by thousands. Rembrandt was a miser. Are his lights and shadows less marvelous? Was he a miser of his palette? Victor Hugo has not always been a pattern of conjugal fidelity. *The Cricket on the Hearth*, ravishing in its virtue, is not, some say, the picture of Dickens' hearth. Are the leaves withered by the twilight? Is the author of *David Copperfield* on that account less of a great writer? No! Let us comprise in art less of sterile and narrow morality and more of love for the beautiful (that is to say, for the good and the true).

To make the works of the artist responsible for the whole of his private life is also unjust and seems to me as absurd as to deny the tone of a fine piano whose case might be of rough wood. I know a celebrated flutist who insisted on playing at his concerts on a presentation flute of massive silver. It had the sharpest sound in the world. Alas! how many silver flutes are admired in the world of art? Of course, I understand that if you are to choose your neighbors it would be more disagreeable to have near you a man, whatever his talents might be, whose morals might corrupt all around him than to have a very respectable imbecile. So, when you purchase a piano to correspond with your furniture, you select one in mahogany or ebony before inquiring if it has a fine tone, but I quite as much contest your right to proscribe the fine inspirations of your artist neighbor of doubtful morals, because you have observed that he goes to church less frequently than yourself, as to deny the beautiful tone of a fine instrument because it is not varnished.

Do you pause when you hear a symphony of Beethoven played by the Philharmonic Orchestra of New York with that intelligent devotion which makes it one of the best orchestras in the world—do you pause to observe if the performers are in full dress, if the piccolo player has his hair carefully combed, and if the violinists in the front rows have their boots blackened? Certainly not; and it is fortunate, for your pleasure would often be diminished.

Poor Poe! He drank! Who knows it now?

The other day in the car, there being no seat, I took refuge in the baggage car, and there I smoked for two hours, seated on the case of my piano, alongside of which, O human frailty! were two other cases also inclosing instruments, now mute, since the principle that made them vibrate, under a skillful touch, like a keyboard, has left them. They were the bodies of two young soldiers killed in one of the recent battles.

◇◇◇◇◇◇◇◇◇◇

Dunkirk [New York], February 14
Conversation between two ladies who spoke in the corridor of the hotel opposite my room: "What an eccentric man this Gottschalk is. He is, however, nothing great. Recently, at Boston, he had to leave suddenly, and his concerts no longer attract anybody!"

Another amusing thing. At St. Louis, an officer speaking of me to a lady, one of my friends being near:

Lady. "Has he received any education?"

Officer. "None at all; but that does not prevent him from being a very good fellow."

Lady. "I thought so."

Officer. "Say nothing bad of him, I beg you; for as I have told you, he is one of my friends."

Lady. "How does he speak French?"

Officer. "Oh, very imperfectly; but you know he is a Spaniard."

O truth, why art thou not petroleum! One would at least know where to dig a well to make thee flow out.

◇◇◇◇◇◇◇◇◇

February 16

Superb concert in Rochester. An anomaly. A crowd, and a *great deal* of enthusiasm.

◇◇◇◇◇◇◇◇◇

Batavia, February 17

No audience, and no applause. Just as we begin, the man who attends to the gas forewarns us that at nine o'clock all the lights will be extinguished.

◇◇◇◇◇◇◇◇◇

Erie, February 18

Arrived at half-past seven o'clock in the evening at the hotel in a sleigh from the station. I was struck by a snowball on the temple and was stunned by the blow. How cruel and brutal the lower class Americans are!

Hardly any enthusiasm at the concert. I asked the reason for it. I am answered, "No one here pays a dollar for a ticket, and it made the people angry to pay that price." What a willful and capricious child the public is! It is vexed to pay a dollar, then why did it come? When the dollar is once disbursed, why not be amused instead of pouting? Let it at least try to get something

for its money. This recalls to me those spoiled children who, because they have not as many sweets given to them as they want,
throw all that has been given them on the ground. Whom have
you punished by being sulky? Do you think that it is me? Certainly
not; because you have paid your dollar and have come to the
concert. You complain that the concert is too short. Why have
you not made it longer? I have never refused to repeat a piece, and
in the six or seven thousand concerts I have given it has not happened one hundred times that I have refused an encore.

I have never seen so many tipplers and drinking places, and
consequently so many drunkards, as in Washington. There are
many degrees of drunkenness (they are all of them most ignoble),
but there is the habitual drunkard, and he is worse than the others.
The newspapers say that Washington is the most immoral
city in the United States. "It is a Gomorrah," says one paper.
Rest assured that, if it ever is on fire, it will not be a fire from
heaven, but from spontaneous combustion.

❖❖❖❖❖❖❖❖

[*Lockport, New York*] *February 18*
On the road from Erie to Lockport, thirteen hours on the road,
the train went off the rails. "It is the first time that it has happened
for six months," is the invariable phrase of the conductor. But I
declare that, in the three months I have traveled in the West, it
is the forty-eighth time that the train on which I have been has
been stopped by an accident, either to itself or from the train that
preceded us and obstructed the road.

At this evening's concert, Lockport, faithful to its traditions,
furnishes us with a Lockport audience—that is to say, one hundred
persons gaping for their money, and who do not applaud. "The
scalded cat dreads cold water." At the first concert I gave here,
there were three hundred persons. They had never seen such an
entertainment, and swore that no one would take them in again.
Since then I have tried my fortune here four or five times, but
always with the same result. This evening, however, they have
varied the monotony a little by hissing.

"Pardon me, O Muse! I have cut thy wings, and instead of

letting thee fly into space, I have used thee to make the pot boil."
It is not for music, no more is it for art, to come and give a
concert at Lockport.

The artist's imagination has no wings save when it is in those
spheres in which it can unfold them and fly. Here it becomes a
gosling, and is only good to make the pot boil. We have not even
that consolation at Lockport.

◇◇◇◇◇◇◇◇◇◇

Utica, March 2

As always a charming audience. I have paid visits to all my good
friends: S[ieboth], a charming man and good musician: Dr.
K[ellogg], my old friend, a man of great merit, who has written
some important works on insanity.[6] I have naturally visited the
asylum and have been recognized by *all* my friends. "Aunt Libby,"
an old woman with pale complexion, immediately recognized me.
She is always dressed in a pink gown, with a very large sash, a
plaited cap decorated with gilt paper, and a little white woolen
shawl trimmed with blue muslin. Small, plain shoes. She informs
us that the Queen of England is enchanted to visit her and gives
her the sum of five hundred thousand dollars. We play and sing
in the principal hall of the asylum. All are standing around us
listening. Aunt Libby, who is conscious of her high position, while
we are playing opens an umbrella with an air of great dignity,
and she holds it the whole time in the air. I ask her to play or
sing, which she does after being well persuaded. I give her my arm
to conduct her to the piano. She requests me with great familiarity
and condescension to hold her fan and her handkerchief. The good
old woman improvises a kind of guitar accompaniment (always
in C), a sort of chant to words also improvised—"I see the Angels,"
tuck, tuck, tuck. "I see the Angels," *ding, dong* (*bell*), *duck, tuck,*
tuck (here she tries a scale), and looking with evident pleasure, first
at the keyboard, then at those around her, she commences "Yankee

---

⁶ This was Dr. Abner O. Kellogg. At the concert, which Gottschalk
shared with Emanuele Muzio, Miss Simons, and Signor Ardavani, a baritone
from the Italian Opera in New York, the pianist played his own *Fantaisie
Nationale* on Root's "Battle Cry of Freedom" and with Muzio a four-hand
version of *La Gallina*.

Doodle," then ends with "God Save the Queen," "King George," *ding, dong*; another flourish in the form of a scale, then she rises from the piano to receive our compliments with a modest air. Poor old woman! She is enchanted, and offers to show me her sanctum sanctorum, which is full of shells and all sorts of curious things. Then another lady is introduced to us, who recognizes L——, to his great consternation, as having been her husband! Later we see a lady who believes herself to have been betrothed to General Washington and bequeathed by him to all the presidents of the United States. She is evidently conscious of the prolific grandeur of her mission, and rejoices in having been the instrument for a population of thirty million souls.

I recognize some of the cases that last year were among the worst. These now are persons of distinguished and modest behavior, who have so well progressed that in a short time they will leave the asylum.

◇◇◇◇◇◇◇◇◇

Buffalo, March 23, 24, and 25

Charming concert. Kind audience. I love Buffalo and Rochester; these are two cities in which I always play with pleasure. Syracuse is cold. I have never obtained there a large audience. The last concert was a "chilly affair." That is what the newspapers say. It rightly adds that the audience and the artist parted mutually disgusted with each other. It is true at least, as far as regards one of them, the audience, if I might judge from its behavior. Not one applause from the beginning to the end. I nevertheless did my best, and I am certain that this audience, under the spur of three or four *claqueurs*, would have warmed up and would have found that charming which today is found wearisome. The beginning of a concert may be compared to the first stage of a grand dinner, before the ice is broken, when everyone is afraid to break the silence and we hardly dare to speak to our neighbor but below our breath. If among the guests there is one who breaks the ice, immediately all speak at once, and, the conversation having become general, each one tries to keep it up. In a concert, if there is a knot of determined persons who, bold enough, dare to give the signal, the crowd immediately follow the current. It warms up, the nerves are affected by it; the excitement causes them to discover points that otherwise would have passed by unperceived. It gives to their perception a susceptibility it would not have under ordinary circumstances, and sometimes even makes them discover imaginary beauties, so great is their impatience to find food for their excitement. But imagine, on the contrary, that there are no *claqueurs*; you play the first piece. The bond is not yet established between the artist and the audience.

The artist is ignorant of the disposition of the audience; the latter may have liked the piece, which being finished, an amateur counting on the enthusiasm of the others applauds warmly—clap! clap!!—but, finding himself alone, he dreads being noticed. Some turn and look at him. Like a tortoise that precipitately withdraws his head into his shell after having stealthily ventured to see what is going on around him, he becomes as small as possible and takes on an indifferent air to divert the suspicions of those who are looking at him. The artist, who does not read the thoughts of the audience and judges its sentiments only by its applause, thinks that he is not appreciated. He becomes oppressed by a feeling of injustice and hastens to finish a task that he believes to be as painful to the audience as to himself. He even skips those passages which he would have lengthened *con amore* under other circumstances if he was sure of being appreciated. Like a flame in a heavy and moist atmosphere his inspirations diminish and end by becoming extinguished. Audience and artist, for want of mutual understanding, and while both are animated with the best intentions, part disgusted with each other. This is what happened at Syracuse, only the audience, whose mind was not very enlightened on all these points, and had only instinct to guide it, on retiring, was satisfied with saying that it was cold and that the concert was long and fatiguing, because, not willing to accuse itself of not being able to appreciate it, it was satisfied and found it infinitely more convenient to accuse the artist with indifference and unwillingness to oblige.

My God, what features! I have never seen anything more artistic or a more striking harmony of contour than in this young face, white as polished ivory, set off by a crown of ebony hair. There is there perhaps the stuff for a great artist or for a superior intelligence. Halt there, my imagination! Do not build up a romance, but pay your dollar to the collector who comes to snatch you from your admiration by asking you to pay for your dinner. As for my Sappho, she is at this moment handing a plate of pork and beans to a traveler. What a fall!

◇◇◇◇◇◇◇◇◇◇

New York, April 3

Set out from New York for California in company with Muzio and his wife. I am engaged by him.

Once, a year ago, I said without thinking much about it, "I will make a trip to South America." Some days later, one of my friends came up to me and asked me when I was going. A month later some newspapers announced that I was leaving the United States to make a long tour of concerts. I understood that I ought to rid the public and my friends of my presence for one or two years.

I was busy tracing out the itinerary of my voyage when an impresario offered me an engagement for some months. The impresario for the purpose of stimulating the reluctant ones, put on the placards, "farewell concerts before his departure." The tour finished, the summer again found me in New York. Saratoga is tempting. I put off my departure for the autumn. Some friends pleased themselves by saying to me in a disappointed manner, "Oh ho, I thought you had left." The newspapers declared my presence in a bittersweet way, by recalling to me that I had put "farewell concerts" on my placards, which was equivalent to deceiving the public. I took up my itinerary again and I bought a large trunk. Another lucrative engagement presented itself. To refuse was easy, but "a bird in the hand is worth two in the bush." I decided to remain. Besides, you have already understood that I had no desire to leave, and that I was burning to find a pretext to offer to Dame Reason to justify my change of plans. The newspapers occupied themselves, some with interest, others with sourness, about my delay in going. My friends overwhelmed me under the weight of an incessant "What, you are still here?" And my disappointed fellow-artists began to cast ferocious looks at me. There was a general alarm. I must resign myself, willingly or unwillingly, at the same time cursing the want of reflection with

which one day I had expressed the possibility of my making a
tour to South America.

For those who live on the outside of art, entering it only
through the public door, one pianist more or less is no more than
a grain of sand carried by the winds of the desert, but for the
unsatiated and famished givers of concerts and their agents one
pianist less is a piece more of cake to divide among themselves;
it is a mean of one hundred concerts during the season whose
receipts come back to the comman mass. It is one hundred thousand dollars that falls to them from heaven, without taking into
consideration the relief to their *amour propre*. The absent are
always in the wrong, and once gone the public thinks little of
an artist whom once it had made its idol.

One fine morning in February 1865, I made a contract with
Muzio to go to California. This contract, which I made as reasonable as possible, was thus conceived "that my impresario in
all probability could not lose much in case of failure and in case of
success would have his share of the profits." For ten years I had
thought of visiting California. In 1855 the great Smith, the old
agent of Jenny Lind, offered me an engagement for San Francisco
which I accepted. He was to go on board the steamer *San Francisco*, I think, preceding me one month, but two hours before
embarking he broke his leg, and in this manner escaped the
terrible catastrophe that took place two or three days later—the
shipwreck of the vessel and the loss of more than one-half of
the passengers. The unlucky one, nevertheless, was predestined,
for he was lost, someone told me, on board the steamer *Baltic*.

Muzio announces a series of farewell concerts in New York,
the last this time, my passage being taken. Some may remember,
perhaps, the marks of sympathy and the magnificent presents that
I received in these last soirées, which were crowned by two concerts in one day, one at the New York Academy of Music in the
morning and the other at Brooklyn in the evening.[7]

---

[7] On March 31, after a performance of the "Battle Cry of Freedom,"
arranged for six pianos, a member of the audience presented Gottschalk with
a silver wreath studded with amethysts and rubies, saying that Americans
would cherish the memory of Gottschalk as Europeans do that of Mozart,
Mendelssohn, and Beethoven. Making no attempt to hide his emotion, he
accepted the wreath, declining, however, to allow it to be placed on his
head. Then he played *Murmures éoliens* (*Courrier des États-Unis*, April 3,
1865).

With a heart swollen and agitated by all the emotions that the moment of separation from those we love brings with it when launching ourselves into the unknown, I embarked April 3 on board the *Ariel*. On leaving New York I felt how happy I had been there. Every face that was familiar to me seemed more tender, more sympathetic, and even the most insignificant became interesting.

It was not until then that I discovered, by feeling them break one by one, by how many invisible threads I was attached to the United States. What did it matter to me that Mr. Dwight, of Boston, maintained in his journal that I was an idiot; that Mr. H——, of New York, affirmed in his that I did not know music. I was recalling only those pinpoint annoyances in contrast to the kind friendships that remained faithful to me, and to the invariable public sympathy that had followed me in so many concerts!! But alas! We always feel grief more vividly than joy. It is true I shall no longer read the bilious effusions of Messrs. Dwight and H——, but is the getting rid of the attacks of these wicked fools a compensation for all that I lose that is good and generous?

~·~·~·~·~·~·~

[Gottschalk distributed this farewell card before leaving for California:

To My Friends and the Public

On the eve of my departure from this country—my native land—the land of my earliest affections—I feel that I must express my heartfelt regret on parting with the public, whose kindness has sustained me throughout my public career. To all my friends, who have given me so many proofs of warm interest, I bid you a warm farewell. The clouds that conceal the future are transparent and bright only in the morning of life. I have already come to the age when they show more deception than joys. Even as I say to all farewell, methinks a distant echo faintly answers "adieu"! A last, a long farewell!

◇◇◇◇◇◇◇◇◇◇

April 8

I have been plunged for four days in Tartarus. Seasickness has confined me to my cabin, but the sea is now calm, and here I am on deck smoking a cigar (which on board is the superlative of boasting), our brave little steamer making eleven knots per hour. My thoughts lose themselves in the past at the rate of fifteen hundred miles per second from New York, and from all those whom I love!

We are over four hundred passengers, many of whom are immigrants. In the first class we form the most heterogeneous assemblage that can possibly be imagined! Singers: Striglia, Misses Phillipps, Messrs. Orlandi, Fossetti, Mr. Muzio and Miss Simons, his wife (they were married the very morning of our departure),[8] Dan Setchell, the talented actor, a United States marshal (of sweet and amiable manners), a judge, a lawyer, a person of gross and sour manners, who meddles in everybody's business and contradicts everyone, treads on your toes without asking pardon, and puts his enormous chair in the most crowded places and where there is the least room. There are also a number of senators and doctors, amiable people who make themselves agreeable to everybody, and three ministers, who preach officially twice on Sunday, and officiously the whole day during the week; some ladies, and a considerable residue of that well-known class of passengers without expression whose business seems to be to repeat from time to time—"Fine weather," "Tolerably hot," "Dinner will soon be ready," and other equally interesting remarks, whose momentary clearness seems only to augment the obscurity into which they again fall after having ventured these remarkable observations.

We have many ladies, but they are all married, two of them having lighted the torch of hymen the day of their departure. One of them, a foreigner, takes the greatest possible care in

---

[8] Verdi and his wife sent their blessing and became godparents to the Muzios' son, Giuseppe. The marriage was ill-fated, however. Their child died and disparities of age and background between them probably contributed to their separation.

being where her husband is not. Flirtation, as far as concerns us old bachelors, is very rare here, and I, isolated and alone, content myself with observing. I see, as the day declines, each happy couple seeking a lone corner, and this involuntarily recalls to me the poor famished ones who suck in the savory flavors that escape from the kitchen window.

◇◇◇◇◇◇◇◇◇◇

April 12

In sight of the port of Aspinwall.[9]

During our dinner a second-class passenger has written for amusement a bill of fare [reproduced on the next page], which he has nailed to the quarter-deck.

The heading is a tortoise, very well drawn, with a chimney on his back and a wheel on each side, representing the steamer *Ariel*, on which we are, and which is known as the slowest steamer on the line.

This proves little in favor of the table. From the first cabin I can judge of the second, and the satire is just and true.

◇◇◇◇◇◇◇◇◇◇

April 12

Eleven o'clock in the morning. Land in sight. We see the mountains of New Granada rising up on the horizon.[1] At two o'clock we can see Aspinwall; some white houses, in the midst of which the American flag floats in the breeze; a little farther on a Protestant church of cut stone and Gothic architecture presents a singular effect in the midst of the palm trees and bamboos that surround it. Aspinwall is still only a village; its population does not exceed one thousand souls, two-thirds of which is composed of Negroes; but, thanks to the flux and reflux of travelers, who every five or six days cross the isthmus from one ocean to the other, it has a certain commercial importance and extraordinary

---

[9] The eastern terminus of the Panama Railroad was named after its chief promotor, William H. Aspinwall (1807–75), a New York merchant. A seaport, it now is known as Colón.

[1] Panama was a part of the viceroyalty of New Granada in 1718, and in 1819 became a part of Colombia. In 1857 Panama left the Granadine Confederation, soon to return to it.

SECOND CLASS—THREE HUNDRED DOLLARS

(Nothing extra for meals.)

BILL OF FARE.

DINNER.

Soups.

Turtle,
(scratched out)

Vanderbistallen,

Oyster.
(scratched out)

Roast.

Turkey,
(scratched out)
Lamb,
(scratched out)

Gutta Percha,

Goose,
(scratched out)
Beef.
(scratched out)

Boiled.

Chicken,
(scratched out)

Owl,

Ham.
(scratched out)

Fried.

Oysters,
(scratched out)

Boot Heels,

Ham and Eggs.
(scratched out)

Vegetables.

Green Peas,
(scratched out)
Jerusalem Arti-
chokes,

Beets (diseased),

Cauliflower.
(scratched out)

Side Dishes.

Baked Beans,
(scratched out)

Hard-tack (à la
Monitor),
Pilot Bread (à la
Ironsides),

Lobster Salad.
(scratched out)

Dessert.

Minced Pie,
(scratched out)
Antediluvian Pie,
C. S. Army Pie,

Custard Pie,
(scratched out)
Dried Cucumber
Pie.

Extras.

Tomato Ketchup,

Ice Water.

Please report any civilities on the part of waiters.

animation. It wakes up immediately on the arrival of a steamer. Hardly at the wharf, the steamer is invaded by Negro porters with large pointed bonnets on their heads which recall those of the astrologers, made from the stringy bark of a tree, and are of the color of tow. We have great trouble to keep off this turbulent, officious swarm, who seize by force every package that is in sight, and without disquieting themselves about the proprietor, and, whether you are willing or unwilling, carry it on land. At a hundred yards from the wharf we find ourselves in a street, about five hundred yards long, in which every house is a hotel. There are twelve or fifteen, one after another, all American. Each is a two-story frame house with a porch. The roof extends above the porch, which is sustained by beams, and forms a veranda on the ground floor.

The Negress fruit sellers abound. They are clad in white muslin gowns, low in the neck, with short sleeves. The color of the dress is sullied by the dust, scorched by the sun, and rumpled by the rain. Eight or ten rows of flounces are ranged one above the other as high as the waist. Bare feet. They follow us, offering us, in poor English, bananas, coconuts, oranges, and some cigars, for which they make us pay ten times their value. I buy some bananas. "How much?" I say to her. "Fifty cents," she answers me. I give her a dollar note, which she returns to me, preferring not to sell to taking paper money.

The sun is burning hot. While awaiting the departure of the train we enter the Howard Hotel, kept by Mrs. Smith, an American. Unfortunately for me, there is a piano in the large hall. The passengers assemble and force me to play. The instrument is from the factory of Raven & Bacon, of New York. One lives fast under the tropics; the strings have not resisted the climate. Some low notes remain. I utilize them by playing a semblance of my *Banjo* and clear out.

The train leaves. It is full. The road is lined with thick jungles of mangroves, bindweed, bamboos, and palms. Sometimes the road widens; then we see one or two farmers' huts. Their architecture is primitive: there are four beams on which is placed, four or five feet from the earth, a roofing of palm leaves. The soil around the cabin is still black from the fire that, by burning the forest, has opened a clearing in the midst of this chaos of vegetation, which grows so rapidly in this warm and humid soil.

The crossing is made from ocean to ocean in two hours and a half. We are running alongside a pretty little river. Six o'clock in the afternoon. Arrived at Panama.

Salvo Atlantic! Garrison in full dress; six Negroes and one mulatto under arms form in line near the wharf. We embark in great confusion on a boat that transports us to the steamer, which is two or three miles out at sea. The city of Panama, proper, extends for some distance. The houses are of Spanish architecture, heavy, massive, and square, which the laziness of the inhabitants leaves to fall in ruins. An American resident assures me that ten houses have not been built since the departure of the Spaniards. Two clock towers overlook the city; it is the cathedral. It is as dilapidated as the rest. The roof lets the rain pass through. The statues of the saints in the interior, of painted wood, are rotten and worm-eaten. The doors are off their hinges and hang on one side at the entrance of the church.

A clever prestidigitator, I was told, found the means of drawing four or five hundred dollars last week from this miserable borough. He announced two performances in the following style: "Homage of the all-Powerful Devil. Mr.—— will give two performances of *magic*, the product of which, after deducting all expenses, will be consecrated to repairing the cathedral roof and making new doors." The hall was filled. The receipts were eight hundred dollars, of which the devil (or his disciple) took one-half under pretext of expenses. Someone assured me that wax lights are wanting for the service of religion, and that there is no money to buy them. Apathy, laziness, and filth everywhere; nobody is willing to work. When their houses (built by the Spaniards, whom they execrate, and to whom nevertheless they owe the little civilization that remains to them) fall into ruins, they prop them up with planks or build them up again as well as they can; they stop up the gaps with stones, which they take from the wall that encircles the town, and which today is everywhere tumbling down under the double attack of time and of the wretched builders who have made a quarry of it.

On board the steamer *Constitution*. A splendid steamer, which makes a still greater contrast with that nutshell—the *Ariel*—which we have just left. The heat is excessive, and produces a malaise that we feel doubly from the absence of ice. Here, as on the *Ariel*, the water is lukewarm. We have to pay twenty-five cents extra for a few small pieces of ice, and again the bar has to be closed, like last night, at ten o'clock.

A pearl fishery exists on a small island (Isle of Pearls) one mile from the coast; few are now found, nevertheless lately a pearl was fished up that was sold for eight thousand dollars to the Prince of Wales. The fishery has become dangerous on account of the number and daring of the sharks that are found swimming close in to shore.

I have said that the *Constitution* is the finest steamer that I have yet seen, but I am not on that account willing to say that there might not be many improvements in various things that concern the interior.

❖❖❖❖❖❖❖❖❖

April 14

I have not slept for three days. I am not in California, and I have already a foretaste of what the contests are apropos of squatters' rights and theories. My body, it appears, was in the possession of a company of squatters, who, when I wished to establish myself, were in full activity, and have defended inch by inch their ground and have chased me away. The mosquitoes of Cuba and of the swamps of Louisiana are certainly disagreeable, but there is something bold in their attack and even in their defeat; there is something in their little trumpeting which commands respect, seeming to say, "Here I am, defend yourself," but these small, obscure vampires—these "B flats"—as one of my lady friends musically calls them, are hateful to me because they crawl silently out of their dens and profit by the darkness to accomplish on their sleeping victims their sanguinary crimes.

I have respectfully suggested that perhaps cleanliness might arrive at a satisfactory result against the invasions of these pioneers, but the steward, a mulatto, belongs to the genus grandiloquent, species insolent, and I draw back confused for having disturbed the serenity of his august temperament.

This does not badly resemble the hotel at St. Louis, which has magnificent corridors but nothing to heat them with in winter, when the thermometer points to the cold of Siberia.

Here is a saloon one hundred fifty feet long and splendid in every way. No ice water, the first thing necessary for an American. Gildings all around, but bedbugs (B flats) everywhere. An hour and a half at table to eat nothing good; abundance of meat and vegetables, all badly cooked.

The dull monotony of the life on board continues to unfold slowly and heavily day by day under the heat of an atmosphere like a lead foundry, like a benumbed boa slowly unfolding his rings to the perpendicular rays of an African sun. The sun cooks us, roasts us, melts us, and reddens us; in the shade it is a hot-air bath, in the sun a shriveling. For fourteen hours in the day we are panting, and every moment frightened at seeing our sweat streaming lest we should be turned to a fountain. The night succeeds the sun with all the splendors of the firmament and the phosphorescent streamings of the sea, but there is no breeze. While we are gasping, suffocating for want of air, breathing painfully like a stranded fish on the beach, I am tempted to cry out as at the Lindell House, "For mercy sake less display and more comfort. Fewer stars and a little more breeze! some air! some air! some air! I suffocate!! "

◇◇◇◇◇◇◇◇◇◇

Sunday, April 16

The Episcopal service is read by the purser—the rule on board limits its duration to forty minutes. A reverend had offered his services, but the forty minutes' clause seemed like an attack upon his dignity and he retired.

The new bride appears the oftenest possible where her husband is not, in which the gigantic proportions of the steamer wonderfully assist her. There would be much to write about humanity such as it appears on board. Sympathies and antipathies, attractions and repulsions have time to manifest themselves. Passengers find their level as the dull calm after the horrors of a storm. Our singers (like all those who make merchandise of music) are already quarreling. To establish harmony among musicians is as impossible as to find an Irish immigrant who would refuse to take from you a glass of whiskey, or a Westerner who would ask pardon for treading on your toes.

Our captain, a fine old fellow who weighs three hundred pounds, evidently likes his dinner; he keeps us an hour and a half at table. When one, in a small company of five of six friends around a well-served table, after having dined well, stops to taste the dessert and under the influence of the delicious lethargy that accompanies a good digestion in taking a glass of wine, prolongs the time by talking, nothing is more sensible. But after having swallowed with a grimace some few spoonfuls of peppered hot water, after having courageously wrestled with a piece of beef hard as bone, one is condemned to an interlude of twenty minutes between each course at a table laid for two hundred persons, in the midst of a deafening uproar, with an atmosphere laden with the combined vapors of two hundred plates of hot water and beef leather, it is more than any one should require from the most indulgent voyager.

I have fortunately taken the habit of going on deck between each course. I have for this purpose a large book, a geographical dictionary, which from its shape gives me a high degree of respectability among many persons who think that it is a Bible.

They are serving the peppered hot water. Five minutes. I go up on deck and read for half an hour.

Neat's leather. Fifteen minutes. Three times longer than that for the soup, the process of deglutition by mastication being at least seventy-five degrees more difficult than that by ingurgitation. Half an hour on the deck to read. We now have disposed of an hour fifteen minutes additional; now comes the curry, which takes a half hour to serve, etc. etc.

The young foreigner (German) having continued more and more to avoid the presence of her husband is, accidentally, it appears, often found in the company of another passenger. The husband, who has some notions about the honeymoon which his young wife does not share in, is heard this evening to make threats of a revolver. Shall we have a drama on board!

◇◇◇◇◇◇◇◇◇

April 19

Acapulco (Mexico) is in sight. After having passed a large rock, the city(?), some huts whose roofs are covered with palm trees present themselves to our view. Seated at the shore of a pretty little bay on the edge of the beach, it runs back to the sierra, covered with forests and thick vegetation. We must take on coal here. Scarcely have we anchored when we see ourselves surrounded by a crowd of canoes made from the trunks of trees hollowed out by fire, manned by Indians. They are clothed in white linen drawers; their heads are covered with broad-brimmed straw hats. They sell bananas, oranges, shellwork, white corals. I was hoping to buy some pearls, but the bay has been so infested with sharks for some time that the fishing has become very difficult. Last week, I am told, they carried off eight imprudent fishermen. On land the beach is covered with Indians, some squatting before piles of fruit, offering their merchandise to us in broken English; others, the greater number, pursue us, offering us necklaces of shells and colored glass and little pins for the head, of shell and glasswork. A little Indian girl begs me; she is most anxious to sell me some. Expressive and singular style, white teeth, olive tint. The absence of clothes (at least they are very scanty) is more than compensated by the abundance of her hair and the largeness of her eyes. She ends by sticking a pin in my collar, which she absolutely wishes to make a present of *"al hermoso caballero."* The proceeding was too gracious for the *"caballero"* not to respond to it. I gave her a *real.* Bad luck for me. In a moment I am surrounded by a swarm of Indians, small and large, old and young, vociferating, disputing the possession of me, who pounce down on me like vultures on a lamb, load me with pins, which they stick in me everywhere. The *"hermoso caballero"* looks like a pincushion. "The Yankees please me, I love blondes, I have made a present to the *caballero,* the *caballero* in return will make me one." The only way I have to get out of the hands of my brown sirens is to give them a handful of *reales,* and I see them rush on another *caballero* and stick him also full of pins.

The houses are miserable huts, the ground plots of which are covered with beaten lime. The streets are not paved, and the footway for the pedestrians, two feet wide, runs alongside the houses from four to five feet above the level of the street.

The church, to all appearances most miserable, is closed; I am sorry, for I wish to see it. The house of the padre is pointed out to me. He is sleeping, his domestic, a very pretty young Indian girl, tells me on my introducing myself. The padre, a fat fellow, is in his hammock. He receives me very politely, and calls the sacristan to let me see the church. It offers nothing remarkable except the decay into which its altars, doors, and statues are fallen. Above the image of a saint there is a paper on which I read, in large writing and in imaginative Spanish orthography, "Everyone too poor to buy medicines for herself will be instantly cured if she makes her devotions with sufficient fervor before this image."

In one corner, suspended from the wall, is a multitude of ex-votos. These are figures of wax or tin, in lead or gilt paper (according to the means of the giver), representing legs, eyes, and ears. When they are suffering from some disease, the devotees suspend before the image or altar of the saint of their preference a facsimile of the sick part and patiently await their cure.

Everywhere the image of idleness, of indifference, of apathy, of ignorance, and of filth. In every house we see women lying in their hammocks, or men indolently squatting down or lying in the shade. Everywhere immobility. Civilization will never be able to galvanize these people, whose soul is buried under the triple layer of torpor, idleness, and inertness.

A long hut, before which some flint guns are ranged on a rack, represents the guardhouse. Ten or twelve Indians, half-naked, lying on their faces around a pack of cards, are playing. A sentinel, lazily leaning on his gun, follows the play eagerly with his eyes.

One of the soldiers asks me if I have any news from "*los Franceses.*" "It is true that the emperor has to recall his troops?" Is the señor an Englishman?" "No," I tell him, "I am a Russian officer." "Ah, the señor," said a sergeant complacently to me, "wished to see great fighting. Don Diego Alvarez"*—with emphasis as one would speak of the great Napoleon—"will teach

---

* Diego Alvarez, an old Indian, is for the Indian Mexicans of the Pacific what Napoleon was for the Old Guard. He is their god, their beau-ideal, their idol. This old general, who is eighty years old, governs the whole Mexican side of the Pacific, and boasts that he has never been conquered [translator's note].

the French manners. He is in the mountains, his son commands here in his absence," then with all the swagger of his race, and straightening himself up into a theatrical pose, "We have killed more than thirty thousand of them in the sierra." After this speech he straightens himself like a bully and gazes around him to receive the tokens of admiration—due to native heriosm.[2]

The Louisiana Hotel is a house of less miserable appearance than the others. The landlord is a fat man who is a Frenchman, not to be mistaken if one may judge by this speech, which he addressed to the Indians lying before his doors.

"Sacré tas de canaille voulez vous bien me ficher le camp," and for a peroration he administered, right and left, some blows to a group of young pin merchants who had again discovered me and hoped to recommence their operations on the *caballero.*

"You are a Frenchman, sir," I say to him.

"No, sir"—with emphasis—"I am from New Orleans."

The love of country is a prejudice I will admit; even I know it.

The traveler's life, which I have led, has singularly enlarged the circle of those whom I regard as compatriots.

From seeing men under every form in all latitudes resemble each other, though changed in name, I have little by little arrived at recognizing that there is really but one nation—humanity; but one country—the globe; but one code, that of justice and morality. Nevertheless, the memories of our first years, our first affections, live at the bottom of our hearts, and this old tavern keeper saying to me in this obscure hole on the coast of the Pacific, "I am from New Orleans," awakening all at once my sleeping memories, in a moment became a friend.

"I also," I said to him, "am from New Orleans." An acquaintance was quickly made. He recounted to me all his affairs, his life, etc. He had kept a restaurant at Lake Ponchartrain.

"What men these Creoles are! Another thing from your Yankees!" (Here he gave way to his hatred for the Yankees.)

The poor man hated the North without being acquainted with it. After having asked me the news about many of the best-known people of New Orleans, he spoke to me of Morphy, the chess player.

---

[2] From 1864 to 1867, Mexico was under the rule of the Emperor Maximilian.

"There is glory for Louisiana! But from his childhood he showed what he would be someday. He is not like another little prodigy, Gottschalk, who promised marvelous things, and whose father sent him to Europe in hopes of making a great musician of him. Nobody has heard anything more about him. What has become of him?" I confess that I found myself a little embarrassed in answering this question. My self-esteem was considerably hurt. I told him the little prodigy was still a pianist, and that without having precisely realized the expectations of his countrymen, he had notwithstanding continued to work at music.

"It is possible, but I have never heard him spoken of," replied the old man, who evidently had a grudge against the infant prodigy who had disappointed the hopes of his patriotic love.

We have an excellent dinner. Some birds whose names I forget, as fat as ortolans. I recommend this old tavern keeper to travelers. At table we are waited on by a thin waiter in shirt sleeves, whose body, squeezed at the waist by a leather band, is surmounted by a countenance wrinkled into folds, set off by long, flat locks of gray hair. The effect of this mummy-like countenance on a body eighteen years old is impossible to describe. "Monsieur is from New Orleans," said this disguised old man, in a falsetto voice with a French lisp, in smartly taking away from me my plate, "a pretty town that has consoled me for leaving Paris. Ah! Paris, sir, my youth, my well-formed leg, and my arm so plump, as the song says. If it was not for *my husband* I should never work for these Mexican savages." I then understood that this young sexagenarian waiter is the wife of my host, who, through an excess of caution, more pretentious than justifiable, had renounced (these Mexicans are such savages) the dress of her sex.

While we are dining, Don Juan Alvarez, the son of the old guerrilla, and the present governor, passes with his family. They are going to visit our steamer. Don Juan is an Indian with insignificant features. His wife and daughter carry umbrellas, wear silk dresses, gold chains and necklaces, earrings, brooches, rings, embroidered shoes, and crinolines. They walk with all the stiffness of Indians with their Sunday clothes on, ridiculously jumbled together; full of pride in parading themselves in these super-

annuated fashions, which must have had their day among the
hucksters of the temple; they attain altogether the height of the
grotesque when they think to attain the summit of Parisian
elegance.

Dull as Acapulco is, it acts as an agreeable diversion to the
monotony of the ship, and it is not without regret that we slowly
return, and soon the huge rock behind which we are disappearing conceals from our eyes the miserable huts, the church, and
even the little dismantled Spanish fort that defends (?) Acapulco,
and here we are again plunged in the dull routine of the steamer.

◇◇◇◇◇◇◇◇◇◇

April 23

A steamer in sight! It is the *Golden City*, which left San Francisco two days ago. The captain comes on board, and, in the
midst of questions from all the passengers who crowd the staircase, hurls these words like thunderbolts: "Richmond is taken,"
"Lee has surrendered," "Lincoln has been assassinated."

The news, more or less true, which has been transmitted to
us since the commencement of the war, has rendered us incredu-
lous. Nothing is more probable than that Lee has surrendered,
since, on the morning of our departure from New York, the news
of the taking of Petersburg was confirmed—but the death of
Lincoln! Some ask for the papers; a passenger has mounted in
the rigging and has been requested to read with a loud voice.
Alas! There is no longer any doubt Lincoln is dead. We do not
know the details of the horrible outrage—the name only of the
assassin is mentioned—Wilkes Booth. I remember having seen
him play a year ago in Cleveland. I was struck at that time with
the beauty of his features, and at the same time by a sinister
expression of his countenance. I would even say that he had something deadly in his look. A literary lady among my friends who
knew him told me that he had as much natural talent for the
stage as his brother Edwin, but that his violent and fantastic
character would not permit him to polish the natural brutality of
his manners any more than to restrain the fury of his acting within
the ordained limits of art.

I never recollect having seen a more affecting sight than that presented by the immense deck of the *Constitution*. The sky is blue, the sun resplendent, the sea is calm, all nature seems to smile above our heads, to render the contrast of our grief more striking with the stillness of all that surrounds us. Strange and inexplicable thing!! The women are those who show the least regrets. Around me, rude features of the seamen leave the badly effaced traces of their tears to be seen. A judge, sitting in a corner, his head in his hands, weeps as if he had just lost a father. All the men seem crushed, overwhelmed under the weight of an incommensurable grief. The women, after having shed some contagious tears, begin to make common conjectures about the motives of the assassin, and the means employed by him. I have for a long time suspected that woman, who weeps so easily for so many superficial griefs, possesses really less sensibility than man. She has her nervous fits, her paroxysms of enthusiasm or of despair, which carry her at one bound to the heights of feeling but do not sustain her there. These are irrational impulses, hysterical crises, which lose in depth what they gain in surface.

In the presence of a great sentiment they are inferior, they are little, and man, whose sensibility for small things is dull under the envelope of his brutishness, takes upon him in the presence of an immense grief, of solemn despair, his supremacy, and becomes again the master, not only through the force of muscle, but through the greatness of his soul. Woman has more frequently the poetry of words than of ideas.

◇◇◇◇◇◇◇◇◇◇

April 24, morning

We are to have a meeting on board to give official expression to the sentiments of grief which, with merely two or three exceptions, are felt by all the passengers. I have said with merely one or two exceptions, because a lady, whose opinions are Secessionist, has pushed her forgetfulness of the respect due to humanity so far as to qualify the assassination of Lincoln as a judgment from God; and one or two other female parrots (a species of female dolls, who are dying for sorrow in not having put on their last new dress), who are exclaiming, with philosophic profundity, that "Lincoln would have had to die *sooner or later!*"

◇◇◇◇◇◇◇◇◇

Evening

The meeting, presided over by Judge Field of the Supreme Court of the United States, has voted resolutions that accord with our feelings of fidelity to the Government, of respect for the memory of the great and good Lincoln, and of horror for the execrable act that has ended his noble and laborious career.

Where are now those frivolous judgments on the man whom we are weeping for today? His ugliness, his awkwardness, his jokes, with which we reproached him: all have disappeared in presence of the majesty of death. His greatness, his honesty, the purity of that great heart which beats no longer, rise up today, and in their resplendent radiancy transfigure him whom we called the "common rail splitter." O Eternal Power of the true and beautiful! Yesterday his detractors were ridiculing his large hands without gloves, his large feet, his bluntness; today this type we found grotesque appears to us on the threshold of immortality, and we understand by the universality of our grief what future generations will see in him.

After the meeting, the Italian singers who are on board sing the Hymn of the Republic, which I accompany on the piano. Miss Adelaide Phillipps[3] sings with electric feeling the patriotic song "The Star Spangled Banner." I play my piece, *Union*. The enthusiasm aroused is without doubt less owing to our music than to the actual circumstances.

◇◇◇◇◇◇◇◇◇

April 25

We shall arrive today, the captain says. Unfortunately the fog has come up, and we are obliged to remain quiet until it disappears. The coast bristles with rocks, and it is very dangerous to approach

---

[3] Adelaide Phillipps (1833–82) was born at Stratford-on-Avon, England, and came to the United States when she was seven. Jenny Lind, on her first visit to Boston, in 1850, advised the young singer to pursue an operatic career. Her Italian debut took place in 1853 under the name of Fillippi. After her New York debut as Azucena in *Il Trovatore*, in 1856, she sang extensively here and abroad and was noted for her intelligent projection of roles.

when the weather is not clear. A general disappointment. Have you taken notice at the theater of the precipitation with which everyone leaves his seat to go as soon as the piece draws near the end? The same persons who for two hours have remained motionless and silent in their seats jostle and crowd each other as if their lives were in danger if they were accused of being in the hall when the curtain falls. For my part, I have often observed, without understanding it, the impatience that seizes travelers who have patiently endured railroad traveling for twenty-four hours and who before the train has had time to stop at the station push each other to see who shall be the first to jump from the car, at the risk of breaking their heads or their limbs. We are nearly in the same condition on board. After having patiently endured twenty-four days in crossing, the few hours we are forced to spend motionless a few miles from port seem insupportable to us.

◇◇◇◇◇◇◇◇◇◇

April 26

Very thick fog. No probability of arriving even today.

◇◇◇◇◇◇◇◇◇◇

April 27, morning

The sky is blue and the air is pure. We shall be in San Francisco today. We see the mountains and the whole coast distinctly. The steamer slowly advances. The mountains unfold themselves majestically to our astonished sight. We are entering into the bay. The pen and the imagination are powerless to portray the splendor of the spectacle that is opened to our eyes. To the left the declivities of the mountains gradually descend, and at last are lost on the shore, enameled with the little white houses of the villages. The canyons, narrow passages where the light entering takes on somber tints; the swelling of the hills, where the reflections of the sun on the patches of verdure are mirrored and colored with the reflex of opals and rubies, and the immense azure vault of a sky like Naples. On the right the Seal Rocks, frowning sentinels over some arms of the beach, and on which for many centuries certain enormous seals have established their quarters, whose shapeless bodies we distinguish lazily sleeping or crawling like gigantic leeches in the fissures of the rock. Planted on a high bluff, the Cliff House overlooks the horizon. From a balcony, many persons with long spyglasses are watching us coming in. The Cliff House is six miles from San Francisco, and is a rendezvous for pedestrians, equestrians, and carriages. They go there to eat oysters, and to see the seals a few yards from the beach carelessly enjoy themselves without being frightened at the approach of the curious, their security never having been troubled, thanks to a local ordinance that prohibits any harm being done to them under penalty of a fine.

We cannot yet see San Francisco, the city being built at the foot of the bay, and the latter making an elbow. Fort Alcatraz* lifts its gray walls from the middle of a little island in the bay. It incloses all the political prisoners compromised during the war, and those accused of burning the steamer *Panama*. Two or three hundred American soldiers constitute the garrison of this desolate and sterile rock, on which there is not a drop of water and not a blade of grass. We are still going ahead! We are turning a promontory on our right, and the port of San Francisco opens on our view.

The Golden Gate, the entrance of the bay, surpasses in magnificence the most beautiful sights I have ever seen. Naples and Constantinople, the two most celebrated bays, do not present to the eye a more imposing, more dazzling spectacle, than the Bay of San Francisco, but the city itself does not answer from the port to the idea one has formed of it. We seen only sand hills with scattered houses of mean appearance. The port is animated, a forest of masts and of flags. Clouds of smoke escaping from the ferryboats, with which the bay is covered, and which are plowing their way, in every sense, give life to the picture. The wharf is covered with an eager crowd. We are approaching slowly. Confusion reigns everywhere, particularly on board. The young female foreigner profits by the absence of her husband, engaged in hunting for his trunks, to go on deck to make a passenger explain the beauties of the landscape to her. The porters

---

* The name Alcatraz—in Spanish, sea bird—comes undoubtedly from the immense number of these birds which inhabit it, and whose eggs, a few years ago, when fowls were scarce in California, furnished a considerable branch of commerce [translator's note].

have already invaded us and seized our trunks. The captain, on the paddle box, is giving his orders. As we approach shore we distinguish the crowd going toward our landing place. Friends are recognizing each other. "Hello, here is Jack! How are you?" etc. etc. Everybody speaks at once. The horses in the wagons get frightened and kick up their heels. The engine roars; the drivers cry out. Conversations are taking place between those on the shore and those on board. Handkerchiefs are in requisition. The women are crying for joy, and the fathers blow their noses energetically. All the passengers regard each other as if they were united in the closest friendship. The judge himself has a less disagreeable air! The young foreigner is in the arms of her husband, and she does not appear to find her companion very disagreeable.

There is a great commotion, "A man overboard!" He has fallen between the wharf and the vessel and has disappeared. Anxiety of the crowd. They fish him out. He is a wagoner; he has escaped safely with only a cold bath.

Some exchange news, others recognize each other. "How are you at home?" Home, that magic word which makes the heart of the most doubting beat. Laugh at it if you will! Call it a weak prejudice! Leave your home; travel, throw yourself into the whirlpool of the world; squander, by throwing to the four winds, the illusions of your heart, its tendernesses, its raptures, until, exhausted by the abuse or bruises of life, it dries up and, insensible, henceforth is associated with your being, only by the material functions it is called upon to fill in the animal economy. Do you say it is dead? Love, ambition, devotion, the follies of youth, lost illusions! Dead, do you say? Reason has taken its place. Return again to your home, there where your first loves blossomed, where your earliest dreams were realized. Behold once more the place where you first lisped in life, spelled love; and this atrophied heart, which you thought was dead, will awaken as from a long lethargy to salute, with all the ardor of its first emotions, as the nightingale sings in the morning the aurora of spring, the memory of this aurora of life—"blessed home!"

For myself this spectacle saddens me. No one awaits me, and those I love I have left very far behind me. The Rev. Mr. Thomas, one of the passengers, is standing next to me. "Is Gottschalk on board?" cries a voice from the crowd. "Here he is," replies the Rev. Mr. Thomas, pointing me out to the crowd. I submit to this exhibition with regret. My looks, considerably deteriorated by seasickness, present the most wretched appearance and offer nothing but what is disappointing to those who always associate the idea of a celebrity of any kind with a certain physical majesty. Of over one hundred persons who know my name without ever having seen me, I have invariably read from their looks that they were quite disappointed in finding me thin and of ordinary height. The frankest contented themselves by saying, "Ah! I thought that you were taller." The ancients who, without understanding anatomy, made such irreproachable statues, obeyed instinctively a natural law when they gave so little expression to their faces. Form always seduces the masses, and the people in their youth become enraptured with the form to the exclusion of the mind.

The elegant Alcibiades was evidently more attractive than the flat-nosed Socrates, and the advocates of Phryne, who took her tunic off her, to cause her to be acquitted (eloquent peroration that carried with it the austere judges of the Areopagus), were decidedly profound philosophers. Sappho must have been pretty. Crowds have only instinct; reason is awakened only by reflection, and the crowd never reflects. It was less by genius that Peter the Great controlled the rude Muscovites than by his terrible fits of passion, seconded by Herculean strength and a gigantic height. If on February 24, 1848, King Louis-Philippe had mounted horse and had shown his fine white head to the Parisian insurgents, the dead republic, born of Lamartine and Ledru-Rollin,[4] would have aborted. If, later, when Louis-Napoleon had been elected because of his name (it is not necessary to seek for any other reason for his elevation, since he was unknown to France, except by two attempts that were looked upon as foolish and absurd because they did not succeed), he had presented himself to the Parisians on foot at the first review of the troops, which took place on February 10, 1850, the Napoleonic dynasty would have been extinguished. His body, too large for his slim little legs, his feet turned out, his awkward gait, his retreating forehead, and large nose, would hardly

---

[4] Alexandre-Auguste Ledru-Rollin (1807–74) was a French radical politician and advocate of universal suffrage. He was provisional Minister of the Interior in 1848 and a candidate for the presidency in the same year.

have found favor with the impulsive, enthusiastic, and unreflecting French people. It would have seemed to them a sacrilege to associate this horse-like head with the profile, like an antique medal, of the great emperor. Thus the president showed himself on horseback, and on the most mettlesome horse of his stables. He is one of the best and most graceful riders in Europe. His fantastic uniform, in which gold played a very important part, concealed the height of his figure. The troops were ranged on the Champs-Elysées as far as the Colonne de Juillet, that is to say in a direction of three or four miles along the boulevards. The drums were beating the march, the bands were playing. "The prince is coming," said the crowd, and all were awaiting impatiently, when all at once the prince debouched at the head of a staff glittering with gold and plumes. His horse, excited by the crowd and the music, rendered furious by the spur, which his rider did not spare on him, advanced, rearing and making immense bounds. The prince, calm and smiling, held the reins with a firm hand and with his right took off his hat before the colors, which were lowered at his passage. He passed like a waterspout, and the crowd, wondering at his grace and his audacity, burst into acclamations. It is thus his popularity began. A name that sounded to the ears of the French like an echo of one of their old glories, and great experience in the art of horsemanship; this is what his great reign is founded upon. It is true that his great genius (good or bad, I do not charge myself with appreciating it) has since been obliged to justify itself to those who applauded without knowing him.

A few grasps of our traveling companions' hands, and the promise (made in good faith but after some hours upon land effaced from our memory) to see each other often, and we go on shore. Mr. Badger, Chickering's agent, was awaiting us, and with the kindest zeal placed himself entirely at our disposal. Our apartments are reserved for us at the Cosmopolitan Hotel. We are gaining knowledge (and I confess that I have a great deal of repugnance for it), with the only scourge of San Francisco—the dust. Built upon sandy ground, and hills exposed to the wind, which blows every day at noon for six hours, the city is enveloped in clouds of dust, which rise in double columns of a grayish color above the city, and, at a distance, recall the smoke that covers the great English metropolis like a canopy. The journey from the wharf to the hotel is made slowly—the horses pull with difficulty, and the wheels of our carriage sink six inches deep into the sandy dust. This thick and impalpable dust, which is dried by the sun during eight months of absolute drought, penetrates into the eyes, the ears, and the mouth.

The Cosmopolitan Hotel is a magnificent square edifice of cut stone, the luxury of whose furniture is equal to that of the first hotels in the United States. A splendid restaurant and a magnificent billiard room are connected with it. The dining room is ornamented with a profusion of mirrors that reflect the gilded ceilings, and the lighted candelabra give to it the appearance of a European palace. The ladies' parlor contains a Chickering piano that, contrary to hotel pianos, is excellent and in good tune. In a portfolio of music that I found on the piano I saw *The Maiden's Prayer—et tu quoque, O California!*

The interior service of the hotel is admirably performed. The waiters, in black suits and white cravats, are polite (they are for the most part French), and neat (the proprietors of hotels in Western cities, B—— and S——, are requested to meditate on this paragraph), and exercise kindness in taking your orders without making you feel the inferiority of your position. The bill of fare would have made Brillat-Savarin and Carême faint for joy. Vegetables in the greatest variety, fruits of all zones, tropical and temperate, and the most artistic dishes appear in the long list. But I am not easily taken by the allurements of these deceptive baits, which the hotels of the West have taught me to distrust. They are generally supernumeraries like those mute choristers whom directors add to their not too numerous choruses, who, opening their mouths and without singing, do very well as a *coup d'œil* but have nothing to do with the music—these artistic dishes have no other purpose but to increase the bill of fare. If, sometimes, an inexperienced traveler falls in the snare, he either receives this answer from the waiter, "There is no more of it," and he thus preserves one illusion more, or the phœnix asked for is served up to him and then he swears, but a little too late, that he will never ask for it again.

This would be the time to make a philosophical digression on the art of cooking, which is more closely connected than is thought with intellectual civilization. One of the aphorisms of Brillat-Savarin (who many think was a celebrated cook but who was only a very honorable judge, whose epicurianism and delicate wit prompted him to write a charming book) was: "It is the beast that feeds, but it is man only who knows how to eat."

In the United States, cookery, like music, painting, and many other branches of a high civilization, has hardly yet been called into being. I will tell you a little story that will lead me by a bypath to the expression of my whole opinion upon our national cookery and our arts.

At the time of the first outbreak of Asiatic cholera, I was then —— I was just about to tell you my age; since the cholera made its first appearance in 1832, by a trifling addition you would have discovered how many springtimes I reckon. My father, to avoid the plague, built a small cottage on the shore of the Gulf of Mexico, in a secluded spot called Pass Christian. Our only neighbors were a few Indians, the only remains of a tribe massacred by the Spaniards, and whose bones were covered by a small mound in the clearings of the wood behind our little mansion.

We had a piano, and it was there, alone, that I began my attempts upon the instrument that, at a later period, was to attract to me so many admirers and detractors, to give me so many joys, and to render Mr. Dwight of Boston so miserable.

One evening when I was playing "Hail Columbia" a large Indian stopped at the door and inquisitively watched my hands running over the keyboard. My father (although a man of great intelligence, he was not without that weakness in which all fathers participate, who think their children phœnixes) said to the Indian, "You see what this little paleface can do." The vanity of the savage was so much the more wounded as he could not deny that the child did what neither he nor his had ever done. He came in and attentively examined the box where the strange sounds had come from. Tea was ready. We passed into the next room without thinking of the Indian. I alone secretly observed him. His great size and hoarse voice inspired me with childish fear. I saw him, after satisfying himself that he was not observed, slowly approach the piano; he looked attentively at the keyboard, then carelessly, and as if by accident, he let his hand fall upon a key, which returned a sound. Scarcely had he heard it when his countenance, which had remained morose, brightened, he sat down at the piano, and with all the force of his arms he began to beat the keys, calling out triumphantly to my father, "You see, I never tried before, and I make more noise than he."

Do you understand my comparison? "No!" Very well, then. Go to B——, and when you are told what someone told me— "Mrs.—— is the best singer here, because you can hear her a mile off"—recall to yourself the Indian of Pass Christian. "This gallery of paintings is the largest we have in America." The Indian of Pass Christian. "Mr. So-and-so is an excellent judge of music; he has spent six months in Europe." Again, my Indian. "Our hotel is as good as the Fifth Avenue or the Continental; look at the number of dishes on the bill of fare." The Indian, always the Indian.

To sing, you require lungs, but it also requires other things; an ox can be heard a mile off. A gallery of paintings, if it possessed two hundred million daubs, would not be worth one miniature of Isabey, or one of Meissonnier's interiors. Mr. So-and-so, instead of six months, might have remained six years in Europe and come back as big a blockhead as before. Your hotel might have as many dishes on its bill of fare as the Queen of Spain has names (I think she has one hundred thirty-two); if they are bad your cooking makes it like a cheap eating house.

But the food of the Cosmopolitan Hotel is excellent, or at least the dishes here are eatable. The town, when you are in the middle of Montgomery Street (the principal street in San Francisco), looks like the beautiful sections of Chicago; the stores are large and luxurious. Built upon a number of steep hills, the streets rise and descend; they have leveled many of them, but much remains to be done. I have seen one spot where the ground is so steep that you have to go up by steps, the roof of the lower house coming to the level of the steps of the one that precedes it, and so with those following. The leveling for the most part being done after the houses are built, they have enlarged them at the bottom. They prop them up and build lower stories to them, so that what was once the ground floor becomes the garret.

It is impossible on seeing San Francisco to imagine that the date of its foundation goes no further back than twenty years ago, and that it has been burned down two or three times. I have been shown the place where the beach was. It is now nearly a mile

from there. They have gained this land from the sea by throwing
into it the sand carried from the hills while they were leveling.
San Francisco numbers three theaters, two large concert halls,
several small ones, an infinite number of saloons for melodeons,
and a Chinese theater. Maguire's Opera House is generally occupied by a dramatic company. Maguire's Academy of Music is a
charming hall that holds from fifteen to eighteen hundred persons
easily, and in which the Italian opera company under the direction
of Maguire is now performing here. The Metropolitan Theater
is a little larger than the Academy of Music, but less elegant in
its interior decorations. Bianqui's Italian Company is playing there
in opposition to that of Maguire's. The name of Maguire is constantly found throughout all California. The one that bears it was,
some say, a sporting character, a boxer. He has made a fortune
and at the same time has built almost all the theaters inland and
in San Francisco. He is very intelligent, very enterprising, and
provides by himself alone almost all the amusements of the northern cities of the Pacific. I have found him very kind and very just
in his transactions. There is, besides, at this moment in San
Francisco, a circus company to which Zoyara the hermaphrodite
belongs. I remember the excitement produced by the "Hermosa
Señorita Zoyara" in Havana when every young person was foolishly interested in the solution of the mystery concerning her sex.
I am told that Mademoiselle Zoyara is married, and that she is the
best husband in the world and the most excellent of fathers. I
suppose from this that the problem is solved.

The cafés and billiard saloons of San Francisco are magnificent,
handsomer even than those of New York. The Bank Exchange is
the most aristocratic of the latter, and at its bar the great merchants every day find a choice collation. Champagne is constantly drunk here throughout the whole day. It is the base of all
the drinks, such as lemonade, cocktails, smashes, cobblers. As to
the California wine, I have as yet seen only one bottle of it, and
I do not believe that a glass a day is drunk of it in all the cafés
of San Francisco. I made this remark to a Californian, who laughingly answered me, "We leave the care of it to you Eastern
people." I know too little of liquors to decide whether he wanted
to say something not at all flattering to our taste in matters of
wine.

The markets of San Francisco are worthy of being seen. They

are floored, and of scrupulous neatness. This country has all the best things of the world in profusion. Fruits and vegetables of every zone and every climate abound here. Salmon (I have seen some two feet in circumference) cost two bits (twenty-five cents) a pound. They are so plentiful that there is a story, true or false, that says the Irish servants stipulate that it shall not be given them to eat more than twice a week. Strawberries ripen the whole year. The apples of Oregon are excellent. The oranges of Lower California are in abundance. The olives are as large and good as those of Andalusia and will become, when the mining fever abates and industry develops the resources of the country, an important branch of industrial production. Almonds, cherries (and what cherries!), peaches, grapes, apricots, artichokes, cauliflowers, beets (the poorest are three times larger than those of the East, and I have seen some that weighed twenty-five pounds); in one word, all the richness of the vegetable kingdom has been accumulated here by Providence on this land of promise, whose climate, a perpetual temperature of spring, would be the finest in the world were it not for the cursed wind that comes up every day from noon until six o'clock and whirls the sandy dust in every direction. The scarcity of trees in and around San Francisco might be easily explained by the action of this wind, which cuts down vegetation and scarcely suffers low plants and bushes to grow.[5]

The mines of copper, silver, gold, and mercury seem inexhaustible! New ones are discovered every day. Very fine opals are found in Calaveras County. The water of the sea near the coast presents large oleaginous spots, which seem to indicate that there must be deposits of oil in the interior of the hills. Some have begun, it is said, to dig wells in many places, and the oil fever promises to make as many victims as its elder sister the gold fever. "Victims!" some may say to me. "How? If the mines are so rich, can they make victims?" I will say nothing myself, but I will answer what a Californian told me to whom I addressed the same question: "The expenses of digging are enormous; roads are difficult to cut in the mountains; water is hard to get to wash the gold, one has to go sometimes five or six miles to find it, and bring it by means of aqueducts. Besides, the diggings often cave in,

---

[5] Conservationists will say that the reverse was true, the scarcity of trees promoting the gusts of wind.

and require the use of enormous timbers, which are very costly; workhands are dear; besides, finally, the chapter of never-ending robberies. There are, perhaps, three thousand mines in California, and there are hardly a half-dozen that regularly make dividends, and, nevertheless, all are rich and productive."

The natural riches of California are marvelous, but it lacks capital. The rate of interest, which is one and a half per cent a month on a first mortgage with good signatures, cannot otherwise be explained. Money rates as high as two to three per cent a month. Capital fails in spite of the immense resources the country presents; it is the oil that would lubricate and put in motion all the wheels of the great machine.

There are, besides the Cosmopolitan (which I consider the best), three other very good hotels. The extraordinary development of the city within the last ten years has naturally caused a great increase in the value of land. Chicago some years ago seemed to have attained the maximum during the speculative fever in land, but nothing approaching the following figures: Last year Admiral Dupont won a lawsuit by which he was awarded thirty-five thousand dollars for a piece of ground for which he had paid fifteen dollars. Mr. Lick purchased for fifty dollars, from a man who had paid five dollars for it, the ground on which he built the Lick House. This ground is today worth, without the hotel, five hundred thousand dollars.

Messrs. Badger and Linderberger, wholesale ready-made clothing merchants, whose large store is situated on the business street of San Francisco, have on the second story a depot for Chickering's pianos, of which they sell a great number. Is it an indication that music is much cultivated? I would not dare to assert it. Music, of all the arts, is the last to implant itself, and takes deep root only in old civilized societies. It is too abstract, it appertains too much to the domain of thought and feeling to flourish, where the physical forces are in full activity. It is an art for idlers and dreamers. Neither the one nor the other is found among men who have to build houses to shelter themselves and who have to seek their food. The plastic arts are the first, after spoken poetry, which suggest themselves to the minds of primitive peoples.

Concerts in San Francisco have never succeeded. Ole Bull[6]

---

[6] If Ole Bull (1810–80) could not succeed at San Francisco, Gottschalk really had cause for worry. The Norwegian violinist, under the early influence

and Strakosch left it in confusion. Paul Julien,[7] who has just spent five months here, has not carried off one thousand dollars net. On the other hand, I regret to say, the circus flourishes, and Miss Adah Menken,[8] after having driven all the people crazy, has carried away with her fifty thousand dollars. You will easily understand that the chaste Muse, sister of Apollo, can go astray only before a public that is enthusiastic at the nudities of *Mazeppa*.

There are many Chinese here. It is supposed that there are more than seventy thousand in California, and at least five thousand in San Francisco. The great majority of them are laundrymen. Stockton Street is lined with Chinese shops; they sell drugs, seeds, make shoes, etc. Some of them are very rich, very intelligent, and speak English readily. I was introduced to Sam Kee, a druggist, I think, who, seated behind his desk, was writing his letters—a ship leaves for China tomorrow.

The neatness with which he wrote his letter from right to left would make the best bookkeeper pale with envy. My guide, doubtless to give him a high idea of the visitor he introduced to him, repeated to him frequently, "Mr. Gottschalk, the great, great pianist," but perceiving that the Celestial opened his eyes without understanding the word "pianist," he added to it a pantomime with his fingers, which he shook rapidly in the air, repeating "great, great."

Sam Kee bowed very profoundly, regarding me with a restless look. It is plain that the pantomime with the fingers did not inspire him with confidence. He accompanied me as far as the door, all the time bowing to me profoundly, as much for the purpose

---

of Paganini, was a flashy player rather than a thoughtful one. He delighted American audiences during his five visits to the United States between 1843 and 1879. Somewhat less successful was his venture into real estate at Oleana, Pennsylvania, where he tried to found a Norwegian colony.

[7] Paul Julien was a young violinist who toured extensively.

[8] The sensational career of Adah Isaacs Menken (1835–68) had not reached its apex even at San Francisco. Poet (frustrated), linguist, actress (she played opposite Edwin Booth), four times married, this native of New Orleans was to become the intimate friend of such literati as Alexandre Dumas and Algernon Swinburne. In *Mazeppa*, a "Grand Equestrian Spectacle" based on Byron's poem about a Cossack chief, she appeared in pink tights, seemingly naked, lashed to the back of a spirited white steed that thundered up a spiral runway.

of complimenting me as from fear that I might use the agility of my fingers to his detriment. I would not be astonished if he had mentioned, on returning to his writing to his correspondents, that he had just received the visit of a celebrated robber of the United States.

One of these rich Chinese made his daughter come over. She was so beautiful that several Yankees, Europeans, and Celestials fell in love with her. The miserable father in his distress did not know what to do to secrete his treasure from the indiscreet regards of the enthusiasts. He closed his door on all visitors. But the type of Rosina in the *Barber of Seville* is the eternal type of amorous damsel. An admirer had some ability in his plan, and one night the house was besieged for the purpose of carrying off the beauty from her jealous father. The old Chinese and his servants barricaded themselves and defended themselves so well that they put the besiegers to flight. The event made such an impression on the honest merchant that he freighted a ship, and forty-eight hours later the beautiful Chinese set out again, sighing for the banks of the Yellow River—where probably she has married a fat, big-bellied mandarin to whom she does not care to speak about her adventure with the young barbarian.

I doubt if the old Chinese has a very flattering idea of our civilization.

I was introduced to Mr. de Cazotte, the French consul. He is the grandson of Cazotte of the revolution, one of the famous Illuminati.[9]

In a narrow street near Stockton Street we see two or three unfortunate creatures concealing their misery under paint and tinsel, and smiling at us with that horrible stereotyped smile of which ballet dancers and courtesans possess the secret.

Two days after my arrival a visiting card was brought me. "The gentleman is waiting for you downstairs," said the servant. I meet again here a young Frenchman, one of my friends, Parisian in mind and heart.

I have been introduced to one of the Crœsuses of San Fran-

---

[9] The Illuminati were members of a short-lived movement of republican free thought, founded in Germany in May 1776. It spread to other countries and attracted authors such as Goethe and Herder.

cisco, whose fortune, it is said, is incalculable. He came here as a Mormon missionary, but quickly perceived that there was more gold to be gained than proselytes to be made. The women were then in such an infinitesimal proportion to the male population that it would have been ridiculous to preach polygamy to those who were forced to be celibates.

He obtained a round sum, which he made use of; money brought then ten or fifteen per cent, and in a few years he had made many millions. He was in his office when I was admitted into his presence, and was amorously caressing the big toe of his right foot with the index finger and thumb of his left hand. "Gottschalk, Gottschalk!" he said to me, without letting go his big toe. "I know that name. Ain't you one of them opera singers? What do you sing, bass or tenor?"

He has, I am assured, renounced the doctrine of polygamy, but he drinks a great deal.

French commerce is represented here by many considerable houses. Contrary to that of other countries where the French play in the money market only a secondary part, they rank here among the first.

Accustomed to the female type of the United States, the foreigner is struck here with the small number of pretty women that he meets with in the streets. Truth forces me to say that the proportion of pretty faces and dresses is remarkably inferior to the Atlantic states. I have, it is true, met in society some charming young girls and married women, but they are rare exceptions.

The newspapers, the *Alta California*, the *Bulletin*, etc., are numerous, and generally are well edited as regards political matters; in matters of art they have too frequently encouraged the circus, *Mazeppa*, and the minstrels, to have true taste, and particularly to treat art and artists with the attention and respect they deserve. We have invited all the newspaper editors to a supper at our hotel, after having paid them a personal visit (which not one of them has returned). Of the twelve or fifteen invited, only two came, and they belonged to the same paper. From the others we have never received any excuse, any card, or anything else indicating that they had the least notion of the elementary laws of politeness. It is true that after my first concert they all gave me very flattering notices, but all I owe them is limited to that, or nearly so. Accustomed to the courtesy of the East, I have felt their indifference so much the more, as the number of pianists who have visited San Francisco gives them less right than the others to be blasé. There is yet too much, decidedly, of Zoyara and of Menken in the atmosphere. Let us not hastily conclude from this that the people here are uncouth. San Francisco is one of the most polished cities in the world, and infinitely more refined than many of those in the West. But a concert for them is a concert, that is to say, an amusement, dearer and less entertaining than other exhibitions, and from their point of view they are right. A dozen apples are worth more than a banana; there are more of them, and they do not cost so much. As for enthusiasm, Menken and company seem to be the only ones who can excite it here. Billy Burk, the minstrel, has left behind him here ineffaceable memories. Many ladies expressed in my presence the void that his departure has caused in the budget of amusements in San Francisco.[1]

Maguire's opera has begun the season with *Trovatore*. Putting aside the infatuation of small towns for everything that is new, the troupe is perfectly justified by its success.

We have announced a series of six concerts. The two opera companies, which are in full activity, will be a severe competition for us.[2] In any other country we would think little of it, but here, where, since Madame B—— (and what an opera), there has been no Italian company, they have all the attraction of novelty.

---

[1] Although Gottschalk's opinion of San Francisco's musical orientation was not very high, it should be noted here that Mendelssohn's *Calm Sea and Presperous Voyage* overture was performed in San Francisco in 1856, when it had as yet been heard in only three major American cities: Baltimore, Boston, and New York. Entitled on this occasion, *The Tranquillity of the Ocean and a Happy Voyage*, it was played by a friend of Mendelssohn, Rudolph Herold (1832–89), conducting the Germania Musical Society—not the same organization, however, as the valiant troupe by that name that arrived in 1848. H. Earle Johnson: "Some 'First Performances' in America," *Journal of the American Musicological Society*, Vol. V (fall 1952), pp. 235–43.

[2] They were definitely too much competition for The Philharmonic Society, which announced the postponement of its activities until the fall. Their third subscription concert was given on September 7, after the close of the opera season. It included works by Beethoven, Meyerbeer, Mozart, Mendelssohn, Schubert, and Weber, and was favorably reviewed by the *Daily Alta California*.

. . .

I was present at the performance of *Ernani* at the Metropolitan Theater. Morelli, the excellent baritone, played Charles V. He still has his fine voice, his intelligent conception of the part, and his good intonation. This last quality will suffice, to my notion, to secure him public admiration—as to sing false has today become a condition *sine qua non* of singers. The choruses, composed in great part of Germans and Italians, were quite satisfactory, as well as the orchestra.

I am not among those who admire Verdi to excess. Some of his operas, *Attila* for instance, seem to me in some parts unworthy of a great musician, but on listening to the quintet in the second act, the duo of the basso, the trio finale, and the finale, I cannot help recalling with bitterness the unskilled judgment which the whole European press, and all the simpletons who compose three-quarters of the public, gave twenty years ago. I was present at the first performance of *Ernani* at the Théâtre des Italiens in Paris. I was in the box of Madame Mennechet de Barival, a writer of merit, an eminent pianist, and the Egeria of Ambroise Thomas. "What detestable platitudes! What vulgarity! What noise! What vacuity!" re-echoed around me. Not one of the beauties of the opera was noticed, and all the little ballad composers fell upon him and tore him to pieces. I myself—who, thank God, have never found enough gall in my nature to make me rejoice at the fall of a confrère—I, myself, in good faith, found everything detestable. Nothing easier, I said to myself, than to make such operas. It has happened to me since to try to write an opera, and the day in which I sketched out a bad duo, I all at once perceived that Verdi possessed genius. I recommend this little exercise to *pianisticules* who deny talents to their confrères, who dare to compose; it cannot fail to be useful to their petty vanity.

◇◇◇◇◇◇◇◇◇

California, 1865

I needed a pianist. I had had executed on fourteen pianos the March from *Tannhäuser*, arranged by myself. Its success was so great that I had to announce another concert on fourteen pianos. On the eve of the concert one of my pianists fell sick. What was I to do? Put off the concert? Never! A warmed-up dinner is never worth anything. In the matter of concerts you must never put off. The public is flighty, capricious, pitiless. Learn to seize the hour when it is favorable to you; if you do not, it escapes you for no good reason.

Announce only thirteen pianos. Another error, still more dangerous. The public wants to hear fourteen pianos, and if you give it one less it will think itself robbed. It demands fourteen pianos in full view on the platform. Should you place some manikins on it, it will be satisfied, provided that it sees there the number of pianos announced. The difficulty was becoming insurmountable. San Francisco, although filled with all the corruption and with all the plagues arising from civilization, then possessed but thirteen first-class pianoforte players. The proprietor of the hall, seeing my predicament, offered to speak to his son, an amateur pianist, he said, of the first class, who played Thalberg, Liszt, and Gottschalk without difficulty, and for whom it would be only child's play to take the part that was wanted for the March from *Tannhäuser*. Experience has taught me for a long time that it is well for an artist to beware of the cooperation of amateurs in general, and especially of those who play everything at first sight, and make havoc in playing the pieces of Liszt and Thalberg. But the father spoke of him with such assurance that I accepted his son's assistance (God protect you, O artists, from the fathers of amateurs, from the sons themselves, and from the fathers of female singers!). The concert was to take place in the evening. I suggested that a rehearsal would be necessary. The son, who in the interval had been introduced to me, expressed surprise, and said it was unnecessary. The part was very easy; he played the fantasies of Liszt. I replied that it was less for the difficulty of execution than for playing together; and that, if he wished, I would play with him to point out to him the movements. He then placed himself at the piano, and like all amateurs, after having executed a noisy flourish, attacked with the boldness of innocence the piece of *Tannhäuser*. At the end of two bars, my mind was made up; I knew what I had to rely on, and I assure you that it was not pleasant. It is not that he played badly, if he played at all. The most complaisant ear would have hardly been able to distinguish any shreds of Wagner's theme floating here and there like waifs in the midst of an ocean of false notes, in a deafening storm of continuous pedal (the storm cannot be described), and of the complete wreck of the measure and spirit of the author; it was no longer to be thought of. My position became horrible. To refuse his assistance—the assistance of the first amateur in San Francisco! elegant and rich, who had probably caused to be circulated among all his friends and all the good society of the city that he deigned to give me the use of his talent! It was impossible! The rehearsal was short. I did not even make a remark; it would have been of as much use as making an Adonis of Aesop. The father, beaming with pride, was looking at me and, wiping his forehead after the piece, said: "Ah ha! What did I tell you!" The young man seemed convinced of his worth, and, with the ease that only amateurs possess when the public is in question, repeated to me many times, graciously smiling, with a satisfied little air, "Oh yes! I think that that does very well! *Besides, it is very easy!*" We parted. I thought seriously of putting off the concert, under the pretense of indisposition, when my tuner, a man of resources, said to me, "Sir, if this young man plays, trouble is inevitable with the other pianos; it is absolutely necessary to prevent his being heard, and the only way to do it is this"—and at the same moment, after manipulating a tool in the piano I had designated for the amateur, a vertical piano, he took out the interior mechanism, and, looking triumphantly at me, added, "The keyboard remains, but I assure you that there will be no more false notes." The method was excellent.

The evening came. The hall was full. My amateur, in white cravat and evening dress, was showing himself in the hall. His friends awaited the moment of his entrance with impatience. He requested me to give him a piano near the footlights in full view (for it must be stated that amateurs, who should be less familiar with the public, have an impassibility and *sang-froid* that we never acquire—again innocence).

I placed his dumb piano in the middle of the stage, close to the prompter.

Before going on the stage, I made my thirteen acolytes take notice, that, in order to produce the greatest effect, it was indispensable not to play any preludes, that thus the public might be more surprised on hearing all at once the fourteen pianos attack the flourish of trumpets with which the March from *Tannhäuser* commences.

One, two, three—we begin. It goes on marvelously. In the midst of the piece I looked at my amateur: he was superb; he was sweating great drops; he was throwing his eyes carelessly on the audience and performing with miraculous ease the passages apparently the most difficult. His friends were in raptures. They applauded to excess. Some enthusiasts even cried out, "Hurrah for ——!" (the amateur's name). "Encore!" "Encore!!" We must repeat the piece. But at the moment of beginning the amateur forgot my recommendation not to play an introduction, and could not resist the temptation to play a little chromatic scale. I see him now! The stupor that was printed on his countenance was inexpressible. He began his scale again. Nothing. The piano was mute. For an instant he had the idea that the ardor with which he had played had been fatal to the strings, but, throwing a glance inside, he saw them all right. "Without doubt it is the pedals," he thought, and, after pushing on the pedals, he began again his little chromatic scale. Then, persuaded that the piano was just out of order, he strove to make me understand that we could not begin the March again.

"Pst! pst!!" said he with a wild air, but I had seen the danger and without loss of time I had given the signal and the March was recommenced. My young man, to save appearances before the audience, made the pantomime of the passages, but his countenance, which I saw from below, was worth painting, it was a mixture of discouragement and of spite. The fury with which he struck the poor instrument, which could do nothing, was very funny.

"That was very well done, gentlemen," I said, on entering into the artists' room, "but the effect was less than the first time."

"The mischief!" said my amateur to me, "my piano broke down all at once."

The secret was kept a long time by my tuner, but it finally leaked out, or at least I had reason for supposing it did from the furious glance that my unfortunate amateur threw at me one day that I happened to greet him on meeting him in the street.

Moral—beware of amateurs.

I have been to Mass at the French church. The priest, from Auvergne, gave us a sermon that would have been only grotesque if it had not been the height of impropriety and absurdity in a temple consecrated to God.

The evidently limited intelligence of this unfortunate priest, placed at the service of a nasal and monotonous organ—like that of the children who repeat, without any inflexion of their voice and without punctuation, lessons they do not understand—had suggested to him a digression on the dogma of the Blessed Virgin, a propos of the month of Mary. After some commonplaces, drawn from the children's catechism, this is nearly the luminous theory he expressed. He wore spectacles and had a nervous tick, every time the flow of his ideas threatened to be exhausted (and this happened every two or three words), of carrying with a convulsive movement his hand to his nose, to be certain that his spectacles were firmly fixed, then he coughed and continued:

"Mes chera freras. Elu Vierge il a été achoinsie a parce qu'il une bonne femme. Ac 'telle qu'alle a élevé à l'enfant Jesus. Veres savez tous combien les mères ont de mal pour éléver leurs enfants. C'est elle qu'a pris soin du sien que elle a nourri. Il lui doit tout à sa mère et alle a pris sur lui le droit de lui demander ses faveurs. Aussi après il a toujours fait tout pour lui être agréable. Aussi, ames chera freras voustre meilleure recommendation est de vous addresser à la Vierge Marie."

The peroration of the sermon is too original for me not to favor you with it.

"Il y a pas beaucoup de monde ici à cette église, ma il y a des paroisses qui ont plus de familles que la paroisse de San Francisco et puis alles ont leurs occupations, et puis beaucoup de ces familles qui en ont sont obligées de rester à la maison pour en prendre soin."

This rigmarole worked on my nerves. It is unworthy of the Catholic religion to permit such indecencies. And I admit that the Protestants would have found fault if they understood French. Fortunately the number of reverends who speak this language, which so much infidel literature has sullied, is in the inverse ratio of their hatred for the doctrines of free thought.

[The presence of Gottschalk in San Francisco was announced by the Daily Alta California on May 5, 1865, which also alluded to his enjoying "a very favorable reputation as a littérateur, from his contributions to the Atlantic Monthly." The next squib, two days later, had a more pragmatic approach, referring to his 95,000 miles of railroad travel, his 1100 concerts, and "the popularity of his compositions 'The Banjo', 'Marche de Nuit', 'Last Hope', 'Cradle Song' . . . said to have yielded to their happy publishers over $250,000 in less than ten years."

From May 10 to 29 there was scarcely a day when the pianist and his operatic confrères did not appear in concert. There were six subscription concerts and several "Grand Gala Matinées." "NEW PROGRAM EVERY EVENING, MUSICAL SENSATION OF THE SEASON," the advertisements screamed as the musicians sought to increase attendance. The concert on May 15, which included The Union, Gottschalk's usual bows to the violin sonatas of Beethoven and Mozart, and a new waltz for piano and voice, composed by Gottschalk for the occasion, was reviewed favorably. On May 18 they performed in Oakland.

Attendance, one gathers, still was not large, but reviews ever more favorable. On May 22, modestly but unmistakably, Gottschalk began to resort to the multiple-piano idea. Together with a local pianist, Gustave Scott, he played the duet from Il Trovatore, in emulation, the press said, of his feat with Thalberg. Four colleagues of Mr. Scott then caught the contagion. By May 24 and 27 six pianists were playing the marches from Faust and Tannhäuser.

On May 25 Gottschalk played at San Jose.

"Gottschalk's 'farewell performance' on Saturday afternoon attracted a very large gathering, nearly all of them present being ladies." The troupe then proceeded to Sacramento, first stop on their tour of "the interior."]

◇◇◇◇◇◇◇◇◇

Virginia City, Territory of Nevada, June 4, 1865
We have arrived at last. The clerk, an impudently pompous genius, extended on his chair behind the desk, his feet as high as his head, after having made us feel by his peremptory tone the incommensurable distance that separates poor travelers from a hotel clerk, grants us permission to install ourselves at the rate of thirty-five dollars per day in a chamber of six feet square. I timidly ask

if there is not a larger one, but he answers me angrily, "No!" in such a way as to make me understand that I must not abuse his patience, under pain of being driven out of the little hole he has been willing to give me. Fortunately, there is attached to the hotel a restaurant kept by a Frenchman, who with all the simplicity of his nation tells me his troubles—always the same—of shares taken in the mines which ought to pay immense dividends and which ruin all who have them.

The town is ugly—built of wood on rough ground. The streets are steep and irregular. The cafés are numerous. The music store is a shoemaker's shop, two-thirds of which is filled with boots and the rest with drawers and loose sheets of music, which would seem to prove that the population walks more over the rugged soil of the town than on the road florid with art. It is not, really, a town. It has rather the appearance of one of those European fairs which once a year attract merchants and purchasers from the four points of the horizon for two months. The dust blinds when it does not choke you, and vice versa, and both at once. Shut up in the midst of steep mountains, the sight perceives as far as it can extend only the gray tints of the arid soil, or the somber masses of sage, the only vegetable that grows. It is meager, sad, mean, and monotonous. I have never really known spleen save in Virginia City. It is the most inhospitable and the saddest town I have ever visited. I have spent eleven days here, during which I have given three concerts. I have not received from the inhabitants one invitation, not one visit, nor any mark of distinction. Fortunately I found here a family from New Orleans, whom the vicissitudes of fortune have temporarily banished here, and a young Louisianian who, by their interest, sometimes contributed to dissipate the ennui of my isolation.

Sunday, sitting in my room, the window opening on my terrace, I was enjoying the only advantage that Virginia City possesses, a pure sky. Whiz, splash, whiff, whew—good God! What does this mean? I was almost inundated and upset by a column of water that continued to invade my room. "That is nothing," said a servant to me, "they are only the firemen who are exercising and amusing themselves."

Every morning I go out with the firm intention of comforting my conscience by letting the truth be known—which, like steam too long compressed, chokes me—that Virginia City is the saddest, the most wearisome, the most inhospitable place on the globe; but the first person that I meet asks me the same question that is put invariably to every stranger who arrives, by every inhabitant of Virginia City who speaks to him: "Well, sir, *how do you find our place?*" and on the countenance of your interlocutor you read so legibly that he expects you to find it with him the gayest, the most beautiful, the richest, and most polished in this part of the world, that you do not feel you have the courage to destroy his illusions and the happiness they cause him. You drive back the compressed vapor of your discontent and answer him with a doubtful "hem!" which he naturally translates as acquiescing in what he thinks, and he adds with an air of satisfied pride, "You bet it is!"

I have been ill for three days. Without exception, nobody, save the doctor and the Louisianians, of whom I have already spoken, inquired after me. When I asked for warm water at eight o'clock in the evening, the pompous clerk refused me. The Frenchman has fortunately the kindness to get some from the French restaurant keeper in the neighborhood.

I begin to suspect that those French infidels so corrupted, and whose literature is so immoral (*vide* Voltaire and Rousseau), are less ignorant than some have supposed of those small virtues, such as charity, generosity, and kindness.

◇◇◇◇◇◇◇◇◇

June 9

I leave for Dayton in the stage. The heat is excessive; fortunately the distance is only six miles. We have four strong horses, in one hour we shall be there. But I reckon without the driver. He passes through the principal street of Virginia City and takes up two other passengers; we are three outside and nine inside. The stage can only comfortably contain eight. We stop before the butcher's, who gives us a basket of meat. "Good day, Joe, very warm today; will you hand this basket of meat to someone near Silver City?" Hua! hia! we set out again. "Joe, my wife wants to go there too. Have you any room?" "Any room? Yes, there is." She gets up. The sun bakes me, the dust blinds me, I begin to lose patience.

"Driver, when will you leave?" "What, mister, are you in such a
hurry?" (This is said with a certain emphasis, suggesting the *idea*
that he is not in a hurry.) Hardly started again, we hear "Driver,
I want to go to Gold Mill." "Climb up, there is room"—a new
passenger gets inside. After a while we find ourselves in the suburbs
of Virginia City. We have added to our load three baskets, a roll
of wallpaper, and a trunk, which is between my legs! A fat man
who is sitting on the hood above me puts, with imperturbable cool-
ness, his boots upon my shoulder; two fat, red-faced women,
flanked with capes, with parasols, under pretence of being timid,
allow Joe to gallantly hoist them in the midst of the other unfortunate passengers inside, where they succeed in depositing their
corpulent bodies. "Cling, clang," we are rolling along. My neighbor to the right speaking to Joe:

"Those people we took up at the International, are they not
a part of the traveling company at a dollar and a half a ticket?"

"Yes," answered Joe. "Ah! Tell me about Billy, he is worth one
dollar and a half; he was dead drunk every night, but a charming
fellow." Thereupon he turned around to notice the admiration
that what he had just said produced.

"Stop, driver, I am going to Dayton!"

"There is room, climb up."

My neighbor above me draws back to make room for the
new passenger, and thrusts his two boots on my right shoulder.
This furnishes an opportunity to the latter to place his upon my
other shoulder, and here I am between the two. We arrive at
the tollgate. I am as red as a lobster, my nose peels. The dust
blinds me. The sweat I wipe off from my face would serve for
mortar. Our driver peaceably continues his journey, taking up
many passengers with his imperturbable "Plenty of room." At the
tollgate I get rid of the trunk between my legs. Between the basket,
which raises my feet several inches above the floor, and the boots
of my companions above me, which make me bend my back, I
had the appearance of one of those Chinese grotesque figures
that ornament what-nots—squatting down, the chin at the top of
the knees. After two hours of suffering we arrived at Dayton. Dayton has but one street, or rather has none, seeing that the town
is confined, or nearly so, to about one hundred houses, which line
the road.

◇◇◇◇◇◇◇◇◇◇

Dayton, Nevada, June 9
A small village, seven miles from Virginia City. Sitting before the door of the inn, I am tranquilly smoking my cigar, awaiting the hour for my concert. All at once I hear at some distance the noise of a large drum. "What is that?" to the landlord. "Why," says he, looking at me, "isn't your concert for tonight? Well, now, they are drumming to call the crowd." A ragamuffin rushed through the street ringing a bell from door to door "to call the crowd," but the finest part of the affair is that for ten minutes the drums and the big drum are quiet. At the moment of making my way toward the theater I am surrounded by two drums, the ringer of the bell, and the big drum, who have come for a "run up to the show." I contrive to escape, and fly like a hare from fear of these cursed drums.

The hall of the theater is lighted (?) by three or four smoking Argand lamps. The stage is so dark that our concert has rather the look of an exhibition of the stereopticon. Our audience consists of a few females, ten or twelve boys, including therein the two drums, the bass drum, and the bell. The rest are miners in large flannel shirts, with pantaloons turned up over their large boots. Their large Californian hats are of gray felt with broad rims. Do not hasten to conclude from this that they were unruly. They listened attentively, and their decent and tranquil manner would cause shame to many audiences that pretend to the refinements of civilization. It is not, besides, the first time that I have had the opportunity of noting this in a Californian audience. Their pretended rudeness, which I have so often heard spoken of, goes back to the primitive times of the miner-colonists. They are now much more refined, better educated than the Far West. I repeat it, I have rarely seen a more peaceful population. It is true that I make my programs as simple as possible. It would be as absurd to play for them pieces very difficult to understand, or classical music, as to give beefsteaks to a newly born infant. They have never heard the piano, and of all instruments it is the most difficult to render comprehensible to an audience who have almost or never heard music. Every instrument that from its nature embraces multiple combinations of sounds, is obscure to an ear that is not accustomed to it. Scarcely is the concert ended when a young girl out of the audience mounts the platform and quietly turns out the only Argand that gave light, whether poorly or well, to this part of the performance. I suppose she is the daughter of the proprietor, and I would wager that she will be a precious acquisition to the husband who shall marry her. At ten o'clock at night we get into the stage again to return to Virginia City. This time I am sitting alone near the driver. The weather is superb. The moonlight is splendid. The sky above our heads is of a somber blue in which, like detached diamonds, the stars shine out. On the horizon the mountains, bathed in transparent vapors, give to the landscape the appearance of a fairy scene.

The mountains are brought so near that, seen from the height where we are, through this blue vapor, they seem to be the waves of an ocean that, by a magical effect, have become petrified in the midst of a storm. The breeze, which blows softly, brings to us the thousand distant sounds from the deep valleys and high peaks. A bird concealed at the bottom of the precipice makes its monotonous song heard, composed of three notes, which it repeats without interruption.

At the turn of the road we perceive at the top of the mountain, along the sides of which our road winds, an Indian. My driver, it appears, has lived a long time among them. They are, said he, very peaceful and less lazy than the majority of their race. They go to Virginia City every day, and are employed in carrying water, burdens, etc. It must be said that they have no stable occupations. The Indian only lives from day to day and would never be able to accustom himself to any permanent work. Their wives are very chaste. She who is unfaithful is condemned by the tribe and put to death. Last year the people of Gold Hill went to gather, at the proper season, pine cones in the woods of the neighboring mountain. A young Indian woman and one of the young men of Gold Hill met. They loved each other. Some time later the two lovers were surprised by an Indian of the tribe coming out of the tunnel of the Ophir Mine. He showed no resentment, and even accepted some money that the young man offered him to secure his silence. The next day the body of the poor Indian girl was found in the tunnel of the Ophir Mine.

◇◇◇◇◇◇◇◇◇◇

June 13, 1865

Left Virginia City at three o'clock. Having timidly asked at the stage office why he took fifteen dollars from me, the clerk answered me, looking angrily (probably because I had spoken politely to him), that he had no reason to give. But if I still must know more? "I tell you that you must pay fifteen dollars, and that ends it; and if you are not satisfied, I will make you pay sixty dollars. Are you satisfied? God damn you!" Amiable people! Yes, I am satisfied that my last impression of Virginia City is such that my joy at leaving it can still be increased, which at first sight did not appear to me possible. For the same reason that the Turks in the greatest heats take steam baths for the purpose of finding the atmosphere afterward comparatively cool, it is necessary to visit Virginia City for the purpose of later finding those places tolerable where otherwise you would be killed with ennui.

For some miles the landscape presents its dull and sickly appearance. The vegetation continues to be mean, but soon the grass begins; a river—the Turkey, I believe—rolls its turbulent waters over a rocky bottom. The trees are numerous. We pass through a forest of pines. The landscape becomes charming. The mountains are again covered with forests. The gray tints are replaced with green verdure. The moon rises and adds to the beauty of the scene. We are nine inside, of whom one is a lady. Feeling sick, I asked a man who occupied a corner if he would change places with me for a moment, as I was suffering (I never could ride backward). He refuses me with the most cruel *sang-froid.* O Christianity! When will thy spirit be implanted in these gross natures? Politeness is a virtue that approaches charity, on more than one side, and, so long as our fellow-countrymen shall affect to despise politeness, they will be savages and not Christians.

"I bet you it is the place to get a good dinner. Virginia [City] is the place, you bet. There ain't a place in the world"—nothing short of the world would do—"you bet, where you can live better than in Virginia." This is from my neighbor, who gives vent to his feelings, having had a bad supper at the previous station.

The night, a dreadful night, fortunately compensated for by

glimpses of a magnificent nature, which the moon lighted up, passed slowly.

The lady at the back complains that her neighbor in the middle crowds her too much, or that the one opposite treads upon her feet; all the awkwardness that I have met with scarcely ever takes place in stages but during the night.

The first rays of day at last illuminate our faces—dirty, covered with dust, our eyes swollen from want of sleep, etc. We arrive at Dutch Flat, a pretty little village, concealed at the bottom of a wooded gorge like a nest in a bush. The neat white houses are covered with magnificent rosebushes whose flowers cover the trellises as high as the roofs. They are small frame houses, very neat, very small, etc.

Concert this evening. Almost one hundred seventy persons. Audience very quiet—very quiet because they do not applaud. It is true that they did not otherwise show their discontent. I very much suspect that they regretted their dollar and a half. "Taken in," said one of them sometime later, and added, to console himself, "It is true that it is only once." It will be the givers of concerts after me who will feel their resentment. I still cannot help remarking the propriety of conduct of these audiences who, however wearisome our music must appear to them, submit to it without protest.

It often occurs to me when playing to look at my audience. There are certain passages where I am so accustomed to see their countenances brighten up that in civilized audiences I am wont to consider it an indissoluble thing like cause and effect. For example, the close of *Murmures éoliens* or even *Last Hope*, or the end of *Ojos criollos*. Here I perceive that it is exactly as if I was speaking Chinese; they hardly understand it, and inquisitively regard me exerting myself with that curious and vacant air which other ignoramuses, for instance, cast upon the hands of a telegraph operator. How many things there are to learn, we often cry out! Come here, and in seeing these audiences, you will see how many things it is possible to be ignorant of.

In order to give you an idea of the artistic ignorance here, it will suffice to copy an account that has appeared today. "Last evening the opera hall was filled to overflowing (there were dances, comedies, etc.). X. was received with thunders of applause, but he is past master in his art. His imitations upon the violin of birds, quadrupeds, are inimitable. His music is what can be felt and understood without any need of being a musician (a blow at me). Everybody understood it." And here is the measure of the tastes of Nevada. O ignorance, when will you cease to be pretentious and insolent!

I have been sick for three days. I cannot recollect in fifteen years of travels and vicissitudes having passed eleven days so sadly as here. I defy your finding in the whole of Europe a village where an artist of reputation would find himself as isolated as I have been here. If in place of playing the piano, of having composed two or three hundred pieces, of having given seven or eight thousand concerts, of having given to the poor one hundred or one hundred and fifty thousand dollars, of having been knighted twice, I had sold successfully for ten years quarters of salted hog, or had made a great fortune by selling dear what I had bought cheap, my poor isolated chamber would have been invaded by adorers and admirers. Decidedly the country of money is not the one of artists. *"Muse, étendez vos ailes et fuyez au plus vite."*

◇◇◇◇◇◇◇◇◇

June 16, 1865

Left Dutch Flat by stage at five o'clock in the morning. Nevada City is thirty miles away, and we shall be there at half-past eleven o'clock. The countryside is charming, less mountainous; it permits the sight to extend over green prairies, which gently undulate and are lost in the pine forests that cover the sides of the distant mountains. At nine o'clock we are in Grass Valley, a veritable garden; laughing, spruce, flowery, coquettish, it has under the morning sun that gilds it the appearance of bidding me welcome. Adieu to my spleen! I have forgotten Virginia City and its villainous mountains, bald and grim, which make grimaces at you perpetually as if they wanted to reproach you for the incessant overturnings to which the cupidity of men condemns them. Here the roses climb to the roof tops, the trees are gigantic, the brooks gayly roll their crystal waters, wantoning amid the rocks in their way. No more briers, but trees and flowers; no more of bald leprous hilltops, but verdure and finally life. I breathe, I live again.

Grass Valley is charming. The streets are carefully planked; this gives them the appearance of a floor. The hotel is excellent.

The journalist comes to pay me a visit. We set out again at eleven o'clock for Nevada City, which is only four miles from Grass Valley. The valleys become larger. The view is magnificent. The trees are gigantic. At a turn of the road we see all at once below us a large valley, a pasture, a garden in the midst of which little houses are at first scattered, afterward they are grouped together, and finally form a village—it is Nevada City. The streets are also planked as well as the pavements, and they are so united and so clean that one might think one was driving over a floor. There are several fine, spacious hotels, furnished with luxury. Large billiard halls are attached to them.

Concert at Temperance Hall. One hundred fifty persons who listen with infinite attention. I would not dare to say that they listened with pleasure, but at least they behaved themselves decently. There is decidedly an improvement in tonight's audience. All are well dressed. Some females have hats. Temperance Hall backs on a steep hill, covered with verdure, on the top of which is hung a charming cottage of Chinese architecture, painted pink, white, and green.

◇◇◇◇◇◇◇◇◇

Nevada City, June 17, 1865

I have already given twelve concerts in San Francisco, made a tour to Sacramento, Placerville, Carson City, Dayton, Gold Hill, Virginia City, and Dutch Flat. I shall not try to give you an idea of the fatigue of these travels. Those who are unacquainted with this country could never conceive what the roads are in the mountains, and the dangers of all kinds accompanying the route from San Francisco to Nevada. Let it suffice to say that I remained in the stage from Placerville to Carson City for twenty hours. Also that I was sick for three days afterward.

California is a humbug. The climate is certainly splendid; the mineral and natural richness of the soil are inexhaustible. The *finest fruits and vegetables* in the world are found here. But what is all this to a man who owns no mines, to know that they produce abundantly (is this always true)? If, like myself, he eats but little, and is not an epicure, what does it matter to him that the most splendid salmon in the world and the most magnificent strawberries are found here? Are the mines, the salmon, the strawberries, etc., a compensation for the thousand and one things wanting, which are discovered at every moment, at every step in the so-called civilization of the Golden City? The women are not pretty, and they dress as if the whole stock of the secondhand clothing shops of Paris had been sent to California.

◇◇◇◇◇◇◇◇◇

San Francisco, July 19, 1865
I have begun a second series of concerts here, which so far has been very successful.

[*He was not exaggerating:*

Gottschalk's matinée, Saturday, was a great success. Each and every time we hear our American genius, the more apparent his great merits appear. There is a delicacy even in his force, and a poetry in improvisation at his command, which no other artiste, to our knowledge, has ever evinced. His trill is bird-like, and his fancy so pure and dreamy that he invariably enlists the whole feelings of his auditory. The vocal portion of the programme was well rendered.
(Daily Alta California, July 17, 1865.)

And only three days before, this paper had reported that, when the operatic portion of the program had to be canceled for lack of preparation, "the audience, who expected to hear the opera, declined to stay for the concert, Mr. Gottschalk consenting at a late hour to 'fill the bill' "!

His popularity in San Francisco now increased perceptibly. He was presented with two large California rugs bearing his name; ". . . the superb overture of Oberon of Weber, for two pianos . . . was rapturously encored at the last concert." Emboldened, he announced "a grand matinée d'instruction" for Saturday, July 28:

This matinée, which the management announces as a 'Piano Forte Recital,' is more especially intended for the benefit of piano students. Such recitals are all the rage in Europe at the present time, and in Paris and New York Mr. Gottschalk has made himself and his music popular through them. He will on Saturday perform ten pieces, some of which are entirely new to our concert goers. We expect to see on such an occasion a crowded house.

The matinée was postponed because of "two injured fingers," then evidently canceled. At Petaluma the audience listened "as though they were a Paris or London public." Next: "Louis Moreau Gottschalk will give TWO GRAND MONSTER CONCERTS and Musical Festivals with TEN PIANOS!" And it was "the greatest musical success of the inimitable artiste's career in California," assisted among others by a "young lady amateur vocalist, Miss Jenny Landesman, daughter of one of our most respected Hebrew merchants." He was taken to task, however, on August 21, for changing to extended arpeggios the little broken chords of Mendelssohn's Spring Song.

At the request of prominent citizens, who affixed their names to the public plea, Gottschalk gave a benefit for himself on September 8. His hard-won success was becoming more secure with each concert. Finally, this announcement appeared in the Daily Alta California, September 16, 1865:

> PIANOFORTE NOVELTY—Gottschalk, who seems to be indefatigable, is composing a piece for THIRTY pianos with orchestra accompaniment. Such an undertaking is truly gigantic, and we hope the eminent pianist will find time and courage to carry through his idea, which is, we understand, to give, as a final farewell to California, a grand festival with all the combined musical forces of the city under his leadership.

And so it would have been. But fate willed otherwise.]

◇◇◇◇◇◇◇◇◇

August 15, 1865

I have left on board the steamer *Julia*, to go to Stockton. After having crossed the bay, we get into a kind of bayou that narrows the passage so that the sides of the boat graze the banks; this tongue of the sea pierces the land as far as Stockton, ninety miles from San Francisco. We arrived at two o'clock in the morning, but I slept until eight, and did not go onshore until nine. Put up at the Weber Hotel. Do not suppose that it refers to the musician, but rather to a German colonist to whom almost the whole town belongs and who possesses a fortune of many millions.

The town, or rather the village, resembles Sacramento on a very small scale: several churches, pretty little cottages concealed, like nests, behind the thick foliage of the large trees.

Concert small, in a mean hall, without platform. Receipts one hundred twenty-eight dollars. The expenses amount to more than the receipts. I have been introduced to Judge Underhill, a charming man, who is an amateur of music and plays the organ in the Presbyterian Church of his friend the pastor Happersett. The latter is a charming, jovial, agreeable old man whose frank laughter indicates a tranquil conscience and the absence of gall. Amiable man! The organ of his little church is charming. His room is on a level with the organ loft, and its recess communicates directly with the pulpit. At the time I paid him a visit I found him writing his sermon for the next Sunday. Large, round, and legible writing, clear and firm, like the good man's character.

The most magnificent fruits ripen here, peaches, figs, grapes, etc.

A small newspaper gives an account of my concert. It has discovered that I trill with the thumb and the fourth finger, and thence concludes that I do not know how to play the piano and that I am a charlatan incapable of playing Beethoven. The same nonsense still!

I have visited the insane asylum; been introduced to a German baron, a very distinguished man, a captain in the Prussian Army, a civil engineer of the greatest worth. He possesses great intelligence, but he is insane and imagines that a band of jealous persons has been organized to follow him day and night, and to ridicule him.

Colfax, the Speaker of the House of Representatives in Washington, is here. He spoke last night to an immense crowd. The placard of the meeting announcing Colfax and that for my concert are next each other. A fat farmer who evidently understood no more about politics than he did about music, mixing the two names into one, inquired, "Who is this Goldax?"

Dined at the Lafayette Restaurant, kept by a Frenchman, and have eaten there, which would have been impossible for me to do at the Weber Hotel.

My second concert has not been much more fruitful than my first. The baron (of the insane asylum) was there, and congratulated me on my great talent. An amateur of the town played a

solo on the flute one tone lower than the piano. The teacher of
the piano is an old German player of the trombone, who, not
being able to play the piano, hums the air to his students. One of
the last pieces given by him for them to practice is *Moïse de
Thalberg*.[3]

I was presented on my saint day with a superb medal. All the
details of the presentation will be found in the following notice:
"For two days the wondering crowd has stopped at the window
of Mr. Tucker, the jeweller, in Montgomery Street, to admire the
beautiful medal presented to Gottschalk on the day of St. Louis,
his fête-day, by his friends of San Francisco, in testimony of their
appreciation of his talent and of their esteem for his personal
qualities. It is to Mr. F. L. A. Pioche, whose well-known liberality
is equalled only by his love for the arts and the protection which
he gives them, that appertains, we are assured, the initiative of this
magnificent offering of respect rendered to a great artist and to an
amiable man, by the élite of the Bank and of the great merchants
of San Francisco. The subscription-list, having at the head the
names of Mr. Pioche and of our worthy and respected consul, Mr.
de Cazotte, was covered in a few hours with forty signatures. Mr.
Mezzara, the eminent sculptor, offered, with the zeal of an artist
whose heart is always ready to associate him with noble thoughts,
to design the model for the medal which Mr. Tucker was called
upon to execute. It was on the 5th of August that the model of Mr.
Mezzara was sent to him, and, although there were only twenty
days for him to accomplish the difficult and delicate task which he
was called on to perform, he has succeeded in making a *chef-
d'œuvre* of jewelry which is certainly unique in America, and which
could not be surpassed in elegance, in delicacy, and in magnificence
in the ateliers of Froment Meurice himself.

"The presentation of the medal took place at the dinner which
the forty subscribers gave, on the 25th August, to Gottschalk. The
menu of the banquet, whose bill of fare must easily have made
the ghosts of Vatel, Carême, and Brillat Savarin leap for joy, was
a marvel of gastronomic research and of culinary chemistry. At the
moment of taking their seats at the table, Mr. Pioche, after a
few well-chosen words, handed to Gottschalk, in the name of all
of them, the casket of red velvet containing the medal. Mr. de
Cazotte, Messrs. Badger, Pioche, Pringle, Caselli, Richard, and

---

[3] Thalberg's Fantaisie on Rossini's opera *Moïse*.

Scott made several speeches à *propos* of the occasion, to which
Gottschalk replied with the modesty and tact which characterize
him.

"The medal is of gold. It is nine inches in circumference. The
principal face is formed of six plates of auriferous quartz of different
colours artistically arranged, on which are fixed the initials L. M.
G. in diamonds, surrounded with a crown of laurels in diamonds
and rubies. The knot of the crown is fastened by a magnificent
solitaire. The reverse of the medal bears the arms of California in
relief, surrounded by a circle of diamonds. Below are these words:
'To Gottschalk: a token from his Californian friends. 25 Aug.
1865.' The attachment of the medal is made of a large ring set
with diamonds, in the midst of which is a lyre also with diamonds.

"The intrinsic value of this jewel, which has cost, we are told,
more than two thousand dollars, is still surpassed by its artistic
merit. It would be impossible, without seeing it, to form an idea
of the delicacy of the work, of its marvelous finish, and of the exquisite taste of this little *chef-d'œuvre*. Let us felicitate Mr. Mezzara on the originality which he has shown in the conception of its
design, and Mr. Tucker on the fidelity with which he has executed
it. Let us congratulate Gottschalk for having been able by his
private qualities and his talent to make friends who know how to
prove in such a significant manner their esteem for him.

"This present is worthy of a monarch, and it appertained to the
Queen City of the Pacific to present to the first musician of America a testimony which was at the same time worthy of the artist
and in harmony with the magnificent generosity and the marvelous
development of the modern El Dorado."

~~~~~~~~

[From "El Dorado" to "purgatory," from victory to defeat,
from honor to disgrace—how else relate the turn of events between the foregoing and the following? At one moment he is
fêted and presented with a jeweled gold medal; next he is south-
bound off Costa Rica, expressing relief that seasickness, keeping
him in his cabin, had at least spared him the scorn of other
passengers. What had happened?

On Sunday afternoon, September 10, Gottschalk and an acquaintance took a carriage drive with two young ladies, students at
the Oakland Female Seminary. The girls were apprehended returning to the college at a rather late hour. It is generally believed that

a version of the story reached the local press by way of an enemy of both Gottschalk and the Chickering representative. A sample of subsequent newspaper comment can be found in The Daily American Flag, September 18, under the headline: "Villians [sic] Who Should Suffer Death." The story vilified "a certain vagabond musician, together with a confederate," etc., in East Lynne prose recommending "tar and feathers" and "horsewhipping" for "bawdy miscreants who should be shot like rabid dogs."

It is very probable that Gottschalk had intended proceeding to South America anyway, but certainly not under such circumstances—boarding the Colorado clandestinely like a hunted criminal.

The slander and persecution of Gottschalk spread eastward throughout the country. Friends came to his defense, notably in Watson's Weekly Art Journal, November 11 and 25. They urged him to defend himself. His answer:

> It is beneath my dignity as a man of honor to notice such slanders. Surely my friends can never credit them, and if believed by those who are not my friends, I only pray kind Heaven give them better minds. A man whose nature allowed him to commit so dishonorable an act could also lie, and disown it! Let the story of my whole life be told, every act scrutinized; and if you can find in it anything to prove me capable of such unmanly conduct, cast me from your regard, blot my name forever from your memory.[4]

After ten days in Panama he spent his last four years skirting much of the outer rim of South America—six months in Peru, one year in Chile, two years in Argentina and Uruguay, seven and a half months in Brazil. Triumph piled on triumph. By 1869, Strakosch was clamoring for his return to the United States. He was also being invited to found a National Conservatory of Music at New York and be its permanent director. But the San Francisco episode was bound to leave its mark on a sensitive artist. The hurt never left him.

Gottschalk, it seems, was always to be plagued with an overabundance of women and pianos.]

---

[4] Hensel: op. cit., p. 162.

Mexico, Panama, South America

1865–68

On Board the Colorado, *September 30, 1865*

I N SIGHT of the coast of Costa Rica.

Purgatory is not what foolish people think it is. I know by experience that it consists for the moment in going at the rate of fourteen knots an hour under a sun that would melt a copper mine, and I am almost sure of going ashore if we arrive at any part of the Elysian Fields. I think that I have sinned in my life, but the sum of all my misdeeds has been cruelly expiated in the first three days of my sojourn on the *Colorado*, during which I have first been purged by the most unmerciful seasickness, which has had at least this good effect—that it has forced me to stay in bed and does not expose me to the remarks of my traveling companions.

I left San Francisco on the eighteenth. The heat in the cabin is suffocating. I go on deck. The moon illuminates with a bluish and transparent light the shore of Costa Rica. The effect of this scene—whose indecisive lines are lost on the horizon in the large, brilliant clouds, the phosphorescence of the sea in these tropical latitudes, where it seems to roll in waves of living silver, and the transparency of the atmosphere—recalls to me the scenes of the theater, where behind a veil of silver gauze is displayed, amid the bluish light of the Bengal fires, the splendor of the enchanted palace of the final apotheosis. The light of the moon is such that I can easily read a volume of Alphonse Karr, which I bought at San Francisco.

The passengers between decks are lying pell-mell on the poop and snoring to see who can do best. Several families of French immigrants form a kind of encampment by themselves. The mothers, the children, and the young girls sleep next to each other, and the brothers and husbands form the frontier. One of my cabin companions, driven, like myself, on deck by the heat, gives me the following details about the Sandwich Islands, where he dwelled for a long time and has lately left.

The details interest me so much the more as King Kamehameha V gave me an invitation to visit his court. The islands of Hawaii, which form the kingdom of the Sandwich Islands, are six in number. They were discovered by Mendoza,[1] but it is generally thought that Captain Cook discovered them. The latter was killed there in a quarrel that arose between his sailors and the natives. Kamehameha I was the Napoleon of Hawaii; chief of a district, he caused himself, by his valor, to be recognized as king of all the islands. Later he armed a brig that he had kept when Vancouver made his voyage of discovery, and with the assistance of two English sailors, John Young and Davis, who had deserted and become his ministers, he conquered all the other islands of the archipelago. The last battle he was engaged in, in which his victory was decisive and gained him the sovereignty, took place in the valley of Nonhouhanon (Cold Valley). Many thousands of the hostile Kanaks, on seeing themselves conquered, rather than yield, threw them-

---

[1] Rather than Mendoza, the name more frequently encountered in this connection is that of Juan de Gaetano. The whole account about Hawaii is less an attempt to record history than an effort to divert a troubled mind.

selves in a body from an immense precipice formed by a huge rock that rises more than three thousand feet above Cold Valley.

Kamehameha was a man of genius. He preached European civilization. Assisted by the two sailors, he applied himself to civilize and polish his people. The Kanaks are mild and hospitable. Their instincts are poetic, and they possess a simplicity and candor almost infantile. The Kanak religion was fetishism. They believed in superior spirits. All their idols were symbolical. They had a singular custom, the taboo.

Kamehameha in his sphere was one of the great spirits of humanity. His height was gigantic, being six and a half feet. The prestige that surrounded him was marvelous. The Europeans themselves felt it, so irresistible is the force of genius. He lived at the beginning of this century.

Polygamy existed, and the chiefs and kings had, most frequently, their sisters and daughters for wives. In every district where the king stopped in traveling, all the women, single and married, rushed to him with the offer to partake of his royal couch. In every chief's family there was one of the daughters who was devoted to the office of learning their traditions for the purpose of perpetuating them.

Queen Kalama, widow of Kamehameha III, has been the one who was best acquainted with the traditions of the country. In this country it is only the mother who ennobles. So far is this carried that if the king himself married a woman of an inferior condition to his own, her children would be strangled in the cradle. It is thus that Queen Kalama, who was not of illustrious birth, saw all the fruits of her union with Kamehameha III perish. This respect for nobility through the female is such that Prince William, son of a chief who does not possess great nobility, but who married the granddaughter of Kamehameha III, considers himself nobler than the actual king, who descends from K. only by the male line. Besides, the father of Prince William behaves with great humility before his son, and shows him all possible respect on account of the great nobility of his wife. In the time of Cook the population was at least three hundred thousand souls. In 1856 the census gave eighty-eight thousand Kanaks and two thousand whites. The Kanak type approaches that of all the other inhabitants of Oceania. Long, glossy black hair; complexion copper-colored, thick lips. The proportions of their bodies attain a perfection that recalls the most celebrated types of antique statuary.

Honolulu, on the island of Oahu, is the capital of the kingdom, and the residence of the court. It has an admirably sheltered port that can hold two hundred fifty vessels. The town is built at the foot of an extinct volcano, of which there are twenty on the island. On the island of Hawaii are found the greatest volcanoes in the world. In 1856–57 no fewer than ninety craters were in a state of activity. A peculiarity: when these volcanoes are in eruption, Vesuvius is also in eruption. In 1859 the lava, ten to fifteen miles in breadth, and for a course of fifty miles, ravaged the country. It filled up valleys, mountains, and, precipitating itself into the sea, filled up many small ports.

The islands are surrounded with coral and madrepore, which constantly increase their size by forming aluvium land. The mountains are enormous. The two principal volcanoes are called Maonnarana and Maonnakea.

Victoria, the sister of the present king, who will reign after him, is very ugly but very intelligent and of dissolute manners. She countersigns the records of the king, in quality of *quinamii*, that is to say, prime minister; it is her function by birth.

The uniform of the king is that of a lieutenant general of France.

The military music is organized and directed by a German. The king was living some years ago with his old wife, Queen Kalama. His palace is superb, in the midst of a park, and is furnished in French style with marvelous luxury. All the portraits of living European sovereigns are there. The receptions at the palace are very brilliant and imposing. The climate is temperate and delicious.

Their manners are dissolute, and the women are addicted to libertinage. They marry at from ten to eleven years of age and at twenty-four are old.

◇◇◇◇◇◇◇◇◇

On Board the Colorado, *September 30*

On the twenty-fourth we reached Manzanillo, a Mexican town concealed in a little bay, encased by mountains whose sides lose themselves in the shore; the town in fact is but a cluster of huts. The Mexican imperial flag floats at the end of a mast on the roof of a whitewashed square frame building, the governor's palace, no doubt. Two or three pirogues loosen from the shore and approach our steamer, one of them manned by three young Mexicans covered with muslin drawers, which descend as far as the middle of the thigh. They use paddles. The youngest of the three is ten years old at most. He absolutely wants to sell me a monstrous tortoise, which he has all the trouble in the world to keep at the bottom of his boat. Not being able to sell it, he seats himself on the back of the monster, who tranquilly crawls along without appearing to notice this increase of his load.

Another canoe has boarded us; it is that of the customhouse. A half-naked Indian whose shirt, with sleeves bound with yellow pipings, is in tatters is an imperial soldier who accompanies the customhouse officer.

Arrive at Acapulco tomorrow.[2] Acapulco, according to the dictionary of Mr. Bouillet,[3] is what in reality it is not, for it is only a small borough. The houses are all low, and consist of only a ground floor. The French returned here four days ago and have landed a garrison of three hundred Mexican soldiers. They are for the most part Indians or mulattoes who go barefoot and are very dirty. There is not one of them whose uniform is perfect, while the greater number have the short coat like the Prussian, which reaches to the middle of the thighs. They are small and repulsively ugly. A large officer of awkward figure like a Don Quixote in uniform of the line parades with his hand proudly placed on the handle of his large sword. He has a long blue coat and cap, wears a watchchain that is loose on his velvet waistcoat, a fanciful cravat, and gray pantaloons spotted with grease. I ask

---

[2] The two entries dated September 30 illustrate the difficulty of Clara Gottschalk's task as editor. If her brother landed at Panama on October 1, as the next entry indicates, he could not have arrived at Acapulco, Mexico, that same day. He might, however, have been "in sight of the coast of Costa Rica."

[3] Marie-Nicolas Bouillet (1798–1864) was a French professor and lexicographer whose works include a *Dictionnaire universel d'histoire et de géographie* (1842), a *Dictionnaire universel des sciences, des lettres et des arts* (1854), *L'Atlas universel d'histoire et de géographie* (1861), and various studies on the classics.

him for his cigar to light mine with, and with that facility of making acquaintance which the Spanish American possesses, he recounts to me his feats of valor. "We have only three hundred soldiers here now, but," he added, bridling up, "all picked troops."

A fat old man with a large straw hat on his head, and his lip covered by a formidable gray mustache, drew near to ask me if I had any recent news from Mexico. "The general," said the lieutenant, who introduces this old Don Quixote to me. The general is, as I have since learned, only a colonel, but it is good taste in the Mexican army, among the subalterns, to exalt the commander before strangers.

The whole town is depopulated. The French had hardly shown themselves when Mr. Diego Alvarez retired behind the mountains that surround Acapulco, with his soldiers, and all the inhabitants followed him. It is really less through hatred of the French than through fear of the terrible Mexican general that this exodus has taken place. In fact during the first French occupation, the army denounced many of the inhabitants for having fraternized with the enemy; they were tried and shot by Alvarez. One Frenchman only, whose little shop bears the sign "Bazar du Pacifique," has had the courage to remain, and we are assured that he has opened only this morning on the arrival of the steamer and will close again on its departure. He sells nothing to the imperialists and lives in the cellar during the day.

◇◇◇◇◇◇◇◇◇

October 1

Landed at Panama. The steamer cast anchor before the island of Tobago, two miles distant from the town. The site is ravishing; the island is a broken coast whose steep and precipitous declivities plunge perpendicularly into the blue sea. A boat comes for us, it will have to make three trips, for it cannot carry at once four hundred passengers, and we are at least four hundred. The wharf is crowded. The Negro porters, sellers of fruit and cigars, quarrel among themselves, as usual, for their prey. Each of us is assailed by six or eight of these ragged monkeys, who offer us their services in English, French, and Spanish, and often impose themselves imperiously upon us by seizing, whether we are willing or not, our trunks. The women sell lemonade, rum, and parrots. It is enough to drive one wild; we are jostled, squeezed, tossed about from one end of the wharf to the other. The first train is just starting for Aspinwall; it is for the steerage passengers.

I succeed in collecting three of my trunks, which are running at random on the shoulders of three busybodies who were in quest of a job and who consent, by means of a forced contribution, to permit me to take possession of my property. A hatbox and small trunk are still missing, but after the departure I shall probably find them, because I took the precaution of writing on them "Panama," which signifies that I stop there and takes from the porters the hope of keeping them with impunity. There remains to them the consolation in perspective of skinning me under the pretext of having had to watch my baggage for two hours.

An omnibus, drawn by two sorry-looking horses sagging in the back, driven by a Negro, takes me to the town properly so-called, which is a mile off. On our road we pass wretched cabins, Negroes in tatters, ruins of stone houses, some tottering walls, the stones of which served for building the few new tottering hovels built in this decrepit town. On a hut a sign in French: "French gentlemen travelers are informed that Jean François, from Paris, washes and does everything pertaining to his trade."

A large square building of cut stone, the whole of which is broken down, and the interior of which has become a medley of climbing plants and trees, is the old Jesuit college. This is the old town, the title might lead one to suppose that the remainder is less in ruins. Vain illusion. Ruins! ruins! ruins! The cathedral is falling down. The wooden balconies of the houses lean toward the street with an evident tendency of throwing into it those who might be so imprudent as to venture into them. The dismantled roofs are covered with vegetation. The clock tower of the cathedral is covered instead of slate with pearl-oyster shells incrusted in the masonry, which sparkle in the burning rays of the sun. The streets are narrow and crooked, and the pavements resemble the brim of a well. The porches serving for entrances to the shops are dark: they sell in them a lot of rags and other mean dirty things.

The Aspinwall Hotel is kept by a Frenchman. The hotel is

dirty and dilapidated; the dinner is passable, although I found many flies in my soup and omelet.

Opposite the hotel a Frenchwoman keeps a shop of super-annuated dresses.

I have been walking on the promenade of the ramparts on the edge of the sea. An old cannon, which keeps itself in equilibrium on half of a gun carriage, is what remains of an immense barrack of cut stone. The walls have crumbled and the roof is falling in. The ground floor still remains. The windows are grated, serving for a prison. A crowd of unfortunates stretch out their hands to me through the bars. *"Un medio, señor."* I throw some small pieces of money to them. *"Dios lo bendiga,"* covered with benedictions, I was about to leave, but the soldiers, allured by my generosity, are at my heels, and I am soon surrounded by a score of black and yellow ringtail monkeys in red caps, who have come out of the guard house. By their caps I guess that I have business with the invincibles of the army of occupation. The uniform consists of a scarlet cap, cotton drawers, no shirt. Some have bayonets at their sides, others a cartouche box hung by a shoulder strap, and no shoes. They were fighting three weeks ago.

◇◇◇◇◇◇◇◇◇

Panama, October 7

A concert, organized by subscription, given in the hall of the *hôtel de ville.*[4] The tickets are a dollar. Receipts one hundred forty dollars. The audience appears to be charmed, while I am playing on a cottage piano that I suspect was the product of an illicit union between a jew's-harp and a large kettle. The climate is so hot and damp that the best piano is not playable at the end of three weeks. Besides they have no tuner. The only person who meddles with them is an unfortunate French secretary at the consulate, who has one-half of his face and nose eaten off by a frightful cancer.

Today I have seen the president of the state, Sobrerano, of Panama. He is a dark mulatto, who received me in his shirt sleeves and slippers, in a nasty, miserable, and unclean little house. His

---

[4] At the instigation of the governor he played in La Salle du Conseil Municipal. The balcony windows were opened so everybody could hear him.

mother is an old Negress who sells preserved guava, which she makes herself, and who goes every morning to market, barefooted, in her chemise. The president is the son of the old Bishop of Panama.

Yesterday I was admiring a pretty girl, eleven or twelve years old, who was making some purchases in the French Bazaar opposite the hotel. She is, I am told, the daughter of the priest—this was said artlessly, as if we had been only speaking of the mayor. Besides her, the priest has also six others—all pretty. She did not hesitate in saying when she made her purchase: "Place that on the account of Papa, el Señor Cura."

The French consul, Mr. de Y——, cousin, I believe, of Mr. Drouyn de L'Huis, is a charming man, who gave me an excellent dinner, which I thankfully accepted and appreciated with pleasure after the infernal cooking on board.

He showed me some superb specimens of the ceramic art of the Indians, found in digging near Chiriquí, two hundred to three hundred miles in the interior. It is curious that the form, design, and color of the vases recall to mind those of the Etruscans. In the necropolis of Chiriquí an innumerable quantity of golden ornaments have been found. The consul has made a collection of them. Some of them are elegant and of remarkable workmanship. They are for the most part animals—lizards, frogs, sharks, and crabs— from one to five inches in length, cast in gold, and they doubtless were suspended from the neck, if I am to judge from the small rings invariably found in all these objects, artistically concealed in the paws or placed in the middle of the sculpture.

The consul, having heard of very rich discoveries, wrote lately to his agent at Chiriquí, ordering him to buy all the ornaments found in the recent excavations. The latter complied, and the consul received at the end of a few days a very heavy box full of shapeless golden ingots—the agent having had the happy idea, he said, of flattening all the objects with a hammer so that they might take up less room!

To give you an idea of the richness of the excavations, the weight of the rough gold in the objects found at Chiriquí has been valued at seventy thousand dollars.

The church is dilapidated; and everywhere the horrible taste of the Spanish religion: silver papers, artificial flowers, horrible paintings. A picture representing, I suppose, purgatory has particularly attracted my attention. The Trinity, painted on a cloud, lets fall indulgences and medals on a crowd of weeping parents. In one corner a little priest, on a little cage in which a spit of souls in trouble are roasting over a furnace, lets fall, as through the chink of a money box, a few pieces of silver that doubtless are to refresh the roasting ones. Finally, at the bottom of the picture, are seen the flames of purgatory, in the midst of which a pope, a bishop, a king, a white man, a black man, and an Indian are burning—to prove doubtless that no one is protected from the flames of purgatory, and consequently could not be excused from paying his debt. There are some farmers who pay the priest for permission to sweep the church out after High Mass on Sunday. They carefully gather up the dust and spread it over their fields, persuaded that it is an excellent fertilizer and that it blesses their crops.

Nothing could give you an idea of the ignorance and the apathy of these people, who constantly see the progress of the civilization of the Americans, and who nevertheless continue to isolate themselves better than the Chinese do behind their Great Wall. They have a horror of innovations. The foreigner is repugnant to them because he represents a summary of ideas and customs different from those which have been transmitted to them by their ancestors. They take great care not to expand their views beyond their small sphere of action, in which they are so circumscribed that they have finally lost all idea of social proportion or historical perspective. They depreciate all foreign events that take place, and exaggerate all those which pertain to themselves.

Their views never extend beyond the circle of little intrigues and petty passions in which they take part. Through constantly occupying themselves only with themselves, they finally lose every idea of proportion; the imperceptible sphere in which they move becomes the center of the world; the universe looks at them—they think themselves great.

◇◇◇◇◇◇◇◇◇

Panama, October 10

The French consul has just told me that I will make the voyage to Lima in company with sixteen French Sisters of Charity, two

Lazarists, and a young Peruvian priest who has just taken orders at Rome. God grant that this holy cargo may procure for us a calm and a happy voyage!

The English steamer is a dozen miles distant from Panama. A little steamer—in which are piled our trunks, upon which the sisters and the priest have seated themselves—takes us off. Singular change! I cast a look of regret on this miserable little town in ruins. I leave there quasi affections, doubtless very premature, but a traveling pianist is outside of all rules, he has little time to lose, he loves very quickly, and I have left behind me many pieces of my heart hanging on the thorns by the road.

There was opposite my hotel a little Indian girl, with large black eyes, and coarse hair that scarcely yielded to the constraint of a large gold comb. A supple figure, beautiful yellow-bronze round shoulders, naked or nearly so—her dress being very light, and open on her bosom. She is a seamstress at the dressmaker's. I have never spoken to her. She has a very wild and timid look— only sixteen years old. I looked at her very often from my balcony. One day as a pretext, I took her a ribbon I had bought and did not want. She was teaching the alphabet to a little Indian sitting at her knees—perhaps her brother. I asked her with my softest voice if it was her brother. She did not answer me, but ran and hid herself behind the shop. My amours stopped there, though, to speak the truth, I affected not to see her any more when I passed her in the street. I often looked at her again, concealed behind my blinds. Grapes—too green! Always the same story; we cannot reach them, and we avenge ourselves on them by a look of contempt. O villainous human nature! Fortunately for me my desire of conquering is never so great as my fear of being conquered, and the uncertain perspective of victory would never lead me to give battle when the issue might be a defeat.

The brave sisters sing canticles, but the little boat begins to rock singularly. The sea is rough, the boat plunges, rises again, and trembles like a restless horse who does not like his rider. It is certain that she shakes herself as if she wished to get rid of her burden. Our trunks tumble down. The poor sisters did not require this catastrophe to interrupt their canticles. Alas, already many of them, with dim eye and pale face, wrestle in vain against seasickness. The superioress herself, after having swallowed her dignity as long as she could, gets up, and disappears at the stern. The fat Polish priest heaves great sighs. The little Peruvian priest is stretched at the bottom of a grotto formed, amid the fray, in the middle of the mountain of trunks, and the little Italian Lazarist, mad, distracted, rolls his large eyes without looking around him, mechanically muttering his breviary, which he interrupts to lean in the attitude of a resigned martyr upon the rigging of the vessel. But as to myself I soon lost the faculty of looking at the ills of others, for the purpose of feeling more my own, and what are they? Seasickness is the most unmerciful, the most terrible, and the most implacable of all evils.

◇◇◇◇◇◇◇◇◇

Opposite Paita (Peru), October 15

Someone lately was relating to me that in a procession in Guatemala during Holy Week, the devotees, no longer satisfied with the large wooden Christ that they promenaded, thought of putting a big, jovial fellow, who was willing, upon the cross. He was attached to it in such a way as to make believe that he was crucified; his feet and his hands having previously been painted scarlet. He had, besides, a female friend, whose services he offered and whom they transformed into the Virgin Mary; both were promenaded in procession as far as the church, where the drama of the Passion was acted *in naturalibus*. The most shocking part of the thing was that the Virgin was to the knowledge of all the mistress of the one who represented Christ!

There is at Guatemala an analogous custom during Holy Week, with this difference only, that Judas is made to appear. They generally confide the part to an Indian drunkard or idiot. They heap upon him insults and bad treatment. The fury of the people hardly knows any limits, and he becomes an object of execration; the poor Judas is generally assassinated, if not during the festival, at least in the following year.

PAITA. As far as the sight can extend only plains of sand. Extraordinary aridity. Not a blade of grass, not a tree. This grieves the heart—one feels as in the presence of a cursed land. The sun lightens up and brings out the somber tints of the gorges and irregularities of the ground. A remarkable phenomenon is that all the cliffs, irregular in their capricious forms, are level at their summits, and form on the horizon a perfectly horizontal line. It never rains here, and the water comes from the interior of the country. There is not a drop of it for thirty miles of our road. It costs one dollar a load in town. I find in Bouillet that Paita is in the middle of an arid plain! What, then, does he call a mountainous country?

Landed. Misery and filth. Five or six streets parallel to the shore extend for almost a mile. All the streets are connected with each other by narrow alleys, two feet in width, that run between every two houses. The houses are of bamboo, covered with macaw trees. The sides are covered with lime, which fills up the spaces between the bamboos. The sun never penetrates into the alleys, which connect the streets with each other.

◇◇◇◇◇◇◇◇◇◇

October 18, 1865

We approach the coast on our left; already the mountains, which merged with the clouds on the horizon, are clearly visible. The activity of the sailors announces that we shall not be long in arriving. They are cleaning up the ship: one polishes the oars, another rubs the copper stair rods. The waiters redouble their zeal, are charmingly gracious toward the passengers (perquisites!). These, after being eclipsed, reappear one by one on the deck, shaven, fresh, and sprightly.

It is at the moment of arrival that vanity finds a place in every heart. It seems that everyone wishes to make up for lost time. The women in general are those who gain the most by this transformation. The slovenly creature that you had hardly noticed, except to curse the effects of seasickness on her, from a chrysalis has changed into a butterfly. She is born again. Ashamed of having for so long a time concealed their charms under the horrible restraint of the least poetic of all ills, the women clothe themselves again in all their seductions, like a warrior, who having just suffered defeat, examines his arms at the moment of returning again to the combat. Besides each one is desirous of making herself finer than her companions.

Seasickness has disappeared. My little priest becomes playful;

he is going to meet his family again. "You will see Lima," he said to me in the fullness of his joy; "it is magnificent, marvelous, and as for the women, they are certainly the prettiest in the world."

"Come, now! What do you know about them, my dear fellow?" replied the French critic, Mr. Fournier, who did not miss any chance of letting an arrow fly at the poor abbé. This last one is the sharpest. Placed between his national self-esteem, which excites him to break a lance for the Peruvian ladies, and his gown, which condemns him to acknowledge his incompetence, he is very much annoyed. For spite, he betakes himself to reading his breviary. Even the sixteen sisters have taken the contagion, they laugh, lay their plans, and sing.

The land appears on our right; we are in the harbor. Before us a forest of masts. The captain at the bow gives his orders in a sharp voice. Callao has no wharf. The vessels anchor some distance out. We are passing a superb Spanish frigate, *La Numanicia,* then a small monitor, constructed in Peru, that has only one cannon, whose engine gets out of order every time they use it, that makes only two miles an hour but has not cost less than two million five hundred thousand francs. Some Peruvian soldiers (Negroes) are sleeping or smoking on this monstrous shell. They have red pantaloons and blue coats, furnishing an opportunity to the abbé to remark that the Peruvian Army is as well disciplined as the French.

We cast anchor. The port is covered with boats that come for the mails and passengers. The boat of the captain of the port, manned by three or four Peruvian navy officers, in gold, resplendent, pompous, and makers of trouble, accosts us.

The sisters are delighted. They just now see two white caps in a boat, approaching. "There they are, there they are," and the handkerchiefs are waving. These are without doubt some sisters whom they have known in Europe. They weep for joy. Is it a long time since you have seen them? I asked. "We do not know them, sir, but they are Sisters of Charity." Poor girls! It is the same with the soldier who sees again the uniform of his regiment.

The mails are got out of the hold with great trouble. It is here that they should possess the method and order of the Yankees! They must wait two hours, and pay the watermen who have already invaded the boat, in order to get them out of the hold. We disembark. Callao presents nothing remarkable. A great many Negroes, Chinese, and Indians, and a great deal of filth. We have our trunks carried to the railroad station; the train runs from Callao to Lima in half an hour.

Four dirty, indolent old men (these are the customhouse officers) examine the contents of our trunks. On seeing that I have five, they upset the first and examine it minutely, for the purpose, a person who was looking on said to me, to tire out my patience and obtain a gratuity in order to spare me the annoyance of opening the others. But they had their trouble for their pains, and the Peruvian administration owes it to me that three of their employees have for once performed their duty conscientiously. Another old man keeps himself behind a Negro who assures him that in changing his piece of gold he has given him a counterfeit.

The train is about to start, and I have not yet got my ticket for my baggage. It is the old man of the counterfeit coin, whose business it is to give it, but he seems disposed for the moment to rest on his laurels, the discussion having ended to his advantage, the Negro, tired of war, having given up the field of battle, carrying off his counterfeit coin.

Finally I obtain a *boleta* for my trunks, and I get into the railroad car. The carriages are like the European, that is to say, in compartments with eight seats like a coach. There are first, second, and third class, and in this the Peruvians are more advanced. At least we are not exposed to the rudeness of drunken soldiers, or to the perilous closeness to ragged immigrants, and I deduce from this that in Peru the fathers of families are almost certain that their daughters will not be exposed, like those of the United States, to hear profane expressions or ungenteel conversation. They shut us up, but we do not leave until half an hour later. Time is not money here. Everything is nearly finished, and it seems that nobody has anything to do at a fixed hour.

At the station in Lima we wait twenty minutes, and a Negro gives us our trunks, which a carter takes to the hotel, a few steps from here, for the modest sum of four dollars. I had already paid six for being landed (a distance of a quarter of a mile). My passage has cost me one dollar, my luggage fifty cents—total eleven dollars. And here is a nation who wonders why the flow of immigration does not turn toward her shores.

Lima, the city of the kings, as it is always called by the old

Spanish writers, is far from meriting, from its appearance now, this pompous title. The streets are, in general, regular, and cross each other at right angles, but their filthiness surpasses all imagination. Piles of dirt, animal carcasses, and all sorts of rubbish ferment under the burning sun, which disengages from it every species of effluvium. The gutters, instead of being next to the pavements, are placed in the middle of the street, and are truly canals, three and four feet in depth, which roll, when they are not stagnant, their poisonous waves, and when I say that *everything* is cast into these open drains, anyone can understand that the air of the city of kings does not bring to mind the roses of Provence.

The houses, mostly built in the old Spanish style—that is to say, massive, heavy, and gloomy—are generally preceded by that part of the building fronting the street which serves for the domestics. Then comes a court, which vaguely recalls, but without possessing their elegance, the patios of Andalusia. The dwelling properly so called is at the back of the court. All this is dusty, dilapidated, and dirty. It is idleness, apathy, and wretchedness such as one invariably finds in all the old Spanish colonies.

The principal square is surrounded by arcades or porticoes, under which swarms a whole crowd of merchants whose booths are filled with odds and ends. One side of the square is shut in by the cathedral, the architecture of which, being of the composite style of the seventeenth century, produces a good enough effect. When I entered it for the first time, it was in the morning; a few lonely female devotees were performing their devotions. Clothed for the most part with the traditional veil, which they wear over the head like a shroud, they recalled to me, by their immobility, those kneeling statues which are found on the tombs of the Middle Ages. The greater part have made a vow, some to dress all in white for a year, some to dress like a Carmelite, some in blue, these generally consecrated to the Blessed Virgin. The effect is picturesque.

The organ is played out of tune, to the disgrace of all religious propriety and of all the rules of music; in spite of all the efforts of its torturer, it however did not succeed in breaking the charm that took possession of me. The chapels still deserted, the large painted wooden saints standing in semiobscurity, twisting themselves into the postures of their martyrdom, or of the actions representing the miracles. The old gildings hidden by the dust, the aureoles of precious stones, all produce a singular effect that, without giving rise to religious meditation, favored the reverie of a traveler.

I have read in the guide to Lima that the cathedral possessed a large picture by Murillo. I asked the sacristan to point it out to me. "Murillo!" said he to me, looking at me with astonishment. "I do not know." I then directed myself toward a priest who had at least seemed to have a vague idea of what a Murillo might be, but he did not know where the picture was. I concluded from this (and later have learned that I was not mistaken) that the Murillo had probably been sold by some rapacious priest who, knowing its value, appropriated it to himself, or that it might have been exchanged for a new picture, very glossy, very bright, one of those ignoble, crude daubs that the priests of South America (are they confined to South America?) are so pleased with.

The city of Lima, the seat of the viceroyalty of Peru, was founded by Francis Pizarro in 1535, forty-two years after the discovery of America.

I found in an old manuscript the following document:

Schedule of the most invincible Queen, Madam June, granted to the Marquis Francis Pizarro, who has been and is governor of the kingdoms which he has discovered and of which he may hereafter discover.

Inasmuch as you, Captain F. Pizarro, residing at the mainland called Castilla Deloro, the venerable Father Don Fernando de Luque, dignitary of the chapter and head master of the Church of Dorieuse de Vacante, which is in the same Castilla Deloro, and Captain Diégo de Almago, inhabiting the city of Panama, have made known that you and your companions, for the purpose of serving us and for the good of our royal crown, have, for five years, more or less, with permission and authorization of Pedro Arias de Avila, our Governor and Captain-General of the said mainland, undertaken to conquer, to discover, to pacify, and people the sea-coast to the south of the said mainland, on the east, the whole at your expense, and that for this purpose you and your companions caused to be made two ships and a brigantine, in which enterprise you spent a large sum of gold pesos, and made said discoveries, in which you have suffered many accidents, and confronted many perils on account of the desertion of your men, who abandoned you in a desert island, excepting thirteen men, who were not willing to leave you, and that with the help of the sailors and people which Captain Don Diégo de Almago offered you, passed from the said desert island, and discovered the said lands and provinces of Peru and the city of Tumbez, in which expedition you and your companions have spent more than thirty thousand pesos of gold; and that with the desire which you have to serve us, you wish to follow up the said conquest and populating at your expense, without our ever being obliged to reimburse you the expenses which for this purpose you have made and will make, except those which in the present article will be granted to you, and that you prayed and requested me to grant you the command of the said conquest, and to grant certain privileges: I ordain that—

Under Captain F. de Pizarro, it may be permitted you to continue for us, and in the name of our royal crown, the said conquest of discovery and population of the said province of Peru, as far as the distance of two hundred leagues, more or less, from the coast, starting from the place called in the Indian tongue Teninipuede, and which you have named Santiago, as far as the village of Chincha, etc. etc.

Followed by a score of clauses in which Madame Jane regulates with profuse prolixity of style and scrupulous accuracy all the details of this curious document.

◇◇◇◇◇◇◇◇◇◇

Lima

The streets of Lima are paved (?) with small spherical stones upon which the foot can never be placed flat; you constantly lose your balance, and your feet are bruised between the cracks of the pebbles, which besides are not made level. The ground is broken, and there are valleys; you suddenly feel the ground slipping from under your feet, and you save yourself with a shock by the *"gracia de Dios."* Two steps farther on you stumble and strike the point of your foot against a hard obstacle—it is a mountain. Then the gutters flow in the middle of the streets and are so deep that they are crossed at intervals by narrow bridges of stones. There are no scavengers at Lima—filth is simply deposited in the middle of the streets, but as it never rains, and the air is dry, the miasmata, which our moist climates would engender, are here unknown; besides myriads of great vultures, familiar and grand, promenade the streets, doubtless relying on the severe laws that prohibit them from being killed, and take upon themselves the cleansing of the city, and perform their duty wonderfully well.

I will take upon myself respectfully to suggest to the municipal authorities of New York the importation of some thousands of these winged scavengers, who have this advantage over others that they do the work intrusted to them and cost the taxpayers nothing.

The houses are two stories high, seldom three, on account of the earthquakes. The architecture is Spanish, that is to say, heavy, massive, and rude; the walls are four feet thick. Immense coach gates give entrance to an interior court that generally has a fountain in the middle and the dwelling in back. These are often of Moorish architecture, elegant and fanciful with arabesques painted in bright colors. Hidden behind the heavy and massive walls that conceal them from the sight, they are like a jewel in its casket.

The Maurin Hotel is full. The refugees from Ecuador, just now in revolution (when is it not?), and from Chile (who has just declared war against Spain, who blockades all her ports), fill all the hotels. There is not a room left.

I set out again with the cart that carries my trunks—Cæsar and his fortune—in search of another hotel. I obtain by force of entreaties a den in a corridor for the night.

It decidedly appears that I could not have chosen a more inopportune moment for giving concerts.

The rebels are twenty miles from the city. The whole country has joined them. The capital alone has remained faithful to the constitutional president.[5] I am wrong in saying faithful; it is truer to say that he still occupies it with all the troops he has concentrated for the purpose of resisting the enemy. It seems singular to an American that the whole country should range itself under the rebel flag, and that nevertheless one city still in the power of the government should be sufficient to prevent the triumph of the rebellion. One battle only, in which the latter should be conquered, would suffice for the reestablishment of order, at least for some time, civil war being the normal state of Peru.

---

[5] Juan Antonio Pezet (1810–79) was the constitutional president at this time.

I have tried to unravel the tangled skein of political affairs of the present time. This is what I understand about it: The Spanish Government claimed from Peru three million for damages done to some natives. The constitutional president acceded, on the consent of the chambers, to the demands of Spain. The vice-president, Señor Canzeco, seized this pretext for accusing the government of Peru of cowardliness, and raised, in the name of the outraged national honor, the standard of revolt. He was arrested. Seeing that his attempt was not successful, he promised the government to leave the country if they would pay him the arrears of his account. "Agreed," said Pezet, who, above all things, wanted to get rid of a dangerous coadjutor. Once the dollars were pocketed, Mr. Canzeco pretended to exile himself, disembarked on the coast to the south, and raised an army.

To raise an army against the government is in Peru, as in all the other Spanish republics, an easy matter. To be in power is to draw handfuls out of the coffers of the state. A party triumphs; the cure is ready: "Myself president," "you general," but as all the soldiers cannot be generals, and all the generals presidents, the friends of yesterday become the enemies of tomorrow. "Get out of there!" is the motto of all politicians in general, but of the Peruvians in particular.

Corruption reigns everywhere. The government is a milch cow —all milk her. An officer lately assured me that the scale of superior officers and generals of Peru corresponds to an army of eight hundred thousand men, and they have hardly twenty thousand troops in time of war! Out of four men two are officers and the others are clerks—all live on the government. A successful revolution is a seesaw movement. One-half of the country rises into power, while the other falls from it. A revolution takes place: one-half of the country is without employment. This gives rise to a conspiracy, and the first ambitious comer finds the elements all prepared. Every employee steals; the government, in pocketing what ought to go into the state treasury, robs its creditors because it spends always more than it gains. The colonels receive three hundred sixty dollars per month and spend one thousand dollars. Besides the gratuities in money that they receive from the general they have assisted in climbing into power, they gain a considerable revenue in the following manner: Their battalion consists of six hundred men; they have in reality only four hundred and fifty men and receive pay for six hundred. In the cavalry it is more profitable on account of the horses. A colonel of cavalry makes a small fortune here by selling the horses of his regiment. The fraud can never be discovered on account of this peculiarity, that, in time of peace, the horses of the regiment are put out to pasture near the city. Our colonel pockets not only the price of the horses, but also that of their forage, which the government allows him for the imaginary horses. Does a general arrive? Does a review take place? The colonel borrows the muleteers from the horse merchants, and on the day of the review he presents his regiment at full strength up and receives the compliments of his general on the fine condition of his troops, and continues his little trade with impunity. In the infantry, as it is not as easy to borrow men as horses, to fill up the deficiencies, the colonels enroll by force the men of whom they have need. And this is the way it is done: Two or three confidential soldiers promenade the streets; they see an Indian; they approach him; one of them garrotes him from behind, while the other throws over him a military cloak and places a cap on his head. They cry out that he is a deserter, and carry him off, tied up like a sausage, to the barracks. Recruiting for the army is not done in any other way. They send some soldiers into the country, and they seize by force the poor Indians, tear them from their families, and lead them, tied, like the beads of a rosary, to a long rope held at each end by a soldier.

The arrogance of the military is insupportable. Their insolence and their haughtiness are equaled only by their folly. Overwhelmed with debts, they would not find credit anywhere if they did not now and then take care to pay something on account to their creditors. This is the way the thing is managed (it is a Frenchman, a dealer in military equipment, who relates it to me): A colonel, I suppose, owes eighty dollars for a pair of epaulets. He comes to bring you twenty dollars on account, and buys a bicorne worth thirty dollars, which he has placed to his account. The account always increases, and the merchant who receives on account does not dare to refuse credit to his customer for fear of losing both the account and the principal.

A poor French tailor who had given credit to the officers

Pezet, at his fall was in for six hundred thousand francs and was ruined.

A colonel went to a Frenchman to purchase ten thousand francs' worth of furniture on credit. The Frenchman refused. The colonel said haughtily to him, "Ah ha! Do you take me for one of those French beggars or foreign adventurers? A pitiful sum of ten thousand francs! I spend it for bonbons!" "The greater reason," the poor man humbly replied to him, "for not giving you credit."

A Bolivian colonel had an account with a French coffeehouse keeper which had become so large that the latter was not willing to give him further credit. The colonel gave his sword to him, and as the sword was worth more than the sum due, the coffeehouse keeper gave him the balance in trade. The sword remained a year at the coffeehouse keeper's, and as the colonel had no other he went to the reviews without any, which did not prevent him, how-ever, from being as proud as Artabazus.[6]

If, however, things go badly in Peru, what shall I say of Bolivia? When the liberator Bolívar cut from the map the territory of each of the nations that his victorious sword carved out from the cap-tains general of Spanish America, he assigned to Bolivia, it is true, an immense extent thereof, but he forgot to give it any seacoast. Shut in, suffocated between Peru on the west and the Argentine Republic on the east, Bolivia felt ill at ease. The only opening she had toward the sea was the little port of Cobija. She longed for the tongue of earth (the Peruvian seacoast) that runs into its territory and robs it of its coast. This is the cause of the war between Bolivia and Peru. The president, Melgarejo, a *cholo*,[7] is a ferocious beast, a drunkard, who hangs, shoots down, kills, mas-sacres, etc. He is a soldier of fortune; his education has been that of the barracks. He lately cut off with one blow of an ax the arm of his favorite aide-de-camp.

◇◇◇◇◇◇◇◇◇◇

Peru

"To catch a bird, put some salt on his tail," they used to tell me when I was a child. The Peruvians believe in this absurd recipe.

---

[6] Artabazus was a Persian general active 480–479 B.C.
[7] Offspring of Indian and white parentage.

When you speak to them about public schools they reply to you, "Peru is yet too young." "Religious liberty!" they exclaim with terror: "God protect us from it! Our people are still too ignorant; wait until they have attained civilization." They might as well say that you must wait until you have learned to swim before taking a bath.

With us a railroad is made between two villages in order that they may become cities. In Peru they construct a line of railroad when the two villages have become cities. Civilization finds every avenue among them closed. Among all other nations the doors are opened to her. In Peru she must gain possession of them by force. Every innovation has to fight against prejudice. The smallest things not recommended by their decrepitude are ostracized. The business of foreigners in Peru is observing her progress; the Peruvians go backward, and progress hardly obtains the swiftness of the tortoise.

I said the other day in a moment of anger (with more truth than politeness), "If your desire to see all the foreigners leave your country were gratified, before fifty years you would return to your national costume—nothing but feathers."

Their hatred for foreigners is rooted in their hearts, infused into their blood.

There is not a point in the Peruvian character in which you do not find the gangrene of venality, of ignorance, of corruption, of sloth, and of boasting. The pashas of Asia Minor have not a more despotic power in the midst of the eunuchs of their harems, and the unfortunate fellahs of their fields, than that which, from the highest to the lowest in the military scale, is exercised by the epauletted janisaries who govern Peru. The Peruvian Government is and has always been a military oligarchy more oppressive, more brutal, and more arbitrary than the autocracy of Russia will ever be. Their good pleasure—this is the law that governs—and every goose, turkey, peacock, cock, capon, or eagle, from the marshal to the lieutenant, wearing a sword, proclaims this law supreme and rules like a despot.

The most unbridled corruption in every branch of government, the most shameless venality among all classes, everything is sold, everything is bought. Sloth, ignorance, and hatred of the foreigner, these are the only beliefs profoundly rooted in the heart of this race, debauched physically and morally. Sad spectacle! And is this what the United States should risk its soldiers, navy, military honor, and millions for? No! A thousand times no! Take all the Spanish Americas and examine their governments:

NICARAGUA, composed of Negroes, Indians, and mulattoes, is governed by an ignorant and barbarous clergy, supported by some imbecile sabers.

GUATEMALA, suffocated in the blood and the murmurs that proceed from an oppressed people, permits itself to be organized by the clergy with the obsequiousness of a conquered province.

HONDURAS and SALVADOR are supernumerary subalterns, who, as in gloomy dramas, show themselves when there is some assassination or strangling to be committed.

COSTA RICA is the only one of these republics that meets the sympathy of honest men by the efforts it is making to enter into the paths of civilization.

ECUADOR belongs to the clergy and the sword.

PERU has this at least in its favor, that it is not sanguinary, and that in its revolutions, except the soldiers killed in battle, history has never registered those bloody proscriptions which sully and dishonor the next day of every new government in the neighboring republics.

BOLIVIA is governed by a mulatto-Indian who calls himself provisional *constitutional* president, although he had killed, with his own hands, the lawful president, and will continue to be provisionally constitutional until his natural death, unless some other assassin in turn kills him, to occupy his place provisionally and constitutionally.

The REPUBLIC OF PARAGUAY is governed by a hereditary president for life (?)—a republic!

And these are the people who cry out against monarchy, while they submit to the most frightful autocracy and accommodate themselves to it because López II, their present tyrant, instead of calling himself sultan, calls himself hereditary president for life. Is this not comical to the last degree? It is absolutely like the *bourgeois gentilhomme*, who was not a merchant (shame on him) but who purchased merchandise for the purpose of exchanging it with his friends for money.

◇◇◇◇◇◇◇◇◇

Midnight, November 3
Battle of Lima.
Nevertheless what happy moments passed at Lima! Of all those to whom I am indebted for them, my friend Dupeyron is certainly at the head of the list.
This evening some friends met together. I played the eternally beautiful *"Bénédiction des poignards,"* [from Meyerbeer's *Les Huguenots*]. This thundering discharge of lyric electricity, as Berlioz said somewhere, excited all my good French friends, who leaped upon their chairs as much on account of the music as for the souvenirs it evoked of their country.
Mr. Dupeyron receives a letter, "Is there news of the revolution?" I said laughingly to him. "Yes, read."
The letter is from an officer at the camp (the president's), who asserts that the two armies are at the distance of a mile from each other. The fight will take place tonight or tomorrow morning. The letter ended more piously than heroically:
"I commend my soul to God," said the officer. Mr. Dupeyron assures me that this brave man is one of the least brave that he knows.

◇◇◇◇◇◇◇◇◇

November 6, 4 o'clock in the morning
Started up awakened by a noise. Firmin, my factotum, calls me. "They are fighting, sir," he calls out to me. Indeed firing succeeds rapidly in opposite directions. It approaches. The whole house is aroused. The battle, if it takes place, will be under our windows, for at the corner of our street, that is to say, at the distance of twenty yards, is the square, or palace of the government and the municipality, which occupies two sides of the square. The discharge of musketry increases. A cannon shot. Are these the revolutionary troops? Is it the people who have risen and attempt to hold out in garrison? Is it only a revolutionary division that has started an uprising and placed Pezet between the fires? We are not able to find out anything. The trumpets in the distance are sounding the

charge. It is a division that is entering the city at a running gait. The drums and the trumpets are sounding the charge and they pass like an avalanche before our windows. Dupeyron has seen them, and by their white hats has recognized the revolutionary troops.

The night is magnificent, the silence profound. Not a bell is heard, every church is guarded by a picket of soldiers, and in each clock tower they have posted men upon whose loyalty they can rely.

Sharp discharges of musketry. They are fighting on the square. The government troops have repulsed the column we saw go by just now. A battery of artillery is placed under our windows. I can no longer resist my desire to see. Concealed behind the blinds, I look down into the street. It is occupied by a compact crowd of soldiers of the revolution, horsemen, covered with large red ponchos, with large round white hats on their heads, and immovable as statues. All at once a discharge of artillery; cries, oaths, a furious tempest. In the gloom I see a whole world of phantoms, striving in the midst of a deafening uproar that rises from time to time above the loud noise of the cannon mingled with the rattling discharges of musketry.

A squadron of cavalry debouches on the square. They are received with a discharge of musketry. For some moments I hear little whistlings very near me, like the noise of a switch beating the air.

A little like the ostrich, intrenched behind my blinds, I am impassible in the midst of the melée. Puff! A dull noise very near me awakens me to reality, and warlike propensities vanish before the instinctive feeling of self-preservation. It is a ball that has lodged in the balcony. A moment later I risk looking out again. The wounded are numerous and cover the pavement.

Who has won? Who has lost? No one will ever understand our suspense. A bell! ! The tocsin is ringing. The church has fallen into the hands of the rebels, who perhaps are so no longer at this time, the way in which things go in this unfortunate country.

The shrieks and tumult under our windows are horrible. It is a hand-to-hand fight. The clashing of swords and the cries of those who fall are heard: "Jesús, María, Dios!" Dupeyron prepares downstairs in the apothecary's shop cots, mattresses, etc., for it is probable that they will open or force the door in a few moments. The only fear we have at this time, besides accidents, spent balls, or stray bombs, is that Pezet is not victorious, and does not return to Lima to dislodge the besieging column. The troops at the palace behave bravely. They have not yielded an inch. It really requires heroism to fight without a flag, without the word of command— blindly; for, like ourselves, they do not know if Pezet is conquered, or if they are fighting sixty thousand men or a column.

◇◇◇◇◇◇◇◇◇◇

Six o'clock

The battle continues. The balls fly and are flattened on a salient part of the wall alongside the house. The children are taken from the rooms fronting the street, and the whole household—Negroes, mulattoes, *cholos* included—seeks shelter in the parlor, which is at the rear of the house. The cries of triumph are drawing near; the discharge of musketry ceases. I place myself again in the balcony, still, like the ostrich, behind my blinds, and I see a strange, charming, indescribable sight. It is at the same time a fairy dream and a nightmare. A band of Indian musicians blowing on horns a sort of savage flourish, composed of four low notes that always follow in the same order, advance running; behind it a long file of Indian soldiers in red pantaloons and round hats like a turban. They are the *cholos* of Canzeco. They go by like an avalanche without any impediment, in the midst of frantic acclamations from a crowd of amateur *cholos* on horseback, who block the pavements and seem to want to lend them a helping hand.

Ten minutes of silence, disturbed at long intervals by single musket shots.

◇◇◇◇◇◇◇◇◇◇

Half-past six o'clock

Bang! A cannon shot. Bang, bang—piff, puff. The battle has re-commenced most beautifully.

The brave government troops have started fighting again. The cannonade is redoubled. Our street is a field of battle. The tocsin sounds. The sun rises. I go again to take my position behind the blinds. Two cannons are leveled before our door against the palace.

The brave troops will not yield. What a sad spectacle! A poor *cholo* stands in a doorway, leaning upon his gun; he has around him a sea of blood; his wound must be serious, for the blood continues to flow and the pool to enlarge. *"O charité chrétienne! où êtes vous et ose t'on bien invoquer Dieu en faisant la guerre?"* (O Christian charity! where art thou, and do we indeed dare to invoke God in making war?)

I can see half of the square through the opening of our street, which opens into the middle of it before the gate of the palace. There is a heap of slain. The revolutionists are in ambush behind, and are firing. They have got on top of the roof of the Hotel Maurin and are shooting. A soldier whose cartridges have given out spies the dead body on the pavement opposite; he searches him after having filled his cartridge box. A little urchin who comes from the scene of action (the type of child found even among the *cholos* of Peru) walks around the dead body and looks at the robbing operation. Afterward, being satisfied that no person sees him, he approaches the corpse and, under pretext of looking at the wound —a musket wound in the forehead—takes off its cap, and I see him quietly put it into his pocket, crying out at the same time, "*¡Viva la revolución!*" and go skipping off.

The firing is against the palace; a breach is opened. They nevertheless still defend themselves. At a distance we see troops advancing. It is a revolutionary division that has been marching for eleven hours and has succeeded in turning Pezet's right. At the head march the bugles and drums; almost all are in uniform; but the greater part have no shoes. All wear a piece of white cloth on the cap, a rallying sign, so as not to be mistaken for the government troops, whose uniform is the same. All are Indians, well made, but small, the identical type of the Egyptians. Many of them are mounted on asses, and accompany the drums on a sort of cymbal. They all pass on to the square, but, as the cannon of the palace enfilades the whole street, they are ranged in two files, which occupy the pavement, two men abreast. The combat begins again more fiercely than ever—as soon as the fresh troops debouch on the square. All at once a general, accompanied by an escort of black cuirassiers—doubly black, for they are Negroes and their cuirasses are of black iron—announces that the revolution has triumphed.

Then, as if by magic, all the windows, balconies, dormer windows, the roofs, and the doors are filled by the curious. They are nevertheless still fighting at the palace. All the time the cannon is thundering. A ball has just flattened itself above my head. I keep it as a relic.

They begin to carry off the wounded. An unfortunate soldier, whose foot has been wounded by a bullet, drags himself painfully along on all fours to get out of the fray. He leaves a long trail of blood after him. So far they have carried all the wounded to the military field hospitals, but at this moment somebody knocks, and, leaning over the balcony, I see three Indian soldiers seriously wounded, whom they are carrying on woolen blankets held at the corners by four assistants. The interior court is square, and from the balcony, which at the second story surrounds it, our eyes look down upon a heart-rending spectacle. Of the three Indians, one has his two thighs pierced by a ball. He will recover from it. The second, a very young Indian, has received two musket wounds in the abdomen; he suffers horribly and groans. A photographer, one of our friends, a Parisian joker, one of those impious miscreants who believe in nothing, has never ceased boasting about nursing and fondling the wounded, and particularly this poor dying man; he gently scolds him and calls out to him, placing himself at a carry arms: "*¡Soldado peruano valiente!*" the only Spanish words the *cholo* understands. "*Sí, Sí,*" said the latter, trying proudly to stand up again. "*Soldado valiente,*" and, vaguely rolling his eyes, already dimmed by the approach of death, he soothes for an instant his pains in a sentiment of national pride

The third has a broken leg. They are all lying on the straw that has been spread all over the court in anticipation of the wounded.

Dupeyron, a brave and worthy soul, his assistant, the whole household, the women (need I say it, for charity, is she not feminine?) are everywhere. The unfortunate creatures from whom they extract the balls suffer with a stoicism to be found only among the Indians. They follow with their eyes the movements of the doctor, and try to learn from his expression the gravity of their wounds. From time to time they heave a sigh and murmur these touching words which, in their language would express "Ah! little father, I love thee" (*tay-tay mira te quiero*). The Indian wounded in the abdomen is dead. The court is so full that they have already had to use his body as a pillow for the new comers. "Go and get some of the Fathers of Santo Domingo," said Dupeyron in the ear of a *cholo* who was consoling his wounded friend—which is the same as saying that there are many dying.

◇◇◇◇◇◇◇◇◇◇

10 o'clock A.M.

A young Indian who received a ball in his left breast is dying. I stop a priest in the passage before the door and make him come in. Squatting on the straw, he confesses the dying man in the Indian dialect. An officer has been shot through the head. He dies in a few minutes.

The palace was taken, after the besiegers had set it on fire. The unfortunate palace guard has surrendered. I need not say (O people!) that, once inside, the conquerors commenced by massacring the vanquished, then in sacking everything. The library, the mirrors, the furniture, everything has been broken and burned. A soldier timidly made the remark that all these things did not belong to the vanquished but to the nation, and that it was at least superfluous to destroy it. He paid for his good sense in the midst of the brutal intoxication, for his officer cut off his hand with one blow of his sword.

The terrace of the palace is covered with the dead. From our house we can make out the uniforms of the corpses. Colonel Pamarra was killed after he had surrendered, as also the commandant of the palace guard, the intendant, and many other superior officers.

It is not one division, but the whole army of Canzeco, that has entered Lima. They have deceived the vigilance of Pezet, have turned his right, and have entered, leaving him behind them, when he was thinking that he had them in front. Gómez Sánchez has saved himself; his energy is such that he has rejoined Pezet, and will decide to come and attack and dislodge the revolutionists. This night's battle is then only the prelude of the tragedy. Pezet has ten thousand fresh troops and forty-six cannons of large caliber. As soon as he discovers that Lima has surrendered and that the revolutionists are behind him, he will attack the city. Generals Balta and Prado scour the streets with numerous escorts of cavalry. They are Indians, officers, Negroes, wearing white ponchos with wide bands of red, violet, and black, blue and green; standards of all colors, arms of all kinds, from the lance to the flintlock pistol. The *montoneras*[8] have muskets and make a very fine appearance, covered to the thighs with ponchos, wearing large hats with white bands and a sort of swelled-muzzle pistol on the thighs.

They are placing platoons of cavalry twenty paces apart through the principal streets. All the churches are ringing the tocsin. It is evident that the victorious troops are expecting, and not without alarm, to be attacked by Pezet's army. A thousand horsemen pass at a gallop like a whirlwind. It is fantastic, marvelous, unheard of, savage. They are the Negro cuirassiers, with dirty faces, their uniforms gray with dust, a large sort of blunderbuss across their saddles. Lancers with violet streamers. Chasseurs on horseback, then the *montoneras* with scarlet ponchos, apple green, sky blue; all these yelling, rushing along, brandishing their swords, with the stamping of the horses, etc.

The screams of our poor wounded become deafening, there are already twenty-nine of them, and they are constantly bringing more in. The corpses cannot remain here the whole night. The wounds are gangrenous, and, the court being covered with glass, all the emanations for want of air rise into our rooms. The odor of the blood is already sickening.

The whole army of Canzeco is moving out. After the regular cavalry follow the free squadrons of *montoneras*. A multitude of large green, yellow, and blue flags; then a regiment of Indians "in bail cloth," the uniform has a singular effect. Old Polish caps of the empire, of canvas, also grayish-white. The music of this regiment consists of little tin flutes, which play a very quick rhythm in a minor key, at a quickstep with a bass-drum accompaniment. Another regiment of Indians, musical instruments of copper— barbarous, fantastic uniforms, arms the same. A squadron of Indians irregularly armed with lances, long flint muskets, some brandishing large axes. Their features make one shiver to look at them. Nothing more truly savage than all these tattered wretches in colored rags. Behind comes a squadron of armed *rabonas*, wives of the Indian soldiers, who follow their husbands everywhere and ride astride; one of them has a parrot solemnly seated on her shoulder. None of the soldiers wears shoes, nothing but sandals.

---

[8] Bands of mounted rebels.

We would like to send our wounded to the hospital, but how are we to transport them? Dupeyron is in despair. Some of the wounds, unless the balls are extracted will become mortal, and almost all will become gangrenous. At last a Frenchman (for not one Peruvian has offered to assist us) has agreed to find a mule, which is harnessed to a cart, and we place three of the wounded upon it on a straw bed. Impossible to find in all the immense crowd of onlookers, of gapers, of heroic soldiers who are strutting in the streets in the midst of a cortege of friends, four men willing to assist us in carrying the wounded as far as the cart!

"Well, gentlemen, what do you teach in your convents and preach to your brothers? The precepts of the gospel which you practice, should they be different from those which make mention of a very modest virtue that is unknown to you: charity?"

Some French miscreants, who were fortunately there, assisted us with a devotion that simulates the Christian charity forgotten here. One, an inquisitive passer-by, actually wanted to enter the court of the pharmacy to look at the pile of corpses. "Go in," I said to him, "but on condition that you work and assist in carrying out the dead bodies." "*Acaso me tomaba por un negro?*" (Did you perhaps take me for a Negro?) he answered, casting on me a withering look of offended dignity. "Ah ha! It is true then that the too frequent contact, the constant manipulation, the daily commerce with the most beautiful things ends in rendering you callous to their greatness and their beauties." These nice fellows take the Communion fifty-two times yearly, have five or six hundred Masses said, follow in all the processions, and yet do not understand the gospel.

◇◇◇◇◇◇◇◇◇

Half-past six o'clock P.M.

Gómez Sánchez, the minister, has escaped, it is not known how, from the troops who have taken the palace, where he commanded up to the last moment. He intrenched himself with a few battalions in the little fort of Santa Catalina at the edge of the city, and has held his ground since this morning against Canzeco's army. A summons to yield has been sent him; he replied that he would sooner die than surrender. The bearer of the flag of truce has returned to say on the part of the besiegers that they would give no quarter to him if he did not surrender before sunset. He has again refused.

They continue to bring in the wounded to us. The cartman has made six journeys, and the last of our wounded have just gone. The dead are carried off in a kind of open coffin. The floor is impregnated with blood; after having aired it as much as possible we cover it with bran, but the smell of the blood is still strong, and still more that of the cold sweat of the dying.

A Lima lady, a neighbor, arrived at the pharmacy at six o'clock this morning to take care of the sick. For twelve hours she has had no food, no rest; her white hands are stained with the blood of all these horrible wounds. She has given the most sympathetic attention, and is everywhere like the angel of charity. (The priests are missing this morning.) Many of the unfortunate creatures are at the point of death. She was kneeling beside them and telling them everything that might console and ameliorate their anguish. "Ay tayta, tayta" (little mother), "am I dying?" "Yes, my son," replied the young girl, "and as you are a brave soldier, the good God, His Son, and the Holy Virgin are awaiting you."

"Ay, tayta! To behold them, I must confess to a priest?"

"No, cholo, if you repeat just what I tell you, and if you hold this crucifix in your hands, you will see them."

And the dear "little mother," leaning over at the ear of the dying, was saying slowly to him an act of contrition which the poor soldier was repeating, word by word; then she made him kiss the crucifix, and, making the sign of the cross, left him, the courageous young girl, to run and carry her consolations to another.

Ah, dear little *tayta*, you have a right to cling to your medals, to your scapular, to your novenas, and to burn incense at the procession. It is certainly not I who would gainsay it, and I think that, without being a Doctor of Theology, like Messrs. the Brothers of Santo Domingo, you know much more about religion than their science will ever teach them.

◇◇◇◇◇◇◇◇◇◇

November 7, 1865

The fort of Santa Catalina has not yet surrendered, and Pezet, like the imbecile he is, did not attack the city during the past night.

He has sent a flag of truce to Canzeco. The result of their

proceedings is not known. Callao has been pillaged and sacked by the revolutionary troops after it surrendered. They seized the customhouse stores and broke open all the cases, burned all the merchandise, forced the strong safes of many of the merchants, etc.

My piano had a narrow escape. It was at the customhouse, and if my friend, Dupeyron, had not had it taken out, it would not have been in existence today.

The crowds in the streets today are immense. On the public square they are engaged in removing traces of the battle. The dead horses remain there. On the cathedral walls lie many hundreds of corpses, which during the combat had been collected in the church. It is a sad spectacle, to which the cries of the women who come to search for those belonging to them, who have not returned home, and whom they recognize among the heaps of the slain, add fresh horrors.

They estimate the number of the dead within the palace at two hundred. One of our neighbors, a charming young girl of twenty-two, remarkable for her beauty, was killed yesterday by a musket ball in her chest, at the moment when, like ourselves, urged by curiosity, she sought to look into the street through the blinds of her balcony. One of the proprietors of the Hotel Maurin had both legs carried away by a ball.

The *montoneras* continue to pass by in squadrons—the musket or ax in their fist. Some of them have the lance, to which is attached a large green standard, which, seen from afar, floating on the wind, has a charming effect in the midst of all the brilliant colors of the ponchos.

◇◇◇◇◇◇◇◇◇

6 o'clock P.M.

It is probable that we are about to have another battle. General Pezet is three miles from the city. In spite of the desertion of one squadron of cavalry, which has gone over to the enemy, his army is still sufficient to dispute the victory with them. Santa Catalina has not yet capitulated. The populace is crowding in the streets near the fort. The commander of Santa Catalina—and he is right— above all, fears that his garrison and himself would be massacred if he capitulated. The magazine of the arsenal contains enough powder to blow up the city if the people set fire to it. Our position is horrible.

We have succeeded, with great trouble, in procuring some bread. Preserves, sardines, pies are a great relief. Forgues is installed in the kitchen, and makes us delicious fried potatoes, which bring to mind those of the *barrière de Clichy*, when at boarding school I treated my schoolmates with my savings (I was then the millionaire by virtue of being the little American).

One of our neighbors, who found himself at Chorillos without being able to get back to Lima, made the whole journey on foot, and met on the road a division of Pezet advancing on Callao.

Things are decidedly taking an alarming turn. Gómez Sánchez has succeeded in rejoining Pezet and has imparted to him a little of his warlike ardor. It appears that as soon as he saw that the city would succumb, he left disguised on horseback and arrived before noon at the headquarters of the president. He left in command General Gutiérrez, a brave man, who made the garrison swear to die rather than surrender. All the men took the oath, and we know how they have kept it. Out of the whole battalion of defenders there remain fifteen men. What is horrible to relate is that all of the wounded we have seen, and all those whose wounds we have dressed, were revolutionists. Not one of the government. Two doctors with whom I have just been conversing have assured me that they have not one in the hospitals, which corroborates what I have just been saying, "that the conquerors killed the wounded and gave them no quarter."

Fort Catalina still holds out. From the turret of the house the view extends over the whole city, and I can see perfectly the tower of the fort for several moments. The balustrade and steps of the turret are riddled with balls; so for only two or three minutes I allow myself the pleasure of enjoying from this elevated and perilous position the magnificent panorama that opens upon the sight.

The number of wounded collected together already exceeds five hundred. They have not yet carried off many dead bodies, which are lying on the terraces of the neighboring houses, where they were posted as sharpshooters. The cathedral towers were full of them. They are bringing them down to take them to the cemetery. A singular episode was that of the general, a brigade commander, brother of the general in chief of the revolutionists. When the palace was taken by assault, he was captured by the conquerors and taken before the general president. The two brothers fell into each other's arms on meeting. Sad effects of civil war!

◇◇◇◇◇◇◇◇◇◇

10 o'clock P.M.

It is just announced to us that Pezet advances toward the suburb of Santa Catalina to attack it. We are barricaded for the night. There are no longer any police, and, the streets belonging during the night to the *montoneras*, it is probable that they will pillage some of the houses. Already last night a jewelry shop was rifled. If they fight tonight they will sack the city. Fortunately the American Legation is not far off, and at the first alarm I shall go to take shelter there. Dupeyron has loaded two revolvers. Forgues has a rifle that fires six times, and another of our guests a pocket pistol. It is not much, but still sufficient to keep in check evildoers during the time necessary for the women and children to escape by the roofs, which, as I have said, are flat and separated from each other by a little wall that can easily be crossed. In the meanwhile I try to sleep and put the iron bar across the door.

◇◇◇◇◇◇◇◇◇◇

November 8, 10 o'clock A.M.

Fort Santa Catalina surrendered last night, but Pezet has retaken Callao and is marching on Lima, from which he is only three miles off. They have shot fifty of the pillagers of Callao.

◇◇◇◇◇◇◇◇◇◇

2½ o'clock

From the turret the advance guard of Pezet is seen advancing toward the city. The artillery and cavalry are in front. The remainder are lost on the horizon in a cloud of dust.

The clock tower of the cathedral, behind our house, swarms with soldiers posted there as sharpshooters. At the end of our street, which opens on the bridge of Rimal, by which Pezet proposes entering the city, they are erecting batteries.

What will become of us?

The revolutionists have besides armed the populace, who are in their favor. There is nothing for me to do, if I am able to leave the house, but to go and demand protection at the American Legation. Unfortunately the fire of the enemy's cannon enfilades our street, and it is more than doubtful that we could get there without being struck.

I have some details respecting the flight of Gómez Sánchez. At half-past eight o'clock in the morning, when he saw that the palace could not hold out, he escaped by the roofs with ten true and devoted followers (devoted? as if there could be such in a country where treason is a consecrated means of making a fortune). They succeeded in getting down into a little street where they found horses, but some revolutionary soldiers discovered them, and thirty horsemen put themselves in pursuit of them. Gómez Sánchez and his suite took to the steep mountain roads; it was flying for life, it was a wild, mad race. The revolutionists, better mounted than they, gained on them slowly, and the distance between them visibly diminished. One of the horses of the fugitives gave out, his rider was killed. The race continued. The balls whistled around the minister. "Surrender," cried out the pursuers to him, and he answered them by sticking his spurs deeper into his horse's flanks. A ball struck the officer near him. The unlucky one tumbled into the dust. The soldiers began to murmur. "Surrender yourselves," said Sánchez to them; "if you are too cowardly to strive for liberty, I will arrive at the president's camp or I will be slain."

Six soldiers stopped and, putting their handkerchiefs at the ends of their swords, they gave the signal that they surrendered. In the meantime Gómez took the lead and after a breathless race of two hours arrived at an advance unit of Pezet's horsemen. Without taking time to rest he divided them into two companies and returned with one of them on his tracks, while the other, by a circuit, was to fall on the rear of the pursuing horsemen. He met the band; a fight took place. Taken between the fifteen lancers of the minister and the fifteen others, who cut off their retreat, they were obliged to surrender, as well as the six deserters who one hour before had abandoned the minister.

Decidedly this little lawyer is in soul a hero, in body a devil (unfinished).

〜〜〜〜〜〜〜

[*Gottschalk gave his first public concert in Lima on November 17, 1865.*]

◇◇◇◇◇◇◇◇◇◇

December 13, 1865

My fears were realized on the subject of the locality that the partial giving way of the theater had forced me to choose, in order to continue the series of my concerts, which had been interrupted. It was in fact doubtful if the society of Lima would not be frightened at the idea of entering the hall and gardens of Otaiza, the Peruvian Mabille, where every Sunday the *tapadas* (veiled women)[9] and their *"amigos"* had their rendezvous, to give themselves up to the stormy *zamacuecas* and other indigenous dances that, although very picturesque, are not such as prudent mothers permit their daughters to indulge in.

In the face of this difficulty there was only one means of overcoming it: raise the price of the tickets so high as to be only within the reach of those privileged by fortune. I put them up to two dollars. It remained now "to bell the cat." The ladies were afraid of compromising themselves, no one was willing to be the first, although they were all dying with curiosity to penetrate into the profane sanctuary about which good and evil tongues had been talking for a very long time. The thick groves, the dark alleys, the kiosks spoke powerfully to the imagination—but, then, what would people say?

One of my friends persuaded his sisters to sacrifice themselves. The rumor spread that General ——— and his family had taken twenty seats. In four hours the hall was full. The first concert was not finished before the seats were already taken for a second.

Besides Otaiza, the proprietor, who has been to Paris, where he has assiduously visited for two years the Mabille Gardens, had done things like a lord. The gardens were lighted *á giorno*. The floor and alleys had been watered with eau de Cologne, and every lady received on entering the hall an enormous bouquet of roses and magnolias.[1]

---

[9] The veil was draped so as to hide one eye.
[1] There were two fifteen-minute intermissions for sauntering in the garden.

At each of my concerts *Banjo, Murmures éoliens, Charmes du foyer, Ojos criollos* (the last has been encored three times) were called for again.

This evening I gave a seventh concert. I played for the first time an important arrangement I have just written of *Un Ballo in maschera.*[2]

We are literally on the eve of a war with Spain, for the decree, people say, is to be published tomorrow. The conflict between the latter and Chile renders imminent the hostile participation of Peru, the Spanish-American republics being so strongly connected with each other by their common origin and their political institutions.

❖❖❖❖❖❖❖❖

Lima, January 13, 1866

My concerts are finished. They have been profitable, and my success has very much surpassed my expectations. Eight days ago a superb decoration was presented to me; the ribbon attached to it is white and red. I am thinking of taking a rest at Chorillos, and to take the sea baths there, for although it is January, we are in midsummer. Chorillos is ten miles from Lima, and I shall be able to come to the city every day. I have the idea of going to Chile, which is eight days from here by steamer, the crossing being as tranquil as on a lake.

❖❖❖❖❖❖❖❖

Chorillos, February 2, 1866

I have been resting for fifteen days in a *dolce far niente*, which had become indispensable on account of the fatigues of my last voyages.

The latest news of the civil war in Spain has thrown all the

After another appearance there, on December 22, he returned to the theater on January 2, 1866.

[2] Verdi's opera *Un Ballo in Maschera*, was first produced in Rome in 1859. Gottschalk's arrangement was scored for harmonium, two violins, and piano, a combination he used for other opera transcriptions during his concerts at Lima.

Spanish Americas into commotion. Being at war with the Peninsula, they rejoice at seeing Spain entangled in affairs at home.

◇◇◇◇◇◇◇◇◇

Lima, March 18, 1866

I have been introduced to Raymondi, an Italian savant, an enthusiast in natural history. He has been traveling for ten years on foot, knows all Peru, and has explored the interior regions, to this day unknown. He has told me a great deal about the coca and its effects. The coca is the leaf of a small tree which holds the same place among the Indians that opium does among the Chinese. There is not an Indian who does not always carry a supply of coca in a little bag hung to his neck.

The effects of this plant, although not ascertained by the physicians, are marvelous. The Indians, under its influence, can sustain journeys of from fifteen to twenty hours laden with heavy burdens, remain without eating four or five days, and do not become weaker for it. Soldiers on foreign expeditions are all always furnished with their supply of coca.

This is the procedure used by the Indians for eating the coca: They take the leaf, after having deprived it of its filaments, and make a ball of it, which they put in a corner of the mouth like a quid of tobacco, then with a little silver or gold pin, the point of which they moisten with their saliva and dip into a little box filled with lime, they prick the ball. The grains of lime adhering to the pin remain in the ball. They then chew, and as it appears that there should be a certain proportion between the lime and the coca, to produce this condition they add sometimes a leaf of coca, or dip again their pin into the lime, according as they wish to augment the quantity of the one or the other.

The effects of the coca are generally felt at the expiration of a quarter of an hour. Their marches are measured by the number of *cocadas* consumed. Such a village is at the distance of ten *cocadas,* which is the same as saying that a peon could go the distance by running, provided that he had ten rations of coca, and a quarter of an hour at each one of the *armados.* These are a kind of station. The peons are seen to arrive panting, their tongues dry, hanging out of their mouths, their eyes projecting and bloodshot, at the stopping place for the *cocada*. They fall exhausted and seem ready to die with fatigue, but immediately they spit out the ball already masticated and proceed to the making of the new one.

Little by little the effects of the wonderful plant can be seen in their organism and in their features, and at the tenth minute they are ready to rise and continue their journey.

❖❖❖❖❖❖❖❖❖

March 20

I have embarked on board the *Limeña* for Islay, a little port about three hundred miles south of Lima. I go there only to get onshore, Islay being only a small borough; but it is animated, being the outlet on the sea to Arequipa, a city of thirty or forty thousand inhabitants, which is situated at the distance of ninety miles in the interior. It is necessary to cross a desert of sand, and the baggage is transported on mules. There are ten *parados*, or *tambos*. The *tambo* is a relay and at the same time a refuge for the traveler overtaken by the night. It is mostly a hut: four stakes covered over with a roof of leaves. One sleeps there or shelters oneself from the heat of the sun and from the rain.

I am going to Arequipa. I am curious to see this focus of insurrection. The *arequipeños* are celebrated for their indomitable character and their warlike disposition. Every revolution commences at Arequipa, and the soldiers are considered brave among the brave.

I remember a dying Indian soldier, last November, of whom I inquired if he belonged to a regiment of Lima, proudly rising to tell me, "*No, señor, de batallón de Arequipa*," as an old soldier of Napoleon's would have answered that he belonged to the Old Guard.

The city of Arequipa is white and has a pretty appearance. It looks like a dove concealed in a nest of leaves, says a poet; with its back to a large volcano covered with snow, it presents the most picturesque view. The vegetation in the environs is fresh and green —a rare thing in Peru, where the country is gray, dusty, and arid.

All those who have traveled from Islay to Arequipa speak of it to me as a Herculean labor. The first journey lasts twelve hours; then you arrive at the Tambo de la Joya, where an Englishman has established a little hotel *with beds,* where you can sleep without much fear of the "squatters."

The water has to be carried thirty-five miles, and costs ten sous a bucketful for the cattle.

◇◇◇◇◇◇◇◇◇

March 22

Arrived at Islay. A few miserable huts hanging to steep rocks. The sea has made grottos under the cliffs and has given fantastic boundaries to the shore. It is not a very long time since one could not land at Islay without being hoisted up from the boat to the top of the cliff in a chair attached to a chain. The landing is less dangerous now, if not more comfortable. It is worked by means of beams held by chains, which form a kind of ladder. One hangs on to them, and with some notion of gymnastics, and getting the feet a little wet, one is nearly certain of getting ashore without being drowned.

What a dreary aspect! Not a leaf, not a plant, only bald gray rocks. The Spaniards being the red phantom of the moment, nobody lands without a passport. A lieutenant and some soldiers receive me on top of the scaffolding and permit me to pass after having examined my passport. It appears they know me, for I hear my name repeated from mouth to mouth. A young merchant, who heard me at Lima, invites me to his house. We are soon joined there by the commandant of the customs and the military commandant. Two travelers who arrive at this moment from Arequipa, and who have made the journey in twenty-four hours at one stage, present such a look of fatigue and of miseries undergone by them that I give up going there. Besides, I learn that the theater at Arequipa has no roof. The lack is not great in a country where it does not rain for nine months, but the winter is beginning, and in eight days the deluging rains will also make their appearance, consequently I should have to wait three months to be able to announce a concert, the public never going to the theater in the winter for a good reason. I will continue my voyage to the south as far as Arica, another little port a hundred fifty miles to the south of Islay. I return to the boat, which has just shot off a cannon—a signal of leaving.

At the foot of the cliff a little cove is formed, where the sea exhausts itself in little soft ripples on a beach of large, flat, white stones. Some young children, all naked, are bathing there. A young Indian girl is swimming among them in water so transparent that I can see that she wears no bathing costume. She has placed a handkerchief over her chest, but in swimming it has got up, and now answers for a cravat. Besides, nobody seems to see her.

◇◇◇◇◇◇◇◇◇

March 23

Landed at Arica, a pretty country town seen from the sea. An immense rock, which runs out into the sea and overhangs the town, is crowned with a battery of large cannons. It is an admirable natural fortification. Last year the governmental Peruvian squadron came to bombard Arica, which had upheld the revolution, but it was obliged to retire, no shot being able to reach as high as this battery perched upon the rock.

With a small effort of the imagination one can see an immense sphynx placed alongside the town and seeming to guard it. Its gray and bald crest extends into the interior of the country and loses itself in a chain of mountains which bounds the horizon behind the town. The city of Arica is, in truth, a little country town. Its importance is due particularly to its proximity to Bolivia.

La Paz is a five day journey on mules from Tacna. Tacna is reached from Arica in two hours by rail.

The whole trade of Bolivia passes through Tacna and Arica. The muleteers are all from Tacna.

There is on board a merchant from Chuquisaca, the capital of Bolivia, who is trying to persuade me to go to Bolivia with him. But five hundred miles of country on mules has nothing to attract me in a land where there are no hotels. As for the dangers, they arise only from fatigue and traveling accidents—robbers are unknown here. Every month hundreds and thousands of dollars are sent in cases made of cowhides, conducted by Indian muleteers, and a *real* is never missing, though the distance traveled is six, eight hundred or a thousand miles. It often happens (the fact has often been mentioned to me by many merchants) that the convoy of silver arrives at Tacna with one mule missing and also the load.

"The animal has died of fatigue a hundred fifty miles from here," says the Indian, "and I have placed it near him—I will bring it to you on the next journey." And true enough, he finds the case of dollars untouched near the carcass of the animal and brings it with him on his next trip.

There is at the present time at Arica a troop of Spanish actors who are going to Buenos Aires by land, playing in every town on the road, an itinerary equal in distance to that from Paris to St. Petersburg. I shall perhaps make this journey, the novelty and hazards of which singularly tempt me.

I have been promenading the town. The church of Arica is like all the Spanish village churches—full of gewgaws and bric-a-brac. A large rock rises perpendicularly on one of the sides of the church square. It is entirely gray and bare. One can hardly form an idea of its height—the eye having no point of departure to establish the proportions of this vast granitic mass that pierces the sky. A few little white lines stripe it like a zebra in opposite directions; these are the paths—a singular optical effect. A battalion of soldiers, not larger than lead toy soldiers, descends from the top. They seem to be only a few yards off. I can distinguish them as clearly as if they were about to touch me, absolutely as if I were looking at an object through the large end of an opera glass.

We have on board an individual who has just been appointed commanding general of the fortifications of Arica. He is a distinguished man, and full of moderation—a rare thing among the Peruvians.

There is a decree of Prado's[3] which subjects to a very severe penalty every Peruvian whose services may be required by the government and who shall refuse to accept its mandate. Colonel V.G. has been obliged to abandon his family to come to Arica to take the command of the fortifications.

He relates to me some of his campaigns in the interior. In the department of Ayacucho there are villages and entire districts whose inhabitants, for the most part Indians, are so ferocious and independent that no one has ever been able to collect the taxes or make them submit to any of the burdens imposed upon the other citizens of the republic, while they exact from the govern-

---

[3] Mariano Ignacio Prado became Pezet's successor in December 1865.

ment the protection it extends to all. They were obedient to the government of Marshal Santa Cruz for forty years, because Santa Cruz was a half-Indian—his mother being a cacique (a descendant of the privileged families of the Incas). Near Ayacucho these Indians elected a governor, who was called for a long time a Peruvian general by his own authority. His son (the general was dead) governed when D. N. Vargas was sent by the republic of Lima to take command with the title of colonel. He was a fat Indian, filthy dirty, who smelled strong of dirt ten feet off. "I made him a present of a pair of epaulettes," said Vargas to me, "but he did not know what to do with them, being naked, with the exception of his sash. He fastened them to it, as well as he could, and demanded that the music of the regiment, which I had brought with me, should parade the streets with him in order that all might see him with his ensign of colonel."

This population is a very savage one. They tear out the eyes of their prisoners, and the bones from out the limbs with horrible refinements of cruelty. They are Catholics; have their churches and their priests, which does not prevent them (in the Sierra Cordillera) from being cannibals.

◇◇◇◇◇◇◇◇◇

Tacna, March 24, 1866

A neat city. I notice in the principal street some French shops, among others, a Parisian perfumer and hairdresser. In the middle of the principal promenade, which is very long and lined with trees, the river flows between two stony declivities on a bed that has been paved. At intervals a stone arch is boldly thrown from one side to the other (a yard and half in width). The river flows tumultuously, and with a noise.

◇◇◇◇◇◇◇◇◇

Good Friday

The Lamentations are sung false by an old Spanish priest. The accompaniment consists of a violin and violoncello. (I mention the latter as a memorandum, seeing that it had only one note.) It is an old Indian who plays the violin, and I forbear saying what he did. While the priest was chanting the Lamentations, he was frolicking, making sometimes trills, sometimes arpeggios, sometimes chromatic scales, ascending, descending—he was frolicking, I say, agreeably on the treble string, precipitating himself from its sharp summit into the depths of the fourth string, where he rested on a tremolo, then came a squib that escaped altogether upward, all of this false, out of tune, strumming without any regard to the key in which the priest was singing.

Besides, I must say that the latter got out of the key in such a way that it would have been impossible to follow him. When he had finished one verse and was taking breath again, the violin, which had traveled insensibly upward or descended a quarter-tone, returned again to the original key, striking a chord, invariably in G, followed by a fluttering little scale. Then the priest began again, and the squibs of the violin recommenced. The effect was strange, when an open string, being on the primitive *diapason*, or pitch, produced the effect of a shower bath every time it returned—oh dear! oh dear!

◇◇◇◇◇◇◇◇◇

March 31

Three Indians have just arrived from Bolivia. Their mules are loaded with silver. These are Indians from Potosí, who come from the mines. They have traveled nine hundred miles, have crossed the deserts, the *cordilleras*, and rivers, have traveled day and night with a load worth fifteen thousand francs. The type of the Indians of Bolivia is uglier than that of Peru. The *cholo* of Peru is fat, small, thick-set; his apathetic features do not lack a certain intelligence: he is mild and generally peaceable. The Bolivian is thin; his skin, of an earthy brown, approaches almost to black; his face is that of a brute; his form angular; he has the appearance of a monkey and that of a bear in movements and conduct; his features are horrible; his mouth is opened to his ears; his long nose, flattened at his birth, and cut sloping to the nostrils, is like a monkey's; his forehead is depressed; above his eyebrows his rough, stiff, dull black hair commences, falling with metallic rigidity in thick locks around his hollow cheeks; his little round eyes, very near together, complete his resemblance to the monkey.

Visited the church at the upper part of the town today, Holy Saturday. They are preparing the church for tomorrow, Easter Sunday; three or four devotees, sitting on some little footstools surrounded by their children, are chatting before the altar. Some Indian servants are cleaning the lamps that are to ornament the altar. The whole neighborhood has been requisitioned, and I give up describing the sight. At first glance this profusion of little mirrors, of children's dolls dressed in little skirts, like balloons swinging between each mirror, the little gilt paper flags, which at a distance produce the effect of penny trumpets; the porcelain cups, the vases of artificial flowers, the chandeliers, the lamps placed alongside each other; on each step of the altar, that heterogeneous crowd of objects that shine in an equivocal manner, all this recalls without mistake those peddlers' booths where for a penny one might win at every chance.

There is an instrument in vogue among the Indians of which I must speak. It is a flute made of reed, and is played like a clarionet. It is called *tristos,* and as it would seem to indicate has a very sad sound of strange rhythm, a funereal and lugubrious tone. Tradition states that the first *tristos* was invented by a friar who was living among the Indians; he lost his *querida,* and made one of these instruments out of the tibia of his well beloved.

❖❖❖❖❖❖❖❖❖

Tacna, April 2

Soirée at S——'s. The society of Tacna is naturally very limited: eight or ten merchants married to *tacneñas,* some young Bolivians who have been civilized by a few months' travel in Europe, and two or three rich families of the country are the elements constituting the *society* of Tacna.

Wealth being almost the only aristocracy recognized among parvenus and republicans, it cannot be gainsaid that the S——'s (the father is English), who are rich, who have a brother in London, who have given soirées, who possess the only carriage in the city, occupy the first rank. I have not the least objection to these assumptions of superiority. That —— should be the center of his little circle I have not the least desire to oppose. But that this imperceptible center of a microscopic circle should persist in believ-

ing himself a center when he goes outside of his little sphere is what
I find ridiculous. Unaccustomed to be seen outside of the factitious
atmosphere where their satisfied vanity exercises itself, these little
centers forget that they are nobodies except when surrounded by
others inferior to themselves. What would be thought of a Lilliputian who, owing to his great height, has been made drum-major
of a Lilliputian regiment, who, thrown into the midst of giants,
should still aspire to the prerogatives of the drum-majoralty?
Absurd!

There is nothing more irritating than those factitious aristocracies that can be explained only by the inferiority of those among
whom they move.

Some very pretty women at the treasurer's. The dances are
quadrilles, the lancers, the polka, the waltz, and the *habanera*,
which they dance here entirely differently from what they do in
Havana. After supper they dance the *mecapaqueña*: it is a kind of
Bolivian Indian quadrille whose music, in a minor key, with a
racking rhythm, reminds one a little of the Arab melodies. The
figures are numerous and complicated. Sometimes the lady, conducted by two cavaliers, advances. The step is always the same
throughout the whole quadrille; it is a skipping from one foot
to the other, rapidly and lightly, which gives to the ladies the
appearance of a shivering throughout their bodies. Sometimes the
lady leads, arms extended, holding a handkerchief by the two ends.
With head inclined, she makes the tour of the room; then all at
once, like a frightened dove, she flies and escapes to one extremity;
then slowly returns, with her head turned backward, as if she
was trying to resist some invisible force that carries her (with
lascivious undulations). It is curious and charming.

The wife of N——, a good little old lady whose round face
looks like a small red apple dried up by the sun, has cacique blood
in her veins.

There are still some Peruvian families who boast of being descended from the privileged, sacerdotal, and governmental class of
the Incas. But as there exists in general a very strong prejudice
against the Indians, and as the principal families hold it to be an
honor to be entirely white, I suppose that the families who betray
too clearly by their color their indigenous stock, save their pride by

claiming an almost royal origin, and take a cacique for their ancestor.

It nevertheless appears positive that this good little old woman of sixty years, round and plump, whose two large black eyes sparkle in their besmutted orbits, and who shows when she smiles two rows of white pearls, descends from the cacique Huáscar. She was a marvelous beauty, they say, and the chronicle of scandals, always busy in small towns, has told me in a whisper the following story:—

Bolívar, that indefatigable hero, who was hewing out territories with his conquering sword and creating with his powerful breath nations on this immense continent of the New World, which he had just snatched from Spain, although less great than Washington, not possessing either his virtue or wisdom, presented in his whole character some features more striking, more romantic than those of his model—the immortal and august founder of the Republic of the United States. There is in Washington something graver, more thoughtful, which becomes the cold genius of the Anglo-Saxon race—it is Cincinnatus and Socrates ennobled by Christianity; while Bolívar was a man of the Spanish-American race. He partakes of the *condottieri* of the Middle Ages by his extravagant depredations, and of the hero by his intrepid valor, his fiery energy, and the sublime sacrifices he made for liberty and his country. Washington will never descend from the serene heights of history, where he dominates in all the majesty of the great, the good, and the true—the greatest representatives of humanity; while Bolívar has been already the type of many Romans. If Bolívar, in the midst of the dissensions which already were commencing to paralyze the flight of the new republics, provoked bitter hatreds, he also inspired the greater part of the nations he had just created with an idolatrous devotion. From the Strait of Magellan to Venezuela, from the banks of the Amazon to the shores of the Pacific, and on all the peaks of the Andes, the name of Bolívar excited transports of enthusiasm.

During one of those short intervals in his life of combat, between two battles, he stopped at Tacna. The hero was fêted: the citizens and magistrates exhausted all the resources that the intoxication of patriotic enthusiasm could suggest. The "Pearl of Tacna," and the descendant of the cacique Huáscar, then in all the

brilliancy of her beauty and youth, attracted his notice. Urged by
the frenzy of enthusiasm, of grateful patriotism, her father, they
assert, presented her to the Liberator. But the restless soul of the
hero would not permit him any repose so long as his task was in-
complete. There still remained half of the continent to be taken
from the Spaniards. He tore himself from love and threw himself
again into the whirlwind of battles. The cannon, glory, and ambition soon effaced the memory of the granddaughter of the Inca
Huáscar. He never saw her again! The poor child!—a moment
dazzled by the aureole that surrounded the hero, thought that in
obeying her father, she was also yielding to the transports of her
own heart; but when alone and abandoned she became a mother;
she interrogated her heart and discovered that she had never loved.
She was then eighteen years old. Concentrating all the treasures of
tenderness which her virgin heart enclosed, she resolved never to
marry, and to devote herself entirely to her daughter. Some years
later, her beauty, which time had only ripened, having attracted to
her the attentions of X——, then also young, she yielded to a desire
that proclaimed itself with so much the more violence as her heart
up to that time had remained mute. She married. Their union was
for a long time happy. But clouds, at first uncertain, then thick and
full of storm, came to darken the peace of the household. This
house was for a long time enshrouded in mystery, and the dark
drama that took place there is in its details still unknown to almost
all. It was confided to my ear, and I relate it here. The natural
daughter of Bolívar had grown; although barely adolescent, she
was as beautiful as her mother. X—— loved her. Did she yield or
not to his wishes? No one knows. She died suddenly, and as no
physician was called in, and as after her death the clouds that
had troubled the peace of the household appeared to be dissipated,
remarks upon them were not wanting. It would seem that the
daughter of the Inca Huáscar, divided between jealousy of her
husband and her instincts as a mother, sacrificed the latter to the
former and poisoned her daughter, her blind passion permitting
her to see in her only a favored rival.

I admit that, ever since, I cannot without an indescribable
emotion look at this good little old woman who offers me a cup
of tea with all the placidity of a good old grandmother whose
conscience has never been sullied by a crime.

⟡⟡⟡⟡⟡⟡⟡⟡⟡

Tacna, April 5

Passed the evening with a Swiss merchant who has married in this country. We have had music, and I have played for them the Overture to *Guillaume Tell* and the March from *Faust*. It was the first time they had heard a composition on this opera, which nevertheless they were acquainted with through the newspapers.

A charming evening! Many ladies sang. A German amateur and a lady sang the duet from *I Masnadieri*, and that of *Rigoletto*. Today I have been invited to eat game taken on the Tacora, a peak of the Andes whose snowy point rises behind the first chain of mountains of the Sierra. It is fifteen thousand feet in height. They shoot wild geese there, which are said to be exquisite. A young clerk left (from Mr. Hay's, the merchant) for Tacora (two days' walk), and has brought back a superb supply.

⟡⟡⟡⟡⟡⟡⟡⟡⟡

Tacna, April 6, 1866

Last evening; second concert at Tacna. Audience passable. My friend, Mr. H., on reaching home, found the door of his stable open; his horse, a superb animal, had disappeared. This morning he called in some Bolivian Indians for the purpose of pursuing the robber and taking his horse from him. A few hours later on they brought the horse to him. It was found covered with foam and sweat, and bearing all the traces of a long race. It is probable that some Indian who had to make a sudden journey last night had taken this commodious means of borrowing H——'s horse.

These Indians whom H—— had immediately called upon, have an admirable instinct for capturing marauders and finding stolen horses or cattle. The tricks employed by the robbers for the purpose of destroying their tracks are worthy of those of the redskin. The footprint betraying the road taken by the animal they put imitation hoofs on him, but the Indians do not let themselves be taken in; they recognize by the greater or less depth of the hoof if it is real or not. Sometimes they put the hoofs of a horse or cow on a sheep, but they gain nothing by it; the Indian has other signs by which he recognizes the animal.

◇◇◇◇◇◇◇◇◇◇

Tacna, April 9

The news of the bombardment of Valparaíso changes all my plans of travel—the intention of the Spaniards being indubitably to go up the coast as far as Guayaquil and burn all the ports.[4] I shall not be able, without imprudence, to go south to Iquique, where I was thinking of giving a concert. What am I to do? Where shall I go?

Bolivia opens before me. Ensconced in the interior of the continent, wedged in the middle of the other republics who serve her as shields, intrenched behind the snowy summits of the Andes, she defies the Spaniards and continues to live in the midst of her normal atmosphere of revolutions, riots, assassinations, and crimes. I have the greatest desire to visit the capital of Bolivia, but it is three hundred miles in the interior, and the journey is made on muleback. It is necessary to cross first a barrier of mountains, traverse a vast extent of desert, cross the Tacora in the midst of snows and the regions constituting the summit of the Andes at fifteen thousand feet above the sea, before arriving at La Paz, which has at least an elevation of twelve thousand feet.

Travelers unaccustomed to the Andes are besides exposed to attacks of malaise, which is felt particularly on the first declivities of the Tacora. The first symptoms are a dimness, nausea, sometimes vomiting of blood. The sudden alternations of cold and heat also cause chapped lips and hands, and the whole skin in general cracks, swells, and degenerates into ulcerations. The perspective has nothing attractive in it, but it presents a magnificent occasion to go to La Paz. Without reckoning the season—which is magnificent, the rains having ceased and the storms of the Andes being over—a caravan of French travelers starts tomorrow on the way to Cochabamba and stops on the road at La Paz. It is composed of French engineers, a number of merchants, and a French baron also, who takes with him the whole equipage for a campaign: tents, wagons, provisions, an Indian servant for cook; mules, arms, and photographic apparatus.

---

[4] Chilean sympathy with Peru in its quarrel with Spain had led to war between Chile and Spain.

The safety enjoyed by foreigners is relative. Bolivia commits
with impunity the most flagrant crimes against the laws of nations
behind these bastions eighteen thousand feet in height, these
giddy defiles, these peaks where the eagle soars or the vicuña
pastures. Her people, strong and warlike by nature, are hardened
by forty years of bloody and desperate strife. Legislation, laws, arts,
have for a long time disappeared before the sword, the symbol
everywhere and here particularly of brutal force, barbarism, spolia-
tions, murders, proscriptions, military executions, and all the
excesses to which a ferocious and licentious soldier of fortune
can give himself who arrives at supreme power sustained by a
victorious and unbridled soldiery. This is the condition of this
unhappy country whose territory is double that of France, whose
mineral and vegetable riches are inexhaustible, and which under a
good government would take the first rank among the strongest
and most favored of the globe.

◇◇◇◇◇◇◇◇◇◇

Tacna, April 21

One of my friends having received a letter from one of his correspondents at Valparaíso, in which the desire of hearing me is
expressed more strongly than ever, I find myself again embarrassed.
On the other side they have written to me from Moquegua (interior of Peru) inviting me to go there to give a concert. There
is a piano belonging to a Spaniard, who on account of my decorations offers me hospitality and his piano for my concerts; but the
road is long. There are no dangers, but much fatigue. The Indians
here are submissive, timid, mild, and honest. They have suffered
so much since the conquest (nearly four hundred years ago), that
energy and human dignity have been extinguished among them,
to give place in the presence of the whites to a docility that borders
on terror and admiration. The whites are for them an infinitely
superior race. Caravans of mules arrive here every day, laden with
ingots of silver, escorted by three or four unarmed, half-naked
Indians. In the rainy season, the roads become broken in the
mountains, and sometimes a mule is mired and disappears with his
load in the mud. He is left on the road. On return of the dry season,
the same Indians pass by the place where the accident happened

and carry off the load (sometimes twenty-five thousand or thirty thousand dollars), which nobody has meddled with, although caravans every day follow each other on the road. What is more singular in regard to this honesty is that the same Indians who would not steal twenty-five thousand dollars will appropriate to themselves, if they can, a strap, a nail, a piece of rag, the smallest trifle worth nothing, that may fall in their way.

The port of Arica, belonging to Tacna (connected with it by a railway eighteen miles long) owes its importance to its geographical position. Almost the whole commerce of Bolivia, its imports and exports, is made through Tacna. Thus the muleteers, the caravans, the long files of laden mules which come from or are going to La Paz constantly encumber the principal street of Tacna. Today I have been more than half an hour in getting as far as my door, which nevertheless was only fifty paces off. A caravan of loaded mules kicking, pushing against each other, became entangled and formed a compact moving mass that would neither go forward nor backward, confined as it was in this narrow street. The confusion of this scene is indescribable. The muleteers swore, made vows to their saints, whipped, jostled; the mules neighed, kicked, reared; the bales knocked against each other; the merchandise was scattered about. All this made a horrible noise.

The President of Bolivia, the most excellent liberator of his country, the very illustrious Señor General Melgarejo (these are his titles) is a mulatto, a sort of tiger with a human face, who gets drunk and becomes ferocious. He then kills everybody around him. He has assassinated with his own hand the ex-president whose place he took. For pastime he caused to be shot, by some soldiers sent for him by his corporals on duty, a young girl, almost at her own home, whose beauty he remarked in passing before her window. In the street he cut off the ears of his adjutant with his saber, cleaved the shoulder of his aid-de-camp with one blow of an ax. He burns, sacks, and gluts himself like a ferocious beast in the midst of all the excesses to which his savage and sanguinary appetites drive him. Last week, one of his adjutants having observed to him that it would be better if he abstained from being present in the condition in which he was, at a religious procession (he was drunk), he placed his revolver on his chest and killed him at once.

. . .

Some of the customs of Tacna.

The marriages of the civilized Indians of Bolivia are extremely curious. The future husband having chosen his godfather, ordinarily a white gentleman, he goes with him to the house of the *novia* (bride). The godfather stipulates with the father or mother (sometimes with the godmother, whom the *novia* has chosen) on the conditions of the marriage. These generally are pieces of pocket money or woolen stuffs, or a sheep, to be given to the bride's parents. Then they send to the neighboring village of the husband and the bride to get, for the husband, red pantaloons, a red coat, a three-cornered hat with feathers, and shoes. For the bride, shoes, a woolen dress, or a silk one when she is rich. These costumes are the same for all, they are lent for the ceremony, and are faithfully sent back again the next day to the furnisher in town. There is nothing so pitiable as the grimaces of these poor husbands and wives, who have never before put on shoes; they are in torture and stumble at every step, their clothes are too large or too small, and they present the most grotesque appearance in the world.

After the benediction at the church, they are conducted into a kind of little grove made of small branches and palms, where they are made to sit opposite each other. Exposed to the remarks of the wedding guests by an opening like a window, they must remain immovable, looking at each other without speaking for many hours. The guests drink, dance, and eat during this time. Then comes the ceremony of conducting them to the nuptial cabin, which is accompanied with very singular customs and practices.

Ordinarily the godfather or godmother sees in the town, at the expiration of a few days, the newly married ones, who come to complain of some trouble that has taken place in the household. These complaints are commonly that the bride is not willing to work, or that the husband appropriates to himself all the pieces of meat or of *chupe* (the national soup). The godfather or godmother is requested to administer some blows with a leather strap to the delinquent, and the couple return to their village. It also often happens that the woman presents herself, all in tears, to the priest. "Padre, my husband does not love me, he has not yet whipped me." The priest then causes the husband to be called, and after having reproached him with his indifference, places in his hands a whip and orders him to administer correction to his better half, who, receiving it with a relish, thanks the priest, and goes away certain that her husband loves her. The humility of these poor Indians, their submission, their fear of the whites, speaks sufficiently of what they have had to suffer from the conquest up to our days.

At every revolution they are treated by both parties like beasts of burden; they are torn from their families and forced to carry enormous burdens for the distance of many hundreds of miles. Many perish from blows and fatigue.

When the woman is about to be confined, the man immediately goes to bed and feigns all the pains of childbirth. He groans, he twists, weeps, and the most curious part of it is that he persuades himself that he is suffering in the same way as his wife. He divides with her the cares that are lavished upon her, drinks broth, stays in bed, and diets during the convalescence of his better half.

I have visited the market. It is a parallelogram, open at the two extremities, by which you can enter from the adjacent streets. On the two sides are lateral alleys, covered like a cloister, under which a crowd of Indians is squatting, selling meat, fruit, etc. The fruit, particularly the grapes, is phenomenal. A priest walked slowly among the merchants and made them kiss a little image of the Blessed Virgin, presenting to them a plate on which they placed a small piece of money. This operation takes place every morning and cannot fail to be very productive to the treasury of the church.

[Chilean music-lovers, receiving reports from Peruvian newspapers of Gottschalk's success, awaited him eagerly. His opening concert in Santiago, the first of fifteen there, took place on May 31, 1866, in the salon of the old Teatro Municipal.

In Santiago, his repertoire assumed ambitious proportions. He presented an arrangement of Weber's Oberon, arias and the chorus and March from Faust, arias from Beethoven's Fidelio, the Pilgrims' chorus from Tannhäuser, a movement from a Mendelssohn symphony, and piano works such as Chopin's "Funeral March" and Beethoven's Sonata "Pathétique," along with the usual lighter assortment including The Banjo, Berceuse, and Ojos criollos.

Remaining in Santiago until approximately mid-August, he continued more definitely his pattern of concert life: enlisting the professional aid of local musicians, contributing the proceeds of his concerts to charity—on July 3 to the Sociedad de Instrucción Primaria—and concluding with a grand festival involving three hundred fifty musicians. Representatives of a grateful citizenry showered him with wreaths, medals, and decorations. As in the West Indies, the streets seethed with wild demonstrations ("¡Viva Gottschalk!"); after the festival he was carried to his hotel by the noisy, adoring throng.

Gottschalk became a public idol also at Valparaíso, where he remained until the end of the year. Then he proceeded northward to La Serena, Chile.]

◇◇◇◇◇◇◇◇◇◇

La Serena (Chile), January 3, 1867
At my last concert at Valparaíso, the municipal council presented me with a golden wreath and a gold medal, inscribed. I have had a great deal of success at my two concerts here. Tomorrow I am going to Copiapó, on the coast.

◇◇◇◇◇◇◇◇◇◇

Copiapó, February 12 [*1867*]
Sad but picturesque incident.

I had noticed at the hotel a tall, thin, shabby man whose distinguished manners led me to conjecture that he was one of those social wrecks with which America so often furnishes us an example. I dined once with him at the French consul's. He was introduced to me. He was an engineer, but his bad health and ill luck prevented him from finding employment, and he was thereby reduced to makeshifts. Day before yesterday they came to inform me that Mr. H—— was dying. Attacked suddenly with a terrible illness, he was sinking. The doctor, called in at once, did not give him an hour to live. We relieved one another in his room for thirty-six hours, during which he was dying. He possessed a vigorous intelligence and a strong mind. He was not conscious, at least in appearance, and we waited for two nights and a day his deliverance, which was momentarily expected. He died today at four o'clock in the afternoon. Burials here are made only at night; the heat prevents the body being kept as long as in Europe. The

French consul requested all the French and myself to come to the Hotel Marcadet, whence we would accompany the corpse to the cemetery. Two hours after his death the body was already decomposed, and spreading its miasma in such a manner that the hotel keeper obliged us to take it away. Fortunately in the court of the hotel itself there is a small circus where cockfighting takes place— they have the poor corpse there.

This evening, at midnight, all the French were assembled at the Hotel Marcadet. I have never been present at the interment of a foreigner, dying far from his country and his family, without having my heart broken with grief. There is also something very affecting in this solidarity of compatriots who come together to render the last duties to him whom they have, perhaps, never known, but who, born like themselves on the soil of their mother country, they have come to claim brotherhood with after death.

This poor departed one, whose history I have learned, was the son of Lieutenant General Marquis de ——, and, with his younger brother, occupied in the elevated sphere of the military hierarchy a distinguished rank in the French army. Timidity, vexation, disappointment caused by failure in life made him throw the handle after the hatchet, and the poor H——, an old scholar of the Polytechnic School, captain of engineers, led a miserable existence, without hope, without any means of escape, except in suicide, of which he often spoke with the *sang-froid* of a determined man. He owed one year's boarding to the keeper of the hotel, an honest Frenchman, who did not venture, knowing his poverty, to remind him of his debt, and who took care of him through charity.

The coffin was placed on a flat hearse, drawn by a horse, and at midnight we are on the road to the cemetery. The driver of the hearse, a peon wearing a poncho, walks alongside the horse, the poor beast stumbling at every step. The roads are bad and hilly. He falls down. We raise him up. A little farther on, one of the straps breaks. We stop to arrange it. The harness is tied together with twine. We were so foolish as to pay the coachman in advance for his journey, and this is the way we are served for it. We are stopped again. This time it is the halter that has broken. The peon informs us that the horse will not be able to go farther. While he is pretending to sweat blood and water, to make strenuous exertions to arrange the harness, I examine this peon. He is a tall, bronzed, roguish fellow, clad proudly in a reddish poncho, to which the hour, the scene, the hearse, the light of the moon give a fantastic aspect. The French consul has employed him. He is a good workman, but the workshop does not suffice for him. "Do you see," said he, with a pleasant seriousness and an innocent impudence, "I have been one of the executioners of R——, and having killed quite a few in my life, I have undertaken first to bury them. I have done it, and, frankly, I can only live with the dead."

The harness is too old and the horse too fatigued. The coachman makes us wait, and the delays are so numerous that a good old French Basque proposes (after having eased his conscience by addressing in French some *kind* words to the coachman, who does not understand one word of them) to ungear the horse and to drag the cart to the cemetery. No sooner said than done. And there we are pulling and pushing. From time to time the inhabitants of the poor hovels lining the road come out on the doorstep to look at this procession, which has on me the effect of a nightmare. We arrive at the chapel of the cemetery. We deposit the corpse in a hall, and the custom is to return next morning to hear Mass. A tottering old man in a black cap, with a lantern, opens the door, and, after having received the coffin, shuts the door and remains with his company. It is a nightmare. I shall not sleep tonight.

The Desert of Atacama extends from the coast of Chile as high as the tropic to Bolivia, a distance of a hundred fifty miles. It is in the mountains of Atacama that the richest silver mine of Chile is found—la Buena Esperanza. It was discovered nineteen years ago (1848), and has yielded very nearly seventy-five million francs. It now yields annually an average of from five to six million francs and still promises certain and infinite riches, since from just the masses and columns left in the galleries it can produce for many years. The manager, a French engineer whose acquaintance I have made during my short sojourn lately at Copiapó, invited me to spend some days at the mine. The distance from Copiapó is eighty miles across the desert. I hesitated, but he sent me an excellent carriage and two horses, one of which was mounted by an experienced driver who led the one in the carriage, and, besides, established relays upon the route. I decided to go. Billet and I left Copiapó at six o'clock in the evening. The weather was magnificent.

Lamarca, the banker, had promised me a revolver (in case of need), but at the moment of leaving he discovered that the pistol had been stolen from him the evening before. Besides, one is rarely attacked.

Hardly are we out of Copiapó than we find ourselves already in that calcareous dust which has the color of sand and is so fatiguing to the eyes. We enter into a gorge. What horrible aridity! Not a blade of grass. The mountains seem to bar the passage to us at every moment, so near do they approach each other, but we wind around them. The ground becomes flat, and in a small plain we perceive some little hovels of dried mud and their paddocks, surrounded with walls also of dried mud—the masonry work of which, made of great square blocks, recalling that of the Assyrians, vaguely gives rise to thoughts of biblical ruins, to which the gray, burned country and the red rays of the sun add the aspect of a biblical land. There is a well here, which explains the few hovels, which are called Pueblo de Indios (Indian village). No industry, no labor; we see now and then a child, who looks with an astonished air at us passing. The father and mother, lying lazily in front of the cabin, half naked, are sleeping or forgetting themselves in the *far niente*, the former smoking a cigarette. As for the rest, the carelessness of these people is favored by the climate. It never rains; it is never cold. When there is nothing more to buy cigarettes with, the father makes a great effort and goes to work, either in the town or at the mine, and, when he has earned a few dollars, he returns to slumber, to eat, to smoke his cigar, and life thus flows onward for them without any event, without suffering, like a sleep.

The last houses of Pueblo de Indios have disappeared. We are entering the Desert of Atacama. The mountains open before us; their chains stretch out instead of surrounding us, and rise on each side of a long narrow plain, like a wall, a sort of palisade, the top of which, illuminated by the sun, renders more somber the first tints of twilight which begin to descend into the plain. The eye gazes in vain over this immense flat and gray surface.

Our coachman often looks behind him. We discover two black points that detach themselves from the horizon. They are two horsemen who are galloping. The coachman watches them with a certain degree of anxiety. The night begins, and I cannot help regretting this encounter and not having arms. The horsemen are drawing near. We are not hasty in reassuring ourselves on see-ing the two horsemen draw off to the right and bury themselves in a gorge where they are lost to view. We are crossing upon our left and are entering the gorge of Taxepote. The road is horrible, but I am wrong in saying road, for there is none. The carriage jolts over fragments of rocks which have rolled down from the mountains—a chaos, an evident cataclysm.

There is a very rich copper mine at some distance. Our first relay is at Chule. There is a well there, and a hovel inhabited by a *cholo* peon, who waters the horses and mules that come down from the mines. The carts, laden with silver-bearing ore that is sent once a week to Copiapó to be worked out, come afterward to Chule. We see a cross on the point of a mountain that advances like a promontory before us. At that spot a miner was murdered by his companion. Both were set at work in this region to discover a mine spoken of in the traditions of the Indians. They found it; it was very rich. After having observed the country with care and established landmarks to find again the place of their treasure, they carefully concealed the entrance of the mine, in order that no other person might dispute the right of their discovery, and took the road for Copiapó, where, according to law, they should immediately present the ore samples, claim the privilege of discovery before the judge, and have the property legally adjudged to them. Tempted by the demon of cupidity, one of them, wishing to possess alone the whole mine, murdered his companion and returned to Copiapó. But his victim was not dead; he had time to drag himself as far as Pueblo de Indios, where before dying the unfortunate man had time to tell the name of his murderer. The other learned that he was accused, and, jumping upon one of these Chilean horses which seem never to tire, he crossed the Desert of Atacama in a few hours and did not stop until he had placed the Cordillera of the Andes and the frontier of the Argentine Republic between himself and his pursuers.

The mine has since passed into the condition of a legend known to all the old miners. It has defied all their searches; they have never been able to find it. The miner, condemned to death, lived many years in the Argentine Republic, and on many occa-sions sent to his friends a rough plan that he had made from memory of the mountains around the mine, and added that the

sun was on his right at the hour for the Ave Maria, while he was
close to the mine, and that before night he had had time to go to
Santa Rosa, but these vague indications served only to further
embarrass the searchers, who have finally given it up. Besides this
there are many celebrated mines that have been lost since the conquest by the Europeans.

Our horses begin to pant horribly. The road is infernal. We
are bounced to the roof, we are thrown from right to left, tossed
about, etc. etc. The road becomes smoother, the stars and moon
lighten up a circular valley surrounded by high mountains. A light
before us! It is a lighthouse in the desert, it is the lantern of the
hovel at Chule. The horses neigh—the poor beasts smell the stable
—a dog barks in the depths of the valley upon our left. I cannot
describe what a singular charm I find in these noises, which banish
in a moment all the somber clouds that the aridity of the country, the solitudes of the Desert of Atacama, and the stories of assassination just heard, of murders committed by miners, had evoked
in my mind. The hovel is preceded by a shed, under which the
peons sleep, and around which the horses, mules, cows, and goats
wander at liberty. There is in the interior but one inhabitable
chamber. It is reserved for us. P—— yesterday sent to inform the
innkeeper about our coming, which explains the luxury displayed.
Two wax candles are on a white wooden table; the walls are covered
with illustrations from the *Correo de Ultramar*. A large man, whose
abdomen, poorly restrained by pantaloons that reach half way
down his legs and permit his shirt (evidently put on in honor of
us) to swell out like a smock—naked feet, humble fat face, sub-
dued, timid, and jovial—bids us welcome. He loses himself in sal-
utations. He evidently does not know who we are, but Don Carlos
(the director of the mine) having the evening before sent him
orders to prepare supper for us, to make our beds, and to entertain
us with all the respect due to persons of high importance, he does
his best so that Don Carlos may be pleased with him. The good
man informs us that he can give us a beefsteak of fresh meat, he
has also fresh eggs and goat's milk. We have ravenous appetites,
and the meal is quickly served up on a small white wooden table.
On each side there is a cot with coverlets and mattress, an unheard-of luxury, but which my traveling experience has accustomed me to distrust. We go to take a look at the kitchen. It

is a shed covered with a few mats of plaited straw. The fireplace, a large fragment of rock upon which are burning, between two large stones which serve for andirons, some firebrands, branches of dried wood. The wife of the innkeeper cuts some slices of meat from a large piece of beef. We request her not to put too many onions in it (they put them here in every thing), and particularly not to drown the beefsteak in grease.

Our coachman has taken possession of the kitchen. We are to set out again at one o'clock; it is now ten. The moon, although only in the first quarter, will give us enough light for our journey. Besides the natives of the country have the instinct of savages to find a place again, and for following the ruts of caravans in the desert, even in the most profound darkness.

Supper is served up. The poor man is evidently worried about the judgment his patrons may pass upon his wife's culinary talents. His large face brightens when we tell him that his beefsteak is eatable.

"Have you any coffee?" we ask. "Yes," he replied, "I have some Costa Rica." Billet makes the coffee himself. It is the best-founded of his pretensions. I believe he thinks more of his reputation as a coffee maker than as a concert violoncellist.

"The coffee is — ——, I cannot express it," said Billet, sipping it. The goat's milk is altogether exquisite. We have excellent cigars. You can hardly have an idea how well off we are, seated on the doorsill of the hovel, with the starry heavens above us.

(Unfinished.)

◇◇◇◇◇◇◇◇◇

Caldera, Chile, April 12 [*1867*]

The incidents that occur in a traveling artist's career are almost always the same. They at first seem interesting through their novelty, but as they are constantly repeated they become a part of the monotony of the daily routine. It is true that, for foreigners who are not acquainted with these countries, there are at every step, in the most ordinary things, in the smallest apparently insignificant details, a thousand interesting observations and curious studies to take notice of. But for myself, whom habitude has rendered callous, and whose curiosity has become deadened, I discover nothing here that does not seem to me normal, and it is only by recalling my remembrances of Europe, by the comparison of the manners of the Old World with those of these societies hardly at the beginning of civilization, that I can seize on the picturesque or barbarous side of the men and things that surround me. I no longer keep my journal so carefully. The constant repetition of the same incidents tires me by its monotony. To arrive, to pass through the invariable routine: visits to the editors of daily papers, to the artists, to smile obsequiously—efforts of mind and body—in one word to perform all those maneuvers that are indispensable to the artist's success: preparatory séances before some judges of the elite; begging for the good will of pretentious and all-powerful fools—such are the preparations on arrival. I pass over the mechanical part, the concerts. More follows, the departure with the inseparable accompaniment of adieus, of bills to settle, trunks to pack, and *a otra parte con la música.*

Life at Copiapó is dull and tiresome generally, but it is particularly so at present on account of the approach of Holy Week.

◇◇◇◇◇◇◇◇◇

[May] 1867

Left Copiapó on April 26 at four o'clock P.M., and left Valparaíso again on April 30.

Great animation on board. All the principal merchants come to accompany E——, who is married this morning to a young German girl, Miss O——. I disappear for three days, during which I pass through the old tortures which you are acquainted with.

Our voyage so far is pleasant. We shall pass through the Strait of Magellan. The seventh, in the morning, we are in sight of land, followed without interruption by high mountains regular and bald, a desolate country, without the least trace of inhabitant. The weather is cold and rainy, the sky is gray, the rolling sea has a leaden tint rendering this desolate nature still more sad. It seems we have passed the entrance of the strait. We must retrace our steps. This coast is uniform, and presents no point of reference to the eye, which makes the task of piloting very difficult. Besides we have against us a cloudy sky that prevents our taking the height of the sun.

Hurrah! It is noon; we are going at full speed toward the strait, of which we have found the entrance at last. The two shores approach each other little by little. The country is still desolate, the silence eternal. We see a little smoke on the left shore, probably a fire lighted by some Indian. The few inhabitants of these desolate regions are nomads, and ferocious. They are the Fuegians, inhabitants of Tierra del Fuego (the Land of Fire). They are stunted, very ugly, etc. etc. Chile possesses a military penal colony at Punta Arenas. We shall be there tomorrow. The navigation being very dangerous, we shall stop tonight. The sea is as smooth as a mirror, the spectacle is grand; the setting sun bathes the snowy tops of the mountains in a flood of light that renders the sides of them still more gloomy. We cast anchor.

◆◆◆◆◆◆◆◆◆◆

May 18

In sight of Punta Arenas and can distinguish a few houses and two English steamers at anchor opposite the colony. A canoe leaves the shore and comes out to us. It is the governor of the colony, Mr. Riobó. He comes to see if we have not some mail for Punta Arenas. Our desire to see the Patagonians suggests the idea of requesting of the governor a canoe to go onshore, which he grants us with the most gracious condescension, only, the number of the curious being greater than the capacity of the canoe, it is agreed that we shall divide ourselves into two parties. The first batch has just left; the canoe will return for us at seven o'clock in the evening. The chaplain of the colony, a Franciscan in frock and hood, comes to go on board. An honest Englishman naïvely asks if he is a Patagonian.

We are embarking in the canoe, the governor accompanying us. We are passing before the *Spiteful*, an English corvette that watches the coast and takes soundings. A few days ago two of the officers embarked in a canoe with which they proceeded along the coast in the latitude we had just passed. Many Fuegians came to meet them. The officers offered them some trifles, buttons, handkerchiefs, etc., to conciliate them, which they accepted with marks of contentment, but when the officers turned toward the shore to rejoin their canoe the Fuegians undertook to prevent them. A fight took place; the two officers were armed with revolvers and killed several Indians, but they received a volley of arrows, two of which wounded them very seriously. I have had an opportunity of examining these arrows. They are very small, the end is a pointed stone and is very slightly attached to the wood, so that when an attempt is made to draw them from the wound the stone remains behind.

These Fuegians are cannibals. Some years ago the governor of the colony, a German, Dr. Phillipi, was killed and eaten by them.

We land at a quay that the governor has just constructed. The night is dark, but the stars are shining. I cannot explain with my pen the strange feeling I experienced on landing on this austral land one hundred miles from Cape Horn,[5] in the Strait of Magellan in Patagonia, at the antipodes of civilization.

The governor, Mr. Riobó, has spent many years in Paris. He is a perfectly polished gentleman, who performs the honors of his little kingdom like a man accustomed to the best society. He precedes us on the road. The ground is covered with short hard grass; it seems as if we were walking on a carpet. We hear the noise of some voices; it is from a group in the darkness on the road. "Who goes there?" It is the passengers of the first canoe returning on board after having explored the colony.

"I am taking you to the palace of the government," said Mr. Riobó. We go up a flight of steps to a street about one hundred yards in length,—the Calle María, etc., from the name, I believe, of a Chilean frigate. The street is lined with small painted wooden houses. It is Punta Arenas. There are four hundred inhabitants, divided in the following manner: sixty soldiers of the regular troops, one hundred children and women, the balance composed of transported *colóns*, for the most part soldiers guilty of desertion, who are laborers, carpenters, blacksmiths, etc. The impossibility of flight has relaxed much of the severity of their captivity. A young Englishman (there are three in the colony), a soldier of the Chilean Navy who deserted, and has been banished here, assures me that he is well contented with his fate.

We reach a small house a little larger than the others, which

---

[5] The Strait of Magellan is about three hundred miles north of Cape Horn.

has a garden in front surrounded with a wooden paling; it is the palace of the government. The governor takes a whistle from his pocket and whistles. In a moment, all that little world which seemed asleep is awakened. A clarion sounds a call. The barrack is opposite, and we see suddenly issuing from the depths of obscurity a sergeant and several soldiers with lanterns, who hasten to receive the governor's orders. We traverse the little garden, in which, by the light of a lantern, we succeed in plucking some very pretty little dwarf roses but without perfume. The governor introduces us to his companions, first to his secretary, then to two little American lions (leopards), charming little animals, which, although only one month old, show very pretty claws and teeth that make me augur the future dispositions of these innocent felines which the governor proposes to shut up in cages in the course of a few days. They are of the size of a cat. Then also two guanacos running at liberty, one male and one female. The guanaco has a body the color of a deer, but with a neck immoderately long, reminding one of the giraffe. It is a ruminant whose flesh is delicate and whose fleece puts one in mind of the llamas. It attacks men only when it is on the defensive, and is very formidable. It then throws itself on its assailant, knocks him down with one blow, and bites him.

The governor escaped by a miracle from one of the two animals at which we are looking. When the guanaco is furious, he ejects a greenish saliva that is very unpleasant.

Separated from the rest of the world, the governor has devoted himself to the well-being of his little colony. His communications with the rest of the world being uncertain, it sometimes happens that for entire months he is without news from Chile.

Game is very abundant. Ostriches and guanacos abound. Admiral P——, who lately passed through the strait, amused himself for some hours with his officers in hunting, and they filled a canoe with their game.

The governor showed us some specimens of coal that appeared excellent; also some fragments of auriferous quartz, found in the mountains of Patagonia.

But I hasten to arrive at the most interesting episode of our visit at Punta. The governor sent for a family of Patagonians. I cannot describe the impression that these singular beings caused

me. The first group to which we are introduced by the governor
is composed of three men and one young woman. The first, one
in particular, is very much above the ordinary height but is not
gigantic. That which is particularly striking is the prodigious development of the bust, the length of the arms, and the enormous
size of the head and features. The nose of the largest is at least
one-third larger than the largest European nose I have ever seen.
The head is enormous, but not monstrous. The features are in
proportion to the head. As to the woman, she is at least six feet
high. She is a young girl of fourteen or fifteen years, admirably
proportioned, slender, with a marvelously beautiful face; Grecian
statuary in its purest expression has never formulated anything
more beautiful. The mouth exquisitely chiseled, of bright red,
reveals on opening the whitest, most polished, and the prettiest
teeth that I have ever seen. Kanucha is the most colossal and the
most beautiful girl in the world. But here I am very much embarrassed in front of this beautiful caryatid, who tenders me a
charming though large hand and shakes with a coquettish movement of her head her copper ear pendants, of which she seems to
be particularly proud. How shall I undertake to tell it you?
Kanucha, the beautiful girl, is a handsome boy! The governor
tells me he is a youth that all the Patagonians despise, because
he has all the instincts of a woman, dresses like one, sews, squats
down, walks, and acts like one. I cannot, without regret, renounce
beholding a young girl, in a form so elegant, a head so fine, and
manners so coquettish.

We offer some cigars to these gentlemen, which they eagerly
smoke. In contrast to their ferocious neighbors, the Patagonians
possess a docility that is rendered very striking by their athletic
forms and colossal proportions. The dress of these poor people
consists of one or several skins of the guanacos, the fur of which
is turned inside. Nothing more. It is a simple mantle that the
women fasten on the chest with a long copper pin, and that is
worn open by the men, notwithstanding the cold, which is piercing. Their legs and feet are also as naked as their heads. They
are very proud of wearing a trinket around their foreheads like a
fillet or diadem. Like all Indians, unfortunately, they are addicted
to drink. For them ardent liquors represent the *ne plus ultra* of
happiness. They prefer a bottle of brandy to everything else. It

is not a rare thing to see a husband offer, with the wife's consent, the latter to one of the *colóns* for a certain time, to procure a few bottles, which both of them go off to swallow immediately. They are not pleased with gold. They prefer the pesos of silver because they are larger and the gold is too small. They live the life of nomads—in small groups, but without government or religion. Even family ties have no existence, since very frequently one or two members of a group will desert and join another for a time. Their character is generally mild, but when drunk they become ferocious. When any one among them dies, they burn everything that belonged to him, and kill his horse upon his grave. The flesh of the horse is immediately eaten. Liquor, finally, is the object of all their ambitions, of all their desires. Many *colóns* have asked me if I would not like to sell them a few bottles of it. They are going on board for the same purpose.

The report of our arrival has spread. A second squad of Patagonians enters. It is the queen, Nata, a woman of thirty years of age, surrounded by several children. Her nose, arched like the beak of a bird of prey, gives a hard appearance to her enormous face, but on examination one discovers a mild and charming expression in it. The features possess an admirable purity. She carries in her arms a little one, a baby of fifteen months, as large as a child of ten years of age, whose robust body, in spite of the cold, is completely naked.

[According to Fors, Gottschalk, after reaching the Atlantic Ocean, disembarked first at Montevideo, Uruguay, in May 1867. He played there on September 20, 1867, gave the inevitable festival on November 9, and helped the cause of popular education with his concert of October 14, 1868. In Buenos Aires his concerts took place in the salon of the Coliseo and at the Teatro Colón, proceeds going to the French, German, and British hospitals and to the victims of the war with Paraguay. He penetrated both Uruguay and Argentina for concertizing and for diversion, and came to know their governors: in the former, General Justo José Urquiza; in the latter, Bartolomé Mitre, general, statesman, journalist, and author. It is also believed that he was acquainted with Sarmiento.

A full account of this period in Gottschalk's life awaits publica-

tion, similar to that concerning his last months in Rio de Janeiro, and by the same author.]

✧✧✧✧✧✧✧✧✧

Buenos Aires, January 13, 1868

Notwithstanding the heat (one hundred six degrees above zero, Fahrenheit), notwithstanding the war with Paraguay, which has already cost the four belligerent parties nearly two hundred thousand men, three-fourths of whom have been destroyed by cholera, typhus, dysentery, and pestilence; notwithstanding the commercial crisis, one of the first effects of which has been the enforcement of a paper currency at Montevideo; notwithstanding the civil war in the interior provinces of the republic; notwithstanding the invasion of the frontiers by Saa, Varela, and I know not how many other brigands who live only by rapine, and whose title of general, which they assume, would not in any other countries than these save from the gallows or the galleys, which they have a thousand times deserved; notwithstanding all these calamities, the company of Parisian *bouffes* brought to Buenos Aires by Mr. D'Hôte, has made its debut at the Argentine theater in *Les Bavards*, by Offenbach.

I suspect that the Latin proverb is wrong for once—and their audacity will not, I fear, be crowned with success. The company is, however, far from being unworthy of the public favor. Mademoiselle R——, the prima donna, is pretty and sings well; Mr. R., the tenor, is an excellent actor; Mademoiselle B. dances pretty well and has fine legs; Mr. D'Hôte himself is a splendid comic actor. But these ladies and gentlemen had not even seen the footlights of the Argentine Theater before they knew to what cause to attribute their failure.

✧✧✧✧✧✧✧✧✧

February 3

My health is passable. I have had to go to the country to escape the cholera that was here. Almost twenty-eight thousand persons have died of it within three months. It is horrible. Happily it has almost disappeared. Naturally there are no concerts, every family being in mourning.

◇◇◇◇◇◇◇◇◇◇

[*Montevideo*] *February 11* [*1868*][6]

Political events have broken up the monotony of our existence. I do not know if I have already spoken of the son of the dictator Flores, of Montevideo, who has acquired through his misdeeds the sad celebrity of a bandit. His name is Fortunato Flores, he is the old bogy of Montevideo. Small and great tremble on hearing this graceful name, which, by a singular chance, seems to be the perfect antithesis of the ferocious character of the one who bears it. Fortunato Flores, literally translated, means Fortunate Flowers. Since my arrival at Montevideo I have been edified respecting his character. They related to me his numerous extravagances, the peaceable and inoffensive persons of the middle classes whom he had assassinated, the boxes on the ear he had given to a Frenchwoman, and his orgies, which invariably ended by shots from his revolvers. Chance threw me in the way of the amiable Fortunato. It was easy for me to see from the manner in which he spoke to me that he would have been happy to have quarreled with me, but my imperturbable politeness and also, perhaps, the salutary fear that the United States inspires in all these tyrants had its effect upon him. I had the pleasure of not seeing him draw his revolver. Since then he has become somewhat gentle with me, and, having one day played the national air of Uruguay for him in a concert, I ended by making a conquest of him. Three or four months ago Mr. Fortunato, finding fault with the politics of the minister of foreign affairs, went to his house and gave him a caning. Then, under the influence of some old spite that he preserved against a certain officer, he sent some soldiers of his regiment to seek him, garroted him, pricked him with bayonets, with a choke pear in his mouth to take from him even the comfort of crying, put him with a manacle on his neck into a subterranean dungeon for twenty-eight hours without the least light, without giving him anything to drink, or to eat, and making him believe

---

[6] By this time Gottschalk had played sixteen times in Montevideo. His *Tarantella* for piano and orchestra produced "*fanatisme.*" Women sought locks of his hair to wear in elegant "*petits 'relicarios' d'or.*" *L'Art musical*, February 13, 1868.

that he was left there to die of hunger, and that neither his family nor anyone else in the world would ever know what had become of him. After many other tortures he gave him a kick and sent him away. He had already been guilty of so many robberies that, in spite of the terror he inspired, and of the number of individuals he had dispatched to the other world with his own hand, a general cry of indignation was heard from everywhere, and the papa of this amiable young man hinted to Fortunato that state reasons required that he should have a change of air. He left for France. His exile was supposed to last two years. He remained seven days in Europe; and two months and a half after his departure from Montevideo, what was the general consternation on seeing one fine morning Fortunato descend from the English vessel arriving from Europe. Soon after, he betook himself to his old ways. Restored by his own authority to the grade of colonel, he began to keep his hand in by torturing his soldiers and his officers. One night he took a fancy to invite several persons to supper. Hardly had the dessert come on when he became, as usual, furiously drunk and gave an order to his aide-de-camp to seize his guests and make them to spend the night in the guardhouse. This took place at the hotel where I lodged.

The whole night the other boarders and myself were on the alert because Fortunato had proposed firing his pistol in the corridors. He broke three hundred glasses, as many plates, all the mirrors, and did not retire until, exhausted by drunkenness and fatigue, he left to go to bed. His young brothers (the youngest is seventeen years old) accompanied him that night as usual (they are also bad, like him, but less satiated than their elder brother), went to an aristocratic club where they knew the political adversaries of their father met; as they anticipated, one of them, an honorable and venerable father of a family, rich and of the better class, was playing billiards when they entered. Young Flores, the one seventeen years old, struck him a hard blow with a cue which stretched him on the floor, pulled out some of his whiskers, kicked him in the face with his boots, and went away, leaving him bathed in blood and unconscious.

Since my departure from Montevideo I have heard at short intervals the fresh misdeeds of Fortunato and his brothers spoken of: some broken heads, women outraged, and other similar peccadilloes, but no more killings, leading me to hope that these gentlemen were mending. All at once three days ago, the submarine telegraph, which crosses the bay and connects Montevideo and Buenos Aires, brings us the following news: *Fortunato and his brothers have risen against their father, have won over the garrison, and overturned General Flores, who has been obliged to abandon the town and has fled to Unión, six miles from Montevideo.* The details soon reached us. Fortunato, tired of the inaction in which the old dictator left him, had had a very animated discussion with him, at the end of which *he boxed his father's ears.* Hurrying to his barracks, he came with his brothers at the head of his regiment and seized all the posts, through the cowardice or the defection of those who guarded them; the whole band marched to the city hall, where Flores and all his family had fled. In vain the old wife of Flores, a very vulgar woman, formerly a washerwoman, whose blind idolatry for Fortunato is the only source of his bad instincts, threw herself at the feet of this wretch. "I do not know you," he cried out to her. "Do you forget," the old general cried out to him, "that I am not only your chief, that before being the first magistrate of the republic, I was your father?" "Get out of the way," Fortunato replied to him, "*or I will fire upon you all.*" And the little brothers, infuriated, brandished their swords to excite their soldiers, for the most part drunk. Poor old Flores, with downcast head, and strangling his tears, retreated and fled, with some forty faithful followers, to conceal himself, as I have said, in Unión, and the whole town remained at the mercy of the revolutionists. But the foreign population, which is infinitely more numerous at Montevideo than that of the natives, was justly alarmed. They had a right to be alarmed at such brigands. The diplomatic corps met and was deliberating as to what means should be taken to protect the property and lives of foreigners, when the news arrived that Fortunato had forced the customhouse stores and seized all the boxes and bales shut up there, to make barricades of them. The foreign ministers immediately transmitted to their respective admirals an order to land their troops. The Americans, the Italians, the English, the Spaniards, the Brazilians disembarked and took possession of the customhouse and the legations. Fortunato, whose audacity has no limits, notified them to leave immediately under pain of seeing themselves attacked by the troops under his orders. "Come if you dare," was the response of the admirals. The hero found it wiser not to try the adventure, and shut himself up in a little fort, which he barricaded, its avenues guarded by cannons. Recovered from their panic, Flores senior and his faithful followers rallied other soldiers and foreigners. They returned to Montevideo. The attitude of the foreigners was too resolute for Fortunato not to understand that he had lost the game. He consented to a parley. The cunning fellow had taken care to keep as hostage an old man, General Balle, Minister of War, and signified that if his propositions were not acceded to he would shoot his prisoner and would not surrender until after fighting to the last extremity. Flores senior was obliged to accept. They agreed not to take the life of any of the rebels, to give thirty thousand dollars to Fortunato and permit him to embark, with his officers, without being molested, and since yesterday we have had the honor of having the celebrated colonel with us. I met him yesterday in the street. I was hoping that he would not know me, but as soon as he saw me he ran toward me extending his arms, and, willing or unwilling, I had to receive his hug.

◇◇◇◇◇◇◇◇◇◇

February 13, 1868

Fortunato re-embarked the very evening of our encounter. It appears that he murdered a Frenchman here a year ago, and the affair having been brought to the notice of the Argentine Government by the French consul, as soon as he learned of the arrival of the celebrated colonel, the latter found it more prudent to pack off. He is on board an Italian frigate, and leaves for Europe today or tomorrow by the English steamer. He will soon be spoken of in Europe, for, with the character I know he possesses, he will quickly make himself known. Apropos, in speaking of politics, I cannot help relating the ignominious fall of Prado, the dictator of Peru, whom his old accomplices in the revolution he engaged in to arrive at power, during my sojourn at Lima, have overturned and conquered in a battle before Arequipa, in which he showed himself as cowardly as he had shown himself up to this time insolent and despotic. He is a wretch who has Indian, mulatto, and Andalusian blood in his veins but has taken from these diverse races only their worst traits. I cordially detest him. A personal enmity separates both of us. I have had to suffer from his despotism and barbarism, and only escaped prison, one day that he sent twenty soldiers to arrest me, by my firmness and the threat I made him to make myself be diplomatically reclaimed by my minister. The fear that these brigands have of American cannons is the only safeguard that we citizens of the United States find in these hostile and dangerous countries.

In Bolivia, a revolution has just broken out against that furiously mad tiger, Melgarejo, dictator of that unfortunate country for the last five or six years. What republics! What scorn and what outrage upon the principles of liberty, equality, and fraternity are cast by these pseudo-presidents of democracies, who trample upon right, justice, and equality in order to wallow in those turpitudes which recall the decadence of Rome and the saturnalia of the lower empire!

◇◇◇◇◇◇◇◇◇

Buenos Aires, February 13, 1868

A priest died lately in a neighboring village; no one was willing to bury him from fear of the contagion. Nevertheless, the odor from the putrefying body was such that it became necessary to arrive at some mode of protection against this new plague. A gaucho (a countryman, always on horseback, whose existence is divided between taking care of herds of cattle, rapine, civil war, and robbery in general) had an idea of making use of his lasso (the lasso is a strap of thirty or forty feet in length, at the end of which is a slipknot, which he throws from his running horse to an incredible distance, and with which he seizes oxen and wild horses either by the head or legs); he threw the lasso, at a great distance, and caught the body by one leg, and drew it to a distant spot on the desert of the Pampas, where he left it to the birds of prey, who would soon dispatch it. Do not let the vocation of the man add anything to the horror with which this proceeding will inspire you. The clergy have shown themselves to be what they have always been here—rapacious, cowardly, corrupt, hideous, egotistic— the receptacle, finally, of all the vices engendered by idleness, ignorance, laziness, hypocrisy, and the impunity with which all their worst passions are satiated. A few Sisters of Charity have alone shown themselves, as always, devoted. They are, I should add, Europeans; but what could five or six good creatures do in the midst of a plague that has carried off twenty-five thousand souls in three months? Those who live among the English or the French Catholic clergy can never know what a bad priest can be. The cassocked bandits of South America must be seen to comprehend the indignation that animates me.

Those of Buenos Aires are authorized by law to collect twenty francs for every corpse buried by them; but the law adds: "When the means of the family of the deceased shall enable it to be paid." They saw that the harvest promised to be fruitful, so they raised this right of burial to forty francs, and, like vultures, fatten upon dead bodies. The more dead bodies there were, the greater the merrymaking among them. The municipality, learning that a great number of corpses were lying deprived of burial on the ground at the gate of one of the cemeteries, the poverty of their relations depriving them of the luxury of possessing forty francs, gave notice to the gentlemen priests that they must notwithstanding bury them, *pro Dei gratia* (for God's sake). These worthy ministers of a religion of devotion, of charity, and of poverty refused to give extreme unction to those who did not pay in advance the expense of their future burial. What a race! What a people! The people of the Argentine Republic are the source whence flow all turpitudes, all corruptions, and every bad human passion. In this nation all are abandoned by Providence. Cowards, vultures, liars, robbers; envious, ignorant, unpolished; cultivating little true warfare—that which is made openly, with the breast bared—but, in lieu thereof, excelling in the use of the dagger, and of the knife, which enables them to stab an individual in the back; theft dispenses them from labor; the word "republic" (an outrage on the elevated principles that this word represents) serves them as a cloak under which they give themselves up to every kind of despotism and vileness. The strong, the ambitious, the brazen-faced take possession by force and suck the milch cow—the public treasury—until another band of powerful, shameless, or ambitious ones without principles hurls them from power. There are murders without end; they cut each other's throats; and this is the

Argentine Republic. Alas! I might almost say, behold the Spanish-American republics; for, except Chile, all the governments of these agglomerations of bandits which sully the banner of American liberty, and which call themselves republics, from Mexico to Cape Horn, are nothing but brigandage, theft, barbarism, and cruelty—organized and unpunished.

◇◇◇◇◇◇◇◇◇

Buenos Aires, May 25

The saddest country in the world, a frog that puffs itself up to become an ox!—everywhere exaggerated pretensions, a universal corruption that begins at the lowest round of the social scale and reaches to those at the highest. Money taking the place of everything, the church a shop, the government a barrack, the army a cutthroat—only one worship, only one religion, that of Plutus. Venus herself is not adored, and even in the most aristocratic circles she is worshiped only under the figure of the golden calf. This takes place in the aristocratic regions; judge of the rest. Sad! Sad! The republic here is an outrage on justice, an odious farce.

◇◇◇◇◇◇◇◇◇

Montevideo, December 15, 1868

I am writing at this moment my grand *Tarantelle* for the piano with orchestral accompaniment, which I have dedicated to Her Royal Highness the Princess Marguerite of Italy. One of my best friends, Count Gioannini, an excellent amateur pianist, ex-minister from Italy to Buenos Aires, has promised to present the composition to the princess, himself, and assures me that it will be worth the new decoration of Italy, which has just been instituted by the king, Victor Emmanuel.*

---

* The composer having died before the presentation of this composition to the Princess of Italy, and even before he had entirely revised it, it happened that, when after his death his trunks were opened and pillaged by the hands of strangers, and even before his family knew of his death, the poor *Tarantelle*, only written on a few detached leaves and very imperfectly, was published by persons of very small scruples, in a state of complete mutilation. Later, the intimate friend of Gottschalk, Mr. N. R. Espadero, of Havana, edited this

I compose also a great deal for Ditson of Boston under the pseudonym of Seven Octaves, and also for Schott of Mayence [Mainz] who asks me for twelve pieces a year.[7]

Tarantelle at the request of Gottschalk's family, from the artist's manuscript, and Mr. Escudier, of Paris, has published it for a full orchestra, also for two pianos, and with quintette accompaniment. C. G.

[7] About this time he wrote also *Morte!* (*She Is Dead!*), which he later described as "*un succès de larmes,* as several of my fair listeners wept at listening to that rather sad and disconsolate of my last effusions, which is my favorite now, and which I consider as being neither better nor worse than old *Last Hope.*" Hensel, *op. cit.,* p. 171.

Postlude

O N April 12, 1867, at Caldera, Chile, the world-weary pianist had admitted: "I no longer keep my journal so carefully . . . and *a otra parte con la música.*" Succeeding pages form a travelogue diverting as usual, but containing little to suggest that it was written by a musician who was winning several more localities in South America.

Then, on December 15, 1868, at Montevideo, the last entry makes more than a passing allusion to music for the first time in twenty months. Gottschalk is under contract to two music publishers and is writing his *Tarantella*, which he has dedicated to Princess Margherita of Italy (later he aimed it toward the king). It requires no great power of clairvoyance to realize what country he intended to be his future field of conquest.

But triumphs still were to be had in the Western Hemisphere. On May 3, 1869, a few days before his fortieth birthday, Gottschalk sailed into the beautiful harbor of Rio de Janeiro.

We are indebted to Dr. Francisco Curt Lange, the eminent Uruguayan musicologist, for a work that traces Gottschalk's activities in detail during the last seven and a half months of his life.[1] Drawing on local newspapers and magazines, firsthand reports by Gottschalk's colleagues and friends and the pianist's own letters, Lange gives as well a vivid picture of the Brazillian capital in 1869. Under the reign of Dom Pedro II, famous for his liberality, scholarship, and devotion to the arts, the music schools, choruses, bands, orchestras, music publishers, and concert halls flourished no less than the theaters. And there was a free press of high caliber.

In Havana, Gottschalk's principal colleague had been Espadero; in Santiago, Federico Guzmán. In Rio the first member of its professional elite whom he sought out was Arthur Napoleão, a Portuguese pianist.[2]

The relationship proved to be mutually agreeable, for Napoleão, opening a music publishing house (Narciso, Napoleão e Cia.), profited from the publication of Gottschalk's works, past and recent. (Curiously, he did not participate in his friend's piano groups.) Next came Luiz Candido Furtado Coelho, actor, theater director, and musician, and two musical amateurs, Henrique Fleiuss, artist and lithographer, whose sketches of Gottschalk in A Semana Illustrada display a keen sense of humor; and Dr. Severiano Rodriguez Martins, a famous mulatto physician, half brother of a son of the composer Padre José Mauricio Nunes García (1767–1830).[3] Gottschalk played for private gatherings in their salons before venturing to play in public. After all, Thalberg had preceded him in 1855, and since then, his own renown. He wanted to excel or at least equal the success of the former and to substantiate the latter.

---

[1] Francisco Curt Lange: "Vida y muerte de Louis Moreau Gottschalk en Rio de Janeiro (1869)," Revista de Estudios Musicales, Universidad Nacional de Cuyo, Vol. II, No. 4, August 1950, pp. 43–147; Vol. II, Nos. 5, 6, December 1950, April 1951, pp. 97–350.

[2] Arthur Napoleão (1843–1925) was born in Oporto of Italian-Portuguese parentage. He studied with Thalberg and Herz in Paris. In 1857 he toured in Brazil, Argentina, and Uruguay; during the following year he went to the United States, remaining two years. In 1860 he was associated with Gottschalk's activities in Havana. After several voyages between Europe and America he settled in Rio de Janeiro in 1867.

[3] The mulatto composers of colonial Brazil were a distinct class. See Francisco Curt Lange: "Estudios Brasileños (Mauricinas), I," Revista de Estudios Musicales, Universidad Nacional de Cuyo, Vol. I, No. 3, April 1950, pp. 98–194, 173–91. Also, same author, Boletín Latino-Americano de Música, Vol. VI, Río de Janeiro, 1946: La Música en Minas Gerais. Un Informe Preliminar, pp. 409–94.

Gottschalk's first concert in Rio took place on June 3, 1869, at the Theatro Lyrico Fluminense. It was an event of the first magnitude. The theater, *"cheio como um ovo"* (full as an egg), was resplendent with *"a mais escolhida sociedade"* (the most select society). The Royal Family, *"Suas Magestades e Altezas Imperiais,"* were present. Local talent assisted Gottschalk: the German Liedertafel Society, a men's chorus; Ricardo Ferreira de Carvalho, pianist, and Furtado Coelho, who played the copophone. Gottschalk's solos were *The Banjo, Morte!,* and *Tremolo.* The two pianists joined forces in Gottschalk's *Grand Fantasy on Il Trovatore* and his *Seus Olhos, Grand Concert Fantasy.* Sr. Furtado obliged with *"Casta Diva"* and his own *Polka Original.*

Four more concerts followed in quick succession. Houses were sold out eight days in advance. Speculators were busy getting seventy-five dollars for boxes, twenty-five for single seats. Following this series, the Italian actress Adelaide Ristori and her company arrived in Rio on June 18. Gottschalk wisely withdrew from the field.

The whereabouts of *"o divino pianista"* from June 25 to July 18 remains a mystery. The press stated that he was paying his respects to *"a gigantesca natureza brasileira."* Lange conjectures that he went to Tijuca, a nearby suburb. Certain it is that he escaped from worldly cares, just as he had a decade earlier in the West Indies.

His return to musical activity was marked by two distinguished occasions: July 19, at the Collegio Imperial Dom Pedro de Alcântara,[4] and July 30, at the Paço de São Cristovão, home of the Royal Family. Immediately after this command performance he fell gravely ill. To read his own account of this attack of yellow fever, the illness that had carried off his father sixteen years previous, is like hearing a distant, ominous drum roll.

---

[4] "All the college met at the banquet. The president addressed me a discourse which was well conceived and well delivered. He spoke, as usual, of the 'great Republic,' for the United States, particularly since the war, are the object of the enthusiasm of all South America, which is proud of the Monroe Doctrine and of the Americanism to which it has given rise. Moreover, I believe that all these South American republics understand that, sooner or later, the United States will be the arbiter of their fate, and Brazil, although ruled by monarchical institutions, is, in point of fact, the most liberal of all these countries, and the most disposed to avail itself of the impulse we have given to civilization." Letter, Gottschalk: *ibid.,* p. 73.

Restored to health through the efforts of Dr. Severiano Martins, he played at Valença on August 23.[5] He failed to impress the public at São Paulo on September 1, much to the embarrassment of the musical *aficionados* among its thirty thousand inhabitants. A second concert there, announced for September 5, had to be canceled. The nearby seaport of Santos, however, saved local honor, responding to his pianistic blandishments on September 6.

Five days later he returned to Rio de Janeiro. Two concerts followed, on September 21 and 29. His Chickering pianos and his tuner had now arrived; all was going extremely well. Grandiose ideas now seethed in Gottschalk's brain. He would conquer as he had conquered before. Rio was ripe for him. On August 3 a concert there had included "the National Hymn played by forty young ladies on twenty-five pianos," the *Anglo Brazilian Times* reported.

On October 2 rehearsals began for his first *concerto monstro*. It took place on October 5. Sixteen pianos were played by thirty-one pianists, and two orchestras under Gottschalk's direction played the Soldiers' Chorus from *Faust* and the March from *Tannhäuser*. A superstitious rumor had prophesied a cataclysm for October 5: Rio was to be inundated by storm and flood. Many fled in terror. Many others, however, decided to brave the musical cataclysm at the Theatro Lyrico Fluminense. Not a seat was to be had. If the police had allowed it, two hanging trapezes left by some acrobats would also have been occupied.

After the concert Gottschalk gave a banquet for his collaborators, at which time a series of concerts for charity was announced. Other concerts were given in October, among them one with the Sociedade Philarmonica Fluminense, of which he was now an honorary member. Houses packed, press idolatrous.

October 24 was evidently a day for attending to his correspondence. Plans for his biggest concert ever were disclosed to friends in the United States. The emperor was giving him complete jurisdiction over the bands of the Army, the Navy, and the National Guard. It was to be a festival of eight hundred performers,

---

[5] On Gottschalk's arrival at Valença, a rocket fired from the church belfry was supposed to be a signal for the town band to assemble and play under his balcony. When he alighted from the carriage, however, only three players, of the cornet, the clarinet, and the big drum, were performing violently. By the time he reached the balcony, a trombonist, a flutist, and a bassoonist, breathless from haste, were joining their colleagues in this musical tribute. (Gottschalk: *ibid*, p. 74.)

all under his direction. "Just think of 800 performers and 80 drums to lead," he wrote.[6] The number actually arrived at was six hundred fifty.

It is impossible to estimate the exact number and grouping of players, as the local newspapers varied, one account mentioning sixty-two snare drums, another eighty-two. But it would seem that there were fifty-five strings, sixteen bass drums, six flutes, eleven piccolos, sixty-five clarinets, sixty trumpets, sixty trombones, fifty-five saxhorns, and fifty tubas and French horns—all grouped into nine bands of the National Guard, four of the Imperial Navy, one of the Army, and one of the War Arsenal, an orchestra of seventy "*professores,*" and two German orchestras.[7]

If deep within him sounded a voice of foreboding at this time, he should have heeded it. Such events had exhausted Berlioz in the 1840's. They had been his own undoing in Cuba, nearly killing him, and in San Francisco leading indirectly to scandal and exile.

But Icarus flew ever higher. He called on his last reserves of energy, already impaired by his recent illness, to rally this time, all the nonpianistic, nonvocal musical elements, professional and amateur, of Rio de Janeiro. Day and night he rehearsed this conglomerate mass, in groups and in entirety. "The rehearsals continue daily," he wrote:

> I go from one barracks to another. I am a symphonic, voltaic pile; a steam engine become man. If I do not go mad, it will neither be my fault nor that of my soldiers. My room

---

[6] Hensel: *ibid.,* p. 174.

[7] As far as sheer numbers go, Gottschalk was conservative. In mid-June, 1869, Patrick Sarsfield Gilmore (1829–92), a bandmaster experienced in directing festivals, conducted the week-long National Peace Jubilee at Boston in a building specially constructed to seat an audience of fifty thousand, an orchestra of one thousand, a chorus of ten thousand, and two batteries of artillery. At the opening concert, Mme. Euphrosyne Parepa-Rosa sang the "*Inflammatus*" from Rossini's *Stabat Mater,* and one hundred red-shirted firemen hammered real anvils in the Anvil Chorus from Verdi's *Il Trovatore.* President Grant, the governor, and other notables attended the Jubilee. It was a financial success. ("I had heard of Gilmore's great undertaking," wrote Gottschalk to his publisher in August. "I am glad he succeeded.")

In 1872, Gilmore's ideas became still more swollen at his International Peace Jubilee, saluting the end of the Franco-Prussian War. He imported Johann Strauss, noted singers, bands of the Grenadier Guards of London, the Garde Républicaine of Paris, a German infantry band, and the Royal Constabulary from Ireland. This time, with a chorus of twenty thousand, it was agreed, Gilmore had overreached himself. There was a deficit.

Mr. Dwight fled from it all.

is a Capernaum, my heart a volcano, my head a chaos! This
will explain to you, as an excuse, this disorderly scrawl that
I am making in haste, while waiting for my third rehearsal
today![8]

Once, momentarily frustrated in his quest for perfection, he
called the performers "imbeciles." They left the stage, indignant.
Alone, contrite, he began to play. They returned. Shaken, tears
in his eyes, he apologized and resumed the rehearsal.

The very music on the stands—some fifteen thousand pages—
was evidence both of his iron will and of his erratic existence. He
had instrumentated it himself, employing eleven copyists to work
around the clock—largely a superfluous effort that could have been
avoided by saving scores and parts from past festivals. It is possible,
however, that on former occasions players had kept the parts as
mementoes.

As if all this was not enough, commitments previously made
were not forgotten. The benefit concerts he had promised the preceding month took place on November 12 and 15, again with
thirty-one pianists. A concert on November 18 followed, with the
Liedertafel Chorus, twenty-five pianists, and two orchestras.

At last, the fateful day, November 24, arrived. The theater had
been sold out days before—oversold, in fact, despite the doubled
price of the tickets. Those unable to enter because of insufficient
seats or their own insufficient funds gathered outside to hear the
opulent sonorities coming through the windows. The event proved,
however, to be a feast for the eye as well as for the ear.

Several preliminaries were given in front of the curtain before
the festival proper. After the arrival of the Royal Family, a comedy
was presented by a local company. Then Gottschalk played a
fantasy on themes from *Faust*, followed by the *Carnival of Venice*,
performed by a violinist, Luigi Elena.[9] Gottschalk's *Tarantella* for
piano and orchestra rounded out this part of the program. By this
time the audience was at a fever pitch of expectancy.

The curtain rose. A cry of delight came from the audience. They
stood up and applauded "the American genius who had the idea to

---

[8] Lange: Vol. II, pp. 106, 107.
[9] Luigi Elena and his brother Annibale, pianist, had made their New
York debuts on December 8, 1849.

present for the first time among us a scene so brilliant, that, if it
had been possible, was worthy of being photographed."

The massed profusion of performers, flags, flowers, and uniforms, illuminated by extra gas jets and eleven extra chandeliers,
created a scene of splendor and pageantry. One reporter could not
resist mention of the 1001 *Nights*. On the front line, so to speak,
were the seventy *"professores."* Then came two amateur groups
facing each other, separated by a pathway for the conductor.
Then a whole flank of drums in semicircle. And finally, rising in
tiers up the stage, the military bands, held in line by their own conductors, who took their cues from Gottschalk. According to a pre-
liminary report, the entire mass was crowned above by the
"bombardas," "ophicleides," and *"saxes,"* below them the trumpets
and trombones, and then the woodwinds.

The festival program opened with the March from Meyerbeer's
Le Prophète and continued with the Overture to Méhul's *Le
Jeune Henri* and the Andante from Gottschalk's symphony,
A Night in the Tropics. The grand finale consisted of a work
written by Gottschalk expressly for this occasion and dedicated
to the emperor, *Marcha Solemne Brasileira*, with battle effects by
a salvo of cannon backstage. It had to be encored.

Next day, November 25, a repeat of the festival was announced
for the twenty-sixth, with a reduction in the price of tickets. Only
by repeating it could Gottschalk hope to profit from this tremendous investment of money, time, and energy. A listing of his
expenses had been published to justify the initial increase in the
price of tickets: performers, rental of theater, music stands, plat-
forms, announcements to the press for five days, tickets, four
thousand programs, lights, movers, carpenters, copyists, employees,
music paper, etc., etc. Even the military bands were paid "not a
remuneration but rather a token of gratitude."

On November 25, the Sociedade Philarmonica Fluminense
gave one of its regular concerts, in which Gottschalk had promised
to participate. He was very, very tired. But "the show must go on."

It could not go on. After playing one of his latest compositions,
Tremolo, he essayed *Morte!* (*She Is Dead!*) and virtually col-
lapsed. Friends assisted him from the stage, and took him to his
hotel. There he stayed the next day, hardly able to rise from his
bed but determined to go on with the repeat of the festival

despite a pain that was gnawing at his vitals. An abscess in the stomach was causing it—probably a late complication of yellow fever. In the evening great crowds poured into the theater, just as before. When Gottschalk did not appear, they shouted impatiently for him. He was backstage, convulsed with pain.

Dr. Severiano Martins, who had been one of Gottschalk's first hosts in Rio and who had brought about his recovery from yellow fever in August, again tried to save him. He stayed with Gottschalk constantly during the agonizing days and nights that followed. On December 8, he and Firmin Moras took the patient to Tijuca in the hope that the quiet and elevation there might bring an improvement in his condition. In a few days the abscess broke, affording some relief—but also flooding his weakened system. The end did not come exactly the way he had feared it would ever since that night at Copiapó. His last words, we are told, were gratitude to Dr. Severiano: "I have traveled much, I have often been dangerously sick; but never have I found a friend as devoted as you. A father, a brother could not have done more, because your efforts are truly superhuman." In the hour just before dawn on December 18, 1869, Gottschalk died.[1]

As the news spread, the city was plunged into profound grief. The embalmed body lay in state at the headquarters of the Sociedade Philarmonica Fluminense. That evening the orchestra assembled there to play Morte! Next day, Sunday, December 19, at five in the afternoon, a leaden-hearted cortege could be seen filing slowly through the streets of Rio de Janeiro. Friends carried the coffin a considerable distance from Rua da Constituição to Largo da Lapa, where it was placed in a funeral carriage. Hundreds of musicians followed, carrying lighted torches, followed by thousands of people in carriages and on foot—Gottschalk's public and, we suspect, many who had not heard him.

Sorrow was reflected in the local press, in musical tributes from his colleagues and in comments from afar. In London his sisters,

---

[1] Dr. Severiano's diagnosis on the death certificate was *"hua pleuropneumonia abcedada intercurrente,"* in other words, empyema, sequel of a ruptured abscess in the abdomen. The doctor and his associates may have realized that only an operation could save Gottschalk, but they probably were loath to take the risk. In those days chest and abdominal operations were extremely rare. Hensel, in fact, reports that an operation was performed, but it is not mentioned by Lange.

stunned, were "broken-hearted."[2] Elsewhere, not only his concerts were recalled, but also social gatherings and quiet hours of friendship enriched by his presence. The return of his body to the United States, ten months later, was consecrated by a solemn Requiem Mass at St. Stephen's Church, New York. Cherubini's *Requiem Mass* in C minor and arrangements of Gottschalk's *Last Hope, Solitude, Pensée poétique,* and his swan song, *Morte!* were performed. He was buried at Green Wood Cemetery, Brooklyn, alongside his brother Edward.

On December 26, 1869, and January 18, 1870, Solemn Mass to his memory had been sung at the church of São Francisco de Paula in Rio de Janeiro. Mozart's *Requiem* was the principal work, preceded and followed by an *Introduction* and *Libera-me* based on such of Gottschalk's works as *Le Mancenillier* and *La Savane.* Both ceremonies were under the auspices of the Sociedade Philarmonica Fluminense, which participated in them.

For years, in the Brazilian capital, the playing of Gottschalk was the criterion by which pianists were judged. Even the grand festival lingered. One took place in December 1871, with 896 performers! And an aerialist advertised himself as "the Gottschalk of the Trapeze."[3]

Immediately after Gottschalk's death, however, some disquieting observations appeared in the Brazilian press: only two Americans were to be seen in the procession of mourners on December 19; there was neither official representation from the Asilo dos Inválidos (Veterans' Hospital), recipient of his largess, nor from the emperor.

To suppose that the number of Gottschalk's compatriots in Rio could be determined in such a vast throng is, of course, absurd. But a representative from the Asilo dos Inválidos would have been

---

[2] The premature loss of her brother evidently produced in Clara a lapse in good judgment. When Firmin Moras tried to gain a legacy for himself through court of law, she accused him of ingratitude and lack of loyalty. But he had given his master ten years of the most selfless service and had acted honorably after Gottschalk's death, turning over the pianist's effects to the American consul. Remaining in Rio, according to information given by Clara in 1899, he married. Thereafter, as we know no more of him, he becomes a source of history lost forever.

[3] Penteado de Rezende: "O Poeta do Piano," *Investigações* (São Paulo, December 1951).

expected to occupy a prominent place, and one from the emperor hardly could have passed unnoticed. Each day during Gottschalk's bout with yellow fever, Dom Pedro II had sent his chamberlain to the pianist, once even his "first gentleman in waiting"—a solicitious if useless gesture repeated during the final illness by Prince Dom Felippe.

Lange suggests that the pianist's continuing penchant for amorous dalliance, of common knowledge also in Rio, was an obstacle to official recognition of his passing. Conjectures abound —Dom Pedro may have been chagrined that the meteoric career of a world-famous pianist had to end in, of all places, Rio de Janeiro, capital of his own realm. He and his family had long admired Gottschalk's compositions. On the pianist's arrival in Rio he had invited him to the palace for an informal visit. The evening of July 30, when, following the concert at the palace, he had conversed with the pianist for hours, was only one of several occasions when his own many-faceted mind found a kindred one.[4] They had discussed "politics, travels, the United States, spiritualism, the music of the future, Offenbach's operettas, fine arts, manners and customs . . . on the Mormons, I was able to satisfy him completely, as I had just read Dixon's New America."[5]

Louis Moreau Gottschalk had come full circle. Toward the close of his career, he was again what he had been at its outset, a representative of his country. As a lad, he had brought American music to Europe; as a mature artist, he interpreted a vast nation, which he knew intimately, to the ruler of an even vaster one. His role as ambassador was recognized in A Semana Illustrada of August 8, 1869, with words that today have a familiar ring: "Such visits are worth more than those of certain political notables and a dozen newspapers subsidized and dispersed around this world."

The respect and admiration that Dom Pedro had for Gottschalk as an American citizen generally was shared by his subjects. Warm references to his nationality were frequent in the press throughout South America. He was "the son of free America! . . . the American genius . . . the glory of America." "In his active life as artist

---

[4] I would like our people to know that there is one emperor who is not a tyrant, and who likes the Americans." Letter from Gottschalk to Mr. F. G. Hill, Boston. Hensel: ibid., pp. 173, 174.

[5] Gottschalk: ibid., p. 72.

he honored his native land, the United States." "It is an amazing example of North American speed, it is the famous *go ahead* applied to music," was the comment (italicized words in English) of the *Jornal do Comercio* of October 9, 1869, on disclosing that Gottschalk had orchestrated the March from *Tannhäuser* and the Soldiers' Chorus from *Faust* by memory in eighteen hours. They marveled, too, at his conducting from memory.

He was regarded not alone as an *estadounidense*, that is to say, a native of the United States, but also as a fellow-citizen of the Western Hemisphere. The most touching example of this Pan-Americanism is to be found in a eulogy delivered at his bier: "But he was an American!" cried Dr. Achilles Varejão, who then asserted that Gottschalk in his cradle had heard the roar of Niagara Falls. The "grandeur of the Americas" was cited from "the White Mountains of New Hampshire" to "the Amazon." "He felt coursing in his veins the blood of those liberated by Washington . . . linked with his name the two continents . . . marked a luminous path from the Arctic to the Antarctic—may it tell future generations what Gottschalk was in the lands of Columbus." Toward the end, Dr. Varejão enlaced the two continents with a reminder of a "fatal coincidence": Gottschalk had died exactly four years to the day after Francisco Manoel da Silva (1795–1865), composer of the Brazilian National Hymn.

Actually, Gottschalk was of a world tripartite: North America, Latin America, and Europe.

To each, he brought all three.

To all, he gave himself.

And he left the imprint of this fruitful interdependence to us in his journal, *Notes of a Pianist*.

A Note on Gottschalk's Compositions

❦

GOTTSCHALK wrote over one hundred works for piano, several songs, orchestra pieces, and three operas. Only ten piano pieces have been reissued in recent years.[1] The rest of his output can be found in collections at the Sibley Library, Eastman School of Music, Rochester, New York; the New York Public Library, the Library of Congress, the National Library, Rio de Janeiro, the National Conservatory, Paris, and in private collections such as those belonging to Abrahão de Carvalho, in Rio de Janeiro, and John G. Doyle, in Mansfield, Pennsylvania. See Bibliography: Doyle, John Godfrey.

The *Tarantella* for piano and orchestra (*Grande Tarentelle, Célèbre Tarentelle*) has a history. Originally conceived for violin and piano at Havana in 1860, it was played there on informal occasions by Gottschalk and his friend José White. In 1861 a version for two violins and piano was performed by Srcs. López, Van der Guth, and Gottschalk at the Liceo de Guanabacoa, Havana. The composer then arranged it for piano, violin, and cello, in which form it was heard at a New York concert on February 26, 1862. At the time of Gottschalk's last entry in his journal on December 15, 1868, he was arranging it for piano and orchestra, although he had already played this version in Montevideo months before. In Rio de Janeiro it became in his own words his "war horse" (*cheval de bataille*). He played it there on June 9, 15, and November 24. The target of Clara Gottschalk's accusing footnote on the *Tarantella* was Arthur Napoleão. Having delegated Es-

---

[1] *Souvenir de Porto Rico, Marche des Gibaros; The Banjo; Ricordati; Bamboula; Berceuse; Le Bananier; Pasquinade; The Last Hope; The Union; Grande Tarentelle.*

padero to make a posthumous edition of her brother's works, she resented Napoleão's editions. Fors and other friends of Espadero joined in her recriminations. Napoleão, however, insisted in his own defense that he published the *Tarantella* exactly in accordance with the way Gottschalk had performed it in Rio. Reconstructed and orchestrated by Hershy Kay from piano scores, since 1957 it has been played extensively by Eugene List, Theodore Lettvin, Reid Nibley, and Ivan Davis with resounding success. Effectively choreographed by George Balanchine as a *pas de deux*, it has become a favorite in the New York City Ballet's repertoire.

Gottschalk makes frequent reference in the journal to his piano piece *Pastorella e Cavaliere*. Even more than Weber's *Invitation to the Waltz* it relies on a romantic scene for its effect. The composer has supplied this commentary:

Fabliau

A gallant Knight in search of adventures, meets on his way a young village maiden. Fascinated by her budding charms and simple grace, he offers her his troth. Bachelette hears him with cruel indifference, smiles at his passion and continues to sing her rustic song. The Knight wages his suit with renewed ardor, but neither vows of love, nor promises of fortune can conquer the scruples of the beauty, whose joyous song is heard by the Noble long after he has left the scene, and with sad and confused bearing has once more turned his palfrey in the direction of the Tournament.

Note by the Author

The performer of this piece should endeavor to emphasize the iterated design of the accompaniment, so as invariably to convey to the listener the idea of the ternary rhythm, i.e. of ¾ time in which it is written. This observation is particularly essential, inasmuch as the melody, in some passages, would seem to indicate the binary rhythm, or 6/8 time. The effect which this piece is capable of producing, if well played, arises in a great measure from the antagonism of these two conflicting rhythms, one of which, as I have already observed, must be subordinate to the other.

After having been informed of the subject of this "Fabliau," the auditor, if it be performed in an intelligent manner, should be enabled to follow all the phases, and the entire action of the little sentimental drama, which the author has endeavored to render into music.

A separate running text is written in above the music, describing the action.

Under the pseudonym of Seven Octaves, Gottschalk wrote several compositions, among them *Fairyland, Schottische de Concert,* which bears the dedication, "To my dear friend L. M. Gottschalk."

Bibliography

❦

Apthorp, William Foster: *Musicians and Music Lovers*. New York: Charles Scribner's Sons; 1908. For John Sullivan Dwight, pp. 277–86.

Arpin, Paul (?): *Life of Louis Moreau Gottschalk.* Translated from the French by H. C. Watson. New York (?): 1852 (?).

———: *Biographie de L. M. Gottschalk, Pianiste américain.* New York: Imprimerie du Courrier des États-Unis; 1853.

Asbury, Herbert: *The French Quarter.* New York: Alfred A. Knopf, Inc.; 1938.

Bacardi y Moreau, Emilio: *Crónicas de Santiago de Cuba.* Barcelona: Carbonell y Esteva; 1909. Three vols. Scattered references to Gottschalk's concerts and the dance *El Cocoye.*

Bartlett, Homer: "First of American Pianists to Gain Recognition Abroad." *Musical America*, January 30, 1915.

Barzun, Jacques: *Berlioz and the Romantic Century.* Boston: Little, Brown & Company; 1950.

Behrend, Jeanne: "Louis Moreau Gottschalk, First American Concert-Pianist." *The Etude*, Vol. LXXV, No. 1 (January 1957), pp. 14, 48, 58–59.

———: "The Peripatetic Gottschalk, America's First Concert Pianist." *Américas, Pan-American Union*, Vol. XI, No. 10 (October 1959), pp. 21–26. Also issued, November 1959, in Spanish and Portuguese.

———: *Piano Music by Louis Moreau Gottschalk.* Bryn Mawr, Pa.: Theodore Presser Company; 1956. Contains eight works, a biographical preface, and editor's notes.

Bolling, Ernest L.: "Our First Musical Ambassador, Louis Moreau Gottschalk." *The Etude*, Vol. L, No. 2 (February 1932), pp. 97, 98, 143.

Breslin, Howard: *Concert Grand.* New York: Dodd, Mead & Company; 1963. A novel based on Gottschalk's life.

Cable, George W.: "The Dance in Place Congo." *The Century Magazine*, Vol. XXXI, No. 4 (February 1886), pp. 517–32.

Carpentier, Alejo: *La Música en Cuba*. Mexico City: Fondo de Cultura Económica; 1946. Pp. 154–63.

Chase, Gilbert: *America's Music*. New York: McGraw-Hill Book Company, Inc.; 1955. Ch. 15, pp. 301–23.

————: *The Music of Spain*. New York: W. W. Norton and Company; 1941. P. 302.

Cleveland Leader, June 18, 1853, to February 4, 1863; intermittent articles on concert course there.

Cole, Fannie L. Gwinner: article on Gottschalk in *Dictionary of American Biography*. Vol. VII. New York: Charles Scribner's Sons; 1931.

Cortot, Alfred: *In Search of Chopin*. New York: Abelard Press; 1952. Gottschalk's portrait by Rubio is mentioned on p. 10.

Doyle, John Godfrey: *The Piano Music of Louis Moreau Gottschalk* (1829–1869). Doctoral dissertation, typescript, New York University, 1960. Available from University Microfilms, Ann Arbor, Michigan. Includes a biographical sketch, an analysis of the music and its folk derivations, a bibliography, and a thematic index indicating the location of each out-of-print work in libraries and collections.

Dwight, John Sullivan: *Dwight's Journal of Music*. Boston: September 30, 1854; July 12, 1862; October 18, 1862; December 12, 1863; January 7, 1865; March 4, 1865.

Escudier, Léon: *Mes souvenirs: Les virtuoses*. Paris: E. Dentu; 1868.

Eyer, Ronald: "Musical Pioneer." *Musical America*, Vol. LXXVI (1956), p. 28.

Fay, Amy: *Music-Study in Germany*. Seventeenth edition. New York: The Macmillan Company; 1897. Pp. 42, 47, 342.

Ferris, George T.: *Great Pianists and Great Violinists*. London: William Reeves. Second Edition, undated. Thalberg and Gottschalk, pp. 202–32.

Finck, H. T.: "Gottschalk's Tour in the United States." *The Nation*, January 5, 1882.

Fisher, William Arms: "Louis Moreau Gottschalk, The First American Pianist and Composer. A Life Sketch." *The Musician*, Vol. XIII (1908), pp. 437–39, 466.

Fors, Luis Ricardo: *Gottschalk*. Havana: Propaganda Literaria; 1880.

Galloway, Tod B.: "A Forgotten American Musician." *General Magazine and Historical Chronicle*. Vol. XXXV (1932), pp. 56–64.

Gates, W. Francis: "A Pioneer American Pianist." *The Etude*, Vol. XVI, No. 8 (August 1898), p. 231.

————: "First American Pianist." *The Etude*, July 1940.

Gerson, Robert A.: *Music in Philadelphia*. Philadelphia: Theodore Presser Company; 1940. Pp. 67, 68.

Gilder, John Francis: "Recollections of Gottschalk." *The Etude*, Vol. XIV, No. 10 (October 1897), p. 271.

Gottschalk, Louis Moreau: "Notes of a Pianist." *Atlantic Monthly*, Vol. XV, Nos. 88, 89, 91 (February, March, May 1865).

———: Articles in *La France musicale*, January 24, 1858; December 11, 1859; October 28, 1860.

———: Articles in *L'Art musical*, July 31, 1862; August 13, 20, 27, September 3, 24, October 15, 1863; May 19, 1864; December 21, 1865. The articles published in this magazine during August and September 1863 under the heading "*Souvenirs de voyage d'un pianiste*" are almost identical with his entries in the journal, June 14–16, 1863.

Gottschalk (versione dallo Spagnolo). Roma: Tipografia A. Befani; 1883. Excerpts from the Fors biography, in Italian.

Hawes, William L.: "Gottschalk's *Last Hope*." *The Musician*. Vol. XIII (October 1908), p. 440.

H. D. (probably Henry Didimus?): *Biography of Louis Moreau Gottschalk, The American Pianist and Composer*. Philadelphia: Deacon and Peterson, Printers; 1853. From *Graham's Magazine*, January 1853.

Hensel, Octavia: *Life and Letters of Louis Moreau Gottschalk*. Boston: Oliver Ditson Company; 1870.

Hoffman, Richard: *Some Musical Recollections of Fifty Years*. New York: Charles Scribner's Sons, 1910.

Holt, Charles: "Gottschalk's Diary." *The Dial*, November, 1881.

Howard, John Tasker: *Our American Music*. New York: Thomas Y. Crowell Company; 1954. Gottschalk, pp. 205–10.

———, "Louis Moreau Gottschalk, as Portrayed by Himself." *Musical Quarterly*, Vol. XVIII, No. 1 (January 1932), pp. 120–33.

Huneker, James Gibbons: *Steeplejack*. New York: Charles Scribner's Sons; 1925. Vol. I, pp. 38, 40, 204, 247.

Kahn, Erminie: *English Biographies of Cuban Composers*. New York: Cuban-American Music Group; 1946.

Kellogg, Clara Louise: *Memoirs of an American Prima Donna*. New York: G. P. Putnam's Sons; 1913. Pp. 106, 107, 295.

Kendall, John Smith: "The Friend of Chopin, and Some Other New Orleans Musical Celebrities." *Louisiana Historical Quarterly*, October 1948, pp. 856–76.

King, Grace, *New Orleans, the Place and Its People*. New York: The Macmillan Company; 1896.

Korn, Bertram W.: "A Note on the Jewish Ancestry of Louis Moreau Gottschalk, American Pianist and Composer." *American Jewish Archives,* November 1963, pp. 117–19.

Lange, Francisco Curt: *Vida y muerte de Louis Moreau Gottschalk en Río de Janeiro* (1869). Mendoza, Argentina: Universidad Nacional de Cuyo; 1951.

Law, Frederick S.: "Some Forgotten Worthies." *The Musician,* June 1908.

Lindstrom, Carl E.: "The American Quality in the Music of Louis Moreau Gottschalk." *Musical Quarterly* Vol. XXXI, No. 3 (July 1945), pp. 356–66.

Loesser, Arthur: *Men, Women and Pianos.* New York: Simon & Schuster; 1954. Gottschalk, pp. 375, 376, 498–501, 510, 511, 515.

Loggins, Vernon: *Where the Word Ends.* Baton Rouge: Louisiana State University Press; 1958.

Louisiana. American Guide Series. New York: Hastings House; 1941.

Lowens, Irving: "The First Matinee Idol, Louis Moreau Gottschalk." *Musicology,* Vol. II, No. 1 (1948), pp. 23–34.

———: Reviews of Records. *Musical Quarterly,* Vol. XLIII, No. 2 (April 1957), pp. 270–73.

———: Music Reviews. *Notes,* Second Series, Vol. XIV, No. 3 (June 1957), pp. 441, 442.

"M": "Gottschalk—A Successful American Composer." *Music,* Vol. II (July 1892), pp. 117–32.

Madeira, Louis C., and Philip H. Goepp: *Annals of Music in Philadelphia and History of the Musical Fund Society.* Philadelphia: J. B. Lippincott Company; 1896. Pp. 160, 161.

Magendanz, Johannes: "Gottschalk in Utica." *Town Topics of the Mohawk Valley,* October 1932–May 1933. Also in manuscript at the New York Public Library.

Henry D. Mandeville and Family Papers. Department of Archives, Louisiana State University, Baton Rouge. Letter written by Josephine Mandeville, New Orleans, April 16, 1853, describing Gottschalk and his playing.

Marmontel, A.: *Les Pianistes célèbres.* Paris: A. Chaix et Cie; 1878.

Mason, William: *Memories of a Musical Life.* New York: The Century Company; 1901. Gottschalk, pp. 205–09.

Mathews, W. S. B.: "L. M. Gottschalk, The Most Popular of American Composers." *The Musician,* Vol. XIII (October 1908), pp. 439–40.

——— (associate editor): *A Hundred Years of Music in America.* Chicago: G. L. Howe; 1889. Pp. 637, 638.

Milinowski, Marta: *Teresa Carreño*. New Haven: Yale University Press; 1940.
Minor, Andrew C.: *Piano Concerts in New York City, 1849–1865*. Master's thesis, typescript, University of Michigan, 1947.
New York *Herald*, January, February 1853; January 1856.
New York *Times*, March, April, May 1853; September, October 1870.
New York *Tribune*, January, February 1853; January 1856.
Odell, George C. D.: *Annals of the New York Stage*. New York: Columbia University Press; 1931. Vol. VI, VII, VIII.
Parry, Albert: *Garrets and Pretenders. A History of Bohemianism in America*. New York: Covici-Friede; 1933. Pp. 19–20, 27, 31, 33, 34, 73, 78, 92, 362.
Pasarell, Emilio J.: "El Centenario de los conciertos de Adelina Patti y Luis Moreau Gottschalk en Puerto Rico." *Revista del Instituto de Cultura Puertorriqueña*, Vol. II, No. 2 (January–March 1959). Pp. 52–55.
Pereira Salas, Eugenio: "La Embajada musical de Gottschalk en Chile." *Andean Quarterly* (published by Instituto Chileno-Norteamericano de Cultura, Santiago, Chile), Winter 1944.
———: *Notas para la historia del intercambio musical entre las Americas antes del año 1940*. Washington, D.C.: Music Division, Pan American Union; 1943
Rezende, Carlos Penteado de: "O Poeta do Piano." *Investigações* (Revista do Departamento de Investigações, Ano III, No. 36 (São Paulo, December 1951), pp. 21–42.
Root, George F.: *The Story of a Musical Life*. Cincinnati: The John Church Company, 1891. Gottschalk, p. 65.
Ryan, Thomas: *Recollections of an Old Musician*. New York: E. P. Dutton; 1899.
Saunders, Whitelaw: "What Gottschalk Said to Carreño." *The Etude*, Vol. XLII, No. 8 (August 1924), p. 526.
Schonberg, Harold C.: "Facing the Music." *Musical Courier*, Vol. CXLV, Nos. 4, 5 (February 15 and March 1, 1952).
———: *The Great Pianists*. New York: Simon & Schuster; 1963. Pp. 204–16.
Sherwood, William H.: "An Appreciation of Gottschalk as a Composer." *The Musician*, Vol. XIII (October 1908), p. 441.
Shpall, Leo: "Louis Moreau Gottschalk." *Louisiana Historical Quarterly*, January 1947, pp. 120–27.
Sohn, Joseph: Article in *The Jewish Encyclopedia*. New York: Funk and Wagnalls; 1925. Vol. VI.
Specht, Will: "Has the Creole a Music of His Own?" *Musical America*, Vol. XLVIII, No. 15 (July 28, 1928), pp. 5, 22, 25.

Bibliography

Stoddard, Charles Warren: "Ada Clare, Queen of Bohemia." *National Magazine*, September 1905.

Tolon, Edwin T., and Jorge A. Gonzalez: *Óperas Cubanas y sus autores*. Havana; 1943. Ch. 5.

Tracy, Dr. James M.: "The World's Greatest Pianists." *The Etude*, Vol. XXV, No. 9 (September 1907), p. 569.

The Universal Jewish Encyclopedia. New York: The Universal Jewish Encyclopedia, Inc., 1946. Vol. V.

Upton, George P.: *Musical Memories*. Chicago: A. C. McClurg and Company; 1908. Pp. 35, 49, 76–78, 104, 221, 233.

Index

Academy of Music, Brooklyn, 193
Academy of Music, Chicago, 243
Academy of Music, New York, 160–1, 268
Academy of Music, Philadelphia, 54, 66, 73
Academy of Sciences and Medicine, 222
Acapulco, Mexico, 277–81, 325
Adrian, Mich., 155
"Agnus Dei" (Marschner), 180
Aïda (Verdi), xxv
A La Claire fontaine (Gottschalk), 83
"à la Sonnambula," 29
"à la Traviata," 29
Albany, 103
Alcatraz, 286
Alexandria, Va., 115, 169
Allard (flutist), 21
Almago, Diego de, 337
Almería, Spain, 138
Alta California (newspaper), 298, 304, 315
Alvarez, Diego, 279, 326
Alvarez, Juan, 281
Amodio (baritone), 75, 78, 230
Anglo Brazilian Times (newspaper), 402
Anna, Grand Duchess of Russia, xxiv, 51, 102
Ann Arbor, Mich., 254, 255
Antilles, 14, 15, 23, 30, 34, 103
Ardvani (baritone), 264
Arecibo, P.R., 20

Arequipa, Peru, 361, 362, 394
Argentina, 320, 342, 389, 395
Argentine Theater, 390
Arica, Chile, 362, 363, 374
Ariel (ship), 269, 271, 272, 274, 275
Army of the Potomac, 67, 115
Ashforth (piano tuner), 145–6
Aspinwall, Panama, 271, 327
Associated Company of Artists, 230–1
Association of French Negroes, 33
Astor Place Italian Opera, 22
Atacama, Desert of, 379, 380, 381
Atlantic Monthly, xii, 95, 230
Atlas (newspaper), xvii
Attila (Verdi), 21, 22, 300
Auburn, N.Y., 88, 210, 211
Autocrat of the Breakfast-Table, The (Holmes), 233
"Ave Maria" (Marschner), 187
Avila, Pedro Arias de, 337
Ayacucho, Peru, 364

Bach, Johann Sebastian, xxi, xxxv
Baden-Baden, 124
Badger and Lindberger, 295
Balanchine, George, 412
Ballo in Maschera, Un (Verdi), 359
Baltimore, 63, 66–7, 91, 168–9, 180, 186
Balzac, Honoré de, 27
Bamboula (Gottschalk), xxii, xxxv
Bananier, Le (Gottschalk), xxii, xxv, xxxiii, xxxv, 23, 194

Banjo, The (Gottschalk), xxv, xxxv, 9, 13, 23, 49, 75, 212, 273, 305, 359, 376, 401

Banks, Nathaniel Prentiss, 65

Barbados, 24

Barbaroussa, Frederick, 14

Barber of Seville (Rossini), 297

Barcelona, Venezuela, 21

Barili, Antonio, 128

Barili, Clotilde, 128

Barili, Ettore, 128

Barili, Nicola, 128

Barnum, Phineas Taylor, xxvi, 45, 46, 51, 95, 156

Bassegio (opera singer), 28

Basse-Terre, Guadeloupe, 23

Bataille de Carabova, La (Gottschalk), 23

Batavia, N.Y., 87, 262

"Battle Cry of Freedom, The" (Root), 181–2, 264

Battle of Prague (Kotzwara), xxiv

Bayou Sarah, La., 11

Beauregard, Pierre Gustave Toutant de, 64, 66

Beecher, Henry Ward, 125

Beecher, Thomas Kinnicut, 125

Beethoven, Ludwig van, xx, xxi, xxvii, xxviii, xxxvi, xxxvii, 63, 120, 183, 305, 376

Behrens (accompanist), 145–6, 170, 177, 183, 187, 194, 195–6, 199, 200, 225, 230, 231, 257

Belgium, 46

Bellevue, Canada, 230

Bellini, Vincenzo, 9, 108

Benvenuto Cellini (Berlioz), xxix

Berceuse (Gottschalk), xxxiv, xxxv, 113–14, 116, 179, 219, 224, 225, 238, 376

Bergmann, Carl, xxi, xxxvii

Berlioz, Hector, xi, xv, xx, xxi, xxiv, xxviii, 124, 174, 403

Bethlehem, Pa., 177–8, 257

Betly (Donizetti), 22

Bianqui's Italian Company, 293

Bierstadt (musician), 259

Billet (violoncellist), 379, 382

Binghamton, N.Y., 189, 190

Bishop, Anna, 166

Bishop, Sir Henry, 166

Bizet, Georges, xv

Blind Tom, 95

Bloomer, Amelia, xxix, 192

Bloomington, Ill., 250

Bolet, Jorge, xxxiii

Bolívar, Simón, 342, 369

Bolivia, 342, 344, 374, 395

Bonheur, Rosa, 105

Booth, Edwin, 282

Booth, John Wilkes, 282

Borchard (prima donna), 78

Bordeaux, 25, 58

Bossuet, Jacques-Benigne, 97, 229

Boston, 47, 76, 91, 157, 166, 232, 234

Bostwick (singer), 163

Boucicault, Dion, 87

Bouillet, Marie-Nicolas, 325, 333

Bourgeois gentilhomme (Fradelle), 164

Bovards, Les (Offenbach), 390

Brazil, xxiv, 320, 400–7

Brazilian National Hymn, 409

Bridgeport, Conn., 156

Brignoli, Pasquale, 52, 53, 54, 56, 58, 73, 75, 78, 145, 146, 160–1, 182, 257

Brillat-Savarin, 290, 291, 318

Brook Farm, xxvii

Brooklyn, 62, 193

Buckley Serenaders, 253

Budan (singer), 25

Buenos Aires, xix, 364, 389, 390, 395, 397

Buffalo, N.Y., 229, 265

Bull, Ole, 295

Bulletin (newspaper), 298

Burk, Billy, 299

Burlington, Vt., 80, 196

Busati family, 21–2

Butler, William Orlando, 131, 186

Cabo Rojo, Puerto Rico, 18

Cádiz, Spain, 8, 15

Caimito, Cuba, 34
Caldera, Chile, 383, 399
California, 267, 268, 285–306, 314–20
Californienne, La (Herz), 181
Callao, Peru, 334, 354, 355, 356
Campos, Juan Morel, xxxi
Canada, xii, xvii, 214, 228–31
Canandaigua, N.Y., 88
Canzeco (revolutionist, Peru), 340, 347, 350, 351, 352, 353
Cape Horn, 386
Cape St. Vincent, Canada, 205
Cárdenas, Cuba, 10, 30, 31, 32, 33
Carmen (Bizet), xv
Carnival of Venice (Gottschalk), 249, 251, 404, 409
Carreño, Teresa, xxv, 91
Carson City, Nev., 314
Castillo Deloro, ancient Peru, 337
Catlin, George, 189
Cazotte, Jacques, 297
Cellini, Benvenuto, 239
Cervantes, Ignacio, xxxi
Chadwick, George W., xxx
Chant du soldat, Le, see *Marche de Faust*
Charles VI (Halévy), 25
Charmes du foyer (Gottschalk), 359
Chateaubriand, François René de, 51
Cherubini, Luigi, 407
Chicago, 57, 99, 101, 102, 112, 146
Chickering family, 194
Chickering Hall, 76
Chickering pianos, 134, 194, 243, 289, 295, 402
Chiclanero, El, see Domínguez
Chile, xxiv, 320, 339, 359
Chiriquí, Panama, 329
Chopin, Frédéric, xi, xv, xx, xxi, xxii, xxviii, 118, 193, 220, 221, 243
Chorillos, Peru, 355, 359
Christy Minstrels, 253
Chule, Chile, 382
Chuquisaca, Bolivia, 363
Church, Frederick Edwin, 105

Cienfuegos, Cuba, 10
Cincinnati, Ohio, 65, 96, 246
Cité d'Orléans, 221
Civil War, xxix, 50–1, 54, 73, 90, 97, 126–8, 130–7, 140–2, 170, 179
Clare, Ada, see McElhinney, Jane
Clermont-sur-Oise, France, 110
Cleveland, Ohio, 91, 93, 96, 238–9
Clyde, Ohio, 241
Cobija, Bolivia, 342
Coca, 360
Cocoye, El (Gottschalk), 9
Coliseo (concert hall), 389
Collegio Imperial Dom Pedro de Alcântara, 401
Colorado (ship), 321, 324
Columbia (Gottschalk), 42
Comettant, Oscar, xv
Compé Bouqui, 11
Compé Lapin, 11
Concertstück (Weber), xxiv, xxviii
Concerto in E Minor (Chopin), 220
Constitution (ship), 274–7, 283–4
Cook, James, 322, 323
Cooper, James Fenimore, 189
Copiapó, Chile, 377, 379, 381, 384
Corday, Charlotte, 132
Cordier (prima donna), 145
Corinth, Miss., see Pittsburg Landing
Corneille, Pierre, 175
Costa Rica, 322, 344
Cortesi (soprano), 30
Courrier de la Louisiane (newspaper), 20
Courrier des États-Unis (newspaper), 17, 18
Cradle Song (Gottschalk), see *Berceuse*
Creation (Haydn), 186
Creole melodies, xi, xxii
Cristina, Queen of Spain, xxiv, 5
Cross of Isabella the Catholic, 5
Cuba, xvi, xxxi, 5, 9, 14, 16, 25, 30, 31, 34, 403

Daily American Flag (newspaper), 320

d'Angri (prima donna), 78
Danish Antilles, 24, 40
Danish government, 14
Dantan (sculptor), 221
da Silva, Francisco Manoel, 409
Davis, Ivan, 412
Davis, Jefferson, 90
Dayton, Nev., 309, 314
Dayton, Ohio, 256
Deberiot (pianist), 220
de Bruslé, Aimée, xiv
de Bruslé, Comte, 12
Debussy, Claude, xv, xxv
de Carvalho, Ricardo Ferreira, 401
de Flavigny, Countess, 48
de Kock, Charles-Paul, 229
de Lagrange, Anna, 202
de l'Isle, Moreau, xiv
de Lucque, Fernando, 337
de Lussan (singer), 73, 75
de Stankowitch, *see* de Lagrange,
　Anna
Detroit, Mich., 91, 242
DeVivo (agent, on tour), 146, 230
D'Hôte (actor and producer), 390
Diario de la Marina (newspaper), 28
Dickens, Charles, 234, 260
Ditson (music publisher), 398
"Dixie," 229
"Dixie's Land," 60, 66
"Do They Think of Me at Home?"
　181
Dodsworth's Hall, 44, 49
Döhler (violinist), 249, 251–2
Domínguez, José Redondo y, 5
Dominica, 24
Donizetti, Gaetano, 110
"Donna è mobile, La" (Verdi), 217
d'Orsay, Count, xv
Douglas, Mrs. Stephen, 91
Dresel, Otto, xxxii, xxxvii
Duckworth, Kate, 257
Dumas *père*, Alexandre, xv, 32, 38
Dumas *fils*, Alexandre, 29, 102, 217
Dunkirk, N.Y., 261
Dunmore (Scots guard officer), 82,
　85

Dupeyron (apothecary shop owner,
　Lima), 345, 346, 349, 352, 354,
　356
Dutch Antilles, 40
Dutch Flat, Nev., 312–3, 314
Dutton, William H., 89
Dvořák, Anton, xxx
Dwight, John Sullivan, xxvii, xxx, 178,
　195, 202, 232, 269, 291
Dwight's Journal of Music, xxvii, 117,
　168

Ecuador, 339, 344
Eichberg, Julius, 158, 166
1812 Overture (Tchaikovsky), xxiv
Eisfeld, Theodor, xxxvii
Elena, Annibale, 404
Elena, Luigi, 404
Elmira, N.Y., 89, 121
El Siglo (newspaper), xxxv
El Toboso, Spain, 7
English Antilles, 40
Erard pianos, 243, 244
Erie, Pa., 93, 262
Ernani (Verdi), 300
Escenas campestres (Gottschalk), 28
Escudier, Léon, xxii, 398
Espadero, Nicolás Ruíz, xvii, 9, 91,
　397, 400, 411
Ewell, Richard Stoddert, 130

Fairyland (Gottschalk), 413
Farwell, Arthur, xxx
Faust (Gounod), 259, 404; *Marche
　(Chant du soldat)*, 49, 190, 226,
　371, 376, 402, 409
Favorita, La (Donizetti), 75
Fay, Amy, xi
Federico el Verdugo (Frederick the
　Hangman), *see* Barbaroussa, Fred-
　erick
Ferdinand VII, of Spain, 124
Feuillet, Octave, 124
Fidelio (Beethoven), 376
Fillmore, Millard, 90
Fishkill, N.Y., 104, 191
Fitchburg, Mass., 144

Fleiuss, Henrique, 400
Flores, Fortunato, 391
Folgueras (baritone), 28
Foote, Andrew Hull, 64
Foote, Arthur, xxx
Forest Glade (Gottschalk), 123
Fors, Luis Ricardo, xix, xxxiii, 389, 412
Fort Cabaña, Cuba, 6
Fort-de-France, Martinique, 23
Fortress Monroe, Va., 180
Fossetti (singer), 270
Foster, Kitty, 89
Foster, Stephen, xxiv
France, xii, xvi, 46, 111
Franchomme, August, xxii
Freischütz, Der (Weber), 108
French Antilles, 40
French Quarter, xiv
French troops (in Mexico), 325, 326
Frezzolini, Erminia, 29
Frezzolinistas, 29
Froment-Meurice, Jacques-Charles-François-Marie, 26, 318
Fuegians, 385, 386
Fuentes (baritone), 28
Funeral Homage to the Bard of the Tropics, 17
"Funeral March" (Chopin), xxviii, 376
Furtado Coelho, Luiz Candido, 400

Gaceta de la Habana (newspaper), xvii, 33
Gallina, La (Gottschalk), xxxv, 264
García, Padre José Mauricio Nunes, 400
Garibaldi's hymn, 74
Gassier (soprano), 30
Gautier, Théophile, xv, 35, 189
Gazzaniga, Marietta, 29, 30
Gazzaniquistas, 29
Geneva, N.Y., 88, 209
Géraldy, Jean, xxii
Gettysburg, Battle of, 143
Gibraltar, 38
Gil Blas (Lesage), 38

Glinka, Michael, xxiii, 49
Gluck, Christoph Willibald, xxi
Gockel (pianist), 49
"God Save the Czar," 73
"God Save the Queen," 25, 84
Gold Hill, Nev., 310, 314
Golliwog's Cakewalk (Debussy), xxv
Gómez Sánchez, 350, 352, 355, 357
Gonaïves, Santo Domingo, 10
Gonzales (tenor), 28
Goria (pianist), 221
Gottschalk, Célestine, 114
Gottschalk, Clara, *see* Peterson, Clara Gottschalk
Gottschalk, Edward, Sr., xiv
Gottschalk, Edward, Jr., 114, 115, 145, 407
Gottschalk, L. Gaston, 114, 115
Gottschalk Waltz, The (Carreño), 91
Grand Fantasy on Il Trovatore (Gottschalk), 9, 401; see also *Trovatore, Il*
Grand Italian Opera Company, 230–1, 243
Grand March (Gottschalk), 26
Grand National Symphony for Ten Pianos: Bunker Hill (Gottschalk), xxiv
Grand Tacón Theater, 9, 26, 27, 28, 31
Grande fantaisie triomphale sur l'hymne national brésilien (Gottschalk), xxiv
Grant, Ulysses Simpson, 171, 210, 241
Grass Valley, Nev., 313
Grau, Jacob, 45
Gray, J. P., 206
Green Wood Cemetery, 407
Grenada, 24
Guadeloupe, 22–4
Guanabacoa, Cuba, 33
Guanajay, Cuba, 34
Guatemala, 332, 344
Guayama, Puerto Rico, 20
Guianas, 21, 40

Guillaume Tell (Rossini), xxiv, 44, 371
Guiraud, Ernest, xv, xxxvii
Guiraud, Jean-Baptiste, xv
Guzmán, Federico, 400

habanera (dance), 368
"Hail, Columbia," xxxv, 60, 66, 291
Haiti, 10, 18
Halévy, Jacques, 25, 31
Hall (Gottschalk's music publisher), 49, 50, 69
Hallé, Charles, xv, xxi, xxxvii
Halleck, Henry Wager, 64
Hamilton, Canada, 60, 215
Handel, George Frederick, 225
Harris (American prima donna), 159
Harris, Edward, 254
Harrisburg, Pa., 128, 129, 130–7, 140–2, 172, 235, 256
Hartford, Conn., 91, 156, 232
Harvard, Ill., 150
Havana, xvi, xxxi, 6, 7, 9, 10, 14, 26, 28, 29, 31, 32, 33, 34, 50, 60, 293, 411
Hawaii, 232
Hawthorne, Nathaniel, 233
Herrera, Juan de, 31
Herron, Francis Jay, 54
Herz, Henri, xx, 15, 26
Hinckley, Isabella, 54, 257
Hoffman, Edward, 167
Hoffman, Richard, 44, 46, 167
Hoffmann, Ernst Theodor Amadeus, 119
Hoffmann, Joseph, xxx
Holmes, Oliver Wendell, 233
Holy Week (Guatemala), 332
Home Journal (magazine), 113, 117, 219
"Home, Sweet Home" (Bishop), xxxvi, 166, 210, 229
Honduras, 344
Honolulu, 324
Horowitz, Vladimir, xxxiii
Houdin, Jean-Eugène-Robert, 72
Hugo, Victor, xv, xx, 88, 260

Huguenots, Les (Meyerbeer), 345
Hummel, Johann Nepomuk, 53
Hunt, William Morris, 233

Idaho, 244
Illuminati, 297
Incas, 365, 368–9
Indiana, 98
Indianapolis, Ind., 98, 112
Indians, U.S., 57, 291, 310; Bolivia, 363, 366, 371, 373, 375; Mexico, 27, 281; Panama, 329; Patagonia, 385, 387; Peru, 341, 347, 348, 351, 360, 364, 366
Invitation to the Waltz (Weber), xxviii, 412
Ione (Petrella), 160, 219
Irving, Washington, 259
Irving Hall, 114
Islay, Peru, 361
Isle of Pearls, Panama, 275
Italy, 46
Ives, Charles E., xxx, 210
Ives, George E., 210

Jackson, Thomas Jonathan (Stonewall), 65, 130
Jamaica, 12, 14
Jericho, Vt., 81
Jerusalem (Verdi), 9, 25
Jeune Henri, Le (Méhul), 405
Jeunesse (Gottschalk), 42
"John Brown," 211
Joliet, Ill., 251
Jornal do Comercio (newspaper), 409
Josephine, Empress, 24
Jota aragonesa (Glinka), 49
Julien, Paul, 296
Jullien, Louis Antoine, 77

Kalama, Queen of Hawaii, 323
Kalamazoo, Mich., 253
Kalkbrenner, Friedrich Wilhelm Michael, 82, 220–3
Kamehameha IV, of Hawaii, 322
Kanaks, 322, 323
Karr, Alphonse, 8, 322

Kaska (singer), *see* Budan
Katzwara, Franz, xxiv
Kay, Hershy, 411
Kellogg, Abner O., 264
Kellogg, Clara Louise, 73, 77, 259
Kennett (contralto), 28
Kentucky, 98
Kingston, Canada, 87, 205
Knights of the Golden Circle, 187
"Kreutzer Violin Sonata" (Beethoven), xxviii, 246

L'Abeille (newspaper), 18
La Belle (organist), 82
Lachine, Canada, 81
La France musicale, xii, 18, 21
La Harp, Jean-François de, 228
Lamartine, Alphonse de, xv, 241, 288
Lancaster, Pa., 175
Landesman, Jenny, 316
Lange, Francisco Curt, 399, 401
L'Ange déchu (Kalkbrenner), 81, 228
La Paz, Bolivia, 363, 372, 374
Larrinaga, de, 26
L'Art musical, xii
La Serena, Chile, 377
Last Hope, The (Gottschalk), xvi, xxxiii, xxxiv, xxxv, 44, 49, 50, 75, 96, 118, 181, 212, 229, 239, 305, 312, 407
"Last Rose of Summer," 211
Latin America, xxxi
Lausanne, Switzerland, 258
Lavater, Johann Kaspar, 117
Ledru-Rollin, Alexandre-Auguste, 288
Lee, Robert E., 126, 282
Le Moule, Guadeloupe, 23
Lesage, Alain-René, 38
Les Misérables (Hugo), 88
Les Natchez (Chateaubriand), 51
Lesser Antilles, 24
Letellier, François, xiv, xv
Letendale (pianist), 82
Lettvin, Theodore, 412
Levy (agent, on tour), 146
L'Huis, Drouyen de, 329
Lick, James, 295

Liedertafel Society, 401, 404
Lima, Peru, xviii, 335, 339, 345–57, 358, 359, 360; revolution, 339, 345–57
Lincoln, Abraham, 74, 115, 171, 210, 282; Mrs. Lincoln, 171
Lind, Jenny, xv, 48
Linda di Chamounix (Donizetti), 9
List, Eugene, 412
Liszt, Franz von, xx, xxviii, xxxvii, 120, 193, 221, 244
Lockport, N.Y., 61, 213, 263
Loggins, Vernon, 21
Lombardi, I (Verdi), 22
London, Canada, 254
Longfellow, Henry Wadsworth, 233
López II, of Paraguay, 344
López (violinist), 411
Lorini (opera singer), 230
Lotti (German tenor), 28, 161
Louisiana, 11, 280
Louis-Napoleon, 288
Louis-Philippe, 288
Louisville, 56, 98
Lucia di Lammermoor (Donizetti), 60, 73, 110, 230
Lucrezia Borgia (Donizetti), 230

Mabille Gardens, 358
McClellan, George Brinton, 76, 90, 126, 136, 137
MacDowell, Edward, xxx
McElhinney, Jane, xvii, 33
Machiavelli, Niccolò, 132
"Madamina" (Mozart), 79
Madison, Wis., 96
Madonna of the Chair (Raphael), 260
Madrid, 5, 8
Magellan, Strait of, 384
Maguire's Academy of Music, 293, 299
Maiden's Prayer, The, 150, 178, 181, 217, 290
Maleden, Pierre, xv
Mamiani, Count, 6
Manatí, Puerto Rico, 20

Ma-na-wau-na-ma-kee (Sioux chief), 57
Mancenillier, Le (Gottschalk), xxii, xxv, xxxv, 407
Manchester, Vt., 144
Mancusi (basso), 54, 56, 58
Manzanillo, Mexico, 324
Marajas, Cuba, 32
Marble Heart, The (Boucicault), 87
March from Tannhäuser (Pilgrims' Chorus) (Wagner), 164, 300, 301, 376, 402, 409
"*Marcha real, La*" (Spanish national hymn), 74, 109
Marcha solemne brasileira (Gottschalk), xxiv, 405
Marche de Faust (Chant du soldat) (Gounod), 49, 190, 226, 371, 376, 402, 409); *see also Faust*
Marche de nuit (Gottschalk), 9, 13, 44, 49, 239, 305
Marche des Gibaros, La (Gottschalk), xxxv, 42
Marche Solennelle (Gottschalk), xxiv
Maretzek, Max, 29, 54, 160–1
Margherita, Princess, of Italy, 399
Marianao, Cuba, 33
Mario, Marchese di Candia, 146, 160
Marschner (composer), 180, 187
"*Marseillaise,*" 110, 229
Marta (von Flotow), 52
Martinique, 21, 22, 23, 24, 25
Martins, Severiano Rodriguez, 400, 402, 406
Maryland, 126, 130
Masnadieri, I, 371
Mason, William, xx, xxxiv, xxxvii, 80, 158
Mason's Musical World, 117
Matanzas, Cuba, xxxi, 10, 34
"*Matinées d'Instruction,*" xxix
Matouba, Guadeloupe, 23, 42, 53
Mayagüez, Puerto Rico, 18
Mayer, Monte, 213
Mazeppa (play), 296, 298
Mazzolini (tenor), 160–1, 183
mecapaqueña (dance), 368

Medea (Pacini), 219
Medori (opera singer), 28
Melgarejo, Mariano, 342, 374, 395
Mendelssohn, Felix, 21, 63
Mendive, Rafael, xxxv
Mendoza, Pedro de, 322
Menken, Adah Isaacs, xxix, 296, 299
"Mercy" (hymn), xxxiii
Mery, Joseph, 35
Metropolitan Theater, 293, 300
Mexico, 277–82, 324–6
Meyerbeer, Giacomo, xxii, 27, 219, 345
Mezzara (sculptor), 318
Milwaukee, Wis., 57, 58, 102
Minnesota, 57
Miolan, Félix, xv
Miolan-Carvalho (singer), xv
Mirate (tenor), 160
"*Miserere*" (Verdi), 24, 60, 231; *see also Trovatore, Il*
Missouri, 62
Mitre, Bartolomé, 389
Moïse (Rossini), 318
Moisonneuse, La (Gottschalk), xxv
Molière, Jean Baptiste, 81
Montaigne, Michel Eyquem de, 52
Montes, Francisco, 5
Montevideo, xix, 389, 390, 391, 397, 399
Montevideo (Gottschalk), xxiv
Montmorency, *see* Duckworth, Kate
montomeras (mounted rebels), 351, 354, 356
Montreal, 81–2, 83, 198, 201, 224, 231
Moras, Firmin, 53–4, 104, 145, 153, 170, 345, 406, 407
Morelli (baritone), 232, 240, 244, 248, 250, 255, 300
Morensi, *see* Duckworth, Kate
Morro Castle, 6
Morte! (Gottschalk), xi, 398, 401, 405, 406
Moscheles, Ignaz, xxxvii
"Mother, Do Not Weep," 181
Mount of Olives (Beethoven), 186

Mozart, Wolfgang Amadeus, xxviii, 80, 108, 305
Mozart Hall, 246
Murillo, Bartolomé Esteban, 337
Murmures éoliens (Gottschalk), xxxiv, 46, 50, 75, 116, 163, 239, 312, 359
Music Hall, Boston, 234
Musset, Alfred de, 86
Muzio, Emanuele, 56, 58, 254, 257, 264, 267, 268, 270
Myers, Leonard, 132

Napoleão, Arthur, 400, 411
Napoleon III, 109
Narciso, Napoleão c Cia. (music publishers), 400
Nashua, N.H., 144
Nastariz (prima donna), 28
Natale, Fanny, 28
Natali, Agnes, 28
Natarre (prima donna), 28
Negrini (actress), 72
Neue Zeitschrift für Musik, xxvii
Nevada, xvii, 305, 313
Nevada City, Nev., 313
Newark, N.J., 80, 103
Newburgh, N.Y., 191, 192
New England, xvi, xxx, 47, 48, 143
New Granada, 54, 271
New Haven, Conn., 91, 159
New Jersey, 163
New London, Conn., 143, 167
New Orleans, xii, xvi, 6, 10, 13, 27, 46, 47, 63, 227, 280
New Orleans Daily Picayune, 54
New York, xvi, xxvii, 15, 39, 44–50, 62, 91, 103, 115, 145, 156, 163
New York City Ballet, 412
New York Seventh Regiment, 76, 135
Niagara, N.Y., 227
Nibley, Reid, 412
Niblo's Theater, xxvii, 46
Nicaragua, 344
Night in the Tropics (Gottschalk), 405
Noces de Jeannette, Les (Massé), 78

Nonhouhanon, Hawaii, 322
Norfolk, Va., 180, 181
Norwalk, Conn., 164
Norwich, Conn., xxx, 167

Oahu, Hawaii, 324
Oakland, Calif., 305
Oakland Female Seminary, 320
Oberon (Weber), 315, 376
Oblate Fathers, 82, 228
Oceania, 323
Offenbach, Jacques, xv, xxv, 390
Ogdensburg, N.Y., 86, 202
"Oh, Susanna" (Foster), xxiv
Once a Month (magazine), 99
Oneida, N.Y., 208
Onslow, George, xxviii
Orfila, Matthieu Joseph Bonaventure, 222–3
Orlandi (singer), 270
orphéons (music societies), 111
Osborne (pianist), 220
Oswego, N.Y., 89, 209
Otuian Hall and Gardens, 358
Ottawa, 85
Overture on Cuban Themes (Roldán), 33

Pacini (composer), 30
Paderewski, Ignace, xxxvii
Páez, José Antonio, 23
Paine, John Knowles, xxx
Paita, Peru, 332
Palestrina, Giovanni, 108
Palmer (American musician), 259
Panama, 270, 274, 320, 326
Pancarri (tenor), 28
Pará, Brazil, 21, 40
Paraguay, 344, 389, 390
Paris, xv, xxii, 6, 15, 22, 47, 48, 221
Paris Conservatoire, xv, 23, 25, 52, 221
Paris World's Fair (1844), xxiv
Parker, Horace, xxx
Parnain (violoncellist), 29
"Partant pour la Syrie," 25, 74
Pasquier (doctor), 223

Pasquinade (Gottschalk), xxxv
Pass Christian, Miss., xiv, 291
"Pastoral" Symphony (Beethoven), 106
Pastorella e cavaliere (Gottschalk), 42, 46, 50, 118, 239, 412
Patagonia, 385, 386, 387, 389
"Pathétique" (Beethoven), xxviii, 75, 376
Patti, Adelina, xvi, 9, 10, 20, 128, 129
Patti, Amalia, *see* Strakosch, Amalia Patti
Patti, Carlo, 61, 129, 145, 165, 170, 178, 185, 196, 201, 210
Patti, Salvatore, 128
Pedro II, of Brazil, 400, 407
Pennsylvania, 126–8, 132, 176–7
Pensée poétique (Gottschalk), 407
Peoria, Ill., 245
Père Goriot, Le (Balzac), 27
Perkins, Charles Callahan, 157
Perpetual Motion (Weber), xxviii, 55
Peru, 13, 320, 332–57, 359; revolution, 339, 344–57
Petaluma, Calif., 316
Peter the Great, 288
Peterson, Clara Gottschalk, xii, 411
Peterson, Robert E., xii
Petite Rivière, Santo Domingo, 12
Petrella (composer), 160
Pezet, Juan Antonio, 339, 340, 342, 345, 347, 348, 350, 351, 353–6
Philadelphia, Pa., 62, 66, 91, 164, 227
Philharmonic Orchestra, New York, 2, 261
Philharmonic Society, Cárdenas, 30, 32
Philharmonic Society, Milwaukee, 58
Philharmonic Society, St. Louis, 63
Phillips, Adelaide, 270, 284
Piano Concerto in B Flat Minor (Tchaikovsky), xxxiii
Pieper (Swedish minister to U. S.), 169
Pilgrims' Chorus (Wagner), *see* March from *Tannhäuser*

Pinar del Río, Cuba, 33
Pioche, F. L. A., 318
Pittsburg Landing (battle), 59, 62, 64
Pittsburgh, 237
Pizzaro, Francisco, 337
Placerville, Calif., 314
Plattsburgh, N.Y., 198
Plazuela, Puerto Rico, 18, 19, 20
Pleyel pianos, 243
Poe, Edgar Allan, 259, 261
Polka Original (Furtado Coelho), 401
Polonia (Gottschalk), 42
Ponce, Puerto Rico, 18, 19
Pope, John, 64
Port-au-Prince, 18
Portland, Me., 79, 91
Portsmouth, N.H., 78, 91
Potosí, Bolivia, 366
Poughkeepsie, N.Y., 194
Powers (American musician), 259
Powers, Hiram, 65
Prado, Mariano Ignacio, 350, 364, 394
Prescott, Canada, 202
Prophète (Meyerbeer), 219, 405
Proudhomme, Pierre Joseph, 52
Providence, R.I., 77, 91, 157, 232
Prudent (American pianist), 221
Puerto-Príncipe, Cuba, xxxi, 110
Puerto Rico, 14, 18, 20, 50
Punta Arenas (Chilean penal colony), 385
Puritani, I (Bellini) 9, 160, 230

Quebec, 82–4, 228

Rachel, xv, 72, 107, 175
Racine, Jean Baptiste, 20, 175
Racine, Wis., 147
Rákóczy March (Berlioz), xxiv
Ramón (gypsy boy adopted in Spain), 137–40
Raphael, 260
Raspail (French doctor), 37
Ratazzi, Princess de Salm, 123–5
Raven & Bacon, 273

Raya, Carlos, 28
Reading, Pa., 187
Rembrandt, 260
Réponds-moi (Gottschalk), 42
Requiem (Mozart), 407
Requiem Mass in C minor (Cherubini), 407
"*Rêverie de Rosellen, La,*" 217
Revue de Villa Clara (newspaper), 16, 17
Ricci (composer), 79
Richmond, Ind., 247
Richmond, Va., 282
Ricord (doctor), 223
Ricordati (Gottschalk), xxxv
Rigoletto (Verdi), 371
Rio de Janiero, Brazil, xii, 399, 401, 402
Ristori, Adelaide, 72, 401
Robert le Diable (Meyerbeer), xxii
Rochester, N.Y., 87, 211–12, 262, 265
Rockford, Ill., 146
Roldán, Amadeo, 33
Rome, N.Y., 89
Root, George F., 182
Rosand, Aaron, xxxiii
Rossini, Giovacchino, xxii, xxiv, 21
Rousseau, Jean Jacques, 307
Royal March (Gottschalk), 84
Rubini, Giovanni Baptiste, 204
Rubinstein, Anton, xxxii, xxxvii
Ruíz, José, 24
"*Rule Britannia,*" 84

Saa (brigand), 389
Sacramento, Calif., 305, 314
Saffo (Pacini), 30
St. Albans, Vt., 81
St. Catherine, Canada, 225
St.-Gervaise, France, 14
St. Lawrence River, 81
St. Louis, 56, 60, 62, 63, 247, 262
St. Louis Cathedral, xiv
St. Lucia, 24
St. Matthew Passion (Bach), xxi
St. Pierre, Martinique, 21, 22, 23, 25
Saint-Saëns, Camille, xv

St. Stephen's Church, 407
St. Thomas, V.I., 13, 14, 15, 16, 18, 125
Salem, Mass., 79
Salvador, 344
Sand, Georges, 221
Sanderson, Harry, 145, 163, 164
Sandusky, Ohio, 93, 94, 240
Sandwich Islands, 322
San Francisco, Calif., xvii, 268, 285–90, 292–304, 314–20, 321, 403
San Jose, Calif., 305
San Juan, Puerto Rico, 20
Santa Catalina (fort, Lima), 352, 353, 354, 355, 356
Santa Clara, Cuba, xxxi, 10
Santa Cruz, 24
Santa Maria (prima donna), 28
Santiago, Chile, 376
Santiago, Cuba, 10, 13, 14, 16, 33, 35, 49
Santiago, Peru, xviii, 338
Santo Domingo, xii, xiv, 10, 12, 14
Santos, Brazil, 402
Sao Francisco de Paula (church, Rio), 407
São Paulo, Brazil, 402
Saratoga, N.Y., 8, 90, 230, 267
Sarmiento, Domingo Faustino, xix
Satter, Gustave, xxxvii
Savana la Grande (newspaper), 16, 17
Savane, La (Gottschalk), xxii, xxxv, 194, 407
Scharfenberg, William, 37
Schenectady, N.Y., 193
Schiller, Johann Christoph Friedrich von, 54
Schott (music publisher), 398
Schottische de Concert (Gottschalk), 412
Schubert, Franz, xxi
Schumann, Clara, xxxvii
Schumann, Robert, xxi, xxviii, xxxvii, 63
Scott, George, 305
Scranton, Pa., 189, 190
Semana Illustrada, A (magazine), 400, 408

Semiramide (Rossini), xxii, 21, 220
Setchell, Dan, 270
Seus Olhos (Gottschalk), 401
"7 Octaves" (pseudonym), 230, 398, 413
Seward, William Henry, 55, 171
Sieboth, Joseph, 89, 264
Siege of Saragossa, The (Gottschalk), xxiv, 5, 25, 109
Sierra Cordillera, Peru, 365
Sierra de Anafe, Cuba, 34, 35, 36
Sikler (violinist), 22
Simons (soprano), 255, 264, 270
Simpson (English tenor), 60, 61
Sisters of Charity, 331, 334, 396
Smith (Jenny Lind's agent), 268
Sobrerano (president, Panama), 328
Sociedade Philarmonica Fluminense, Rio de Janiero, 405, 406, 407
Society of the Friends of Education, xix
Solemne Marcha Triunfal a Chile (Gottschalk), xxiv
Solitude (Gottschalk), 407
Sonnambula (Bellini), 9, 60, 108, 194
Sousa, John Philip, xxx
South America, xii, xviii, 267, 321–406
Souvenir de Porto Rico (Gottschalk), xxxv
Spain, xii, xvi, 5, 7, 15, 28, 31, 46, 340, 359
Spanish America, 15, 31, 43, 344, 359
Spanish Antilles, 40
Spanish Main, 21, 40
Spanish people, xxiv, 38
Spohr, Louis, xxxvii
Spring Song (Mendelssohn), 316
Springfield, Ill., 114, 249
Springfield, Mass., 80, 91
Stamaty, Camille-Marie, xv, xxi, 220, 221
Stamford, Conn., 160, 165
"Star-Spangled Banner, The," xxxv, 284
Stebbins (American musician), 259

Stefani (tenor), 230
Steinway piano, 194
Stockton, Calif., 316
Stowe, Harriet Beecher, 125
Strakosch, Amelia Patti (Mrs. Maurice), 93, 128, 129, 134, 144, 210, 224
Strakosch, Maurice, 129
Strakosch, Max, 43, 94, 128, 129, 130, 132, 133, 134, 135, 137, 142, 143, 145, 153, 170, 190, 196, 216, 218, 226, 228, 257, 320
Strauss, Johann, 119
Striglia (singer), 270
Stuart, James Ewell Brown (Jeb), 130
Sulla Poppa (Ricci), 79
Susini (baritone-bass) 54, 56, 58, 78, 257
Switzerland, xii, xvi, 14, 46, 258
Swedish Antilles, 40
Syracuse, N.Y., 208, 265

Tacna, Chile, 363, 365, 367, 374, 375
Talleyrand, 52
Tambo de la Joya, Peru, 361
Tannhäuser (Wagner) xxxii; *Pilgrims' Chorus, see March from Tannhäuser*
Tarantella (Gottschalk), 397, 399, 404, 411
Tassera (poet, Spanish minister to U.S.), 73
Tchaikovsky, Peter Ilich, xxiv
Teatro Colón, Buenos Aires, 389
Tedesco (opera singer), 28
Teninipuede, ancient Peru, *see* Santiago
Tennyson, Alfred, 234
Testa (tenor), 28, 230
Thalberg, Sigismond, xx, xxii, 9, 86, 220, 221, 243, 318, 400
Théâtre des Italiens, Paris, 300
Théâtre d'Orléans, New Orleans, xv
Theatro Lyrico Fluminense, Rio de Janiero, 401, 402
Thomas, Ambroise, 300

Thomas, Theodore, xxviii, xxxvii, 91, 145
Thumb, Tom, 156
Ticknor and Fields, 233
Tierra del Fuego, 385
Tijuca, Brazil, 401, 406
Timm, Henry Christian, xxxvii
Titiens (actress), 72
Toledo, Ohio, 59, 60, 92, 241, 256
Toronto, Canada, 87, 215, 223, 224
Toussaint l'Ouverture, Pierre Dominique, 13
Traviata, La (Verdi), 29, 30, 77, 255
Tremolo (Gottschalk), 401, 405
Tremont Hall, 234
Trinidad, Cuba, xxxi, 10
Triumphal Hymn (Gottschalk), 26, 27
Trobriand, Philippe Regis de, 82
Trollope, Anthony, 63, 236
Trousseau (doctor), 223
Trovatore, Il (Verdi), 9, 24, 60, 75, 77, 116, 230, 231, 299; *Miserere*, 24, 60, 231
Tumbez, ancient Peru, 338

Ullman (theatrical producer), 72, 77
Uncle Tom's Cabin (Stowe), 8, 15
Unión, Uruguay, 393
Union, The (Gottschalk), xxiv, xxxii, xxxv, 66, 73, 75, 116, 171, 284
Urquiza, Justo José, 381
Uruguay, xxiv, 320, 398
Utica, N.Y., 90, 206, 264

Valença, Brazil, 402
Valladolid, Spain, 137
Valparaíso, Chile, 372, 373, 377
Valse poétique (Gottschalk), 13
Vancouver, George, 322
Van der Guth, Francisco, 9, 411
Van der Guth, Juan, 9
Varejão, Achilles, 409
Varela (brigand), 389
Varela, José Pedro, xix
Vargas, D. N., 364, 365

Variani (American soprano), 167, 168, 170
Venezuela, 13, 14, 20
Verdi, Giuseppe, xxv, 21, 22, 58, 232, 270, 300
Verdistas, 232
Vespucci, Amerigo, 203
Vestvali (contralto), 173
Victoria, Hawaiian princess, 324
Villa Clara, Cuba, 17
Violette, La (Herz), 228
Virginia, xvii, 115
Virginia City, Nev., 305, 311, 314
Volpini (tenor), 28
Voltaire, 213, 229, 307
von Bülow, Hans, xxxiii, xxxvii

Wagner, Richard, xxi, 63
Wallace, William Vincent, 46
Wallenstein (Schiller), 54
Washington, 54–5, 73, 171, 263
Watertown, N.Y., 86, 206
Watson's Weekly Art Journal, 320
Weber, Carl Maria von, xxi, xxiv, xxviii, 55, 108, 180
West Indies, vii, xxx, xxxi, 5–38, 401
White, José, 411
Whittier, John Greenleaf, 233
William, Hawaiian prince, 324
Williamsport, Pa., 126, 129, 188
Willis, Richard Storrs, 99
Wilmington, Del., 67, 257, 259
Wisconsin, xvii, 57–8
Wolfsohn, Carl, xxxvii
Worcester, Mass., xxiii, 75

"Yankee Doodle," xxxv, xxxvii, 60, 66, 95, 210, 249
Yonkers, N.Y., 91

Z—, Maurice (orchestra leader), xxii
Zanesville, Ohio, 93, 98
zarzuela (traditional Spanish opera), 28
Zayara (actress), 293, 299
Zimmerman (of Paris Conservatoire), 52, 221

A NOTE ON THE TYPE

◇◇◇◇◇◇◇◇◇◇

THIS BOOK is set in *Electra*, a linotype face designed by
W. A. DWIGGINS. This face cannot be classified as either
modern or old-style. It is not based on any historical model,
nor does it echo any particular period or style. It avoids
the extreme contrasts between thick and thin elements
that mark most modern faces, and attempts to give a feeling of fluidity, power, and speed.

Composed, printed, and bound by
The Haddon Craftsmen, Inc., Scranton, Pa.
Typography and binding design by
HERBERT H. JOHNSON